⌖ THE CRIME IN MIND ⌖

THE CRIME IN MIND

Criminal Responsibility
and the
Victorian Novel

LISA RODENSKY

OXFORD

UNIVERSITY PRESS

2003

OXFORD
UNIVERSITY PRESS

Oxford   New York
Auckland   Bangkok   Buenos Aires   Cape Town   Chennai
Dar es Salaam   Delhi   Hong Kong   Istanbul   Karachi   Kolkata
Kuala Lumpur   Madrid   Melbourne   Mexico City   Mumbai   Nairobi
São Paulo   Shanghai   Taipei   Tokyo   Toronto

Published by Oxford University Press, Inc.
198 Madison Avenue, New York, New York 10016

www.oup.com

Oxford is a registered trademark of Oxford University Press

Library of Congress Cataloging-in-Publication Data
Rodensky, Lisa.
The crime in mind : criminal responsibility and the Victorian novel /
Lisa Rodensky
p. cm.
Includes bibliographical references and index.
ISBN 0-19-515073-2; 0-19-515074-0 (pbk.)
1. English fiction—19th century—History and criticism.
2. Crime in literature. 3. Legal stories, English—History and criticism.
4. Law and literature—History—19th century. 5. Criminal liability in literature.
6. Responsibility in literature. 7. Criminals in literature.
I. Title.
PR878.C74 R63 2003
823'.809355—dc21   2002015617

1 3 5 7 9 8 6 4 2

Printed in the United States of America
on acid-free paper

⊰ ACKNOWLEDGMENTS ⊱

My thanks are owed first and foremost to Christopher Ricks for his detailed and unflagging engagement with this work. My debt to him is a large one. I am also very grateful to Julia Prewitt Brown and Laura Korobkin for their advice throughout. To William E. Cain and Margery Sabin I offer my thanks for their invaluable guidance and encouragement. So too I have profited from the generous counsel of other friends and colleagues: Judith Aronson, Nicolas de Warren, Kenneth Haynes, Laura Johnson, Ann L. Kibbie, Jane Kokernak, Peter Lurie, Joellen Masters, Timothy Peltason, Jeanne Follansbee Quinn, Jonathan Ribner, and Jane Thraillkill. My thanks go as well to the anonymous readers for Oxford University Press from whom I learned much. My reliable and efficient research assistants, Beth Davis and Alexa Bedell-Healy, were a real help to me. I would also like to thank Elissa Morris and Jeremy Lewis at Oxford University Press for their unstinting attention to this project.

I am grateful to the Syndics of the Cambridge University Library for permission to quote from the letters of Sir James Fitzjames Stephen, and to Austin Sarat for permission to publish passages from the talk that he gave at the 1998 Meeting of the Working Group on Law, Culture, and the Humanities.

My husband, Kerry Timbers, has been and continues to be, among other things, an inestimable legal resource, much needed at moments when my own legal training and practice failed me. And when I lost my sense of humor, he kept his own intact.

Without the support of my mother, Joanna Rodensky, I could not have finished this book.

⧉ CONTENTS ⧉

CONTENTS

❈ THE CRIME IN MIND ❈

Introduction

The general rule is, that people are responsible for their actions, but to

this there are several exceptions of great importance and interest.

— JAMES FITZJAMES STEPHEN *(1883)*

There is a dignified simplicity in the way the Victorian jurist Sir James Fitz-james Stephen, writing not only as a criminal lawyer but also as a journalist, statutory draftsman, high court judge, and legal historian, begins his discussion of criminal responsibility in the second volume of *A History of the Criminal Law of England*,[1] the only history of criminal law published during Victoria's reign and still indispensable to the study of the English criminal law.[2] Stephen proffers the general rule—that people are responsible for their actions—with an appealing straightforwardness, as appealing as the way he recognizes, without paltering, the exceptions to that rule. They are important and interesting. But they are neither simple nor straightforward.

"The general rule is, that people are responsible for their actions." The legal discourse of criminal responsibility in the nineteenth century—and I include here legal opinions, statutes, treatises, histories, articles—reveals the necessary fractures in Victorian ideas and ideals about criminal responsibility. Victorian jurists were aware of such fractures, and while some documents manifest attempts to suppress their existence, more often than not Victorian jurists confronted them. The very nature of a legal opinion—a document that may and often does include the arguments of both majority decision and dissent—cannot but acknowledge disagreement. And disagreement there was, particularly around questions pertaining to criminal states of mind and to the relations between states of mind and acts. Determining whether or not a defendant had committed a crime meant (and means) judging an external and an internal element. How would the relations between these elements be defined and applied? Such a question foregrounds an even more potent one: by

3

whom would the limits of criminal responsibility be determined and named? Not, to be sure, by courts alone.

⇥ Novels with a Purpose ⇤

Nineteenth-century legal documents tell rich and complicated stories about cultural attitudes toward criminal responsibility. But there was another kind of discourse assuming cultural power at midcentury that also claimed the right to weigh in on such matters. In 1865, the Irish politician and historian Justin M'Carthy announced in his *Westminster Review* article "Novels with a Purpose" that

> The novelist is now our most influential writer. If he be a man of genius his power over the community he addresses is far beyond that of any other author. Macaulay's influence over the average English mind was narrow compared with that of Dickens; even Carlyle's was not on the whole so great as that of Thackeray. The readers of "The Idylls of the King" were but a limited number when compared with the readers of "Jane Eyre"; nor could Mr. Browning's finest poem pretend to attract as many admirers, even among people of taste and education, as were suddenly won by "Adam Bede."[3]

But to identify the novelist as the most influential writer is not yet to identify the areas within which such influence was to be exercised. "Is it given to the novelist to accomplish any social object, to solve, or even help toward the solution of any vexed social question"? asks M'Carthy.[4] Not given, but the Victorian novelist nonetheless took up vexed social questions and attended to solutions and in so doing shaped his or her own narratives as well as the questions themselves. The novelist occupied a complicated position in social affairs since his or her authority was unofficial yet undeniable.[5]

Though novels issue no legal verdicts, the Victorian novel's influence over matters of justice was significant. Far from being unacknowledged legislators, novelists who promoted social, political, legal reform—Charles Dickens, most potently—were singled out for praise and blame. Stephen often called attention to the dangers such novels posed. In a footnote to one of his earliest essays, "The Relation of Novels to Life," Stephen reports that

> It has indeed become a sort of commonplace, or what may perhaps be called a secondary commonplace . . . to extol the representations of novelists and memoir writers over the more authorized mediums of obtaining historical and social knowledge. This surely is confounding facts and possibilities. It may be very true that more knowledge about the relations of the Saxons and the Normans after the Conquest is gained from *Ivanhoe* than from Hume's *History*, but that is surely owing to the fact that, for one person who studies Hume and Hume's

authorities with sufficient attention to place a clear picture of the twelfth and thirteenth centuries before his mind, thousands will read *Ivanhoe*.[6]

So authoritative (though not authorized) were Dickens's representations of legal history, that in 1928 William Holdsworth, the great legal historian of the twentieth century, produced a small volume, *Charles Dickens as a Legal Historian*. On the very first page Holdsworth holds forth on Dickens's novels as legal histories, observing that the accuracy of detail in Dickens's treatment of law "entitles us to reckon one of the greatest of our English novelists as a member of the select band of our legal historians."[7] That such authority should be attached to Dickens had been a subject for discussion in the Victorian press. In a May 16, 1857, article entitled "Judicial Dignity," an anonymous writer for the *Saturday Review* took Lord Chief Justice Campbell to task for bringing the high character of his honorable office into question by repeatedly referring to Dickens:

> In the morning papers of Tuesday last we find a report of the trial of a man who was convicted of selling improper publications, in which the following remarks fell from Lord Campbell, in answer to a plea of ignorance on the part of the defendant: — "It was no excuse for him to say that he also sold the *Household Words* and other publications of a most interesting, moral, instructive, and beautiful character, for which the country was indebted to Mr Charles Dickens.[8]

Having considered Dickens's famous letter on the execution of the Mannings, with which Lord Campbell had "entertained the House of Lords during a motion for the abolition of public executions," this commentator poses a not altogether rhetorical question: "Is it conceivable, for example, — to take the last manifestation of the kind — that Lord Campbell should really feel so strongly the excellence of the morality of Mr. Dickens's publications as to be called upon to go out of his way to puff them from the Bench?" So too in his own *Saturday Review* articles Stephen, no friend to Dickens, would attempt to expose and contain Dickens's influence. What he would most illuminate, though, was Dickens's power to shape public opinion on the most consequential social questions. Of novelists who undertake to write fictions seeking reform, Stephen remarks:

> They are the most influential of all teachers — the teachers who make themselves friends and companions during those occasional intervals of rest and enjoyment which to many minds are far the pleasantest part of life. The production, among such readers, of false impressions of the system of which they form a part — especially of the falsehood which tends to render them discontented with and disaffected to the institutions under which they live — cannot but be a serious evil, and must often involve great moral delinquency. Except the relations between

men and their Maker, no subjects can be more grave than Legislation, Government, and the Administration of Justice.[9]

This rebuke does more than reflect Stephen's conservatism. It considers the place that certain novelists occupied in Victorian culture, and it names novel-reading as an activity more intimate and potentially more impressive than many others. For Stephen, the issue is not merely that novelists take advantage of vulnerable readers but also that they do so in order to pursue their own legal-political programs. Certain novelists and novels—and Dickens in particular—had to be called to account. Stephen concludes: "Looking, therefore, at the sphere of Mr. Dickens's influence, we are compelled to think of him seriously. He is not entitled to the protection of insignificance."[10]

The serious thinking that Dickens compelled Stephen to pursue provokes him to imagine how far Dickens's novels might go, and his train of thought leads him into the criminal court: "If Mr. Dickens has in his hand an instrument which enables him to teach us all about the Court of Chancery, and to procure its reform, why should he not employ it in criminal as well as civil justice? Why not write a striking tale in a magazine or newspaper, to establish, before trial, the guilt or the innocence of Palmer or Bernard?"[11] I consider this passage and Stephen's reactions to literary representations of criminal responsibility in chapter 4; for the purposes of this introduction, the passage calls forth Stephen's resistance to the influence the novel and novelists exercised. Such resistance arose in no small part out of the knowledge that the novel had already entered the courtroom, since readers of novels included judges, lawyers, jurors, and defendants. While Dickens may not have tried and sentenced a particular defendant prior to trial in any of his "striking tales," the representations of crime that his novels produced were deeply involved in the very questions of criminal responsibility that concerned Stephen. Dickens was moving closer to producing the "striking tale" that Stephen was anxiously imagining.

Stephen offers the hypothetical "striking tale" as his worst nightmare. In it Dickens acts not only as judge and jury for an actual criminal defendant but also has at his command all of the powers and may take advantage of all the license of the novelist while doing so. My study considers in some detail one power in particular: that which gives the novel's third person narrator imaginative access to the minds of his or her characters. It need not be by inference from external evidence that third person narrators offer the thoughts of their characters; they can hold themselves out as representing thoughts directly. Novels invite readers to imagine that they are in the mind of the criminal. This access to the mind distinguishes fiction—and the novel in particular—from law, from history, from psychology, and even from other literary genres, like biography and drama.[12] While drama can make action physically present in a way the novel cannot, the novel can enter the mind, and the Victorian novel explored the interior life of its characters as never before. The epistolary novels of Richardson give voice to first person narrators who generate evidence of their own minds and may make inferences about the minds of other characters from their actions, but they cannot go inside those minds. The third person narrators of Fielding's novels may indeed go inside those minds, but they choose not to do so. I locate the most intensive exploration of the inner life in the Victorian novel, and having identified the inner life as an object of extreme interest and detailed representation, I ask the following question: what might the consequences of such representations be for social and cultural attitudes toward the basic elements of crime and toward criminal responsibility more generally? This question immediately raises at least one potential objection about the place of Dickens in this study. The overt theatricality of Dickens's novels seems to make his work curiously out of touch with the narratives of the inner life I aim to explore, yet his first great crime novel, *Oliver Twist*, thrillingly imagines Fagin's criminal state of mind.[13] Relations between the internal and external elements of crime are at the heart of the novel and this study. The Victorian novel's power to represent the interior life of its characters both challenges the law's definitions of criminal liability and reaffirms them.

Although Dickens had one of the largest readerships, he was certainly not the only novelist framing questions of legal and moral responsibility. Well beyond the Newgate novels of William Harrison Ainsworth and Edward Bulwer-Lytton (from both of whom Dickens distanced himself) and the Sensation novels of Wilkie Collins (which Dickens promoted), the novels of Trollope and Thackeray required (and require) of their readers serious thinking about responsibilities, both civil and criminal, legal and moral. Yet beyond even Trollope and Thackeray are the deeply complicated representations of responsibility in the novels of George Eliot. Eliot's name may not be the first to come to mind when one considers fictional representations of crime in the nineteenth century—Dickens's name may be—but her novels create crimes and engage more fully the possibilities that fiction presents for exploring the relations between elements of crime and the questions of responsibility these relations raise. I choose Eliot's novels not only because I admire them but also because these texts forcefully represent the crime in mind—the crime from the inside out.[14] Still, even as Dickens and Eliot exercise their power to make criminal intentions (for example) uniquely present, they also appear judiciously cautious—and at times ambivalent—about exercising such a power. Should criminal states of mind replace criminal acts as the key (if not the sole) factor on which responsibility rests?

I place the work of James Fitzjames Stephen along with and against the work of Dickens and Eliot because it often responds to the novel and its practices. As a barrister and later a judge, Stephen was most obviously engaged in shaping narratives of criminal responsibility and in understanding and even constructing the relations between the internal and external elements of crime. Moreover, Stephen sought to provoke discussion about the responsibilities of the novelist and the novel's representations of social problems. While I take up Stephen's legal writing throughout this study, I make use of

7

other legal texts as well, including legal opinions, treatises, encyclopedias, statutes, and histories. In moving between the literary and the legal in the course of my argument, I show how the literary and legal texts and practices of the period supported, illuminated, and critiqued one another. This approach owes much to the substantial work done by law and literature scholars whose work precedes mine, and particularly to the work of Brook Thomas, whose arguments about American literature are animated by close attention to the narratological and historical relations between literary and legal texts.[15] And, although I take issue with some of its premises (as I will later discuss), I have learned and continue to learn much from Alexander Welsh's *Strong Representations: Narrative and Circumstantial Evidence in England*, a work that commits itself to close readings of legal and literary texts and to an historically informed argument. My aim here is to bring to bear rhetorical and historical analyses in a way that does justice to law and literature. The legal texts are neither subordinate nor superordinate to the literary, and the literary functions neither as supplement to nor master of the legal.[16]

Literary and legal representations of the criminal act, and particularly of the internal component of the criminal act, did not occur in a vacuum but rather formed a part of the body of Victorian writing about the workings of the interior self, and — more broadly — about personal identity, no small topic in the nineteenth century. Discussions that took as their topic criminal states of mind happened in a larger historical context that also included a newly developing Victorian psychological discourse. Victorian psychology both influenced and was in its turn influenced by law, literature, philosophy, economics, and politics. No doubt representations of interiority — criminal and otherwise — emerge out of specific social and cultural conditions, and I am indebted to philosophers and historians who have themselves put their minds to modern identity, which is so closely connected to conceptions of consciousness and inwardness, and on which our own ideas about criminal responsibility depend. Charles Taylor's *Sources of Self*, to name one example, specifically focuses on the development of inwardness, claiming that "our modern notion of self is related to, one might say constituted by, a certain sense (or perhaps a family of senses) of inwardness."[17] Taylor moves through the work of Augustine, Montaigne, Descartes, and Locke, describing in turn the development of the relations between inwardness and human agency.[18] Literary critics have also attended to the historical development of interiority and its influence on and representation in literature. In *Inwardness and Theater in the English Renaissance*, Katherine Eisaman Maus fully substantiates her claim that the idea of inwardness not only existed during the Renaissance but was a significant part of the culture, refuting other critics who argue that inwardness developed most fully in the eighteenth century, concomitant with the rise of the middle class and the novel.[19]

Unlike Maus, I need not enter into the debate about the historical moment at which inwardness becomes a significant force in the development of the self. It is safe to say that by the nineteenth century the interior has become a topic of interest and study. On the first page of the first chapter of *Charlotte Brontë and Victorian Psychology*, Sally Shuttleworth makes reference to "the new theories of subjectivity that arose in the nineteenth century," theories that offered an "interiorized model of selfhood."[20] Shuttleworth also presents a detailed and astute assessment of the importance and popularity of phrenology and the ways its popularity resonated in various aspects of Victorian culture.[21] Although phrenology, like mesmerism with which it is often paired, was in some ways marginalized in the nineteenth century, the abiding interest in these enterprises signifies a persistent attraction to the possibility of getting access to the interior self. But even if I am on safe ground in asserting the centrality of interiority in Victorian culture, readers who conceive of interiority as bound up with a liberal, middle-class economic, social, and political agenda that privileges individuality may still object that any discussion of the interior must necessarily work to devalue and debunk it. Although my argument depends on neither the valuing nor devaluing of interiority, it is true that I myself value representations of the inner life in the work of Dickens, Eliot, and in the work of a host of other writers. I am aware that giving life to the interior suggests a value that some would reject. I do not.

As usual, terminology matters here. In the 1870s, Fitzjames Stephen drafted (though never finished) a letter to his children "on the nature of belief and knowledge" in which he attempted (among other things) to analyze the language of "the operation of our minds":

> If any part of our language could be expected to be exact, it would be that which applies to the operations of our minds, for of them at least, we are immediately conscious. They have no existence at all except in the fact of our being conscious of them. Yet no part of our language is more obviously inadequate. Every word which describes the operations of the mind, is a metaphor, taken from some external objects. "Intend" – "attend" a metaphor from taking aim, probably with a bow and arrow. "Comprehend" "apprehend" and the like, metaphors from grasping with the hand, or catching with the hand.[22]

The relations between the internal and the external within the language itself suggest to Stephen difficulties that are presented when trying to describe the operations of the mind, and his analysis details his interest in and frustration with this enterprise. The language of interiority counted, though certainly not for the first time (or the last) in history.[23] Still, the first instance of "inner life" that the *Oxford English Dictionary* (*OED*) gives is from George Eliot's translation of Feuerbach's *Essence of Christianity*: "The inner life of man is the life which has relation to his species." This example falls under the second definition offered for the adjective "inner," when "Said of the mind or soul (as the more inaccessible or secret, or as the more central or essential part of man, or as distinguished from the external or outer world), and of things belonging or relating thereto." "Inner self" also appears under this definition, sometimes to suggest (as in Eliot) that the inner self is the essential part of the human being. This passage from J. W. Palmer's 1860 translation of Jules Michelet's *Love* (*L'amour*) gives the inner self as essential: "A feeling that the woman's inner self will not be reached, her soul not attained." By 1930 the phrase has also become a part of psychiatric discourse; the *OED* gives the following quotation from the *American Journal of Psychiatry*: "The Former is derived from *persona* meaning the essential or inner self." Even in the late nineteenth century, the phrase had been taken up into scientific discourse: Carpenter's *Mental Physiology* (1879) has: "The Cerebrum, — the instrument of our Psychical or inner life." These entries render the ways the phrases "inner life" and "inner self" moved between religious, scientific, philosophical, and literary texts. These *OED* examples also make apparent that the phrases on occasion attempt to distance themselves from the moral weight they carry, but without success. Other terms require the same consideration. The *OED* entry for "mind" produces, not surprisingly, a rich set of meanings, not only when the word is used in phrases that suggest recollection (e.g., "call to mind") but also in those that evoke "thought, purpose, intention" (e.g., "To know one's own mind" — a phrase that the *OED* records as entering the language in the early nineteenth century), as well as "desire or wish." Then there are the meanings that encompass not just a particular thought but all thought. Under this heading are meanings that restrict "mind" to the intellect, "as distinguished from the will or emotions": the head as against the heart, in other words. "Consciousness" is its own quagmire, both before and after Freud. There are a number of other terms in addition that one might fruitfully explore; for example, the *OED* gives "interiority" as both the neutral "quality or state of being interior or inward" and a definition that suggests that the word may define a person's being — "inner character or nature; an inner element." "Inwardness" includes not only "inner nature, essence or meaning" (and so overlaps with many other terms discussed earlier) but also "depth or intensity of feeling or thought," "subjectivity" (a meaning that according to the *OED* enters the language in the early nineteenth century), and "relation to or occupation with what is inward or concerns man's inner nature, as opposed to occupation with externalities; spirituality." The uses of "mental" as against "inner" also open themselves up to consideration. While my own purpose here is not to offer anything even remotely close to a full history of these fertile terms (that would be a different enterprise), I do wish to note that I am mindful of these historically grounded subtleties.

The ability to reveal the inner selves of characters "at will" is, in the words of Dorrit Cohn, "the singular power possessed by the novelist."[24] Cohn's book *Transparent Minds*, as well as her more recent work on narrative, is itself singularly powerful. Cohn's approach to narrative is typological; she usefully names and explores basic techniques (she names three) for representing the inner self in fictional narratives.[25] Her types suggest the richness of and possibilities for the narration of the inner self. Though I do not use Cohn's types (her distinctions give rise to other difficulties that are not germane to this study), I recognize in my readings (particularly of George Eliot's novels) that such narratives may proceed differently: readers may be offered an interior monologue that represents the character's unspoken thoughts in his own "mental language,"[26] or narrators may describe the thoughts of a character using the narrator's idiom.

To identify these differences is to recognize that the third person narrator mediates the inner life of characters (as does language itself), but such mediation is different in kind from that of, say, a lawyer, judge, psychiatrist, or a narrator in a work of nonfiction—including a historiographer or a biographer. These figures can only (though not merely) make inferences. The narrator of *Oliver Twist*, to take one example, does not infer. And his unique knowledge is unchallenged by the novel. So potent is this "cognitive privilege"[27] that post-Foucauldian literary critics, most notably D. A. Miller but also John Bender, have focused on the narrator of the late eighteenth- and nineteenth-century novel as an omniscient figure (a term I examine hereafter) with the ability to plumb the depths of its characters in an invasive way, at one with the culture of surveillance with which the novel was complicit. Of the realist novel and its narrator, Bender remarks, "fictional consciousness is experienced as actuality through the convention of transparency, epitomized by the device of free indirect discourse, which presents thought as if it were directly accessible."[28] This claim foregrounds Bender's larger argument—that the narrative strategies of the novel (and other forms of prose fiction and art as well) "enabled the conception and construction of actual penitentiary prisons later in the eighteenth century."[29] Miller makes similar claims about the relations between the novel and the police, claims in which the omniscient narrator's capacity to represent the interior self play a prominent role.[30] In seeking to expose the nineteenth-century novel's disciplinary powers and to debunk the idea of it as a liberal, liberalizing form resistant to authority, Miller's and Bender's texts often make homologous the novel and the other institutional forms under examination (for Miller, the police; for Bender, the prison). My claims also depend on the powers of the third person narrator; however, my argument does not present the criminal law and the novel as homologous forms. Nor do I choose between identifying the novel as a liberalizing force or as a disciplinary technology. Such a choice is, in the end, unproductive, for it reduces the novel to an either/or. Instead, I pursue a mode of analysis that considers the way the narrator's special access both takes the novel outside of the law's epistemological boundaries and at the same time questions the consequences of its own transgression. What happens, for example, when a novelist creates an intent that is as active and material to the reader as an act? How are attitudes toward criminal responsibility altered, and what is the novel's response?

Third person narratives give access to an inner self in ways that profoundly alter our experience of the criminal act, but I am not arguing that the third person narratives of the Victorian novel are the only kinds of literary narratives that imagine the interior life. Consider, for example, *Paradise Lost*, in which the bardic narrator can move us into the minds of Satan, Adam, Eve. I would overplay my hand if I were to argue either that the novel as a form is

defined by narratives that give special access to the interior lives of its characters or that the novel is the only kind of fiction that gives such access. What
one can argue, though, is that in the nineteenth century, novels are the most
influential and popular kinds of fiction and that the third person narrative
rises to power in that century. One of the ways it uses its power is to represent
many different kinds of characters from the inside out.

Moreover, though I call attention to third person narratives here, I recognize that they do not limit the narrative practices of the novel, which include
first person narratives (with the further complication of the epistolary novel)
as well as novels that shift from first to third person narratives (for example,
Dickens's *Bleak House*) and novels that proceed largely through dialogue.
These different practices make a difference in the way one experiences the
minds of characters. First person narratives offer access to the inner self of
the narrator and indirect access to the inner selves of the characters with
whom the narrator comes into contact (though there are necessary distinctions within this category that arise from first person narrators who go beyond this description and third person narrators who on occasion use the first
person—I discuss these later), but even the access the character gives to his
own mind might be distrusted, not unlike the way a witness's testimony might
be called into question.[31] Is the character posturing? Is he concealing from
his audience unappealing aspects of his intentions? Are all aspects of his own
intentions accessible to him? There are some famously unreliable first person
narrators—Nelly Deane in *Wuthering Heights*, for instance. We might ask the
same questions of narrators in epistolary novels, whose willingness to expose
their inner lives is influenced by the anticipated recipient of the letter. Third
person narratives are not free from this family of concerns, since it is entirely
possible for readers to think that the representation of a character's inner self
given by a third person narrator is not believable, that it is inconsistent with
the character as a whole or simply beyond the bounds of credibility. But here
a different issue is raised. It is not that our access to the inner self is inferential or that we have to consider the dramatic limitations of a narrator of which
the narrator himself is not aware. It is instead that the novelist has not the skill
(or will) necessary to make the interior life believable.

The relations between first and third person narrators are explicitly at
issue in Audrey Jaffe's *Vanishing Points: Dickens, Narrative, and the Subject of
Omniscience*, where Jaffe argues that

> omniscience is not a fantasy limited to third person narrators, but one
> whose epistemological implications transcend particular narrative
> modes, breaking down distinctions between first and third person.
> Thus nineteenth century first person narrators, such as David Cop-
> perfield or Charlotte Brontë's Jane Eyre or Lucy Snowe often perform
> the kind of reading usually ascribed only to omniscient narrators, col-
> lapsing the difference between the supposed limitations of first per-
> son and the unlimitedness of third person narration.[32]

While Jaffe's thinking about first and third person narration is salutary, even Jaffe has to take back in part her claim that the differences between them are collapsed, for in the same paragraph she concedes that the narration David Copperfield (for example) provides is "not the same as mind reading."[33] And yet I agree with Jaffe that distinctions between first and third person do on occasion break down (though they are also repaired). To say that first person narrators never attempt to assume the power to enter the inner lives of those they describe is to say too much. The first person narrator of Melville's *Billy Budd* offers the kind of access to the minds of the characters that one expects from a third person narrative, though as others have shown, Melville exposes his narrator as unreliable in ways that mark a significant difference from third person narrators (Eliot's narrator in *Middlemarch*, for instance).[34] At some moments the narrator appears omniscient; at others he lacks such power. In his rich discussion of the novella, Lawrence Douglas explores these "jarring shifts in access," finding that the narrator experiences a "crisis of omniscience" not only but most notably at the moment when Vere tells Billy what his sentence is. Like other critics before him, Douglas zeroes in on this scene because it provokes him to ask why it is that "a narrator who elsewhere claims sweeping access to the consciousness of Billy Budd and Vere should now, in this critical moment, be barred from hearing a mere exchange of words."[35] Douglas argues that the breakdown demontrates that "the judge and the condemned exist in separate normative universes which cannot be made one."[36] The narrator's omniscience reassures readers, concludes Douglas, while its failures reveal its limits. Douglas ends his own reading by noting that "the text frames the distinct discursive limits of both artistic and juridical rendering."[37] While Douglas does not consider the representations of the relations between internal and external elements of crime, as I do here, his reading of *Billy Budd* (like mine of the novels I examine) probes the instances in which a literary text recognizes its own limits (and limitations) and puts those limits up against those within which the law must operate. Tellingly, questions of narrative access are central to *Billy Budd*'s legal/literary critique.

I mention George Eliot in the previous paragraph as a novelist closely associated with third person narratives, yet even in Eliot's novels—novels that proceed as third person narratives—we frequently find narratorial passages presented in the first person. A much-discussed chapter in *Adam Bede*, aptly entitled "In Which the Story Pauses a Little," uses the first person narrator to anticipate the objections of "lady readers" to the story's depiction of its cleric, the less-than-perfect Mr. Irwine, but it would be perverse to name *Adam Bede* as a novel that unfolds as a first person narration.[38] This chapter of the novel sets out Eliot's artistic principles; it does not attempt to offer access to the inner lives of the novel's characters. It makes sense, then, that this is the chapter in which Eliot's narrator compares herself to "the witness in the witness box narrating my experience on oath" (177). The first person narrator operates here much like a dramatized character who must make suppositions, like the rest of us. So too it is significant that the chapter is set off from the rest of the novel, for while a witness has access to his own mind, he does not have access to the minds of others, except by inference. When the "I" of chapter 17 recedes into the background (as it does in the chapters that precede and follow) and the third person narrative reasserts itself, we move back into the minds and hearts of the characters. (We learn in chapter 18, for example, that seeing Hetty come down the stairs in her Sunday best, Mrs. Poyser is "provoked at herself" (186) for smiling at the sight of such prettiness.) Still, it would be ill judged to argue that the distinction between first and third person narration in Eliot's novels was hard and fast. The narrator on occasion shifts unobtrusively between first and third person narration. As the narrator takes readers into the village church, we are asked to have a good look at Mr. Irwine, who is himself looking around at his parishioners:

> I think, as Mr. Irwine looked round to-day, his eyes rested an instant longer than usual on the square pew occupied by Martin Poyser and his family. And there was another pair of eyes that found it impossible not to wander thither, and rest on that round pink-and-white figure. But Hetty was at that moment quite careless of any glances—she was absorbed in the thought that Arthur Donnithorne would soon be coming into church, for the carriage must surely be at the church gate by this time. She had never seen him since she parted with him in the wood on Thursday evening, and oh! How long the time had seemed! (197–8)

The narrator's "I think" makes the observations continuous with those of a very knowledgeable historian, yet as this passage unfolds, the first person narrator recedes, and the third person narrator returns to provide access to the interior lives of both Adam Bede (who finds Hetty irresistible) and Hetty, whose internal voice we hear so clearly at the end of the passage. The porousness of the narration here (and elsewhere in Eliot's novels, and in Dickens's for that matter) does not, I would argue, invite readers to call into question the reliability of the third person narration. The sense that we are in the mind of Hetty is not undermined or subverted or corrupted by the earlier presence of an "I." For one thing, Eliot does not call attention to the move from the "I" to the third person narrator. Once she turns back to the story of Adam Bede after the "pause," she takes no interest in breaking the illusion she creates of a narrator who can enter the minds of the characters. Contrast, for instance, Thackeray's narrator in *Vanity Fair*, a figure who introduces himself as "the Manager of a Performance" and then plays many roles in the story itself, delighting often enough in exposing his fiction as a fiction.[39] Chapter 15 of *Vanity Fair* begins with this challenge:

> What think you were the private feelings of Miss, no, (begging her pardon) of Mrs. Rebecca? If, a few pages back, the present writer claimed the privilege of peeping into Miss Amelia Sedley's bed-room, and understanding with the omniscience of the novelist all the gentle pains

and passions, which were tossing upon that innocent pillow, why should he not declare himself to be Rebecca's confidante too, master of her secrets, and seal-keeper of that young woman's conscience?[40]

These are not questions the narrator goes on to answer: the point is that the answers are obvious. Thackeray pricks his narrator's authority (not only here but elsewhere), exposing omniscience as a fiction, more proof (though we probably do not need more) that postmodernist self-consciousness was alive and well long before anyone thought of the term postmodern. Still, Thackeray is careful to separate the narrator from the novelist. The narrator who operates in *Vanity Fair* as a dramatized character borrows the privileges of the novelist to whom such privileges (like the privilege of inventing a character who can read the inner thoughts of other characters) rightly belong. The passage tweaks omniscience, gesturing comically to its limits. As different as Eliot's narrators are from Thackeray's, the porousness through which Eliot's third person narrations move into the first person does something similar and similarly valuable; it protects the narrator from the term *omniscience*. Though these third person narrators go very far into the minds and hearts of their characters, they are not gods.

J. Hillis Miller has identified the omniscient narrator as "so crucial to nineteenth-century fiction, so inclusive of its implications, that it may be called the determining principle of its form."[41] Though Miller himself uses the term "omniscient," he is quick to qualify it. Instead of operating as God, "standing outside time and space of the action, looking down on the characters with the detachment of a sovereign spectator who sees all, knows all, judges all from a distance,"[42] the Victorian third person narrators have a "perfect knowledge" that is "rather that of a pervasive presence than that of transcendent vision."[43] While Miller is careful to distinguish between God and the third person narrator, he does insist that the narrator's knowledge is "perfect." ("It is an authentic perfection of knowledge. The omniscient narrator is able to remember perfectly all the past, to foresee the future course of events, and to penetrate with irresistible insight the most secret crevice in the heart of each man."[44]) Unlike Miller I do not use the term "omniscient" to describe the third person narrator, because while the third person narrators I examine in this study have access to minds in ways that mere mortals do not (and I agree with Miller that the narrator "can know the person better than the person knows himself"), even these narrators do not make the mind completely known, without ambiguity.[45] Can the minds of characters be known, be explained fully, totally, completely?[46] The preceding discussion offers passages through which we are allowed to experience Hetty's confusions through interior monologue, and what she does not know about her own mind is significant to our judgment of her. But what of the narrator herself? In her analysis of Virginia Woolf's *To the Lighthouse*, Martha Nussbaum grapples with this problem, though for a very different purpose.[47] Using Woolf, Nussbaum explores "the problem of other minds"—that is, the way that other minds are in-

THE CRIME IN MIND

accessible to us—and concludes that Woolf's work is germane to this philosophical knot "through her depiction of the sheer many-sidedness of the problem of other minds, by her indication that it is not a single problem at all, but many distinct human difficulties that are in complex ways interrelated."[48] The difficulties Nussbaum names are pertinent here, for while she argues that "we know things about the minds of others when we read novels of consciousness," she details the kinds of limitations (inadequacies of language to represent the human mind, for instance) that even Woolf's "novel of consciousness" cannot overcome.[49] While Woolf's radical model presents these problems with a singular insistence, George Eliot precedes Woolf in confronting them. These limitations are in part what make the external act so important to the thinking about moral and legal responsibility at work in the novels I consider in the chapters that follow.

⇥ Foucault's Criminal Soul ⇤

When the critics D. A. Miller and John Bender identify the third person (what they would call the omniscient) narrator in the novel, and particularly in the Victorian novel, as complicit with the disciplinary technology of criminal law, they acknowledge their debt to Michel Foucault's *Discipline and Punish* (*Surveiller et punir*). Indeed, Foucault makes some complicated historical claims in that text about the transformation of crime as an object of punishment in the nineteenth century, and he is notably interested in the way the law treats states of mind. What Foucault's analysis highlights are the ways the boundaries between judgment of a specific act and judgment of character become, at best, more difficult to determine and, at worst, more readily manipulated to contain transgressive behavior and to coerce those who will not conform. He targets, more specifically, changes in nineteenth-century jurisprudence that, in effect, shifted attention from an act to an intent, from external behavior to internal drives, from conduct to character. "Under cover of the relative stability of the law," writes Foucault,

> a mass of subtle and rapid changes has occurred. Certainly the "crimes" and "offences" on which judgement is passed are juridical objects defined by the code, but judgement is also passed on the passions, instincts, anomalies, infirmities, maladjustments, effects of environment or heredity; acts of aggression are punished, so also, through them, is aggressivity; rape, but at the same time perversions; murders, but also drives and desires. But, it will be objected, judgment is not actually being passed on them, if they are referred to at all it is to explain the actions in question, and to determine to what extent the subject's will was involved in the crime. This is no answer. For it *is* these shadows lurking behind the case itself that are judged and punished. They are judged indirectly as "attenuating circumstances" that

introduce into the verdict not only "circumstantial" evidence, but something quite different, which is not juridically codifiable: the knowledge of the criminal, one's estimation of him, what is known about the relations between him, his past and his crime, and what might be expected of him in the future. They are also judged by the interplay of all those notions that have circulated between medicine and jurisprudence since the nineteenth century (the "monsters" of Georget's times, Chaumié's "physical anomalies," the "perverts" and "maladjusted" of our own experts) and which, behind the pretext of explaining the action, are ways of defining the individual.[50]

And later in the same paragraph:

The criminal's soul is not referred to in the trial merely to explain his crime and as a factor in the juridical apportioning of responsibility; if it is brought before the court, with such pomp and circumstance, such concern to understand and such "scientific" application, it is because it too, as well as the crime itself, is to be judged and to share in the punishment.[51]

Note that these passages ask us to attend to states of mind, motives, intentions as both "shadows lurking" behind cases and as elements that are explicitly introduced at trial with "such pomp and circumstance." Since Foucault wants to expose "mercy" as a form of discipline, perhaps this explains part of his resistance to "circonstances atténuantes."[52] Yet, one is surprised to find that "circonstances atténuantes" are to be determined by a jury and not by a judge or some other expert. The early pages of *Discipline and Punish* are dedicated to showing the way judges vested power in experts with regard to degrees of punishment. Stephen's analysis shows that, at least with respect to "circonstances atténuantes," an alarming amount of power was vested in the importantly nonexpert jury, a fact that makes Foucault's analysis hard to interpret. One of the central ideas here—that the soul is being judged as much as the act itself—is not a new one, nor is it one that the law has not overtly struggled with and over. We have, for instance, longstanding (unresolved and unresolvable) arguments in jurisprudential treatises well before and well into the nineteenth century that assert that criminal law requires evidence of a wicked state of mind. Such a mental state does not appear in court "merely to explain his crime" nor is it offered as a pretext for explaining an action; it is identified as an object of judgment in and of itself. Foucault plays down the criminal law's overt emphasis on state of mind as an object of judgment so that he can argue that in the nineteenth century in particular the law as an institution began to conspire with psychiatry to use the courtroom not to punish acts but to discipline minds, to diagnose and not to sentence. Taking up Foucault's analysis and applying his arguments to the relations between the novel and psychiatry, Sally Shuttleworth, in *Charlotte Brontë and Victorian Psychology* puts the case more straightforwardly:

As Foucault has argued, the nineteenth century witnessed the emergence of a new economy of individual and social life, centered on the regulation of the forces of the body and controlled through surveillance. A new interiorized notion of selfhood arose and, concomitantly, new techniques of power designed to penetrate the inner secrets of this hidden domain. Psychiatry and phrenology emerged as science, dedicated to decoding the external signs of the body in order to reveal the concealed inner play of forces which constitute individual subjectivity.[53]

Criminal law and its old techniques of power have long been and still are very much in the business of "decoding the external signs of the body in order to reveal the concealed inner play of forces which constitute individual subjectivity." However, I take the point that what is particular about the Victorian period, as Foucault and then Shuttleworth might claim in response, is that as more extensive medical testimony about mental states entered the courtroom, the testimony about mental states became more elaborate and the relations between the internal and the external necessarily shifted. I would note, though, that Foucault does not account for the great conflicts between law and psychiatry, conflicts so deep that Fitzjames Stephen—in his chapter on the relation of madness to crime in *A History of the Criminal Law of England*—takes special notice of the oppositional interactions between law and medicine:

> [T]he subject has excited a controversy between the medical and the legal professions in which many things have been said which would, I think, have been better unsaid. Cruelty, ignorance, prejudice, and the like, are freely ascribed to the law and to those who administer it, on the grounds that it is said not to keep pace with the discoveries of science and to deny facts medically ascertained. The heat and vehemence with which such charges are made makes a perfectly impartial discussion of the whole matter difficult. It is hard for any one not to resent attacks upon a small body of which he is himself is a member, such attacks being often harsh and rude, and almost always connected with if not founded upon misconceptions. The interest and possibly the importance of the task is, however, upon a par with its difficulty, and it certainly should be said, in extenuation of the violent language which medical writers frequently use upon this matter, that they are sometimes treated in courts of justice, even by judges, in a manner which, I think, they are entitled to resent.[54]

So the "interplay of all those notions that have circulated between medicine and jurisprudence since the nineteenth century" was not as free and easy as Foucault's description suggests, and the law's resistance to the evidence of the mind brought in by medical experts indicates that that evidence and those experts were not wholeheartedly (or even halfheartedly) embraced. Foucault's observations should, however, be read in the context of the significant differences between the French and English systems of justice in the nineteenth century, differences Stephen vividly describes in his earlier work *A General View of Criminal Law*: "The English system of criminal procedure is almost exclusively litigious; the French almost exclusively inquisitorial."[55] By this Stephen means to bring to his reader's attention the way the French trial "is nothing less than the last stage in an elaborate public inquiry, carried on by an organized public department."[56] While the prosecutor in an English criminal trial received almost no support and had to make his case like a private individual, the prosecutor in a French case, like all the other officials in the case, was an agent of the government. This significant procedural difference probably influences Foucault's analysis of the relations between law and medicine.

The questions Foucault raises concern moments in which criminal law appeared to be judging not an act but a type, and not conduct but character. Even if we leave aside whether or not the "something quite different" that Foucault names is or is not "juridically codifiable," we need to pay attention to the fact that the criminal law has certainly moved cautiously around the introduction into court of such elements as "the knowledge of the criminal, one's estimation of him, what is known about the relations between him, his past and his crime." Stephen himself reports in his *Digest of the Law of Evidence* that evidence of a past criminal act was not admissible to prove that a defendant committed the act for which he was then on trial, even if the past act constituted a similar crime. Moreover, prosecutors were prohibited from introducing facts whose purpose was to show "a tendency to commit such crimes."[57] For example, in *Russell on Crime*, Turner describes *R. v. Cole*, an 1810 case (unreported) that determined that character evidence could not be introduced at trial as proof that the defendant committed the act of which he stood accused. Identifying the case as involving "a prosecution for an unnatural offence," Turner goes on to explain that *Cole* "held that an admission by the prisoner that he had committed such an offence at another time, and with another person, and that his natural inclination was toward such practices, ought not to be received in evidence.[58] Not surprisingly, there were exceptions to the rule, and "when there is a question whether an act was accidental or intentional, the fact that such act formed part of a series of similar occurrences in each of which the person doing the act was concerned, is relevant."[59] Stephen gives the following example.

> The question is whether the administration of poison to A, by Z, his wife, in September, 1848, was accidental or intentional. The facts that B, C, and D (A's three sons) had the same poison administered to them in December, 1848, March, 1849, and April 1849, and that the meals of all four were prepared by Z, are relevant, though Z was indicted separately for murdering A, B, and C, and attempting to murder D.[60]

This seems a significant exception, large enough to swallow the rule itself, but, continues Stephen, the general rule that makes such evidence inadmissible remained of more importance than its exceptions, and, further, "in criminal cases the Courts are always disinclined to run the risk of prejudicing the prisoner by permitting matters to be proved which tend to show in general that he is a bad man, and so likely to commit a crime."[61] Even with this explanation in mind, one registers a tension between the rule and its exceptions. Evidence of past acts did enter the courtroom, to prove not only that the accused committed a criminal act but also that he was a man of corrupt disposition.

Victorian criminal law identifies the difference between holding a person responsible for what he does and holding a person responsible for who he is, even as it allows room for the kind of boundary-crossing I have just described. When does character become conduct? In attending here and in my next chapter to the relations between conduct and character, I am often thinking about them in relation to the external and internal elements of crime, but one needs to recognize that conduct is not conterminous with the external, and character is not conterminous with the internal. In judging an individual's character, we consider what he or she does and what we imagine, on the basis of those actions, he or she thinks (and is). Character sometimes suggests more of a totality of circumstances—both internal and external. Two of the definitions the *OED* ascribes to "chararacter" illuminate its ambiguity. Character can be "reputation" and so be based on opinions of internal qualities and external actions. It also more narrowly means "mental and moral constitution."[62] Likewise, descriptions of conduct often advert to a certain state of mind. To speak of medical treatment as torture or of a killing as a murder suggests the particular state of mind that attaches to the conduct in question. Yet when conduct and character are paired, as they are, for example, in Dickens's preface to *Oliver Twist*, one's impulse is to see these terms as distinct, even oppositional. The same can be said of other familiarly paired terms. Absent 'subjective,' 'objective' has a large range of meaning; paired with 'subjective,' 'objective' turns into its opposite. These familiar pairings are both necessary and inadequate, even perilous, since they invite us to imagine that ideas easily fall under one heading or the other. Such pairings also create the opportunity to deceive, to suggest that one is limited to this or that alternative. There is a clear need for the distinctions presented by terms like objective/subjective, conduct/character, internal/external, but we must also recognize, as Dickens and George Eliot ask us to do, that these distinctions will eventually fail us. When Dickens and Eliot imagine the possibility that the activity of the mind may be judged as conduct—so much so that Gwendolen in *Daniel Deronda* believes that she has murdered her husband with her mind—they contest the distinctions between the internal and external. Still, in the novels of both Dickens and Eliot, we are turned back to a world in which the distinction between an act and a thought, conduct and character, is steadfastly maintained.

⚜ The Novel, Inside and Out ⚜

The pairing I am most obviously interested in throughout this study is the pairing of the criminal law and the novel. The pairing leads me to ask what difference it makes that the novel has the license to represent interiority not by inference but directly. In undertaking this work, I have been much indebted, as so many scholars working in this field are, to Alexander Welsh and his indispensable book *Strong Representations: Narrative and Circumstantial Evidence in England*. The central argument of his work is that the criminal law's preference for circumstantial evidence over testimony in the eighteenth and nineteenth centuries influenced the narrative practices of legal and literary texts of these periods: novels became narratives of circumstantial evidence, narratives in which external circumstances are arranged to tell a convincing story. While I am both persuaded and inspired by much of Welsh's argument about the relations between evidence and the structure of fictional narrative, I question the way Welsh lines up legal and literary texts. For Welsh, Scott's representation of evidence for or against Waverley (to take one example) and our experience of those representations are no different from what we would get from an exceptionally good lawyer or from a very well-managed legal narrative. Welsh proceeds as if when we read a novel or other work of fiction our access to the inner life is as limited and as inferentially bounded as the access we are allowed when we observe a trial or read a legal narrative. He assumes that, as in a court of law, we must ascertain motive and intent from the outside, that the narrator and we must work by inference. I disagree. When Welsh turns his attention to Scott's *Waverley* as a narrative of circumstantial evidence, he does not account for the way the third person narration invites us into the mind of Waverley. Yet when Welsh describes the scene in which Waverley is arrested for desertion and inciting mutiny, he remarks, "Thus Waverley not only accedes to the formalities of his arrest but inwardly weighs the evidence against him. He knows his innocence, because he has not held any wicked or criminal intention in what he has done. At the same time, he realizes that his intentions will be judged by the circumstances, whatever he says."[63] While it may be true that characters who participate in *Waverley*'s fictional legal proceedings—including the advocates for the prosecution and the defense—rely on outward circumstances (including Waverley's own testimony), we as readers do not rely on them. Not only do we have access to the mind of Waverley at the moment of his arrest, we have had access to his mind during his dealings with Fergus Mac-Ivor. We know what Waverley's motives and intentions have been and what they are now. Welsh's analysis of *Tom Jones* is a good deal more convincing, since in that novel Fielding limits the access one has to the mind of the characters. Welsh adeptly shows us that Fielding's narrator occupies the position not of witness but of a "manager of evidence, analogous to a prosecutor or a judge and to later defense attorneys."[64] Fielding's narrator, then, does not have any more access to Tom's motives than an expert who assembles and reviews the facts of the case. What is unpersuasive throughout Welsh's impressive book is the way Welsh assumes that the novel abides by the same limitations as a legal narrative and that as readers our relation to these two narratives is the same. When Welsh moves from eighteenth- and early nineteenth- to later nineteenth- and early twentieth-century novels, he argues that novelists begin to reject the narrative of circumstantial evidence and offer instead narratives of experience. Novelists, Welsh claims, turn to testimony (including confession) as the preferred form of story-telling. But it is not the case that these are the only choices open to novelists. Novels can and regularly do reach beyond circumstantial and testimonial evidence. Which is not to say, then, that I reject the claim that legal trials exercised influence over the shaping of literary narrative in the nineteenth century. However, literary narratives are not bounded by the same epistemological limitations that apply in a court of law (and in life). I am interested in thinking about the relations between different kinds of evidence presented in a text—not only testimonial or indirect (circumstantial) evidence but also evidence that can be presented precisely because we are reading a novel.

There is a telling moment in *Strong Representations* when Welsh recognizes that the novelist's representation of the inner self might be distinguishable from that produced in a legal text or in the course of a legal proceeding, yet this recognition confirms for him that literary texts are no different from legal or philosophical texts. In considering the power of the narrative of circumstantial evidence in the eighteenth century, Welsh notes that one of its most significant features was its ability to use perjured testimony against the accused as evidence of intent. Since lying under oath undermined the accused's credibility in other ways, it could be used against him, and the perjured testimony was not, therefore, simply excluded: "The great triumph of circumstantial evidence over direct testimony—including confession," states Welsh, "is that it can turn even false testimony to account." From this Welsh concludes with these provocative but in the end problematic remarks:

> Thus motive and intent can be wrested away from both defendant and witness and reconstructed from circumstances over which neither had anything like complete control, just as, in the larger eighteenth century scene, confessions, memoirs, letters, and eyewitness history are giving way to more complete but connected narratives, in which even states of mind can be described from the outside. Not altogether surprisingly, Burke's trust in "the sagacity of the observer" and Bentham's more intricate review of particulars will one day be turned around by Michel Foucault to proclaim a narrative based on "surveillance." The movement in the English novel from first person to third person narratives should not be seen as an isolated literary development, and in novels as elsewhere, circumstantial evidence might emerge as a threat to private being. One of the designs co-opted from Defoe and Richardson by strong representations was the privilege of narrating a character's own thoughts.[65]

It is not quite clear what Welsh means when he calls our attention to narratives "in which even states of mind can be described from the outside." I take this to mean that outsiders described the states of minds of others and not merely their own mental states, though I wonder how an eyewitness history (of any historical period) could be expected to provide anything but a description of others' states of mind "from the outside." The larger problem in the passage, though, is that Welsh produces the third person narrative of the eighteenth- and nineteenth-century novel as if it were no different from the narratives of Burke and Bentham. The passage suggests that nineteenth-century English novels threatened "private being" by using circumstantial evidence to invade the mind of the subject, to narrate "a character's own thoughts." One thing to say in response is that circumstantial evidence was used as evidence of state of mind long before Burke and Bentham, since the law required evidence of intent, and that evidence always (by necessity) came "from the outside," even when it was gleaned from testimonial, that is to say direct, evidence. Still, I take Welsh's point: the criminal law of the nineteenth century was delving more deeply into the mind of the accused, as I will later discuss. I am most interested, though, in the matters that Welsh considers in the last part of this complicated passage. To paraphrase Welsh: nineteenth-century novelists assumed the "privilege" of narrating a character's own thoughts, a privilege Defoe and Richardson enjoyed in their first person narratives of the prior century. Welsh's observation should prompt us to think about the relation between first and third person narration. While the first person narrators of the novels of Defoe and Richardson can reveal their own thoughts, desires, and intentions, Welsh observes that the third person narratives reveal the interior life of other characters, but do so by inferring those mental states from external signs, by means of (in other words) circumstantial evidence. A necessary question follows: why would the third person narrators of the nineteenth-century novel need circumstantial evidence to narrate a character's own thoughts? These narrators do not have to infer thought from circumstance. They give us direct access to the thoughts themselves. Even if one argued that in third person narratives a novelist was imagining and then inferring from the circumstances he created what a character might think, the structure of the narrative as presented to us is not one in which those thoughts are inferred from circumstances. We inhabit the mind of a character without needing to make any inference from outside circumstances. The Victorian novel's investment in the third person narrator marked its distinction from and at moments superiority to other disciplines—law and psychology, for instance—that had to infer knowledge. As Audrey Jaffe argues, the "explicit and implicit insistence on narratorial knowledge," including "the sharp epistemological distinctions between narrator and character," signals "an emphatic display of knowledge," a display that, I would add, no other discourse could claim so fully.[66]

More recent law and literature studies have explored the relations between first and third person narration beyond those animated by Foucault.

In the course of *Testimony and Advocacy in Victorian Law, Literature, and Theology*—a detailed and adept response to Welsh's *Strong Representations*—Jan-Melissa Schramm briefly considers third person narration in legal and literary discourse, but she too, on occasion, elides legal and literary practices.[67] Schramm's study persuasively tests Welsh's claims about the demotion of testimonial evidence in the nineteenth century and exposes the influence that the introduction of defense attorneys empowered to speak for their clients had on testimonial evidence and on trials more generally. Schramm is most often sensitive to the differences between legal and literary narratives, particularly "the ethical agenda of both types of discourse,"[68] and she notes (for instance) that novelists need the limitations of the law to "find their own imaginative space in which to pursue their own quest for justice."[69] Schramm looks in detail at the consequences of the Prisoners' Counsel Act of 1836, through which advocates gained "the right to narrate a suspected felon's thoughts or intentions."[70] Real advocates, according to Schramm, operate like their fictional counterparts and like authors themselves: in Schramm's analysis, the right to narrate the thoughts and intentions of the accused is a right that advocates and fictional lawyers and authors "share."[71] But there is a potential and suggestive problem here, and it is a tricky one that Schramm's astute analysis does not quite face, for that analysis does not account for the special position that the third person narrator (a figure that one may need to distinguish from the author) occupies. While both lawyers and third person narrators may present details about the thoughts of the accused, it is worth considering the difference it makes that the details presented by the third person narrator exist in an imaginative context in which that narrator may have unique and unchallenged access to those thoughts—the kind of access that no person (whether or not a lawyer) could ever hope to have. The third person narrator need not wait for the accused to tell his story; that narrator can enter his mind directly. While Schramm rightly asserts that the novel is not a trial and that "authors are . . . liberated by artistic license to snatch a protagonist from the gallows, to reverse judgements at will or to act on the basis of information which would not have been available to a court [because of the exclusionary rules of evidence],"[72] she does not take up what might be a more telling difference: that the narrators they create can read minds. Schramm argues on the last page of her book that Victorian law and literature went their separate ways at mid-century because authors remained committed to the idea that the best and most trustworthy evidence of intention depended on "access to the story of the accused"[73] in the form of testimonial evidence ("the defendant's own words and his or her assessment of his or her accountability"[74]) and that argument persuades as far as it goes, but the novel's representations of the interior life produce yet other complications, for the third person narrator produces a narrative of that interior life that goes beyond—even beneath—testimonial evidence. My own argument often turns on this distinction.

Thinking about the difference between real people and characters in novels, E. M. Forster—a twentieth-century writer who situated himself at "the fag end of Victorian Liberalism"[75]—gets to the heart of the matter. Though Forster does not bring the law into his argument, in placing the historical against the literary (the nonfictional against the fictional) narrative, his observations speak to a central difference between legal and literary narrative:

> The historian deals with actions, and with the characters of men only so far as he can deduce them from their actions. He is quite as much concerned with character as the novelist, but he can only know of its existence when it shows on the surface. If Queen Victoria had not said "We are not amused," her neighbours at table would not have known she was not amused, and her ennui could never have been announced to the public. She might have frowned, so that they would have deduced her state from that—looks and gestures are also historical evidence. But if she remained impassive—what would anyone know? The hidden life is, by definition, hidden. The hidden life that appears in external signs is hidden no longer, has entered the realm of action. And it is the function of the novelist to reveal the hidden life at its source: to tell us more about Queen Victoria than could be known, and thus to produce a character who is not the Queen Victoria of history.[76]

A bit later, he adds that

> the historian records whereas the novelist must create. Still, it is a profitable roundabout, for it brings out the fundamental difference between people in daily life and people in books. In daily life we never understand each other, neither complete clairvoyance nor complete confessional exists. We know each other approximately, by external signs, and these serve well enough as a basis for society and even for intimacy. But people in a novel can be understood completely by the reader, if the novelist wishes; their inner as well as their outer life can be exposed.[77]

It's easy enough to call Forster naive for thinking that historians (or lawyers, for that matter) do not also "create." In my chapter 4, I take up the complications of historical creation when I explore James Fitzjames Stephen's response to Macaulay's historical treatment of the Maharajah Nuncomar, Warren Hastings, and Elijah Impey. It is also true that Forster oddly overstates his case when he claims that "people in a novel can be understood completely by the reader," though I suppose by adding "if the novelist wishes" he makes a useful distinction. There are certainly some characters who hold no mystery for us and in whom we are usually the least interested. Notwithstanding these reservations, Forster's central claim—that "novels reveal the hidden life at its source"—remains a potent one, and the distinction he maintains between the novel, history, and everyday life is one that deserves our attention.

⊰ The Inner Life of the Criminal Law: ⊱
"Actus Non Est Reus Nisi Mens Sit Rea"

Since this study depends on understanding and exploring the representations of and relations between the external and internal elements of crime, I need to begin with a brief discussion of the elements themselves. Apart from strict liability offenses, crimes consist of two elements: an *actus reus* and a *mens rea*. The *actus reus* comprises the external element of crime—the act and its consequences—and the *mens rea* concerns the internal elements, or, as H. L. A. Hart conceives of them, "the mental and intellectual elements" that are "many and various and are collected together in the terminology of English jurists under the simple sounding description of *mens rea*—a guilty mind."[78] In strict liability offenses, no *mens rea* is required. Statutes regulating the sale of food and drugs often define such offenses. In the 1846 case of *R. v. Woodward*, for example, the defendant was shown to have had no knowledge or reason to know that tobacco in his possession was bad, but he was convicted of possession of bad tobacco nonetheless.[79] While strict liability offenses require no *mens rea*, certain other crimes are defined such that the defendant need only act negligently, which means that the defendant should have been aware of some circumstance whether or not he was in fact aware of it. Disagreement has arisen about criminal negligence as a *mens rea*. Does a negligent act require a culpable state of mind, or are negligent offenses really strict liability offenses? There is an argument to be made that a negligent accused can and should be said to have a culpable state of mind. The most that Glanville Williams, in his highly influential English criminal law textbook of the last half century, can say is that "Negligence in law is not necessarily a state of mind; and thus these crimes are best regarded as not requiring a *mens rea*."[80] Tucked into "not necessarily" and "are best regarded" is a concession that these crimes may be regarded as requiring proof of *mens rea*. Moreover, J. W. C. Turner, in his edition of *Kenny's Outlines of Criminal Law* (one of the more important and most accessible documentations of the English criminal law, which first appeared in 1902), lists negligence as among the elements of *mens rea*, though he goes on to argue that at common law, negligence cannot constitute the mental element of a crime, notwithstanding the fact that it may be made culpable by statute.[81] The philosopher Anthony Kenny asks the question directly: "Is negligence a form of *mens rea*? Some argue that unawareness is not a state of mind and so negligence is not *mens rea*; others argue that because negligence is voluntary and culpable unawareness, the requirement of *mens rea* is present in crimes of negligence."[82] What is clearer is that offenses of strict liability—offenses in which the defendant may not have had even a careless or negligent state of mind—are defined as not needing a prosecutor to adduce any evidence as to mental state. But strict liability criminal offenses are the exception, not the rule.

To identify the elements of criminal responsibility—the *actus reus* and the *mens rea*—is already to get into the thick of things, for no treatise on English criminal law has yet been written that does not include as still good law the great pronouncement of Justice Brian, from the reign of Edward IV, to wit, that "the thought of man is not triable, for the devil himself knoweth not the thought of man,"[83] a dictum that hardened into a maxim. Glanville Williams cites it on the first page of his work on criminal law as "a favourite legal quotation."[84] Brian's maxim is appealingly logical. The law cannot put on trial that to which it has no access. The epistemological limitation structures the law itself. At best, the law can know and therefore judge an act—a visible occurrence. But it is of the nature of maxims to be open to countermaxims. "It is not correct," writes Fitzjames Stephen in *A General View of the Criminal Law* (1863), "to speak of any visible occurrences as constituting crimes, either by themselves or collectively. A mental element is a necessary part of every crime."[85] The invisible element of crime must be made visible in a court of law. As J. W. C. Turner remarks:

> By the end of the Middle Ages the courts had abandoned the notion that the mind of man cannot be investigated. Bowen, L.J. in 1891 declared such a principle to be fallacious and said "so far from saying that you cannot look into a man's mind, you must look into it, if you are going to find fraud against him; and unless you think you see what must have been in his mind, you cannot find him guilty of fraud." Once it had been admitted that some degree of wickedness was a requisite in criminal guilt, it followed logically that *mens rea* must eventually become a subjective matter of an increasingly subtle kind.[86]

So not just a criminal state of mind but wickedness itself becomes a requisite of criminal guilt. Whether or not *mens rea* imports into crimes an element of moral blameworthiness is a question about which Victorian jurists disagreed. Fitzjames Stephen argued that the term was "ignorantly supposed to mean that there cannot be such a thing as legal guilt without moral guilt, which is obviously untrue, as there is always the possibility of a conflict between law and morals."[87] Still, the term *mens rea* carries moral weight, and the twentieth-century legal philosopher H. L. A. Hart concedes that "traces of this view [that *mens rea* means an evil mind] are to be found in scattered observations of English and American judges—in phrases such as 'an evil mind with regard to that which he is doing', 'a bad mind', or references to acts done not 'merely unguardedly or accidentally, without any evil mind.'"[88]

Not many readers would, I think, be surprised by Turner's emphatic statement that as the criminal law developed, *mens rea* was to "become a subjective matter of an increasingly subtle kind," and yet even in Turner one detects a tension. Turner cites Bowen, L. J., who claims not only that we do look into the mind of the accused, but that we "must look into it." However, what the jury is required to find is "what must have been in his mind," which is a different thing from saying that the jury is required to find what was in fact in his mind. What must have been in his mind is inferred from other evidence. Perhaps what must have been in his mind is what we imagine would have been in our minds, should we have been in his place, or what must have been in the mind of some imagined reasonable man, or what an accused claimed to have been in his mind. The historical developments that made *mens rea* "a subjective matter of an increasingly subtle kind" (to use Turner's phrase) necessarily come up against the limitations of knowing what is in a person's mind.[89] Tellingly, as Edward Griew remarks, "Little, certainly, relating to mens rea or its proof in the nineteenth century is consistent or clear."[90]

The essential point that Turner through Bowen makes—that the thought of man goes on trial—is undeniable because, *pace* Brian, "*Actus non est reus nisi mens sit rea*": "The act is not criminal unless the state of mind is criminal." Here is a maxim more famous than that of Brian. It appears in Coke's *Institutes* but not only in Coke. Pollock and Maitland cite Augustine's *Sermones* as providing that "*Ream linguam non facit nisi mens rea*."[91] Revised by Coke in the early seventeenth century as "*Et actus non est reus nisi mens sit rea*,"[92] the phrase was "the best known maxim of English criminal law"[93] in the nineteenth century. Stephen notes that the phrase "is sometimes said to be the fundamental maxim of the whole criminal law.[94] The maxim gives us the two parts of criminal responsibility: an act and a state of mind. To pass judgment on a criminal defendant is to try what Brian says cannot be tried and to know (at least beyond a reasonable doubt) what cannot be known, and what cannot be known is what some have identified as an essential element that makes an act a crime.

So perhaps a criminal state of mind is the key element, the one we most care about in holding persons accountable. In his *Report from the Committee of the House of Commons* prepared as part of his prosecution of Warren Hastings, Edmund Burke in the eighteenth century took the opportunity to comment on the nature of crime. "In all Criminal Cases, the Crime (except where the law implies Malice)" remarks Burke, "consists rather in the Intention than in the Action."[95] Or, as Oliver Wendell Holmes surmised more memorably: "Even a dog knows the difference between being stumbled over and being kicked." In his zeal to incriminate Warren Hastings, Burke took the bold step of privileging the internal. But a crime is not a crime without an act. In his edition of *Kenny's Outlines of Criminal Law,* under the heading "*Mens Rea* Alone Not Enough," J. W. C. Turner puts the case clearly enough: "In law an *actus reus* is always required, although in ethics a guilty mind alone may be held sufficient to constitute guilt."[96] And this observation turns Turner's attention, unexpectedly, to Dr. Johnson. Johnson in conversation about actors and acting inquired of the actor J. P. Kemble whether he was "one of those enthusiasts who believe yourself transformed into the very character you represent," and after Kemble responded that he did not believe himself to be transformed, Johnson concluded, "if Garrick really believed himself to be that monster, Richard the Third, he deserved to be hanged every time he performed it."[97] What draws Turner to this passage from Boswell's *Life of Johnson* is the way it highlights the law's boundaries, for the law will not, as Turner notes, "inflict penalties upon mere internal feeling, when it has produced no result in external conduct."[98]

Trying to save Johnson from any such mistake about the law, Turner asserts that "Dr. Johnson's remark was not a serious argument but a neat *jeu d'esprit*. For the actor, when on the stage, was a mere simulacrum of a man long since dead and gone, and the feeling was against another such lifeless creature; any moral censure therefore could only be levelled against the character portrayed."[99] Turner simplifies the problem a good deal here, since Johnson specifically imagines a transformation of the actor. The actor believes himself to be a murderer and intends to commit murder, so that the actor is no "mere simulacrum." Once the actor undergoes the transformation, might he not be said to have the *mens rea* of a murderer? There is no murder—but is there an attempt? Johnson's comment to Kemble says something not only about the transformation of the actor but about the power of the drama to inspire the actor to imagine himself as a murderer and the power of imagination itself to transform us. When we shift our attention from drama to novels, the question is not so much one of a transforming performance (though certainly Dickens's famous readings of his novels were very much performances and transformative ones at that) as of the possibilities in novels to render the interior and test the boundaries between acts and intents.

I name intents here, but as the preceding discussion suggests, intention is not a necessary element of all crimes. Recklessness may be sufficient for a charge of manslaughter, for instance. However, intention, as H. L. A. Hart remarks, was and remains "probably the most prominent . . . and in many ways the most important" of the mental elements that are taken up into the term *mens rea*.[100] The relations between the intentional and the *voluntary*—another term that is at the center of jurisprudential considerations of *mens rea*—produce deep and lasting complications for judgments about responsibility. In his chapter on criminal responsibility in *A History of the Criminal Law of England*, Fitzjames Stephen makes plain that responsibility for all crimes (except crimes of omission) depends on a finding that the alleged criminal act was voluntary: "In order that an act may be criminal it must be a voluntary act done by a person free from certain forms of compulsion."[101] Deciding whether or not an act was voluntary itself turns on probing different mental elements, including intentions. Stephen gives these examples:

> A man who stumbles forward to save himself from falling acts mechanically and cannot be called a voluntary agent in doing so. In the same way if there is no intention, if the movements of the body are not combined or directed to any definite end, there may be action, but it is not voluntary action. A man receiving news by which he was much excited might show his excitement by a variety of bodily movements, as, for instance, by the muscular movements that change the expression of the face, but the question whether they were or were not voluntary would depend on the further question whether they were intentional.[102]

Voluntariness, intention, knowledge, foreseeability: here is a set of terms that jurists (and nonjurists) use to describe an act and its consequences. These terms shape our judgment of criminal responsibility. Figuring out whether an act was or was not voluntary leads us into intent, and intent, in its turn, raises further questions: did the accused have sufficient knowledge of circumstances to render his act intentional? Did he foresee the consequences of his act? Intentions lead us far into the mind of the accused.[103]

Focusing as I do on the relations between the internal and external elements of crime, I necessarily take up causation, a term that, though not at the center of my study, is on occasion at issue. Criminal law must, of course, address causation as a topic. In their seminal study *Causation in the Law*, H. L. A. Hart and Tony Honoré note that causation in both civil and criminal law works not only to attach but also to limit responsibility:

> as in tort, so in criminal law courts have often limited responsibility by appealing to the causal distinctions embedded in ordinary thought, with their emphasis on voluntary interventions and abnormal or coincidental events as factors negativing responsibility. Indeed, the general course of decision in the two spheres is strikingly similar.[104]

Nan Goodman's work on the influence of the newly bourgeoning doctrine of civil negligence on representations of accidents in nineteenth-century American legal and literary narratives details the ways that changing notions of causation complicated judgments of civil responsibility and assessment of damages for industrial accidents. The recognition that one could identify many potential causes (as opposed to one "objective cause") of any given accident created significant cultural anxieties. Who would be held responsible for the damages?[105] When I turn to George Eliot's *Adam Bede* in chapter 2, I examine the novel's representation of the anxieties that arise out of the potentially limitless consequences caused by an act, and that examination calls into play notions of causation and, more significantly, the relations between these external elements of responsibility and the internal element of responsibility, that is to say, *mens rea*. Whereas Goodman in her study of the civil law need not take up representations of mental states, they stand at the center of my own. So different is the criminal from the civil law in its treatment of mental states that the criminal law can hold an accused responsible for inchoate offenses (conspiracies and attempts, for instance), offenses in which the harm to another person or piece of property has not yet even been caused.

⊰ Novels and "The Mysterious Complexity of Our Life" ⊱

While the maxims first from Brian and then from Coke take us far, we need George Eliot's censure of the "man of maxims" to expose their limitations:

> All people of broad, strong sense have an instinctive repugnance to the men of maxims; because such people early discern that the myste-

rious complexity of our life is not to be embraced by maxims, and that to lace ourselves up in formulas of that sort is to repress all the divine promptings and inspirations that spring from growing insight and sympathy. And the man of maxims is the popular representative of the minds that are guided in their moral judgment solely by general rules, thinking that these will lead them to justice by a ready-made patent method, without the trouble of exerting patience, discrimination, impartiality, without any care to assure themselves whether they have the insight that comes from a hardly-earned estimate of temptation, or from a life vivid and intense enough to have created a wide fellow-feeling with all that is human.[106]

This critique from *The Mill on the Floss* has an anti-Kantian flavor to it. It produces a harsh criticism of both the moral and the legal maxim in its invocation of the "ready-made patent method" that is used to "lead them to justice." Eliot makes clear in some just measure the narrowness of a mind that is guided "solely by general rules," as opposed to minds guided by, say, a George Eliot novel, a form that resists the restrictions of formula, invites the "divine promptings and inspirations that spring from growing insight and sympathy," and celebrates the "mysterious complexity of our life." One registers the poise of Eliot's resistance to maxims when she figures the embrace of maxims as a form of imprisonment. Those who adhere to maxims become laced up in formulas, so that the embrace becomes a restraint to feeling. Indeed, novels do not carry the responsibility of reducing the many possibilities they present to a single decision. They do not issue verdicts. But the law does.[107] The practical and urgent necessities of the law require it to be guided by general rules and, in the end, to reduce the complexities and ambiguities of a case to a particular holding. This, among other things, distinguishes the work of law from the work of art, though (as I will later argue) Eliot's own art is made the better for its being in touch with the limits—if not the limitations—of the law.

What, more specifically, sets apart certain novels from the law (and from the ordinary limitations of life) is that while in law the devil himself knoweth not the thought of man, in the novels I examine in this study we can know the thought of man and devil. Dickens gives intimate and unsettling access to Fagin, at once both man and devil. The third person narratives of *Middlemarch* and *Daniel Deronda* have the freedom to move into the thought of man; they give a representation of the "hidden life," as Forster remarks, "at its source."

In chapter 1 of this book, I consider questions about the relations between judgments of conduct and judgments of character as they are fictively and vividly imagined in Dickens's first crime novel, *Oliver Twist*. I argue that the novel requires its audience to confront the foundations on which judgments of criminal responsibility are based and does so by taking full advantage of the novel's license to enter into the minds of its characters. This chapter focuses on the crime of being an "accessory before the fact" to murder, the crime for which Fagin is hanged — or is he hanged for some other crime? The ambiguity is germane to my discussion, as is the ambiguity of the category of accessory itself. Amid the turmoil of political, legal, and social reform within which both Dickens and his novel were centrally situated, *Oliver Twist* rethinks the nature of criminal responsibility and copes with habitual criminality. When Oliver Twist — Dickens's Principle of Good — reforms Nancy, the novel disconnects her from her criminal past and from the criminal acts she has already committed. She is no longer the agent of her own acts as she becomes more and more like Oliver, whom Dickens has long since disconnected from his own acts, past and present. The relevance of past criminal acts to present conduct has always been a bone of contention in the criminal law, but in the nineteenth century, as the problem of the habitual criminal became paramount, the difficulties intensified. When *Oliver Twist* contests and reaffirms the boundaries of criminal law, the novel reflects a Dickensian and perhaps a larger cultural ambivalence about the reach of criminal law.

Chapters 2 and 3 move further into the mind of the accused as I take up four novels by George Eliot: *Adam Bede*, *Felix Holt*, *Middlemarch*, and *Daniel Deronda*. While Eliot's early work ambivalently locates responsibility in acts and consequences, the later work resituates responsibility more fully in the activity of desires and intentions. Eliot asserts the superiority of the novel to know more than the law can know but also respects the boundaries in which the law must operate. The novels reflect a continued commitment to external behavior as part of criminal and moral responsibility. Though they take us very far into the minds of Nicholas Bulstrode and Gwendolen Harleth, they stay connected to the criminal law's requirement of an act. The heightened consciousness of the complicated relations between the mind and the act, the intention and the deed, brings not only a moral but also a juridical impulse into Eliot's novels while the same consciousness complicates the boundaries between the elements of crime.

The final chapter of this study examines James Fitzjames Stephen's book *The Story of Nuncomar and the Impeachment of Sir Elijah Impey*, which takes as its point of departure Thomas Macaulay's popular 1841 *Edinburgh Review* essay on Warren Hastings. Stephen is not likely to be a figure most readers have come across, so a short biographical outline will, I hope, prove useful. Of James Fitzjames Stephen, his younger brother Leslie Stephen wrote: "The cases are rare indeed where a man's abilities have been directed precisely into the right channel from early life. Almost all men have to acknowledge that they have spent a great portion of their energy on tasks that have led to nothing, or led only to experience of failure. . . . Fitzjames's various labours came to a focus in his labours upon the Criminal Law."[108] Fitzjames Stephen's "labours upon the Criminal Law" produced some of the most revealing and complex thinking and writing on criminal law in the nineteenth century. Not all of his writing took the criminal law as its topic, nor did his most sustained philosophical work, *Liberty, Equality, Fraternity* (1873) — a response to John Stuart Mill's work *On Liberty*. But more often than not Stephen involves examples from the criminal law as central to his arguments. Fitzjames Stephen's labors upon the criminal law constituted the great work of his life, work in which he would bring to life the criminal law of England's past and present.

Stephen was called to the bar of the Inner Temple in January of 1854 and was, by the following year, a member of the Midland Circuit. It makes a difference that Stephen was a practicing barrister, that he represented clients of different classes, that he made his way among other barristers who were not the sons of Sir James Stephen. In short, his first experiences of the law were far from rarified. His unpublished letters during his years as a barrister describe in some detail the impression the real life of the law made on him.

Concurrently with his earliest work as a practicing barrister, Stephen was also publishing articles in the *Saturday Review* and other magazines on a wide variety of topics, including, not surprisingly, the controversial criminal trials of the day and other subjects arising out of the evolving criminal law in England. In his biography, Leslie Stephen reported that during this time Fitzjames

> was deeply interested in the criminal cases, which were constantly presenting ethical problems, and affording strange glimpses into the dark side of human nature. Such crimes showed the crude, brutal passions which lie beneath the decent surface of modern society, and are fascinating to the student of human nature. He often speaks of the strangely romantic interest of the incidents brought to light in the "State Trials"; and in these early days he studied some of the famous cases, such as those of Palmer and Dove, with a professional as well as a literary interest. In later life he avoided such stories; but at this period he occasionally made a text of them for newspaper articles, and was, perhaps, tempted to adopt theories of the case too rapidly.[109]

Crossing the ethical with the romantic, the professional and the literary, Leslie Stephen gives us our own strange glimpse into the complexities these cases generated for and with Fitzjames Stephen. The sordid cases of William Palmer and William Dove straddled the professional world of the law and that of literature.[110] Because Fitzjames Stephen began his legal career not only as a barrister but also as a journalist, he was attuned to the interactions between legal and popular texts. He remained engaged in the way the interactions between legal and literary narratives defined and were defined by conceptions of criminal responsibility. I disagree with Leslie Stephen that he "avoided such stories" in later life. The last major work of his life, *The Story of Nuncomar and the Impeachment of Sir Elijah Impey*, brought him very far into such a narrative.

In 1869, Stephen was appointed legal member of the Governor-General's Council in India, a position that had been held by Macaulay before him. During his tenure, he continued the work on the Indian Penal Code that Macaulay had begun, and he drafted administrative regulations.[111] When he returned to England in 1872, he led the movement to codify the criminal law of England, though without success. Such a comprehensive code was never adopted. In 1879, he was appointed judge of the Queen's Bench Division. During his time on the bench, he wrote his three-volume work *A History of the Criminal Law of England* and revised *A General View of the Criminal Law*, which had been initially published in 1863 and had been one of the first works of its kind. When, in late 1889, Stephen presided over the well-publicized trial of Florence Maybrick, an American accused of the murder of her husband, reports began to surface that Stephen was mentally incompetent. Such questions continued to be raised, and in 1891, Stephen resigned from the bench. He died on March 11, 1894.

The Story of Nuncomar and the Impeachment of Sir Elijah Impey was published in 1885 and was Stephen's last major work.[112] A rich and penetrating text, *The Story of Nuncomar* censures the fictionality of Macaulay's legal history and his representations of the motives and intentions of Hastings and of Chief Justice Impey, who was accused of judicial murder. Macaulay's essay claims at once the authority of historiography and the license of fiction, the license to go directly into the interior lives of the figures it presents. Stephen takes Macaulay to task for obscuring the fact that he proceeds inferentially. The inferences from act to intent that Macaulay necessarily makes are, after all, matters of conjecture in Macaulay's narrative—as they are for the rest of us. But Macaulay, like the third person narrator of *Middlemarch*, articulates his story as if he has access that we do not have. Stephen's response to Macaulay's "Warren Hastings," as well as his own representation of the case, invite us to consider the responsibilities of narrative and suggest the dangers as well as the possibilities that art presents when it imagines into the mind of another.[113]

I close my study with a brief discussion of Thomas Hardy's late century novel *Tess of the D'Urbervilles* (1891) and two decidedly twentieth-century crime narratives by Truman Capote: *In Cold Blood* (1965) and *Handcarved Coffins* (1975). My concluding remarks seek to test the limits of the analysis I present in the preceding chapters, and raise questions about whether the work I have done with criminal responsibility and with the internal and external elements of crime in narratives could be carried forward in any meaningful way into novels shaped by the influences of modernity and postmodernity. I think it cannot, and in my conclusion I consider the reasons why.

↦ ONE ↤

Organizing Crime
Conduct and Character in *Oliver Twist*

There is not much of a coherent plot in *Oliver Twist*, and what there is does not drive the novel. A child, soon to be orphan, is born to a destitute mother who dies shortly thereafter. The mistreated boy falls into the hands of criminals but is later saved by a gentleman who, we later discover, was a friend of the boy's wellish-to-do father, and Oliver is reclaimed by this man and his newly discovered aunt, an angel into whose life he has previously dropped (through a window). For the most part, the plot is propelled by the game of lost and found Dickens plays with Oliver, a device that moves Oliver back and forth from good hands to bad, and Dickens plays the game more than once. About halfway through the novel, Oliver drops out of our sight almost entirely (and happily since we don't really miss him), and Dickens attends to other characters, all criminal—Nancy, Fagin, Sikes, Monks—and their relations with and to the upstanding citizens in the book. A good deal of plot exposition happens in the space of a couple of chapters near the end of the novel in which Mr. Brownlow interrogates Monks, formerly Edward Leeford, Oliver's half-brother. Throughout, Dickens is able to launch attacks on the New Poor Law, on the summary justice of a bitterly (but not unamusingly) cruel magistracy, and various other issues of the day.

All of this is well and good, but much of our interest in *Oliver Twist* is in character, in who Nancy and Bill Sikes and Fagin are. But more than this, Dickens invites us to pay close attention to the dramatically realized relations between their character and their conduct. The novel's plot necessarily moves as a result of the actions of these figures, yet the movements of the plot sometimes feel like afterthoughts. While some readers of *Oliver Twist* may remain involved in the question of Oliver's origins and his rightful inheritance, one

35

registers how mechanical this part of the plot has become. Once Oliver is safe and sound, it is hard to work up much of a lather over his activities with the Maylies. Even when the crime story supplants the inheritance story, we might expect a more plot-driven narrative. Not so. It is surprising to think how un-plot-driven this book is, even as it is reasonable to assume that a plot will structure and control a Victorian crime novel. The great turn in D. A. Miller's essay on *Bleak House* in *The Novel and the Police* comes when Miller shows how the shift from the chancery/inheritance plot to the murder plot in *Bleak House* produces clarity of agency and of resolution, of action/reaction and cause and effect, which chancery thwarts but murder delivers. Miller suggests, then, that the shift from the civil to the criminal offers the fantastic and the longed-for simplicity of who did what to whom. *Oliver Twist* is a novel about inheritance and about crime, but the criminal world created in *Oliver Twist* does not offer up the simplicity of action that Miller imposes on *Bleak House*.[1] It does not ex-actly surprise us that Bill Sikes swings, but that he is (and is not) lynched — that is a different matter. The lynching complicates our attitude toward Sikes, who suddenly at the moment of punishment appears more victim than villain. The aftershocks of the extralegal punishment exacted on Sikes produce the satisfaction of revenge for the murder of Nancy without an affirmation of the fact of punishment; the reader's opprobrium moves from the condemned criminal to the raucous mob. Dickens reforms Sikes in ways I will later dis-cuss, and indeed, *Oliver Twist* is itself committed (though inconsistently) to the reform of both systems and persons, but Dickens's reformative agenda pro-duces a different set of seemingly intractable problems, for if reform precedes judgment, then one finds oneself in the unenviable position of judging a character who seems powerfully unlike the one who committed the crime. What, after all, do we do with a reformed criminal like Nancy? She is a figure who is reformed before a lawful punishment attaches. If Nancy's character has been reformed, do we hold her responsible for acts that, one could argue, someone else — some unreformed character — has committed? Sikes's instan-taneous change from simple brute to complex agent after he murders Nancy imagines the problem differently but still maintains the problem. After the murder Sikes is almost unrecognizable. This is the crisis Dickens presents in *Oliver Twist*, a crisis that he has the space to explore most fully because he can enter into the minds of the figures he creates.

Discontinuities of character destabilize the relation of the self to its own conduct and unsettle criminal law's authority to judge and punish. I am not here arguing that Dickens attempts to produce a fixed coherent subject and fails; instead I am suggesting that Dickens exposes the troubling conse-quences of the reform he promotes. The reformed criminal may no longer be an appropriate subject for official punishment. He has become a different person. Such consequences, as it turns out, are pretty hard to face. Which is why the two moral poles presented in the novel — Fagin and Oliver — remain themselves fixed points. While it is true that Fagin at his trial looks less like cagey fence and more like insensible and even, perhaps, sympathetic old man, his last words are consistent with all that we know of him ("'Bolter's throat as deep as you can cut. Saw his head off!'" [363]), and it is no accident that in his last hours Oliver is with him, attempting to lead him to redemption through prayer, a path Fagin readily rejects, except as a ruse for possible escape.

But Fagin does more for Dickens than occupy the position of Oliver's opposite. Though Bill Sikes murders Nancy, it is Fagin who is legally executed as an accessory before the fact to a murder he did not actually—that is to say, physically—commit. Arguably Fagin dies not for what he does but for what he is, and Dickens uses the category of accessory before the fact to make us at once confident in and uncomfortable about the reach of criminal law. Fagin's vividly represented criminal intents are manifested in the act of Sikes. By separating intent from act, Dickens enacts a gap that, like the tensions between conduct and character, upsets our assumptions about criminal responsibility.

The persistence of the questions Fagin's crime raises—from the nineteenth century through our own decade—is provocative. As I will discuss later, readers have disagreed about what, precisely, Fagin hangs for. Why does this crime give rise to such continued and sometimes heated discussion? John Sutherland reports the question about Fagin's crime as one of the most frequently asked in connection with Dickens's work.[2] The question remains fertile because the crime as Dickens represents it at once contests and reaffirms the limits of criminality. By deactivating Fagin's act (as I will later explain), Dickens tests the limits of liability. At the same time, though, he stabilizes those limits by making Fagin's intent fiercely active. The novel *Oliver Twist* can make an intent as materially present as the acts it represents. In so doing, it affirms the legal judgment passed on a fictional accused. We have a window into the guilty mind of the fictional accused, to which we never have access outside the fictional world. Yet we are also made nervous about a judgment that does not rely on an act. Should a man of bad intention be held criminally responsible for the act of another? By allowing us to experience directly that which can never be known and experienced so directly or unambiguously in a court of law—the thoughts of the accused—Dickens refigures the boundaries the law erects between act and intent. And yet, what would it mean to a Victorian audience to be asked to affirm a death sentence based not on an action but on an intent? *Oliver Twist* asks its audience to accept the long reach of criminal law (how else could it catch a figure as wily as Fagin?), but its own anxiety about that long reach informs much of the novel, for the long arm of the law reaches not only Fagin but also, and much more frighteningly, the innocent orphan Oliver Twist, though it finally lets Oliver go. While the novel cannot entirely repair the fractures it has generated, by representing Fagin as internally and intentionally vile—by turning Fagin inside out, as it were—Dickens reestablishes the line between the criminal and the noncriminal that his audience could easily accept. Can any reader with any common sense seriously challenge the claim that Fagin *is* a criminal? We read his thoughts. The narrator's authoritative description of Fagin's consciousness gives us access to what Fagin feels. We know what he is. The activity of Fagin's mind reassures us that the law gets its man.

This chapter takes up Dickens's response to a crux in criminal law (and in life): what happens when a person and his acts become dissonant, incongruent, or even disconnected? In *Oliver Twist* Dickens explores the repercussions that arise out of the relations, and particularly the dissonances and incongruities, of conduct and character, and I argue that the judgments of guilt and the punishments (legal, extralegal, and illegal) represented in the novel attempt to negotiate between conduct and character. Those negotiations produce at times a richer understanding and at others an evasion of the logical consequences of the judgments made (and not made). From the criminal law, Dickens imports a legal category—accessory before the fact—that mediates between conduct and character as a way of handling and ultimately disposing of Fagin. One could take up the same set of issues without the legal category since moral philosophy is as involved in imagining relations between conduct and character. That Dickens uses legal categories marks his own commitment to legal judgments. This category allows legal judgment to pass in large part on an act not actually done by the accused; what then gets unexpectedly illuminated is the uneasy relation between who we are and what we do.

When Dickens presents the interior lives of his characters, the potential disjunctions of and incongruities between who they are and what they do become intensely realized. One immediate response to this assertion is that Dickens is not a novelist who generally imagines a difference between inner and outer: the characters perform who they are. In Gradgrind or Miss Flyte or Mr. M'Choakumchild, the inner finds perfect expression in mannerism, costume, name, action. Dickens teaches us to locate self in these outward manifestations.[3] And there are certainly characters in *Oliver Twist*—the Artful Dodger and Mr. Bumble, for example—who fit this bill exactly. However, *Oliver Twist* is more experimental than such an approach would suggest. The novel offers the potential conflict between inner and outer, and this difference is particularly consequential for this crime novel.[4] When, for example, Mr. Brownlow first inspects Oliver, he calls into question what he believes he has witnessed with his own eyes—that Oliver has committed a crime. Looking closely at Oliver's face, Brownlow must ask: "*Can* he be innocent? He looked like—."[5] Musing over this question, he taps "his chin with the corner of [a] book" (61). What, after all, is the face evidence of? Can one judge a book by its cover? For Brownlow, the face, often taken as a reflection of character (the *OED* records a passage from Sterne's *Sentimental Journey* that makes character mean "the face or features as betokening moral qualities"), is at odds with the conduct he believes he has witnessed (though he is a poor witness at best). Much rides on the question he raises—*Can* he be innocent? In Oliver's case, the answer is a resounding yes—the face reflects his character perfectly no matter what situation he finds himself in or what he has seemingly done—but the question remains, if not in Oliver's case then certainly in Nancy's.[6] Why realize these epistemic gaps, these potential conflicts, in a crime novel? Perhaps the answer is that the conflict is not just potential but most potent, most dangerous, in a novel about crime. What emerges from a comparison of Dickens's novel negotiations and those in the criminal law (in and out of the nineteenth century—these are perennial difficulties which turn up elsewhere) is the fullest sense, the largest sense of the difficulties that attend on negotiations between the internalities of character and the externalities of conduct. For the criminal law, the struggle often involves attempting to distinguish judgments of conduct from judgments of character and to exclude evidence of character altogether. On the other hand, the law does expect a wicked act to tell the story of a wicked mind. By illuminating the incongruities of conduct and character, Dickens presses us to consider the boundaries between them. Both the congruities and incongruities in the novel give Dickens the opportunity to critique the limitations of the criminal law. But that opportunity comes at a price, for Dickens not only critiques the criminal law but also is critiqued by it. There are moments when *Oliver Twist* can do no more than the criminal law and moments when it does a good deal less, particularly at the moments when the novel evades the very problems it sets up.[7]

Naming the categories "conduct" and "character" implies a misleading clarity: we need to ask at the outset "what is conduct?" and "what is character"? These are large questions, which I touch upon in my introduction as well, and I mean only to suggest the complexities without attempting a systematic analysis or resolution. Conduct can be understood as an act or a series of acts at a given moment and over time. An act in itself may be conceived of as momentary or as something that moves over time. Some criminal acts, for example, by definition require a reiteration; I am thinking here of stalking or other kinds of harassment. J. L. Austin, in his "A Plea for Excuses," lights on this problem: "we need to ask how we decide what is the correct name for 'the' action that somebody did—and what, indeed, are the rules for the use of 'the' action, 'an' action, 'one' action, a 'part' or 'phase' of an action and the like."[8] The issues raised when attempts are made to describe and define acts are legion. The philosopher Anthony Duff argues: "To ask which is 'the action itself' is as absurd as to ask what 'the event itself' is when the roof of a house is damaged in a storm—is there just one event (the roof being damaged) or are there 'really' many events (each individual tile being damaged)? Actions and events are identified and individuated only by our descriptions of them."[9]

What is included in our definitions, then? A crime, as I discuss in my introduction, requires both a *mens rea* (a criminal state of mind) and an *actus reus*, which means, following Glanville Williams, "all the external circumstances and consequences specified in the rule of law as constituting the forbidden situation."[10] The shift from act (or *actus reus*) to situation suggests the ambiguity of "act." As Duff avers, much depends on our definition of the act.

Temporal aspects are more obviously constitutive of character, and the continuance through time of a character and, by extension, a personal identity has itself a complex historical and philosophical pedigree.[11] Here we face problems cognate to those sketched earlier for the synchronic and diachronic views of "act." The nineteenth century's particular commitment to imagining character as it developed over time is undeniable. So most famously in the novels of George Eliot, one marks a working out of an idea much respected in the culture: that the past (including, importantly, past conduct) shapes character, manifests character, and must be assimilated by character. Eliot offers a continuity of character over time; we register the connections between past and present in, for example, *Middlemarch*'s Dr. Lydgate or Dorothea Brooke. Still, to say that there are marked differences between the way character development proceeds in *Middlemarch* and the way it proceeds in *Oliver Twist* is not to say much that is surprising or new, yet the striking discontinuities of character at work in Dickens's representations of criminal figures—Sikes and Nancy in particular—raise a potentially dangerous set of questions about legal judgment. I am not arguing here that novelists are obligated to present characters who behave with perfect consistency and whose conduct is perfectly congruent with their character (no doubt we can think of such figures from novels, and they are often the least compelling figures). While not all (or even most) seemingly inconsistent action disrupts character, the extreme changes that we see in Nancy and Sikes—changes that turn them into different people, almost unrecognizable to us—deserve special attention. Moreover, when such extreme discontinuities of character take place in the context of a novel interested in raising questions about criminal responsibility they suggest that something more is at stake. In *Oliver Twist* Dickens promotes reform, and reform requires alteration. When Nancy is transformed from prostitute to savior, how are we to judge the criminal acts she has committed in the past?

In his chapter on "Collective Memory and the Actual Past" in *Literary Interest: The Limits of Anti-Formalism*, Steven Knapp critiques the value of any recovery of what he calls a "past social reality," and in the course of this discussion, takes as a subject for analysis the logic of imposing punishment for past criminal acts.[12] Punishment, as Knapp explains, is the "social practice, that perhaps more obviously than any other, assumes that past events have an intrinsic relevance to present action."[13] Though Knapp is not interested in continuities or discontinuities of character per se, his analysis assumes that notions of punishment depend on an ideal of continuous identity. While Knapp does not cite John Locke's *Essay Concerning Human Understanding*, he well might have. In Locke's chapter "Of Identity and Diversity," he famously defines a person as "a thinking intelligent being, that has reason and reflection, and can consider itself as itself, the same thinking thing, in different times and places."[14] The definition continues:

> For since consciousness always accompanies thinking, and 'tis that, that makes every one be what he calls *self*; and thereby distinguishes himself from all other thinking things, in this alone consists *personal identity*, i.e. the sameness of a rational Being; And as far as this con-

sciousness can be extended backwards to any past action or Thought, so far reaches the Identity of that Person; it is the same *self* now as it was then; and 'tis by the same *self* with this present one that now reflects on it, that the Action was done.[15]

Later in the chapter, his section entitled "Person as a Forensic Term" intersects questions of legal responsibility and continuous selfhood explicitly: a person is "a Forensic Term, appropriating actions and their Merit, and so belongs only to intelligent agents, capable of Law, and Happiness, and Misery. This personality extends itself beyond present existence to what is past, only by consciousness, whereby it becomes concerned and accountable, owns and imputes to itself past actions."[16] Of penal sentences passed on such agents, Locke argues, "The Sentence shall be justified by the consciousness all Persons shall have, that they *themselves*, in what Bodies soever they appear, or what Substances soever that consciousness adheres to, are the *same*, that committed those Actions, and deserve Punishment for them."[17] The justness of legal punishment depends on "the sameness of a rational Being," according to Locke.[18] F. H. Bradley makes a similar point in *Ethical Studies*, where he observes that "the first condition of my guiltiness, or of my becoming a subject for moral imputation, is my self-sameness; I must be throughout one identical person."[19] So too, claims Bradley, it must be true that to be guilty the accused must "be the very same person to whom the deed belonged."[20] Knapp's challenge, though, is to ask "whether it makes sense to treat a person existing in the present as still the appropriate object of attitudes appropriate to an action she performed in the past."[21] To do so, argues Knapp, one needs to suppose that we treat a person in the present as if she were continually "performing the act she once performed." To hold Nancy responsible for her bad acts—of thievery, prostitution, kidnapping—is to treat her as a person who continues to perform the acts she once performed. But to do that is to be out of touch with the way *Oliver Twist* unfolds. *Oliver Twist* destabilizes the attribution of responsibility for past conduct by producing an inner life that had seemed not to exist in the past. Yet at the same time the novel is very much in touch with the Lockean notion of the "sameness of a rational Being." The consequences of Nancy's acts are continually with her—the circumstances of her life, the danger into which she has placed Oliver—and she is conscious of such consequences. Sikes too both does and does not fulfill the prerequisites of Locke's definition of a forensic person. At precisely the moment that Sikes is punished (though extralegally) for the murder of Nancy, he gets not only a conscience but a consciousness. He acquires a past and becomes a person in the Lockean sense only after he has committed this crime, and as the eyes of Nancy follow him from place to place, it is as if he is called on to commit the crime over and over again; he continues to perform the act he once performed.

The preface Dickens composed for *Oliver Twist*[22] is dominated by questions of conduct and character and of the relations between the two. Responding to the critics of his novel and more specifically to critics of his Nancy, Dickens maintained in his preface that

> It is useless to discuss whether the conduct and character of the girl seems natural or unnatural, probable or improbable, right or wrong. IT IS TRUE. Every man who has watched these melancholy shades of life knows it to be so. Suggested to my mind long ago—long before I dealt in fiction—by what I often saw and read of, in actual life around me, I have, for years, tracked it through many profligate and noisome ways, and found it still the same. From the first introduction of that poor wretch, to her laying her bloody head upon the robber's breast, there is not one word exaggerated or over-wrought. It is emphatically God's truth, for it is the truth He leaves in such depraved and miserable breasts; the hope yet lingering behind; the last fair drop of water at the bottom of the dried-up weed-choked well. It involves the best and worst shades of our common nature; much of its ugliest hues, and something of its most beautiful; it is a contradiction, an anomaly, an apparent impossibility; but it is a truth. I am glad to have had it doubted, for in that circumstance I find a sufficient assurance that it needed to be told. (lxv)

Dickens's defensive posture here is understandable enough. The novel, though a success in the marketplace, had met with criticisms from reviewers that the author no doubt had anticipated. Dickens knew his thieves would be viewed as far too crude and his child-hero far too good for the tastes of some of his contemporaries. He may also have anticipated certain readers' resistance to Nancy, that "poor wretch" who rests "her bloody head upon the robber's breast." This preface is of a piece with many others that justify as factually accurate some fantastical element of the story—the talking raven Grip in *Barnaby Rudge* or, more famously, Krook's spontaneous combustion in *Bleak House*. But this preface does more than defend. Notwithstanding the sentimentality of some of its rhetoric ("the last fair drop of water at the bottom of the dried-up weed-choked well"), it reveals the central paradox of the novel. The novel promises to and sometimes does hold these two possibly and at times impossibly contradictory elements—conduct and character—together; it also moves between them (as Dickens does in this paragraph) and can, on occasion, accept them, even embrace them.[23]

During the last thirty or so years of Dickens criticism, readers have generated analyses of *Oliver Twist* that focus on one or another of the inconsistencies in the book. These readings effectively demonstrate that the novel lacks a stable argument.[24] What strikes me, though, about this concluding passage of the preface is how deeply important illogic, inconsistency, and paradox itself are to Dickens in this novel. The penultimate sentence of the paragraph accepts and then asks the reader to accept what is in essence a definition of a paradox—a figure that is contradictory and at the same time true. More telling still are two of the elements that make up the paradox:

conduct and character, two separate elements that come under scrutiny here and in the novel proper: "It is useless to discuss whether the conduct and character of the girl seems natural or unnatural, probable or improbable, right or wrong. IT IS TRUE." The passage provokes even as it tries to set the critics straight, to lay matters to rest. It draws our attention to seemingly contradictory pairs, but it also gives us "conduct and character": at once a single unit and separate elements.

First things first. How do we interpret the word "character" here. What does it mean? It seems to mean that which is our self, what George Eliot calls in *Adam Bede* the "inward facts," our interior life (315). Still, though we may seek to know the inward facts, we do so by looking to outward manifestations; we expect character to be manifested in conduct, as it so often is. In law as in life, character is known through conduct, including speech. Part of what distinguishes fiction from nonfiction is that what fiction offers is an opportunity to know character separately from conduct as well as from circumstances. *Oliver Twist* gives us directly that which in life can only be produced by others indirectly; thoughts, intentions, desires come to the reader in a fictively immediate way. We are, as it were, in Nancy's or Fagin's or Bill's head. When this interior life is presented, conflicts between conduct and character might be played out fully, richly, deeply. To notice conduct and character separately, as Dickens does in his preface, is to register some difference between them. If character includes conduct, why not just refer to character, or vice versa? The pairing itself is common enough so that we might read it as perfectly natural. Indeed, it turns up eight other times in Dickens's fiction (three times as "conduct and character" and five times as "character and conduct").[25] None of the other uses raises the potential disjunctures that the preface raises, and the majority of these other instances are for obvious comic effect. Here, though, something more is at issue. The difference between who Nancy is and what she does is no sooner displayed than it is erased. The two are made into one in the singular "seems" and not the plural "seem," and for the remainder of the paragraph, conduct and character are represented by "it." Close attention is required before one realizes that the "it" that is so central to the meaning of the passage actually refers back to these two elements.

All of the pairings in the passage—conduct/character, natural/unnatural, probable/improbable, right/wrong—work to produce a sense of something binary in the story, though Dickens is careful to shield his creation from too much analysis by giving it the unequivocal stamp of truth. Still, the pairings make us think of relations, as does the definition of his "it" that Dickens explicitly produces. He explains "it" as "a contradiction, an anomaly, an apparent impossibility": conduct and character are divided against as well as within themselves, but the bits are yet held together, and held together by "and," not (as are the other pairs) "or." The novel realizes both the necessity of discrimination and the necessity of forgoing this discrimination. The truth the passage illuminates concerns the difficulty of discrimination. At some level, conduct is character. As T. S. Eliot observes about belief and behavior in *Notes*

Towards the Definition of Culture, "The reflection that we believe is not merely what we formulate and subscribe to, but that behaviour is also belief, and that even the most conscious and developed of us live also at the level on which belief and behaviour cannot be distinguished, is one that may, once we allow our imagination to play upon it, be very disconcerting."[26] *Oliver Twist* plays on these disconcerting possibilities.

Criminal law has long depended on distinctions between conduct and character; it has been and continues to be on its guard against questions of character, defensively declaring that those on trial are to be judged and punished not for who they are but for what they have done. Moreover, the only acts to be scrutinized are those relevant to the crime for which the defendant is tried and not past bad acts (with notable exceptions). While this may stand as the criminal law's official position, Foucault and the historians and critics who follow his lead expose the strategies of the legal technologies of the nineteenth and twentieth centuries that bring character into the courtroom, not only as evidence of the crime but as an object of judgment and punishment in and of itself. The passage from *Discipline and Punish* that I include in my introduction is pertinent here. Foucault censures the law's attempt

> to introduce into the verdict not only 'circumstantial' evidence, but something quite different, which is not juridically codifiable: the knowledge of the criminal, one's estimation of him, what is known about the relations between him, his past and his crime, and what might be expected of him in the future. . . . The criminal's soul is not referred to in the trial merely to explain his crime and as a factor in the juridical apportioning of responsibility; if it is brought before the court, with such pomp and circumstance, such concern to understand and such "scientific" application, it is because it too, as well as the crime itself, is to be judged and to share in the punishment.[27]

Though Foucault cites no evidence of his own in support of this claim, I take this challenge seriously because it considers the consequences of what happens when character becomes an object of judgment in the courtroom.

"What is the principle of admitting character evidence into criminal cases?" begins Sir William Erle, in the 1865 case *R. v. Rowton*.[28] It was not a question the court was eager to answer; the justices maneuvered in and around the dangers this practice raised and would raise. The case involved an alleged indecent assault by a schoolmaster—James Rowton—on George Low, "a lad of about fourteen years of age."[29] During the course of his trial, Rowton produced witnesses who testified that he (the defendant) had "an excellent character."[30] To refute such evidence, the prosecution called on one of Rowton's former pupils who, having been asked to speak on the general character of the accused, replied thus: "I know nothing of the neighborhood's opinion, because I was only a boy at school when I knew him; but my own opinion, and the opinion of my brothers who were also pupils of his, is that his character is that of a man capable of the grossest indecency and the most flagrant im-morality."[31] Rowton was convicted, and the case was appealed.

When asked to rule directly on whether evidence of good character was admissible in a criminal court, Sir Alexander Cockburn answered in the affir-mative that what had been a practice would now be a rule: "The issue of gen-eral good character of the prisoner is not a collateral issue in the ordinary sense of the term: it is one of the elements in the case from which a jury are to find their verdict."[32] This of good character, but what of bad character? The practice rule in England was clear enough: once evidence of good character was admitted, then and only then might the prosecution introduce evidence of bad character. None of the justices writing opinions for *Rowton* was com-fortable with the admission of bad character into evidence, fearing as they did that such evidence would prejudice a jury against a defendant (with one judge, Willis, saying outright, "I should have been glad if the court could have come to the conclusion that it [evidence of bad character] should be re-jected").[33] Still, following many years of regular practice and textbook decla-rations, the court acted as if it was pressed to confirm and then did confirm the rule that would allow such evidence into a criminal trial. Nevertheless, the testimony of the witness against Rowton was disallowed, and the case was overturned. Stepping carefully around the rule just affirmed, Cockburn, speaking for the majority, held that the witness had given evidence of an indi-vidual opinion and not of the defendant's general reputation—and not just individual opinion of reputation but individual opinion of what Cockburn calls (without defining it) disposition. Much is required of the word "general" in Cockburn's opinion, as he announces that "evidence of general character must be general evidence in the sense of reputation, and that evidence of par-ticular facts to establish the disposition or tendency of the mind of the ac-cused, and to show his capability of committing the offence charged, is inad-missible."[34] *Rowton* distinguishes within character between reputation and disposition, the former being admissible and the latter not. Those on the court who agreed with the ruling as a whole rejected Cockburn's reasoning, with one judge concluding: "The best character is generally the least talked about; the man whose honesty has never been thought to be in question is not talked of, and, therefore, the value of general rumour is doubtful."[35] But this is precisely the idea. What the majority opinion does is dilute character by turning to reputation and away from disposition. This move from disposition to reputation, from individual opinion to community opinion, suggests a move away from the introduction of character evidence into the courtroom. As opinion gets more and more diffused, the persuasive punch of such testi-mony must likewise be diffused.

When Michel Foucault suggests in *Discipline and Punish* that evidence of general bad character becomes central to the criminal trial of the nineteenth century, he ignores an even more complicated tension with which the crimi-nal law struggled. Perhaps the difference between French and English criminal procedure explains Foucault's assumption. Fitzjames Stephen notes these differences in *A General View of the Criminal Law*, though that description may indicate his Anglophilia and Francophobia. Of these differences in relation to character evidence Stephen writes:

> A man's general bad character is a weak reason for believing that he was concerned in any particular criminal transaction, for it is a circumstance common to him and hundreds of thousands of other people; whereas to the opportunity of committing the crime and the facts immediately connected with it are marks which belong to very few — perhaps only to one or two persons. If general bad character is too remote, *a fortiori* the particular transactions of which that general bad character is the effect are still further removed from proof; accordingly, it is an inflexible rule of criminal law to exclude evidence of such transactions. This is a peculiarity of our law. In France, every circumstance of a man's life may be, and often is, produced against him. We owe this in a great measure to the litigious view of the criminal law. In France the judges seem to consider that it is their duty to exercise a sort of moral supervision over every one who comes before them, and to investigate, and, if necessary, stigmatize as wicked, every part of the life of a bad man. An English judge thinks only of the point at issue.[36]

But the rule was not inflexible, as Stephen's own *Digest of the Law of Evidence* would demonstrate, and even here Stephen recognizes the way evidence of character enters the courtroom, for in his next paragraph he observes:

> On the whole, no doubt the English rule is humane and just; but, in practice, it is subject to one important qualification. The judge knows the prisoner's character, though the jury do not. When many charges are brought against a prisoner, and when the depositions in all of them are submitted to the judge, as they always are, his mind can hardly be altogether uninfluenced by the circumstance; and this influence may weigh fearfully against the prisoner.[37]

Fearfully indeed. Stephen, like the *Rowton* court, is very much on his toes about the introduction of such evidence. The criminal law must negotiate carefully between character and conduct, and it must be mindful of the fearful consequences of a bad negotiation. Before the nineteenth century, the more ad hoc proceedings of the criminal law allowed judges and juries wide discretion in trying and convicting defendants: "Who the prisoner was — his character and reputation — was as critical a question as what he had done (and even in some cases whether he had done it), and it was centrally the business of the trial to find the answer."[38] But with the rise of utilitarianism and the ensuing reforms of the criminal law, the discretionary powers of judges and juries were more limited, and practices became more systematic and predictable, including the development of more formal rules of evidence.[39] The reformers prized consistency and predictability, yet as recent cultural critics (following Foucault) have shown, the Victorians remained deeply interested in questions of character. These critics have dedicated their energies to demonstrating the way institutional changes in the nineteenth century—not only the growth of a police bureaucracy but also changes in public health structures, educational programs, and philanthropist organizations—produced a society obsessed with surveillance and self-discipline. *The Novel and the Police* names the novel and the Dickens novel in particular as one more disciplinary technology designed to control the will, to suppress the irrational, and to construct the individual. But this conviction at once oversimplifies and overlooks the way the criminal law and the novel (the two particular institutions I examine here) confront questions about the relations between character and conduct.

In *Oliver Twist* Dickens situates himself and his readers among some complex areas of the criminal law, areas in which the relations between character and conduct, and in turn their relation to criminal responsibility, are at issue; he puts before us the problems of accessory liability and of innocent agency. At one end of the spectrum, we have the accessory (Fagin), who does not murder Nancy but is the only figure put on trial for that crime. On the other we have the innocent actor (Oliver) who performs the action out of which a harm arises (a housebreaking), but who is not adjudged responsible for the harm done. What this spectrum reflects is a range of response to crime in the nineteenth century. The growing interdependence of activities among strangers in Victorian England made the possibility that one could become "associated with"—or, as Oliver Twist himself says, in "accidental companionship" (114) with—some wrongful activity seem all too likely. Note, for example, that when Mr. Fang the magistrate turns his attention from the accused to the accuser—from Oliver to Brownlow—he seems on the verge of arresting Brownlow for having inadvertently held onto the book he was perusing before the attempted robbery. Fang threatens Brownlow, an obvious representative of middle-class values, in no uncertain terms: "I consider, sir, that you have obtained possession of that book, under very suspicious and disreputable circumstances; and you may think yourself very fortunate that the owner of the property declines to prosecute. Let this be a lesson to you, my man, or the law will overtake you yet" (66). Still, the intricacies of criminal activities in themselves—the growth of criminal syndicates, as it were—required criminal laws that could reach beyond direct participants in crime. Moreover, as Weiner notes in *Reconstructing the Criminal*, "as the brutality of the law was lessened, its reach was extended to cover more persons and more forms of behavior. Vagrants, drunkards, and the other 'immoral' and 'disorderly' persons, on the one hand, and white-collar offenders on the other, were brought more fully under the purview of the criminal law."[40] In the nineteenth century, as in the twentieth, the culture was caught between a fear that the criminal net would be cast too broadly in an ever-growing society of strangers and the anxiety that those most culpable for misdeeds would slip through a net too narrowly cast.

⚔ Fagin and Poetical Justice ⚖

As early as 1879, readers puzzled over the nature of Fagin's crime, so much so that an anonymous reviewer of some of Browning's works for the *Saturday Review* could mention it in passing without imagining that it would excite much response. This reviewer of *The Dramatic Idylls* could not only take issue with Browning's juridico-poetic creations ("Ivan Ivanovitch," "Martin Relph," and "Ned Bratts," in particular) but could also use the space to object offhandedly to a case of Dickensian sleight of hand. In moving his censure from Browning to Dickens, this reviewer asks why readers should have to tolerate Browning's poetic procedures that turned English judges into liars and murderers, when "it was bad enough in Dickens, who was wonderfully ignorant of many common things, to hang the Jew Fagin, for no definite offence except that he was one of the villains in the novel. . . . Fagin was tried in due form, though for some unknown crime."[41] Such an attack was not taken lightly, and a response was published forthwith in the pages not of the *Saturday Review* but in the July volume of *Notes and Queries*:

> The *Saturday Review* of 21 June brings a charge against Dickens which, if there were any foundation for it, would prove the great novelist to have been guilty of a piece of gross ignorance; but happily there is no foundation for it, and as I do not think that such an imputation on Dickens's common sense should be allowed to go forth to the world supported by the high authority of the *Saturday Review*, I come forward in the absence of a better champion, not only to defend, but I trust entirely to clear, Dickens from this stigma. The *Saturday* in the course of a review of Mr. Browning's *Dramatic Idylls* says [that Fagin was hanged for no definite offence]. So far the *Saturday* reviewer. Now mark what follows. In *Oliver Twist*, chapter 50, I read, "'The sessions are on,' said Kags: 'if they get the inquest over, and Bolter turns King's evidence: as of course he will, from what he's said already: they can prove Fagin an accessory before the fact, and get the trial on Friday, and he'll swing in six days from this.'" An accessory before the fact in a case of wilful murder, far from having committed no "definite offence" is regarded by the law of England as a very definite offender indeed, and even in these comparatively mild days he would be *liable* to be executed, although he would probably get off with penal servitude for life. At the date of *Oliver Twist*, which is, I suppose, from forty or fifty years ago, he would undoubtedly, in Mr. Kags's expressive vernacular, have "swung" for it.[42]

Dickens's defender here is probably right, but he overstates his case. How many readers of *Oliver Twist* can actually name the crime with which Fagin is charged? If only a few, Jeremy Bouchier of *Notes and Queries* being one, why is it that we can't say and what difference does it make? It does seem at least odd that Mr. Kags of the "expressive vernacular" is able to name so technical a charge as "accessory before the fact," though given what Kags's profession is, he, more so than Dickens's readership, would have been familiar with such exact legal terminology. John Sutherland, in a most recent discussion of the same crux, argues that it certainly is not clear that Fagin is being hanged for his participation, albeit from afar, in Nancy's murder.[43] What one might first observe is that the charge Kags states isn't quite complete, for we must infer the principal crime to which Fagin has been an accessory. Kags announces that "they can prove Fagin an accessory before the fact." Given that this scene at Jacob's Island with Kags (and the rest) follows close on the heels of Nancy's murder, we assume that what Kags means is that Fagin will be tried as an accessory before the fact to Nancy's murder, though it is not absolutely clear that Fagin is so charged. True, Kags says that "Bolter turns King's evidence" (340), but Bolter knows about other crimes (theft, for example) to which Fagin might be charged as an accessory. But in that case Fagin would probably have been charged as a receiver, and receiving stolen goods was not a capital crime while being an accessory to murder was unquestionably capital. I find this ambiguity a telling one, since by failing to name the principal's (that is to say Sikes's) crime, Dickens turns all of our attention toward Fagin's. Moreover, by erasing (literally) the principal act (the murder itself), Dickens makes the charge brought against Fagin—an accessory before the fact without specifying what the fact is—feel all the more like a matter of who Fagin is and not what he has done.

So the problem remains: what does it mean to be an accessory? The response by Dickens's *Notes and Queries* defender to the not unreasonable claim that Dickens executed Fagin "for no definite offence" does not dispose of the problem the *Saturday* reviewer raises. So too Sutherland's provocative discussion, while attesting to the continuing interest in the ambiguity of Fagin's crime (though he is unaware that the controversy was in full swing as early as nine years after Dickens's death), does not work through the questions provoked by naming a defendant as an accessory in the first place or their relevance to this novel. In the discussion that follows, I examine at some length the history of "accessory before the fact" in order to suggest how odd this criminal category is and its significance to the way the novel represents criminal responsibility.

After a review of various descriptions and definitions of accessory liability, one might reasonably conclude that, under certain circumstances, to be convicted as an accessory is to have been convicted of no definite offense. To justify the incrimination of an actor who does not himself commit the principal act, the criminal law turns, not surprisingly or ineffectually but not altogether comfortably, to theories of agency and to distinctions between derivative and principal liability. *Accessory* is a term the criminal law uses to discriminate a different kind of participation; it is more specific than the term *accomplice* (a term Dickens uses twice in *Oliver Twist* to describe Monks), which more loosely describes "every person who is in any other way associated with another person in committing or attempting to commit any criminal offense."[44]

To make a person an accessory is to put that person in a particular relation to the act of another. The criminal law itself is at once entirely committed to and uncomfortable about such liability. To be an accessory before the fact to a crime is to be indirectly involved in the commission of that crime, and such indirect involvement will make one a party to a criminal act, subject to both judgment and punishment: about this much criminal law is clear, even well settled.[45] Sir Matthew Hale's chapter on principal and accessory liability in the *History of the Pleas of the Crown* (1736) begins with no justification of accessory liability, since none was needed.[46] What is less clear, what is not so easily settled, are the nature and boundaries of such indirect criminal involvement. The difficulties raised by accessory liability are differently raised in different historical periods, but the difficulties themselves are perennial.

Let's take the simplest case first. A person acting alone shoots and kills another. The accused becomes a principal in the first degree because he has "actually and with [his] own hands committed the fact."[47] If this were the only kind of crime imaginable, there would be little more to say about parties to a criminal act.[48] We would still be left with the ambiguities and challenges of defining the internal and external elements of crime, but we would not be left to scratch our heads over the nature of the accused's participation in this act. He is the principal in the first degree, the one and only perpetrator.

We move, then, from the lone gunman to the complications of principals in the second degree and of accessories before the fact. The criminal law registers differences not only in degrees of crime (murder in the first and second degree, manslaughter) but also between alleged parties to the same crime. The impulse behind such distinctions feels as if it has always been with us: there are distinctions to be made between those whose participation in a crime appears unmediated and those whose participation appears indirect or attenuated. To recognize such differences, the criminal law defines principals in the first and second degree and accessories before the fact.[49]

Historically, the distinction between principals in the second degree and accessories before the fact mattered procedurally because accessories before the fact could not be prosecuted unless and until the principal who committed the crime was duly convicted. By contrast, the crown could proceed against the principal in the second degree at any time.[50] The only substantive circumstance that differentiates the principal in the second degree and the accessory before the fact is that the principal is present[51] during the commission of the felony at issue and the accessory before the fact is not.

When liability gets apportioned to a principal in the second degree or an accessory before the fact, it is for something different from the act that is the immediate cause of the harm that the law forbids. But what is it that the principal in the second degree or accessory must do to come within the scope of a penal statute or the common law? The law, as far back as Coke in the early seventeenth century (and farther—in Bracton writing in the early thirteenth) marshals a set of terms to describe and inscribe the liability of accessories before the fact. In *The Second Part of the Institutes* (1642), Coke, for example, takes

up an analysis of certain terms defining accessory liability contained in the
Statute of Westminster I:

> (1) [Commandment] *Praeceptum*. Under this is understood all those
> that incite, procure, set on, or stir up any other to do the fact, and are
> not present when the fact is done.
> (3) [Aid] *Auxilium*. Under this word is comprehended all persons
> counselling, abetting, plotting, assenting, consenting, and encourag-
> ing to do the act, and are not present when the act is done; for if the
> party is commanding, furnishing with weapon or aiding to be present
> when the act is done, then is he principal.[52]

Coke unfolds these terms—*Praeceptum* and *Auxilium*—to take in the circumstances he invites the statutory language to take up. The problem is not only
one of translation—though this no doubt is relevant—but also of turning
nouns into verbs, situations into actions. Coke turns the noun *praeceptum*, or
commandment, into actors—"all those"—and then into a series of possible
actions: incite, procure, set on, or stir up. Out of *auxilium* (aid), Coke again
spins out first actors ("all persons") and then actions: counseling, abetting,
plotting, assenting, consenting, and encouraging. It is an impressive list; at
the very least it is impressive that a word that Coke might, in another context,
translate as "aid" takes in meanings as various as these. What moves Coke to
interpret *auxilium* as, for example, consent or assent? Coke's reading of the
Statute of Westminster suggests the breadth of his understanding of the different forms that accessory liability might take, but with this breadth of understanding comes a certain anxiety about any lacuna through which some
possibly culpable defendant might slip. The criminal law is always worrying
over loopholes; however, in Coke the closeness of the verbs listed marks a
heightened anxiety.[53] There simply was not much of a difference between
consent and assent in the early seventeenth century.[54] Still, as close as the
terms were and are, the distinction Coke could draw reveals the reach of
accessory liability as he imagines it through the Statute of Westminster I.
Latent in the *OED* citations for "consent" and "assent" is the difference between "consenting to" and "assenting with," where the former moves toward
an overt agreement between at least two parties and the latter happens only
in the mind of one of the parties concerned. *Consent*, in other words, feels
more like an overt act while *assent* does not. Coke wants both terms to be
in play.[55]

Hale entitles his chapter on principal and accessory liability "Concerning
commanding, counselling, or abetting murder and manslaughter," yet his very
first definition changes his terms: "He, that counsels, commands, or directs
the killing of any person."[56] If we account for this shift simply by accusing
Hale of sloppy draftsmanship, we overlook the way definitions of accessory liability permit this shifting of terms. The eighteenth century's Michael Foster
produces the most extensive and the most influential treatment of what he
calls "the law of accomplices" in his seminal treatise *Crown Cases* (1776).[57] The

trouble with the law of accomplices, Foster complains, arises out of the inconsistent statutory language that defines liability:

> Some statutes make use of the word accessories simply without any other words as descriptive of the offence. Others have the words, abetment, procurement, helping, maintaining, and counselling. One describeth the offence by the words, command, counsel or hire; another calleth the offenders, procurers or accessories. One having made use of the words, comfort, aid, abet, assist, counsel, hire, and command, immediately afterwards in describing the same offence in another case useth the words counsel, hire or command only. One statute calleth them counsellors and contrivers of felonies; and many others make use of the terms counsellors, aiders and abettors, or barely aiders and abetters.[58]

Foster presents this list to address a problem in statutory interpretation: would a prosecution be limited to the literal meanings of the words explicitly used in the statute at issue, or would the prosecution be allowed to bring into these statutes the range of words linked to accessory liability that had been developed in the common law? Foster argues for the latter position: "We are not to be governed by the bare sound, but by the true legal import of the words."[59] The contrast Foster sets up—the bare sound as against the true legal import—should give us some pause, for what is the contrast to which Foster wants us to attend? Foster's "bare sound" suggests that for him the given words of a statute on secondary participation at once contain and lack meaning, and that the "true" meaning can and cannot be found in a statute. Moreover, Foster's "true legal import" suggests some settled true, legal idea of what it means to be an accessory, an idea distinct from any words used.

Foster's treatment of accomplice liability leads the twentieth-century jurist J. C. Smith to conclude that "the actual words [of any given statute] are of no significance once it is clear that they were intended to incorporate the common law concepts of secondary participation."[60] The actual words of a criminal statute are of *no* significance? True, there were and are common law concepts of secondary participation to which jurists might turn, yet it is a bit strange when the actual words of statutes passed to define accessory liability are brushed aside as mere placeholders for common law concepts.[61] Moreover, Smith's shift from word to concept is revealing, as it is consistent with what happens in Foster's analysis of accessory liability. What Foster wants is a broad idea of rather than a specific language for accessory liability, and in support of this position, Foster cites and then takes a good deal of trouble with *Macdaniel and Others*, a 1755 case that upheld a conviction of defendants as accessories before the fact. *Macdaniel* concerned a sort of illegal sting operation cooked up by the defendants whereby one of their number would dupe others into joining with him to commit crimes against unknown victims. But the targeted victim would, in actuality, be another member of this gang, who would then turn the dupes into the police and collect a reward. Not surprisingly, this Dickensian design failed, and all were arrested, tried, and convicted. The defendants who had been involved in the plan but had not in fact spoken to or plotted with the dupes (who had actually attempted the robbery) argued that they could not be convicted as accessories because their activity did not fall within the statute that defined accessory liability. That statute attached liability to those who comfort, aid, assist, abet, counsel, hire, or command another to do a criminal act; defendants argued that "without a personal immediate communication of counsels, intentions, and views, from the supposed accessories to the principals, there can be no accessory before the fact."[62] The judges rejected this argument, declaring that the defendants had *procured* the felony and that such procuring fell within the statute. "For what," concluded the judges, "is there in the notion of Commanding, Hiring, Counselling, Aiding, or Abetting, which may not be effected by the intervention of a third Person, without any direct immediate connection between the first Mover and the Actor?"[63] Though in the form of a question, the judges offer this not as a question but as a statement of fact. One needs to speculate, at the outset, as to why such terms as *commanding, hiring, counseling, aiding*, or *abetting*, which, though related, are not synonyms, come to be thought of by the court as a single *notion?* At bottom lies the sense that the words do not much matter. More important is what the judges here call a "notion," some more "general idea," to use Foster's terms, about secondary participation. *Macdaniel* may seem to us an easy case—we wouldn't want the "first movers" to be shielded by the intervention of third parties—but the readiness with which the judges and, more overtly, Foster as commentator go beyond the actual words of the statute in order to accommodate "procure" marks a certain approach, not only to statutory interpretation but also to accessory liability. So what we see in *Macdaniel* and in Foster's commentary is an impulse that defied the usual practice in criminal law, a practice in which statutory language was always given the narrowest reading when that reading was in favor of the defendant.[64]

Foster turns for support to an earlier case on accessory liability as precedent, a case in which an indictment "was held to be sufficient though the words of the statute . . . were not pursued."[65] Foster's justification for such a holding is telling:

> I take this case to be good law, though I confess it is the only precedent I have met with, where the words of the statute have been totally dropped. And I the rather incline to this opinion, because I observe that the Legislature in Statutes made from time to time concerning accessories before the fact, hath not confin'd itself to any certain Mode of Expression; but hath rather chosen to make use of a variety of words, all terminating in the same general idea.[66]

To make his case, Foster takes a case that he admits is anomalous, and his concession leads him into a less confident position with respect to the relation between statutory language and accessory liability. His support weakens the more he pushes himself to justify it—the no-nonsense tone of "I take this case to be good law" fades into a weak-spined "I the rather incline to this opinion"—and the explanation he offers (in short, that the words of any given statute don't matter because different statutes that address accessory liability use different terms) itself terminates in a loose, baggy, and finally not quite accurate conclusion. First, Foster never himself articulates what the "same general idea" is that issues out of all of this statutory language. Second, the statutory language that Foster produces gives us not one but several ideas about accessory liability. Are accessories criminally responsible because they *assist* another perpetrator or because they *encourage* that perpetrator? Though one can imagine a situation in which assistance could also be encouragement, the general idea (to use Foster's language) of assistance is different from that of encouragement. What Foster won't address is why so many different modes of expression are used to describe the offense, why he resists finding a language for accessory liability and wants instead an idea of liability.

To have an idea of accessory liability that does not have, and in Foster's opinion does not need, "any certain mode of expression" but arises in some vague way out of a variety of words (words about which we are instructed not to attend to "bare sound" but to some "true legal import") is to give real breadth to the law of accessory liability.[67] Moreover, unlike so many other reforms of the criminal law in the nineteenth century, the reform of principal/accessory liability tended to make this broad area of criminal law more and not less severe. The changes made it more likely that an accessory would be charged with a capital crime rather than less so. One of those key changes in the nineteenth century concerned the question of whether an accessory before the fact could be tried before the principal offender. As Stephen reports, "From the earliest times till the year 1702, the rule was . . . that 'no accessory can be convicted or suffer any punishment where the principal is not attainted or hath the benefit of his clergy.'"[68] To justify such a rule, Foster and others explain that the accessory's offense is derivative of the principal's and, as Stephen says, "cannot subsist without it, and in consequence of this connection the accessory shall not without his own consent be brought to trial till the guilt of the principal is legally ascertained by the conviction or outlawing of him, unless they are tried together."[69] In 1826 a statute was enacted that appeared to end this procedural distinction between principal and accessory by making accessories triable before, with, or even instead of the principal. Tellingly, however, the courts refused to recognize that the legislature had enacted such a change and instead interpreted the statute as continuing to hold that accessories were still untriable until the principal had been convicted.[70] Notwithstanding this judicial resistance, 11 & 12 Vic. c. 46 s. 1 (1848) made clear what was thought to be clear twenty-two years earlier: that an accessory could be tried before the principal. This provision was reenacted in the Aiders and Abettors Act of 1861, the controlling statute on accessory liability that remained in force until it was repealed and, in essence, reenacted, by the Criminal Justice Act of 1967.

The initial judicial resistance to the change in law that would allow the accessory to be triable before or instead of the principal marks an important moment in the criminal law of secondary participation. Though the issue is settled in 1848, what one registers during the early decades of the nineteenth century is the very tension revealed in Foster's work in the eighteenth. For even as Foster argues that the guilt of the accessory is dependent on the guilt of the principal, he also shows his impatience with rules that protect the accessory from prosecution when the principal, for example, refuses to answer to the charge ("stands mute"). Against such a scenario, Foster bristles at the fact "That the accessory, who frequently is the leader, contriver, and *real principal* in the Villainy, should be permitted to bid defiance to the justice of the kingdom; merely because the instrument employed by him cannot be prevailed upon to deny the charge, and put himself upon a legal trial."[71] Yet just a few pages earlier we find Foster casting an approving eye over the rule that requires the conviction of the principal before the trial of the accessory: "This rule is founded in good sense and natural justice. The accessory is indeed a felon, but guilty of a felony of a different kind from that of the principal. It is, if I may use the expression, a derivative felony connected with and arising out of that of the principal and cannot exist without it."[72] Foster's logic here suggests a certain hierarchy of blame: the principal commits the crime out of which arises the supplementary guilt of the accessory. This hierarchy is at odds with a version of accessory liability that makes the accessory the real villain and the principal an instrument. Twice Foster uses the locution "no more than accessories," which likewise identifies the primary guilt of the principal and the lesser guilt of the accessory.[73]

The common and statutory laws concerning liability for principals in the second degree and for accessories constitute the laws of criminal complicity, as modern commentators have defined it, laws that work "to determine the circumstances when one party . . . by virtue of prior or simultaneous activity or association will be held criminally responsible for another's (the perpetrator's) wrongful behavior."[74] Or, as another commentator has put it, "secondary liability differs from primary liability in that, fairly obviously, the accessory is convicted not for himself committing the *actus reus* of a particular offence, but because of his association with the commission of such an offence by the principal offender. The exact nature of that association is a matter of some difficulty."[75] Indeed, there is something immediately provocative about including in this definition both "activity" and "association," as it seems to suggest that either activity or association is a sufficient basis for criminal liability, and association begins to look less like conduct and more like character. Does the criminal law recognize no distinction between activity and association? This recent definition begs the question: how do we make individuals responsible for acts they do not actually do? Those preparing the Law Commission's 1993 consultation paper on secondary participation had to acknowledge "the absence from the case law of any properly articulated theory of the nature of the connection between the accessory's conduct and the principal's offence."[76] What we do say of accessories is that their guilt is derived from the guilt of the perpetrator, but even that, as I have shown earlier, is a dicey business. These are the issues Dickens raises when he charges Fagin as an accessory.

Fagin is apparently tried as an accessory before the fact to Nancy's murder, but Fagin could not before 1848 have been tried as an accessory to Sikes's murder of Nancy because his liability was still contingent on Sikes as principal. In other words, Fagin could be tried for the crime if and only if Sikes had been tried and convicted of the murder in the first place. Sikes, one should recall, falls to his death several chapters before Fagin faces legal judgment. But in *Oliver Twist* this is beside the point. Dickens does not produce anything like the form of a criminal trial, notwithstanding the 1879 *Saturday* reviewer's claim that "Fagin was tried in due form." Due form? Dickens gives us something of a trial, but since it is all filtered through the mind of Fagin, Dickens can dispense with the formalities of proof, not to mention the thousand other niceties that make up an English criminal trial. The presentation of Fagin at trial in the penultimate chapter of the novel, "Fagin's Last Night Alive," is a great triumph, a moment of feeling wholly within this disintegrating person, but it evades the legal, moral, and social tensions that accessory liability raised and raises. He wants the legal judgment without the legal process. In charging Fagin as an accessory before the fact, Dickens sets for himself the task of putting on trial this crime that is neither one thing or another, of testing the limits of criminal responsibility but in the end he dodges the very task he makes up. The book is itself powerfully in touch with the urge to dodge responsibilities, either artfully and comically, as is the case with the dodgings of the Artful Dodger, or more crudely, as with the boltings of Morris Bolter (once Noah Claypole), whose first instinct is always to run.

Having brought these issues to the table, I do not wish to insist that knowing whether Fagin could have been tried as an accessory before the fact defines our experience of this character or this novel. It would be both heavy-handed and misguided to suggest that novels are required to abide by the same rules as legal trials. Indeed, my argument depends on one's seeing that novels can go beyond the boundaries of a legal trial. However, that Dickens's readers—from the *Saturday* reviewer and Jeremy Bouchier in the nineteenth century through John Sutherland in the twentieth—so persistently take up the question of Fagin's crime distinguishes it from other representations of the law of which this and other novels make use. This persistent interest wants closer attention. Moreover, and more importantly, this novel in particular calls on readers to take seriously the attacks on legal categories, processes, judgments, and punishments that it mounts. Fitzjames Stephen recognized that Dickens's work necessitated this scrutiny, and while it is true enough that Stephen's often all too literal-minded readings of novels reveal his own limitations as a critic, he understood well enough that Dickens's influence reached beyond the fictional worlds he created, into the courtrooms and jury docks. Like Stephen, as we look "at the sphere of Mr. Dickens's influence, we are compelled to think of him seriously. He is not entitled to the protection of insignificance."[77]

Dickens's decision to dispense with many (or any) of the formalities of Fagin's trial allows him to do something that the law cannot, and this license not only gives him the freedom to produce a powerful experience of the suddenly enfeebled mind but also permits him to sidestep the very problem he had created for himself and for us. Dickens invites sympathy for Fagin at the moment of legal judgment, just as he invites it for the haunted and hunted Sikes, who is chased to his death after Nancy's murder. In Fagin's case, Dickens distances us from the court scene by making us feel how distant Fagin himself is from this scene. Much of what is so moving in this scene is how we are made to feel Fagin's eerie detachment (a detachment eerily like that in T. S. Eliot's *Eeldrop and Appleplex*) from this forum in which judgment on him is passed. Dickens brings us as close as we have ever come to Fagin, as close as we have been to any other figure in the book, including Nancy and Sikes (after the murder), yet he removes us and him from the trial itself. I do not pretend that the trial of the Artful Dodger or of Oliver before the dreaded Fang provides anything like a treatise on the procedures of criminal law in the nineteenth century, nor should it be required to do so or dismissed for not having done so; still, both of these previous scenes allow us some objective view of the way business gets handled. We know the charges brought; we know the witnesses who testify; we understand how and why affairs, fairly or unfairly, proceed as they do.[78] Not so in the trial of Fagin. Is this choice significant? I think that it is.

Dickens's defender in the 1879 *Notes and Queries* protests against the *Saturday* reviewer's attack and uses Kags's remarks to substantiate his defense, but, as I noted earlier, Kags only says that Fagin will be tried as an accessory before the fact. He never specifies the crime to which Fagin is accessory. This ambiguity makes the charge Dickens has brought against Fagin—an accessory before the fact without specifying what the fact is—feel all the more like a matter of who he is rather than what he has (or has not) done. As the *Saturday* reviewer concludes, Fagin appears to be tried for no reason "except that he was one of the villains in the novel." John Sutherland in his 1997 analysis reaches the same conclusion. Even the fully confident *Notes and Queries* man fudges the character/conduct line ever so subtly. Rebutting the *Saturday* reviewer, he remarks that "An accessory before the fact in a case of wilful murder, far from having committed no 'definite offence,' is regarded by the law of England as a very definite offender indeed." The shift from offense to offender, to *having committed* no definite offense to *being* a definite offender, marks that which makes accessory liability different from many other kinds of liability. Since Fagin is not actually a participant in or present at the murder scene (and therefore is not a principal in the murder), his crime is more a condition than an action, more a part of character than a part of his conduct. While a murderer murders, an accessory can't be turned into an action: an accessory can't "accessorize," as it were.[79]

These tensions can be adduced from what is one of the most significant cases on secondary participation from the nineteenth century, a case that is, not surprisingly, from the Victorian period and on which James Fitzjames Stephen was one of the sitting judges. The case, *R. v. Coney, Gilliam, and Tully* (1882),[80] involved arrests following an illegal prizefight. These arrests included not only those of the fighters and ringmen but also of three members of the audience, Coney, Gilliam, and Tully, who were charged as principals in the second degree to the crime of assault.[81] Though *Coney* was decided late in the century (1882), the opinion exemplifies how vexed the issues attendant on accessory liability had been and continued to be throughout the nineteenth century. Following an earlier case (*R. v. Murphy*, 1833) and the first edition (dated 1806) of Sir William Oldnall Russell's *A Treatise on Crimes and Misdemeanors* (also known as *Russell on Crime*), the trial judge instructed the jury to find Coney, Gilliam, and Tully guilty as charged if the jury concluded that the defendants encouraged the fighters. To help the jury make its determination, the judge added:

> there is no doubt that prize fights are illegal . . . and all persons who go to a prize fight to see the combatants strike each other, and are present when they do so, are in point of law guilty of an assault . . . in the words of Littledale, J., *Rex v. Murphy* . . . "If they were not casually passing by, but stayed at the place, they encouraged it by their presence, although they did not do or say anything."[82]

The jury found the three defendants guilty, but their finding reflected the very ambiguity that the judge's instructions sought to avoid. Though the verdict was guilty, the jury added that the three were not guilty of aiding and abetting. So what were they guilty of? As this verdict was on its face utterly contradictory, the case was appealed. The problem in *Coney* was in large part evidentiary. The only evidence of encouragement introduced at trial was evidence that the three had been present at the fight. On appeal, the majority found as a matter of law that mere presence of these defendants at the fight was not sufficient evidence on which a jury could base a finding of guilt for the crime charged.

What is telling about this case, first and foremost, is the way it demonstrates how little was required to make someone guilty of a crime. *Murphy*, decided in 1833 (some forty-nine years before *Coney*, though only six years before *Oliver Twist*), has liability turn on whether or not presence might be deemed casual, but, as the *Coney* court recognized, *Murphy* could be read as holding that presence was conclusive proof of encouragement, whereas for the *Coney* court, mere presence was held to be only *evidence* of encouragement, which could not, on its own, form the basis of a guilty verdict. *Coney* increases the prosecutorial burden, but not by a lot. There is much reliance in *Coney* on the word *mere*; the court is uncomfortable with mere presence forming the basis of liability, but anything beyond "mere" could legitimately support a guilty verdict. What I find more revealing, though, is what I think un-

derlies the decision: who are Coney and Gilliam and Tully? To Cave, writing
for the majority, the evidence adduced is "quite consistent with their being
labourers working near, or persons going quietly home from the races, who,
observing a crowd, went up to see what the matter was, and, finding it was a
fight, stayed some short time looking on."[83] To Mathew, writing for the dissent, the evidence was consistent with a view of the defendants that would
make them a part of

> a class of persons to whom prize fights are attractive; and that
> pugilists fight in public for the gratification of those persons; and that
> the chief incentive to the wretched to fight on until (as happens too
> often) dreadful injuries have been inflicted, and life endangered or
> sacrificed, is the presence of spectators, watching with keen interest
> every incident of the fight. . . . there was evidence that they were pres-
> ent as spectators, and for the purpose of seeing the fight and for not
> another purpose, and that those who fought and those who watched
> the fighting were assembled in furtherance of a common criminal
> character . . . [84]

The contrast is stark and turns in large part on questions of character: the decent, hard-working laborers going quietly home are set against a "class of persons to whom prize fights are attractive."[85] The spectators are depicted as
much less appealing than the fighters themselves, the sacrificial lambs whose
blood gratifies those who greedily watch. The action is all in the watching,
while the fighters themselves get offered up as passive agents ("until dreadful
injuries have been inflicted"). The judge reads presence at the prize fight in
terms of a class and not individual character—for the majority, presence is accidental to the returning working men; for the dissent, presence is a deliberate part of the lives of men of a certain class to which these three men unhappily belong.

When Dickens presents Fagin's trial from the point of view of this now
nearly mentally incompetent old man, he evades the very troublesome questions about secondary liability—about the reach of the criminal law, about the
relations between conduct and character, about the relations between act and
intent—which his novel has so persistently and provocatively engaged. By
making the trial an internal event, he mystifies both the judgment against
Fagin and, perhaps, Fagin himself. Of Fagin, Dickens wrote in a letter to
Forster that he "is such an out and outer, I don't know what to make of him."[86]
Dickens describes Fagin as the perfect type of scoundrel, but so obvious is the
thing he is ("such an out and outer") that Fagin eludes him. The locution "what
to make of him" is itself made strange in light of the fact that Fagin is entirely
of Dickens's own making. Placed in obvious contrast to the hulking Sikes,
Fagin's violence is internalized. Our first vision of Fagin, through Oliver's
eyes, is of a shriveled old man huddled in front of the fire whose face is cov-
ered with red hair. Though not above throwing the occasional pot or throttling
the occasional boy, Fagin is no Sikes. Fagin is primarily (though not only) a

fence; he receives stolen goods and reoffers them to the marketplace. He is a kind of money-launderer, though what he launders are "wipes" rather than pounds (the wipes, of course, turn into pounds). As passive receptor, Fagin lives as a middleman. His acts of violence pass through others or are turned inward and manifested in him as lip- and nail-biting. His evil thoughts aren't often voiced, and his crimes are as much in the mind as in the heart. So this "out and outer" moves very much within himself. Fagin alone is shown cooking up a plan ("intent upon the thoughts that were working within his brain," 3o5) that would rid him of Sikes and put Nancy squarely under his thumb, though his role in this plan is most indirect. Considering Nancy's lately inconsistent behavior, he imagines that she has formed a new attachment to a new man. His first thought is that he should press Nancy to kill Sikes:

> Sikes knew too much, and his ruffian taunts had not galled the Jew the less, because the wounds were hidden. The girl must know, well, that if she shook him off, she could never be safe from his fury, and that it would be surely wreaked—to the maiming of limbs, or perhaps the loss of life—on the object of her more recent fancy. "With a little persuasion," thought Fagin, "what more likely than that she would consent to poison him! Women have done such things, and worse, to secure the same object before now. There would be the dangerous villain: the man I hate: gone; another secured in his place; and my influence over the girl, with a knowledge of this crime to back it, unlimited." (3o5–6)

And then a bit later: "He cast back a dark look, and a threatening motion of the hand, towards the spot where he had left the bolder villain; and went on his way: busying his bony hands in the folds of his tattered garment, which he wrenched tightly in his grasp, as though there were a hated enemy crushed with every motion of his fingers" (3o6). Much indebted to Iago's premeditations, his thrilling imagining of possibilities, Dickens's Fagin considers his options, but the premeditations remain unspoken (though Dickens at moments gives us Fagin's thoughts in what Dorrit Cohn calls "quoted monologue"). And while Fagin is willing to go through the motions of performing a violent act with his "threatening motion of the hand" and "bony hands in the folds of his tattered garment," he with his hidden wounds will do no more than mime a murder. Dickens skillfully reduces Fagin's motions from hand in the air to hands in his garment to the motions of fingers within the garment. The hands within the folds of the garment offer a vivid image of Fagin's surreptitiousness and his inwardness. Although it is Fagin who sends Morris Bolter to follow and report on Nancy, and Fagin who gets Bolter to tell Sikes of Nancy's midnight rendezvous, Fagin does not murder her, nor does he direct or solicit or procure Sikes to murder her. Perhaps the most chilling moment in the novel comes when Fagin, clutching Sikes "by the wrist, as if to prevent his leaving the house before he had heard enough" (32o), gives Sikes a last and purposefully ambiguous suggestion:

"Bill, Bill!" cried the Jew, following him hastily. "A word. Only a word."

The word would not have been exchanged, but that the house-breaker was unable to open the door: on which he was expending fruitless oaths and violence, when the Jew came panting up.

"Let me out," said Sikes. "Don't speak to me; it's not safe. Let me out, I say!"

"Hear me speak a word," rejoined the Jew, laying his hand upon the lock. "You won't be —"

"Well," replied the other.

"You won't be — too — violent, Bill?" whined the Jew.

The day was breaking, and there was light enough for the men to see each other's faces. They exchanged one brief glance; there was a fire in the eyes of both, which could not be mistaken.

"I mean," said Fagin, shewing that he felt all disguise was now use-less, "not too violent for safety. Be crafty, Bill, and not too bold." (321)

There can be no mistake here. Or can there? Dickens makes us certain that Sikes registers Fagin's intentions with respect to Nancy ("there was a fire in the eyes of both, which could not be mistaken . . . he felt all disguise was now useless"); still, Fagin takes care not to say the word *murder* or to voice the means by which such an act should be done or even what act should be done. The narrator displays more of the external circumstances than the internal ones here. We get the heated conversation and their fiercely expressive eyes, and though the narrator adds that the fiery looks "could not be mistaken," he seems to read the internal from the external evidence (instead of "was not mistaken" he gives "could not be mistaken"). I take note too of the fact that the narrator describes Fagin's final words to Sikes as "shewing that he felt all disguise was now useless." "Shewing" invokes a display, and it is preceded by "I mean," a phrase that cues us to believe that what follows will reveal in full exactly what Fagin's meaning is. It does not. Ambiguity remains. John Sutherland notes that in watching this scene "it is not clear whether Fagin is trying to restrain Sikes's homicidal rage, stoke it up still further, or direct it into a devilishly cunning act of blood."[87] These are very different intentions, and Sutherland is right to register each. There is a world of ambiguity in "as if to prevent his leaving the house before he had heard enough." The "as if" gives us the possibility that Fagin restrains Sikes for some other reason. We feel most powerfully the presence of Othello and Iago here, but Iago does what Fagin does not; Iago uses the imperative, commanding the Moor though he is his inferior ("Do it not with poison; strangle her in her bed").[88] Fagin whines; he does not command, and to the extent that "'Be crafty, Bill, and not too bold'" is an imperative, it is arguably to restrain Bill rather than to incite him.

In his *Digest of the Criminal Law* (1877), Fitzjames Stephen looked to Fagin and to Iago (he couples them up) as recognizable examples of accessories that might help his reader distinguish between criminal and noncriminal behavior. Stephen's discussion of these dramatic and novel cases makes clear that in Stephen's eyes neither Fagin nor Iago has done an act necessary to make him an accessory before the fact to murder. Taking up accessory liability for the crime of murder, Stephen gives this illustration: "A tells B facts about C in the hope that the knowledge of those facts will induce B to murder C, and in order that C may be murdered; but A does not advise B to murder C; B murders C accordingly. A has not caused C's death within the meaning of this Article."[89] Much hangs on the distinction between "tells" and "advises" in Stephen's hypothetical; "advises" makes A the cause of C's death while "tells" relieves him of responsibility. Moreover, by using causation as a limitation on A's liability (A is not an accessory because he does not cause the death of C), Stephen sidesteps the difficulties accessory liability generates. Is A any less the cause of the murder when he tells B about C than when he advises him about C?[90] Stephen's footnote to his hypothetical murder produces both his attempts to limit liability for accessories and the special power that Iago and Fagin held in defining the scope of that liability. By way of explanation, he provides these remarks:

> The law as to accessories and incitement, appears to show the limit to which participation in a crime can be carried. Unless the line is drawn there, it is impossible to say how far it would extend. Illustration (6) is a prosaic version of *Othello*; or, to take a humbler instance, of the catastrophe of *Oliver Twist*. Iago and Fagin receive poetical rather than legal justice.[91]

That poetical justice should come into Stephen's mind I find particularly evocative. Poetical justice is ideal because it dishes out to its recipient that which he has dished out to others. We know from what Fagin tells Bolter earlier in the book that he, Fagin, has peached on other associates, and such information has helped to hang other inconvenient companions. How appropriate, then, for Bolter to peach on Fagin. We also know that others have been hanged for Fagin's crimes. How appropriate, then, that Fagin should hang for another's crime. The issues that Fagin and Iago raise are complex, so complex that even Stephen has trouble providing a consistent answer on the question of guilt for accessories. Considering the issues attendant on liability for remote causes of death in *The History of the Criminal Law of England* (1883), Stephen once again turns to *Othello*, but this time he concludes that Iago would be guilty as an accessory, whereas in *A Digest of the Criminal Law* he had acquitted him: "In Othello's case," says Stephen, "I am inclined to think that Iago could not have been convicted as an accessory before the fact to Desdemona's murder, but for one single remark—'Do it not with poison, strangle her in her bed.'"[92] Iago's words are a direct incitement to the act, and that makes a difference to an accessory charge since a line has to be crossed.[93] And in Fagin's "A word. Only a word" we register the care Fagin is taking (and that Dickens allows him to take) to stop short of directing Sikes; he is taking care to speak certain words only. Accessory liability depends often enough on words alone to establish liability, and the criminal law has long recognized words as acts, but Fagin isn't telling Sikes to do anything here.

What stacks the deck against Fagin in this scene aren't the words he speaks to Sikes but rather the narrator's superior knowledge of the intent behind those words that the narrator shares with the reader. The novel gives us what can never be known so unambiguously in a court of law: the thoughts of the defendant. True lawyer that he was, in judging Fagin, Fitzjames Stephen limits himself to the evidence that could be adduced in a court of law. But we are under no such limitation. And this is what, I would argue, makes the justice in *Oliver Twist* not just poetical but novel, for while Shakespeare offers us Iago's great soliloquies as evidence of the workings of that malignant mind, those soliloquies leave us both thrilled and dazed. Iago remains, famously, motiveless and malignant. Whatever we know of Iago's intents we have gleaned from his own speeches—his performances for us and for the other figures in the play. The novel *Oliver Twist* need not abide by such limits. It brings us fully within the mind of Fagin and brings his intents vividly to life. While at the end of *Othello* Iago can pronounce defiantly "What you know, you know" (5.2.352), readers of *Oliver Twist* can know more. They can enter the mind of Fagin.

Fagin himself seems to have the limits of the law half in mind when he speaks to Bill. Ever cautious, Fagin knows enough not to command or order or advise or even suggest murder. His words to Sikes are often carefully couched negations ("You won't be," twice, and then "not too violent" and "not too bold"). Of course the witness against Fagin, Morris Bolter, could testify to Fagin's restraining Sikes and to his words but to little else. Yet we as readers register that something between Fagin and Sikes is being exchanged here, and exchange is central to this passage. The words get exchanged between Sikes and Fagin (note that it is Sikes who brings the word "safe" into the scene and Fagin who turns it into "safety" and "crafty," as if Fagin is doing no more than crafting the thoughts he wants Bill to have) and then, more significantly, we have the exchange of that "one brief glance." There is a special mutuality here—"a fire in the eyes of both"—that makes the reader believe that something has passed from Fagin to Sikes.[94] I have often thought that there should be a chapter or less formal break of some kind between Fagin's talk with Sikes and Sikes's murder of Nancy, but the continuity of the scene suggests that Fagin's intent works through Sikes. We cannot help but feel that at the moment Sikes strikes the fatal blows, much of Fagin is with him: "The housebreaker freed one arm, and grasped his pistol. The certainty of immediate detection if he fired, flashed across his mind even in the midst of his fury; and he beat it twice with all the force he could summon, upon the upturned face that almost touched his own" (322). The special conjunction of "fired" and "flashed" introduces the idea that the thought itself is being fired, though it is first fired by Fagin (in the previous scene), not by Sikes. The act is Sikes's, but the thought—that the firing of the gun will mean certain detection—is Fagin's. Fagin's ambiguous direction and the intent behind it become, for the

purposes of criminal law, a part of the murder Sikes commits. That Fagin's intentions are bad Dickens makes crystal clear. Here he is thinking on Nancy's
betrayal and his loss of power over her just moments before Sikes appears at
his door:

> Mortification at the overthrow of his notable scheme; hatred of the girl
> who had dared to palter with strangers; an utter distrust of the sincer-
> ity of her refusal to yield him up; bitter disappointment at the loss of
> his revenge on Sikes; the fear of detection, and ruin, and death; and a
> fierce and deadly rage kindled by all; these were the passionate con-
> siderations which, following close upon each other with rapid and
> ceaseless whirl, shot through the brain of Fagin, as every evil thought
> and blackest purpose lay working at his heart. (318)

Against the thoughts that shoot and whirl, Dickens is quick to add that Fagin
sits "without changing his attitude in the least, or appearing to take the smallest heed of time" (318). The violent action is all in the thought. A recent commentator on accessory liability notes the importance of this kind of bad
intent, given what are the admittedly weak conduct standards in Anglo-
American criminal law: "the rather loose conduct requirements for complicity are narrowed down by the fault requirements: a small act of assistance may
suffice, but only if done with intent to assist or encourage the commission of
the principal's crime."[95] It is in this context we should situate the radically unambiguous nature of Fagin's bad intents and the ambiguous words Fagin says
to Sikes. Fagin's ambiguous instruction bespeaks his savvy about erecting, or
attempting to erect, a barrier between his speech and Sikes's act. It must be
the case that Fagin is at least as savvy as the inconsequential Kags who seems
to know, along with the rest of the thieves' gang, what it means to be an accessory before the fact. If, as Stephen argues in *A History of the Criminal Law of
England*, Iago would not be an accessory but for "Do it not with poison; strangle her in her bed," Fagin may have a not unreasonable idea that he isn't *saying* anything that will form the basis of a crime. Here, though, this novel and
novelist demonstrate their epistemic superiority to the law. We can know
what Fagin is thinking, and in so knowing we can justly execute him, notwithstanding what he does or does not say to Sikes. The words—the acts, then—
become irrelevant to our judgment of Fagin. What is relevant? That which
Fagin *is*—what he imagines and intends, and not what he does. A later edition
of *Oliver Twist* tips the scales even more unambiguously against Fagin and may
betray Dickens's own unease about the nature of Fagin's liability. Dickens
added running heads to his 1867 edition of the novel, and the headlines he attached to his chapter 47—"Goading the Wild Beast" and "The Wild Beast
Springs"—suddenly define a specific relation between Fagin and Sikes; now
Sikes is no more or less than Fagin's instrument, as exempt from legal responsibility as one who is insane or inhuman. Perversely, Sikes as wild beast
(with his "dilated nostrils and heaving breast," 322) becomes a less-than-
human agent that cannot be held accountable for its acts. Fagin then turns

into the principal. The law, in essence, erases the would-be principal and assigns full responsibility to the party ordering the act. No responsibility could attach to a wild beast. The running head thus simplifies what the text complicates, but such a simplification leaves the questions raised by the text unanswered. To be a bad man is no crime; Fagin is certainly a bad man. Is he and should he be held criminally responsible for a murder? The novel is obviously in a position different from that of the criminal law: it holds out the possibility of dramatizing and exploring alternatives without being held responsible for a legally defensible judgment and sentence. But the last chapters of the novel — the trial and Fagin's meeting with Oliver — are evidence that Dickens wanted the force of the law behind Fagin's conviction and the death sentence that follows (even as he vocally opposed capital punishment and attested to its evils). Yet even as Dickens brings the force of the law to bear on Fagin in a way that satisfies his readers, he evades the very negotiations about responsibility that he introduces and that the law must face.

⚞ Oliver Twist and Guilt by Association ⚟

The criminal category of "accessory before the fact" that Dickens invokes in *Oliver Twist* bespeaks his knowledge of and stake in representing more elusive criminal behavior. Indeed, the crimes *Oliver Twist* delivers include not only immediately recognizable criminal acts — murders, frauds, thefts — but also acts that are marked as criminal before a crime takes place or acts that become crimes because they are attached to or derived from some other criminal act. The plans of Fagin and Monks to recapture Oliver form a part of a conspiracy to commit a crime. Like accessory liability, inchoate liability — liability that rests on an incipient and not a completed criminal act, as in conspiracies and attempts — reveals criminal law's efforts to define and determine criminal conduct and discriminate it from criminal character. The novel *Oliver Twist* involves itself in questions of inchoate liability. As with attempted crimes, it is hard to lay out the criteria for and to make good an accusation of a conspiracy. The net of conspiracy is wider, and as a crime it implicates more would-be defendants than other crimes. A conspiracy must necessarily have more than one perpetrator. Dickens involves us in inchoate crime and, more generally, in the way a crime implicates more than the person who has committed what we necessarily think of as the criminal act itself. Fagin, explaining his operations to Morris Bolter (whom we have previously known as Noah Claypole), explains how the criminal world works:

> "In a little community like ours, my dear," said the Jew, who felt it necessary to qualify this position, "we have a general number one; that is, you can't consider yourself as number one, without considering me too as the same, and all the other young people."
> "Oh, the devil!" exclaimed Mr. Bolter.

"You see," pursued the Jew, affecting to disregard this interruption, "we are so mixed up together, and identified in our interests, that it must be so." (293)

And then a bit later: "To keep my little business all snug, I depend upon you. The first is your number one, the second my number one. The more you value your number one, the more careful you must be of mine; so we come at last to what I told you at first—that a regard for number one holds us all together, and must do so, unless we would all go to pieces in company" (294).[96] Fagin's fast-talking is part of a masterful performance, and it comes as no surprise that Fagin delights in impressing Bolter "with a sense of his wily genius" (294) without telling him anything directly about his "operations" (294). The passage has also been cited as evidence of Dickensian anti-Benthamism in its satire of the individualist ethic built into a collective creed (the greatest happiness for the greatest number). I see that, but I also see that the passage suggests the new complications of a criminal organization. The sense of mutual dependence that Fagin talks up in the passage makes it more difficult to pin down and contain a criminal act. Liability is corporate and not separate, shared and not individual. What we focus on is the connection between the criminals and not any specific act, and we are just as interested in the one who does the act as we are in those he implicates. Throughout the novel, the criminal figures live in fear not only of getting caught in the act but of being implicated by the others who are doing the acting. "It appeared to me that to draw a knot of such associates in crime as really did exist . . . would be to attempt something which was greatly needed, and which would be a service to society" (lxii), writes Dickens in his 1841 preface to *Oliver Twist*, and such language suggests a criminal tie that binds.

Often enough to warrant our notice, the novel offers guilt by association in addition to guilt by action; at the same time as Dickens resists the idea of guilt by association (Oliver's being the case in point), the novel also fosters it.[97] The figures in *Oliver Twist* are defined not simply by what they themselves do but also by what the other figures to whom they are attached do. In this novel, character is formed through inexorable attachments: Nancy to Sikes, the boys in the gang to Fagin, Fagin to Sikes, Nancy to Fagin. These attachments make us feel on occasion that criminal responsibility is assigned as much by association as by action itself. Sikes implicates Fagin as Fagin does Sikes. Nancy's attachment to Sikes implicates her, though in the end it is she who gets him executed. The idea is simple enough—once attached is always attached. This is the great plot Fagin cooks up for Oliver: "'Once let him feel that he is one of us; once fill his mind with the idea that he has been a thief; and he's ours! Ours for his life!'" (126). The language bears close examination here because it is has less to do with the act of crime than the idea of it—"the idea that he has been a thief." There is no getting out of the implications of crime, even if one hasn't actually done a particular criminal act. Dickens can also turn the consequences of such attachments into a legal joke, as when

Bumble rails against the law's assumption that the husband is responsible for the crimes of his wife. When the jig is up and Bumble realizes that Brownlow has discovered his part in Monks's conspiracy, Bumble's first thought is, in true Bumble fashion, for his "parochial office," and when Mr. Brownlow assures him that he is a parochial officer no more, his defense is in earnest:

"It was all Mrs. Bumble. She *would* do it," urged Mr. Bumble; first looking round, to ascertain that his partner had left the room.

"That is no excuse," returned Mr. Brownlow. "You were present on the occasion of the destruction of these trinkets, and, indeed, are the more guilty of the two, in the eye of the law; for the law supposes that your wife acts under your direction."

"If the law supposes that," said Mr. Bumble, squeezing his hat emphatically in both hands, "the law is a ass—a idiot. If that's the eye of the law, the law's a bachelor; and the worst I wish the law is, that his eye may be opened by experience—by experience." (354)

Brownlow's claim that Bumble's presence at the "destruction of these trinkets" forms a central part of his liability is correct, since, as *Coney* and *Murphy* (before *Coney*) demonstrate, presence is one of the elements that the law weighs in determining whether one is an accessory to a crime. But what else has Bumble done? He has married Mrs. Bumble, and having done so he is responsible, under the fiction of marital unity, for her acts. We enjoy this moment, certainly, yet what has turned into a well-known Dickensian joke about the law is no joke when Fagin hangs as an accessory, and we are at once asked to feel that he is more responsible for the crime and less so than Sikes.

For every moment that Oliver lives among the criminals and in their den, the possibility exists that the little hero will be seen by others in the novel, and perhaps by readers too, as implicated in that criminal life and even a criminal himself. The rather extreme forms of protection Dickens constructs on Oliver's behalf, particularly as the novel unfolds, appear designed to keep anyone from assigning any criminal taint to Oliver. Using a kind of belt-and-suspenders strategy, Dickens not only critiques the reach of criminal law when it latches onto Oliver, he also ensures Oliver's innocence by, in essence, making him unconscious at certain key moments in the text. That Oliver should emerge from the den of thieves unscathed by their potentially deforming influence is a fact stated in no uncertain terms in the novel's preface, where Dickens forthrightly attests to Oliver's purity: "I wished to shew, in little Oliver, the principle of Good surviving through every adverse circumstance, and triumphing at last" (lxii). But Dickens wants Oliver to represent more than a principle of good; Oliver must be pure innocence, without the slightest taint of corruption or immorality, and to achieve that among the likes of Fagin and Sikes would be a triumph indeed. Oddly enough, Dickens does not himself make this triumph happen in a completely satisfying way. Having so boldly put Oliver among the criminals, Dickens seems to have had a failure of nerve. No doubt Dickens places Oliver in danger, most potently when Fagin tells his entertaining stories "of robberies he had committed in his younger days" (120). And yet, although the narrator describes Fagin as working at "instilling his soul with the poison which he hoped would blacken it, and change its hue for ever" (120), Oliver remains utterly the same. While Dickens may risk Oliver's life, he never risks his soul. Dickens makes good use of the looser kinds of liability in order to hang Fagin, but he ensures that Oliver is impervious to any implication that he is ever an accessory to or a co-conspirator in any criminal act, whether he is present at the commission of a criminal act (as he often is) or not.

That Oliver always has good intentions we can be sure, but in the world in which Oliver and we live, it is difficult to prove what our intentions are or have been. We must rely on what Dr. Losberne in a key scene calls "worldly considerations and probabilities." In this scene—just after the half-dead Oliver has appeared on the Maylie doorstep—Losberne patiently draws out the legal complexities of Oliver's case for a confused Rose, who insists that Oliver's story "faithfully repeated to these men, will exonerate him" (198). The doctor knows better, as, perhaps, did Dickens: "'I doubt it, my dear young lady,' said the doctor, shaking his head. 'I don't think it would exonerate him, either with them, or with legal functionaries of a higher grade. What is he, after all, they would say? A runaway. Judged by mere worldly considerations and probabilities, his story is a very doubtful one'" (198). And then later he further explains:

"viewed with their eyes [the eyes of the police], there are many ugly points about it; he can only prove the parts that look ill: and none of those that look well. Confound the fellows, they *will* have the why and the wherefore, and will take nothing for granted. On his own shewing, you see, he has been the companion of thieves for some time past; he has been carried to a police-office, on a charge of picking a gentleman's pocket; he has been taken away, forcibly, from that gentleman's house, to a place which he cannot describe or point out, and of the situation of which he has not the remotest idea. He is brought down to Chertsey, by men who seem to have taken a violent fancy to him, whether he will or no; and is put through a window to rob a house; and then, just at the very moment when he is going to alarm the inmates, and so do the very thing that would set him all to rights, there rushes into the way, a blundering dog of a half-bred butler, and shoots him." (198–9)

In large part, the problem Losberne poses is evidentiary. How can Oliver prove that he was barely conscious when Sikes put him through the Maylie's window? Or that he was about to "alarm the inmates" just before the butler shoots him? His testimony, it seems, will do him not good before the law. The evidence, including the evidence that "he has been the companion of thieves for sometime past," looks bad indeed. Losberne's lecture reveals the limits of the law: it can only know what it can know.

The novel and its readers can know more, but tellingly, Dickens does not rely even on the novel's power to represent Oliver's pure intentions. It is not enough that we see inside Oliver and appreciate that he did not intend to do any criminal act or be a part of any criminal plan; Dickens must actually render him unconscious (or semiconscious) before any hint of criminality might attach to him. Perhaps Dickens worried that one's intentions could never be pure. For all Oliver's innocence, he does understand why Sikes is taking him on the ill-fated journey. In one of the most powerful moments in the novel, Dickens demonstrates that Oliver knows he is being taken along for some criminal purpose. As Nancy is taking Oliver to Bill just before the ill-fated journey, Oliver puts the question to Nancy in a startlingly straightforward way:

> "Am I to go with you?" asked Oliver.
> "Yes; I have come from Bill," replied the girl. "You are to go with me."
> "What for?" asked Oliver, recoiling.
> "What for!" echoed the girl, raising her eyes, and averting them again, the moment they encountered the boy's face. "Oh! for no harm."
> "I don't believe it," said Oliver: who had watched her closely. (131)

Making Nancy responsible for his being taken to Bill also makes Oliver responsible for knowing what he is in for. Dickens works hard to clear Oliver utterly and completely, and the harder he works, the more we feel how easily criminal responsibility might attach. At the age of twelve, Oliver is too old to be automatically excused from liability as an "infant," since in the nineteenth century only children under the age of seven would be (by operation of law) exempted from criminal liability. A child between the ages of seven and fourteen could be tried, but the prosecution would be required to rebut the presumption that the child was incapable of knowing right from wrong. Stephen remarks in passing of this presumptive rule that it "is practically inoperative, or at all events operates seldom and capriciously."[98] Hale explains: "if it appear by strong and pregnant evidence and circumstances, that he had discretion to judge between good and evil, judgment of death may be given against him."[99] We have no doubt that Oliver has the discretion to judge between good and evil, for at the moment that Oliver sees the Dodger and Charley Bates light-finger Brownlow's handkerchief, we know that he knows what's what: "In an instant the whole mystery of the handkerchiefs, and the watches, and the jewels, and the Jew, rushed upon the boy's mind. He stood, for a moment, with the blood so tingling through all his veins from terror, that he felt as if he were in a burning fire" (58). The hellfire Oliver experiences arises out of his certain knowledge of the evil of the act, and it is crucial to Dickens's creation of this "principle of good" that he is born with a knowledge of right and wrong. But with knowledge begins responsibility.

As a "companion of thieves," to use Losberne's terms, Oliver is vulnerable to criminal accusation, and while Dickens makes us feel sure that this is wrong when applied to Oliver, the novel as a whole seems also to confirm our assumptions about those who associate with the likes of Fagin. Soon after Oliver is returned to Fagin's den following his brief vacation with Brownlow and Mrs. Bedwin, Fagin explains to Oliver, with all the civilities for which he is duly famous ("with great friendliness and politeness of manner") that should Oliver attempt to contact the police, Fagin will produce evidence against him, as he has against others, that will get him hanged. Oliver's response to Fagin's threats is telling: "Little Oliver's blood ran cold, as he listened to the Jew's words, and imperfectly comprehended the dark threats conveyed in them. That it was possible even for justice itself to confound the innocent with the guilty when they were in accidental companionship he knew already" (114). It is the idea of "accidental companionship" that I want to attend to here, because within "companionship" is both the sense of association and of fellowship. While not every association becomes a fellowship, the coupling we get in companionship registers more than an association. But when might companionship be accidental? What can it mean to have an accidental companionship? Companionship needs this special modification to ensure that Oliver is somehow disconnected from the very connections he makes. So too when a compassionate Rose Maylie looks on Oliver for the first time, Rose asks incredulously: "can you really believe that this delicate boy has been the voluntary associate of the worst outcasts of society?" (191). The problem with "associate" is that it assumes voluntariness, so it is strange that the word should require modification. Whether consciously or not, Dickens gives us the very tension he often suppresses in and through Oliver. Can Oliver remain an innocent lamb when in the company of wolves, or must he become entangled in the "knot of such associates in crime as really did exist"? Does and should his "association" make him criminally responsible? If we recoil at the thought that a kidnapped person might become responsible for her actions while in the presence of her kidnappers, one need only recall the case of Patricia Hearst.

The difficulties Dickens has exonerating Oliver are not his alone. Except for certain so-called victimless crimes, every crime has a victim, and, as K. J. M. Smith remarks, "all 'victims' are necessarily incidental "accessories" and, further, the "tight limits and uncertainty of the concept of complicity-free 'victims' are indistinctly illustrated by a thin scattering of inconclusive case law."[100] It is, at first, an absurdity to think of victims as accessories, but there are cases in which the victim seems at once both party and victim, and those cases are ones that, although certainly distinguishable from Oliver's case, illuminate the issue as a whole. A key Victorian legal judgment on the question arises out of *R. v. Tyrell*,[101] an 1894 case in which a fifteen-year-old girl was charged as an accessory to an act of unlawful intercourse, an act made criminal by the Criminal Law Amendment Act of 1885, which prohibited intercourse with a girl under the age of sixteen. The court held that the girl would not be liable as an accessory because the Criminal Law Amendment Act "was passed for the purpose of protecting women and girls against themselves."[102] In short, the court found that the girl was a party made victim by the statute itself.

So how can Dickens make what Oliver does (associate with criminals) congruent with what he is (perfectly innocent)? The answer is simple: Dickens keeps him from doing much of anything. The novel sometimes has, as other critics have been quick to point out, the feeling of a waking dream, the kind of waking dream that Oliver, at two critical moments in the novel, famously experiences.[103] Just before Oliver senses the presence of Monks and Fagin at the Maylies' window, Dickens defines that middle state between consciousness and unconsciousness into which Oliver falls: "There is a kind of sleep that steals upon us sometimes, which, while it holds the body prisoner, does not free the mind from a sense of things about it, and enable it to ramble at its pleasure" (227). Dickens creates an Oliver unable to act but not unable to be — to be cognizant of the situations around him. Prevented from acting by the powers of sleep, Oliver can neither participate in nor control what happens to him or around him.[104] The same kind of *cordon sanitaire* is erected when Oliver is watching Fagin finger the loot he has collected from lately-executed colleagues. And when Oliver is called on to answer for what appear to be incriminating circumstances, Dickens takes him out of commission before he will be in any way compromised. Hauled up before Fang for picking Mr. Brownlow's pocket, Oliver teeters on the verge of total collapse, leaving the policeman, comically, to answer for him.[105] Likewise, once rescued by the Maylies and Dr. Losberne and having duly reported his sad history to them, a convenient delirium keeps him from lying to the Bow Street Runners about his association with Fagin and Sikes, leaving the doctor to do it for him as a makeshift defense attorney — though, tellingly and amusingly, Cruikshank's illustration of this scene shows an Oliver wide awake and apparently well enough to speak on his own behalf.[106]

All of this fainting and half-sleeping effectively removes Oliver from the scenes of the crimes, even though he is bodily present. So it makes sense that J. Hillis Miller should argue (in the service of a different claim — to show that the novel is a fairy tale) that hanging "is the fate which awaits Oliver if he lifts a finger in any positive action. In a way he is most in danger when he asks for more, and when he fights Noah Claypole for having insulted his mother. . . . His only hope is passivity."[107] Dickens evacuates Oliver of intention and makes him an innocent agent, which, as Glanville Williams explains, is "in law . . . a mere machine whose movements are regulated by the offender."[108] An innocent agent is a tool that commits the criminal act without committing the crime. So when the journey to and the break-in at the Maylies is described, we often register that Oliver has no volition of his own. We get "Mr. Sikes, dragging Oliver after him" (136), "Mr Sikes accompanied this speech with a jerk at his little companion's wrist; Oliver, quickening his pace into a kind of trot, between a fast walk and a run, kept up" (136), "He was awakened by a push from Sikes" (138), "Sikes pushed Oliver before him" (140), "'Down with it!' echoed Toby . . . 'Tell him to drink it, Bill.' . . . Frightened by the menacing gestures of the two men, Oliver hastily swallowed the contents of the glass, and immediately fell into a violent fit of coughing" (141–2), "Oliver: who was completely stupefied by the unwonted exercise, and the air, and the drink that had been forced upon him: put his hand mechanically into that which Sikes extended for the purpose" (142), "Before Oliver had time to look round, Sikes had caught him under the arms" (143), "Toby . . . placed his hand upon the boy's mouth, and dragged him to the house" (143). In addition to all of this pushing and dragging and shoving, Sikes continually threatens Oliver with his loaded pistol. At the moment Oliver breaks into the Maylies' house, Dickens has Sikes keep physical control over the boy ("Sikes . . . put Oliver gently through the window with his feet first; and, without leaving hold of his collar, planted him safely on the floor inside," 144). And then, to make clear that Oliver is more inanimate than animate, he is described simply as "more dead than alive" (144).

Problematically, though, Oliver isn't dead, and problem it is. One way of reading Dickens's solution is to say that he does kill off Oliver—or at least he puts him in a state of suspended animation. By making Oliver inanimate or unconscious, he evades the questions of complicity that Oliver's acts raise. There is a marked sentimentality and a marked lack of generosity in Dickens's assuming that if Oliver is at all tarnished by the tawdry world in which he for a time lives, he will lose all entitlement not just to readerly sympathy but to legal protection. His Leeford family inheritance is contingent on his not doing any wrongful acts that show any degree of meanness or cowardice. The will, as Mr. Brownlow renders it, contains a potent contingency related to Oliver's acts. "If it were a girl," the will says, "it was to inherit the money unconditionally; but if a boy, only on the stipulation that in his minority he should never have stained his name with any public act of dishonour, meanness, cowardice, or wrong" (351). Brownlow explains the stipulation as reflecting the dying father's "confidence in the mother, and his conviction—only strengthened by approaching death—that the child would share her gentle heart, and noble nature. If he were disappointed in the expectation, then the money was to come to [his first son]; for then, and not till then, when both children were equal, would he recognise your prior claim" (351). I don't want to make more of this business than it is. While Brownlow is determined to get Oliver's money for him—he is willing both to forgo criminal prosecution of Monks (if any such prosecution could be mounted) and to risk Nancy's life to get the information he needs—we as readers have long since lost interest in this "object." When the good doctor Losberne proposes grabbing every scoundrel in the thieves' den, Brownlow pacifies him by recalling him to their "object":

"What object?" asked the doctor.

"Simply, the discovery of Oliver's parentage, and regaining for him the inheritance of which, if this story be true, he has been fraudulently deprived."

"Ah!" said Mr. Losberne, cooling himself with his pocket-handker-chief; "I almost forgot that." (281)

We too have long since forgotten what the object is, as has Dickens. He has to recall us to it in this mechanical way in order to bring the plot to a conclusion, but who, really, is worried about Oliver's parentage or his inheritance? Once Oliver is safe in the Maylie world, he drops out of the novel. It is unexpected, though, that when justifying the illegitimate boy's inheritance, Dickens makes it turn on a public act of dishonor, meanness, cowardice, or wrong. Critics rightfully have made much of the fact that *Oliver Twist* turns bastardy into a sign of innocence while evil is conferred on legitimacy, but Dickens's way of legitimating Oliver means that he can have not a single moment of moral weakness. The consequence of such a weakness for little Oliver would be that he loses the money and his legitimacy—though, I would add, there is a Dickensian wobble here. Since the act of wrong under the will must be public, Dickens seems to recognize that some private moment of weakness might be allowable. Dickens might allow his "principle of good" to survive even if Oliver in a private moment considers some cowardly act, as he perhaps does.[109]

Were this all, the book would not be as powerful as it is. What is best in this novel pushes us to face the paradox that Dickens describes in his preface about Nancy ("It is useless to discuss whether the conduct and character of the girl seems natural or unnatural, probable or improbable, right or wrong. IT IS TRUE") and to confront the necessary and difficult task of having to pass a judgment, and then even more exactingly a sentence, on a figure who embodies the contradictions Dickens at times so deftly realizes. When Rose Maylie implores Nancy to quit her life with Bill, Nancy replies rather unexpectedly and quite unsentimentally, "I am chained to my old life. I loathe and hate it now, but I cannot leave it. I must have gone too far to turn back,—and yet I don't know, for if you had spoken to me so, some time ago, I should have laughed it off" (316). There is a lingering sense of the old Nancy here, the Nancy who so cheerfully and entertainingly helped Fagin and Sikes haul Oliver back into the thieves' den, of Nancy as she is first introduced to us in the novel with her friend Bet, as young ladies who "wore a good deal of hair: not very neatly turned up behind; and were rather untidy about the shoes and stockings. They were not exactly pretty, perhaps; but they had a great deal of colour in their faces; and looked quite stout and hearty. Being remarkably free and agreeable in their manners, Oliver thought them very nice girls indeed. As there is no doubt they were" (55). The piling up of adverbial phrases here invites us to enjoy the shabbiness of this pair and to feel Oliver's innocence about such women. The freedom that Nancy and Bet express not only in their manners but also with, impliedly, their bodies marks them as part of the criminal world.[110] The affectionate but not altogether un-judgmental bantering in "As there is no doubt they were" echoes in a later scene when Nancy, trying to make her way to Rose Maylie, is rebuffed by a porter and other servants. But now Dickens's affectionate banter has a dis-cernible edge to it; we are to disapprove of those who would sneer at Nancy for her shabby (or worse) appearance: "This allusion to Nancy's doubtful character, raised a vast quantity of chaste wrath in the bosoms of four house-maids, who remarked, with great fervour, that the creature was a disgrace to her sex; and strongly advocated her being thrown, ruthlessly, into the ken-nel" (269). Dickens has long abandoned the caricature of the cheerful young lady with which he introduced Nancy and offers instead the contrast be-tween the kind of conduct Nancy's physical appearance suggests and the character she has become. Even her grammar and diction have undergone a dramatic improvement: she speaks like Oliver now. Yet she still *is* a woman of doubtful character. Faced with the possibility of leaving Sikes, Nancy thinks aloud about whether, in fact, she is chained to a life that she would otherwise leave if it weren't already too late, or whether she stays in the life because it is her life. How are we to judge her decision to stay? Her choice is both freely made and fated.

Writing to Forster on November 3, 1837, Dickens remarked that he wanted "to do great things with Nancy,"[111] and part of the great thing he did do with her was to imagine these tensions. When Dickens has Nancy, speak-ing to Mr. Brownlow and Rose Maylie, say tersely of Sikes and herself "bad life as he has led, I have led a bad life too" (313) and then later "I have been a liar" (314), we are being asked to weigh these considerations against others which press against them. The fullest realization of these tensions comes as Nancy is on the verge of meeting again with Rose Maylie and Brownlow:

> Adept as she was, in all the arts of cunning and dissimulation, the girl Nancy could not wholly conceal the effect which the knowledge of the step she had taken, worked upon her mind. She remembered that both the crafty Jew and the brutal Sikes had confided to her schemes, which had been hidden from all others: in the full confidence that she was trustworthy and beyond the reach of their suspicion. Vile as those schemes were, desperate as were their originators, and bitter as were her feelings towards the Jew, who had led her, step by step, deeper and deeper down into an abyss of crime and misery, whence was no es-cape; still, there were times when, even towards him, she felt some re-lenting, lest her disclosure should bring him within the iron grasp he had so long eluded, and he should fall at last—richly as he merited such a fate—by her hand.
>
> But, these were the mere wanderings of a mind unable wholly to detach itself from old companions and associations, though enabled to fix itself steadily on one object, and resolved not to be turned aside

by any consideration. . . . she had refused, even for [Sikes's] sake, a refuge from all the guilt and wretchedness that encompassed her—and what more could she do! She was resolved. (301)

What Nancy will do next is not in question: she will meet with Rose and Brownlow. But who is this girl who will now do this act? Is the act she now undertakes—the act to protect Oliver—in or out of character, and, perhaps more to the point, what character are we talking about: the girl Nancy whom we once knew or the girl Nancy whom we know now? On the one hand, we locate a continuity of character here, with the narrator reminding us that Nancy is and has been a liar, that she is in "an abyss of crime," that she is surrounded by guilt and wretchedness of which she herself is a part. Yet the narrator detaches Nancy from the criminal character he has created. She can now judge Fagin ("richly as he merited his fate") as the narrator himself judges him: it is as if these voices have merged. She has become an intellectually and emotionally mature figure, like the narrator himself. To mark the separation of the reformed Nancy from the unreformed one, the narrator unaccountably dismisses her thoughts of Sikes and Fagin as "the mere wanderings of a mind unable to detach itself wholly from old companions and associations." Why "mere"? There is something inapt in "mere" and in "wholly" here (twice), since the wanderings are not mere and Nancy is never able to detach herself from old companions and associations.[112] Dickens destabilizes the character of Nancy but then fixes her again by having her mind "fix itself steadily on one object." However, to be fixed on a new course of conduct does not mean that one is detached from an old character, and a new character cannot detach itself from old conduct. When Brownlow gives voice to the idea that Nancy can disconnect, we, like Nancy, identify it as a pipe dream. Brownlow imagines that he has the power to place Nancy so far from her "former associates" (315) that she could be made to have disappeared without a "trace"; she dismisses him after only "a short struggle" (316).

Nancy is not tried for the crimes she commits (kidnapping among them), but she is punished for them, as she herself predicts: "I must go back," she insists to a persistent Rose, "Whether it is God's wrath for the wrong I have done, I do not know; but I am drawn back to him through every suffering and ill-usage: and should be, I believe, if I knew that I was to die by his hand at last" (274). God's wrath for wrongs done isn't the same as the law's wrath for wrongs done, and since the novel never realizes any trial of Nancy or invokes the law to affirm or substantiate her punishment (as it does of Fagin), the ambiguity we are left with about Nancy—the one Dickens details in his preface—feels decent, permissible, even necessary; for what would the criminal law do with Nancy? It would do what it would have to do: try her (for theft, or prostitution, or kidnapping), convict her, sentence her, and this is too brutal to face. That she prostitutes herself, that she steals, one cannot doubt. That she *is* a whore or a thief—now we are in difficult, even treacherous territory. Recall Stephen Knapp's argument about responsibility for past actions. Her past acts are incongruent with present character. Nancy pays for her crimes, but she is not put through the torture of a public trial or execution for them.

In *Eugene Aram*, a novel published in 1832 — six years before *Oliver Twist* — Edward Bulwer novelized the historical case of Aram, a murderer who had lived a respectable and scholarly life until the murder he committed many years before was exposed and he was arrested, tried, convicted, and executed. Given Aram's reformation, it was a case in which readers had to confront the incongruity of a past act and present character. However, while the novel's third person narration generates readerly interest in and sympathy with Aram's inner torment, Bulwer does not (perhaps he could not) bring the reader so fully into Aram's mind, and as a result, the potential conflicts I describe in Dickens's representation of Nancy are not realized. It is significant that Bulwer had first composed a drama about Eugene Aram, only to abandon that enterprise in favor of a novel. The novel bears the marks of the earlier attempt (with Aram waxing poetic in his soliloquies). Moreover, reformed though Aram may be, he remains violent, at one point losing his temper and coming close to murdering the character who threatens to expose him, so the relations between character and conduct are less troubling than the synopsis of the case might suggest. Bulwer also had the comfort of a legal judgment already passed on Aram; his readers would have known Aram's fate. Dickens, by contrast, had no such safety net. Unwilling and perhaps unable to render a judgment on Nancy, Dickens leaves judgment to God: in her last act, Nancy holds up the handkerchief that Rose has given her "as high towards Heaven as her feeble strength would allow, breathed one prayer for mercy to her Maker" (322–3). Nancy can be redeemed without our having to produce a legal judgment on her. Such judgment is deferred, as it is in the sentencing of Magwitch in *Great Expectations*. Though the sentence of death is actually passed on Magwitch, as it is not on Nancy, that earthly judgment is displaced by a greater one. Pip observes at the moment of sentencing: "The sun was striking the great windows of the court, through the glittering drops of rain upon the glass, and it made a broad shaft of light between the two-and-thirty and the Judge, linking both together, and perhaps reminding some among the audience, how both were passing on, with absolute equality, to the greater Judgment that knoweth all things and cannot err."[113]

⚔ The Inner Sikes? ⚔

Nancy is the paradox that Dickens renders in the last paragraph of his preface to the novel, but the contradiction between conduct and character Dickens gives in that paragraph is figured not only in Nancy but in Sikes as well, though it is difficult at first to see any contradiction in Sikes at all. *Oliver Twist* is justly famous for producing the real criminal, for showing criminals "as they really are" (lxii), and no one fits that bill as well as Bill Sikes. Of Sikes, Dickens prefatorily writes:

I fear there are in the world some insensible and callous natures that do become, at last, utterly and irredeemably bad. But whether this be so or not, of one thing I am certain: that there are such men as Sikes, who, being closely followed through the same space of time, and through the same current of circumstances, would not give, by one look or action of a moment, the faintest indication of a better nature. Whether every gentler human feeling is dead within such bosoms, or the proper chord to strike has rusted and is hard to find, I do not know; but that the fact is so, I am sure. (lxiv–lxv)

Dickens here responds to criticisms that Sikes is too much of a bad thing, that he lacks any "of those redeeming traits which are objected to as unnatural in his mistress" (lxiv). Given his thorough badness, we should find in Sikes a perfect congruence between conduct and character, and for much of the book we do. Notwithstanding Dickens's insistence on his realistic treatment of Sikes ("nothing overdrawn"), he is a caricature. Introduced as a great hulking mass of a man, a "stoutly-built fellow" with "a very bulky pair of legs" and "large swelling calves" (76) whose first words are threats, Sikes embodies violence; he is a figure who will inflict violence or on whom violence will be inflicted.

There is a strong sense in Dickens's presentation of Sikes of what-you-see-is-what-you-get: no punches pulled, no surprises to come. In his preface, Dickens defends such descriptions "of the everyday existence of the Thief"—Sikes, the Dodger, Nancy—as part of his principled decision to have nothing disguised and, eschewing such disguises as he sees in Gay's Macheath or Ainsworth's Jack Sheppard or other Newgate novel figures, Dickens undertakes to show these characters in their least romantic incarnations. And Bill Sikes as he really is gives us "not the faintest indication of a better nature." What we have in Sikes for most of the novel is the congruence of the internal and the external. The internal itself is turned into external action, criminal behavior, violent conduct.

Sikes should be for us one of the easier cases to handle in the novel, since he has about him the same kind of caricatural simplicity as Mr. Brownlow or Rose Maylie. They are simply good; he is simply bad. We are, moreover, not as interested in how Sikes got to be the bad sort that he obviously is as we are in the fact of his badness. Dickens's preface attends more to the creation of a Sikes type than the book itself does. "I fear," says Dickens in 1867, "there are in the world some insensible and callous natures, that do become utterly and incurably bad." The first version of the preface in 1841 had read, "I fear there are in the world some insensible and callous natures that do, at last, become utterly and irredeemably bad." Dickens's "become" in both 1841 and 1867 calls up the idea that Sikes, though born "insensible and callous," has turned bad—utterly bad. The shift from "irredeemably" to "incurably" registers a move from moral condemnation to a resigned acceptance of the situation. "Irredeemably" in 1841 indicates that Sikes lacks the capacity to undergo moral and spiritual redemption or that, by choice, he resists it. "Incurably" gives

Sikes a disease and implies that the blame for the absence of antidote cannot fall solely on him. Still, while it is a significant shift in Dickens's thinking about Sikes, it is not one that he plays out in the novel proper.[114] The novel is no doubt in touch with arguments about free will and social determinism — *Oliver Twist* is, after all, a reform novel—but whether Sikes was born bad or environmentally determined so is, in the end, beside the point.

Sikes's conduct tells us what we need to know about him, including what little interiority he must have. He is Bill Sikes the housebreaker first and foremost. After he murders Nancy, he becomes Sikes the murderer. The change in terminology is telling, and it is a change Dickens reflects almost immediately. In the moment before Sikes strikes Nancy with the fatal blow, we have him as the housebreaker. Seconds later, he is "the murderer staggering backward to the wall, and shutting out the sight with his hand" (323). How unexpected it is, then, that in the next chapter, the first after the murder, he is again "the robber," hiding out in a public house. How odd too that in all versions of his preface, Dickens, in replaying the scene of Nancy's murder, turns Sikes back into the robber: "From the first introduction of that poor wretch [Nancy] to her laying her bloody head upon the robber's breast" (lxv). Dickens's reluctance to call Sikes a murderer suggests that the judgment we are to make against him has less to do with his criminal act than with who he is: he is a criminal—a housebreaker and a thief—but not a murderer.[115] This is perhaps what Humphry House means to tell us when he says that "Fagin and Sikes are never despised, even though what they do is despicable."[116] Note a shift from *are* to *do*. What House gestures toward here is the difference between who they are and what they do. If, as House suggests, we feel sympathy for Sikes after the murder, it is in part because we feel a sudden discontinuity between his conduct and his character.

Paralyzed by the murder he has committed, Sikes stays in the room with the dead Nancy: "He had not moved; he had been afraid to stir" (323). Certainly this is the first time Dickens gives us a fearful Sikes, and his inability to act changes our attitude toward him. What we begin to experience after the murder of Nancy is the drama of the conflict between what Sikes has done and who or what he is. This requires Dickens to create an inner self for Sikes, and experiencing the inner Sikes is disorienting. As with Old Rudge in *Barnaby Rudge*, Sikes is haunted by his victim, is desperate for refuge, and will do anything to get his mind off his terrible deed. In his preface, Dickens had proclaimed his desire to distinguish himself from the so-called Newgate school of novelists and to show the real consequences of crime, and these postmurder chapters fully realize Sikes's torment. As Sikes must see again and again the face of his victim, we hear the moralizing narrative voice: "Let no man talk of murderers escaping justice, and hint that Providence must sleep. There were twenty score of violent deaths in one long minute of that agony of fear" (327). Dickens insists here, quite some time before Sikes actually meets his Maker, that Sikes has been punished enough. To suffer "twenty score of violent deaths in one long minute" does sound like overkill, and what other justice but the justice that Providence determines could we wish on Sikes? Knowing, as he was likely to have known at this point in the composition of the novel, that Sikes was going to meet his fate extralegally, Dickens assures the reader that, as with Nancy who accepts "God's wrath for the wrong [she has] done" (314), his sentence will come from God, and so the kind of weighing attendant on a legal judgment suddenly becomes irrelevant. Once that has been managed, what drives these chapters is not the suspense of Sikes's demise; rather, Dickens draws us into a different problem. Sikes begins to lead a double life, acting the part of a good man who comes to the aid of his neighbors. Where physical action has been that element that has defined Sikes, that has expressed most fully his character, the chapters following the murder present the paradox of the preface. Sikes acts out the role of savior here by throwing himself into the dangers of a nearby fire. True, he works through his desperation and paranoia by helping extinguish the fire, but we are within our rights to ask why Dickens chooses to represent Sikes as a good Samaritan. Sikes wants to be part of a community. He works tirelessly and selflessly to put out the fire, but as soon as the crisis is over, he must return to "the dreadful consciousness of his crime" (329). "Consciousness" used here attaches to Sikes personality; he becomes Locke's forensic person, an appropriate subject for judgment and punishment.[117]

That Sikes suddenly has something to hide does not in itself make his conduct (helping the neighbors put out the fire) explicable. He has spent the whole of his life in hiding—moving, like Fagin and the others, from hideout to hideout. Here, though, we have a Sikes who has done something not of himself, and his sudden irresolution, his weakness (what a strange thing it is that Charley Bates almost beats him to a pulp), and his discomfort when people look at him with suspicion (wasn't he always viewed thus?) enact the disjunction of what he has done from who he is. Having decided to make his way to Hendon to find lodgings, he begins his journey: "Thither he directed his steps,—running sometimes, and sometimes, with a strange perversity, loitering at a snail's pace, or stopping altogether and idly breaking the hedges with his stick" (324). This strange combination of fury and idleness *is* perverse, invoking as it does the sense that Sikes hasn't any idea what he is supposed to be doing. He has ceased to be a caricature and has become a character in tension with and not consonant with his conduct. To produce a character is to produce the paradox.[118]

Though Bill Sikes was Dickens's first murderer, he was not to be his last. The homicidal figures who operate in Dickens's middle and late novels— *Martin Chuzzlewit*'s Jonas, *Our Mutual Friend*'s Bradley Headstone (though he does not actually succeed in killing Wrayburn), *The Mystery of Edwin Drood*'s John Jasper (if one believes he murdered Edwin)—invite consideration of Dickens's representation of the criminal mind. Instead of offering a general discussion of murder in Dickens, what I would like to present is a very brief and specifically focused contrast between Sikes and these other major Dickensian murderers. Dickens's representation of Sikes remains remarkably distinct, not only because Sikes is so fully a part of disrespectable, criminal society (while Chuzzlewit and Headstone and Jasper are not) but also because the murder of Nancy creates him as a figure who suddenly experiences a conflict between conduct and character. In *Dickens and Crime*, Philip Collins investigates Dickens's turn from Sikes the low-class brute to the middle-class murderer figure like Jonas, a figure who must suppress his wickedness until it erupts into an act of supreme violence.[119] The tension between the external respectability and the internal corruption in Headstone, for example, presents the opportunity for Dickens to imagine a complicated psychology, as Collins (and others) have considered. Still, though Dickens creates an interior life for Jonas Chuzzlewit and Bradley Headstone, we register no genuine disjuncture between who they are and what they have done. We know that what they do is a sham (in *Our Mutual Friend*, the narrator calls Headstone's daytime activities a "disciplined show" and a "performance of his routine of educational tricks, encircled by a gabbling crowd").[120] Dickens's representations of the interior lives of these figures create continuity, not conflict. Bradley Headstone's attempt to murder Eugene Wrayburn is consistent with what Dickens allows us to know of him, of that which is "animal" in him.[121] Before Headstone attempts to murder Wrayburn, the narrator tells us quite straightforwardly: "The state of the man was murderous, and he knew it."[122] One might argue that Sikes anticipates Chuzzlewit and Headstone in the horrors he endures after he murders Nancy (his paranoia, for instance), yet while the terror that Sikes experiences is of a piece with that which Dickens represents in Chuzzlewit and Headstone, those later interiorized descriptions are not at odds with our previous experiences of these figures (Collins notes that Headstone is "seen from within" throughout the novel.)[123] The passages that bring to life Headstone's postmurder movements of mind are terrific, but they do not come as a great surprise to us. Headstone feels no remorse ("He had no remorse," the narrator tells us without paltering[124]), and while he does commit the crime over and over again in his mind, he does so not because he cannot stop reliving the horror of it but rather because he tortures himself with the idea that the act might have been done "more efficiently."[125] Nor are we taken aback by Jonas's paranoia. Sikes, by contrast, becomes a figure who can embody a conflict only after he murders Nancy, late in the novel, at which point the complexities of judgment present themselves. Given these differences, Sikes, I would argue, presents a special and distinct case.

What Dickens does not resolve about Sikes and Nancy got resolved, or perhaps erased, when Dickens rewrote these crucial chapters of *Oliver Twist* for his public performance of them as part of his 1868 reading tour. From the novel he extracts a drama that begins with Nancy's meeting with Mr. Brownlow and Rose Maylie on London Bridge and ends with Sikes's self-execution. His performances of *Sikes and Nancy* (its new title) were famously triumphant and famously disastrous, contributing as they did to his own death in 1870. Dickens's comments in letters to Forster and other friends about his revisions to the chapters and his later reading performances do more than invite

the interpretations biographers and literary critics have given them; so overt
is he in identifying himself with Sikes that such an interpretation is not
merely anticipated by Dickens but positively cultivated by him. More to the
point is the major rewriting of these scenes that Dickens undertook in 1868
for his Farewell Reading Tour. Philip Collins reports in his *Charles Dickens:
The Public Readings* that the performance text of this part of the novel "contains rewriting more interesting than in any other Readings."[126] Many of the
revisions seem motivated by the obvious need to economize. Others may be
explained as inspired by the pleasure Dickens would get in reading certain
lines out loud. More often, though, Dickens makes the performance text
more straightforward than the novel text. Pathetic as Nancy sometimes is in
the novel, she becomes little more than the television movie-of-the-week victim in the performance text. The moment that I have already included here in
which Nancy considers why she is staying with Bill ("I am chained to my old
life. I loathe and hate it now, but I cannot leave it. I must have gone too far to
turn back, — and yet I don't know, for if you had spoken to me so, some time
ago, I should have laughed it off") is deleted. The reply of Nancy in the performance text comes from another chapter in the book — the first meeting between Rose and Nancy — and is a piece of high melodrama: "I am chained to
my old life. I loathe and hate it, but I cannot leave it. — When ladies as young
and good, as happy and beautiful as you, miss, give away your hearts, love will
carry you to all lengths. When such as I, who have no certain roof but the cof-
fin-lid, and no friend in sickness or death but the hospital-nurse, set our rot-
ten hearts on any man, who can hope to cure us!"[127] Having prepared for the
murder in this way, Dickens proceeds apace to give us in performance Fagin
waiting for Sikes's return, Fagin's meeting with Sikes, the murder itself, the
escape and pursuit of Sikes, and his fall from the roof. Once past Nancy's
meeting with Brownlow and Maylie, one registers how quickly Dickens wants
to get his audience to the murder itself. Deleted are most of the passages
from the book that present Fagin deep in thought, considering the ways in
which he might dispose of Nancy and revenge himself on Sikes. By repro-
ducing the scenes as drama, Dickens submerges the tensions the novel plays
out. Most of the dialogue between Sikes and Fagin remains intact (as one
might expect in a dramatic reading), but the emphasis in the performance
text is on Sikes's action and less on an exchange between Sikes and Fagin.
Two key moments of exchange are deleted from the text. The murder scene
itself proceeds with few changes. Then, perhaps most significantly, Dickens
deletes many of the sections that show the sudden paradox that Sikes presents to us as readers. After Sikes has murdered Nancy, we get a few of the passages in which we find him haunted by the dead girl's ghostly presence, and
then, almost immediately, the mob shows up to chase him up to the roof and
then, finally, down to his death. Dickens's audience would be anxious for
punishment after so gruesome a murder, and to introduce the complexities
of Sikes after the murder would have changed the relation between Sikes
and his criminal act.

But it is nevertheless this altered relation that is at issue. It is not just that Sikes feels remorse or fear but that the remorse and fear are of a piece with the consciousness suddenly created at this moment—created at the moment he awakens to find he has murdered Nancy. The negotiation between what Sikes is, what he was, and what he has done allows the paradox but cannot in the end maintain it. Like Nancy, Sikes is punished without a legal judgment having been rendered; the punishment is inflicted outside the authority of criminal law, and our sympathies are clearly with the man against the mob. If tried in a court of law, justice would probably demand that Sikes be convicted of manslaughter, if not murder, but what person, or "forensic person," to use Locke's terms, would be subject to the judgment then passed and the punishment then inflicted? To release Sikes from responsibility is unthinkable; to judge him legally means facing that which we do not want to face, that which cannot be resolved.

Prologue to
George Eliot's Crimes

Taking up the distinction between law and morals in *The Concept of the Law*, H. L. A. Hart explains:

> The most famous attempt to convey in summary fashion their essential difference is the theory which asserts that, while legal rules only require "external" behavior and are indifferent to the motives, intentions, or other "internal" accompaniments of conduct, morals on the other hand do not require any specific external actions but only a good will or proper intentions or motive. This really amounts to the surprising assertion that legal and moral rules properly understood could not ever have the same content; and though it does contain a hint of truth it is, as it stands, profoundly misleading. . . . None the less there is something of importance caricatured in this confused argument; the vague sense that the difference between law and morals is connected with the contrast between the "internality" of the one and the "externality" of the other is too recurrent a theme in speculation about law and morals to be altogether baseless.[1]

This theory, "inherited by jurists from Kant's distinction between juridical and ethical laws,"[2] does mislead, but productively. It is easy to see with Hart how misleading a view this is: homicide laws, for instance, certainly depend on distinctions between different states of mind. One only has to review any set of statutes or cases on homicide to register how engaged the law is in asking questions about the life of the mind. Still, Hart calls on and calls up a distinction that by its very persistence in the cultural imagination and social practices invites attention. From H. L. A. Hart—the most important legal philosopher of the twentieth century—I turn now to James Fitzjames Stephen, who, if not his counterpart in the nineteenth (Hart practiced law but was not appointed to the bench, and Stephen was not as accomplished or committed a philosopher), was at least his equal. Writing on criminal law in 1863, Fitzjames Stephen anticipates Hart on the relation of the legal to the moral:

> in regard to that part of the criminal law which ought to be based on morality, it must be borne in mind that it is never possible to make the legal definition of a crime satisfy the moral sentiment which the crime excites. . . .
>
> Every action is, as I have already shown, a complex matter made up of bodily motions and states of mind inferred from them. The moral sentiment with which an act is regarded depends far more on the state of mind inferred from the bodily motions than on the bodily motions themselves. On the other hand, both legal and moral definitions of necessity look, in the first instance, to the bodily motions, and regard state of mind merely as an ingredient necessary, indeed, to constitute the action, but to be assumed to exist.[3]

Morality may assign more weight to state of mind than to an act; it may even regard the act as a means to an end—a way of getting at state of mind—but still it must take account of bodily motions. Both the legal and moral definitions must, as Stephen says, begin with bodily motions ("in the first instance") and must recognize ("of necessity") that a state of mind is a constituent part of those motions. One is surprised to find state of mind "merely as an ingredient" even in the first instance, since no one knew better than Fitzjames Stephen (except, perhaps, John Austin, the most important early nineteenth-century legal philosopher, writing before him) how large a role states of mind had to play in the criminal law. Even so, Stephen's main point has the force of common sense: both the law (in this instance the criminal law) and morality depend on bodily motions—on the manifest elements of an act—to understand (and judge) state of mind.

In the novel, and particularly in certain novels of George Eliot where the third person narrator offers such full access to the inner life of characters, we need neither action nor spoken word to manifest state of mind. The third person narrator produces that to which we have no immediate access in ordinary life: the thoughts of another. As I remark in my introduction, I do not claim for the third person narrator the power of omniscience. Yet Eliot's narrators go very far, a good deal farther than we can go in our daily lives. This formal difference becomes both opportunity and challenge in Eliot's work, since it puts her in the position of regarding a desire without the evidence of bodily motions as signs of that desire. She is, as Dorrit Cohn notes of the novelist more generally, "the creator of beings whose inner lives [s]he can reveal at will."[4] Unlike the narrator but like the rest of us, Eliot's characters famously misread the signs that other characters produce. In *Middlemarch*, for instance, Dorothea misinterprets the signs of her husband-to-be, Edward Casaubon, and finds herself yoked to a man and a scholarly project that bear no resemblance to her own premarital interpretation of either. But Eliot gives her narrator and her reader access to inward states that the characters may not themselves understand. Given this access, what is striking is the interest Eliot takes in representing murderous states of mind and the complex relations among state of mind, act, and consequence. In representing these elements, Eliot takes advantage of the novel's power to enter into the minds of its characters, but she also attends to the limits that acts and consequences impose. These limits are in part what turn the novel back to the necessity of an external act.

In the following two chapters, I explore four of Eliot's novels — *Adam Bede*, *Felix Holt*, *Middlemarch*, and *Daniel Deronda* — and I suggest the ways Eliot's work reflects a shift in focus and emphasis from consequences to intents, motives, desires — a shift from the external to the internal, from the objective to the subjective in assessing accountability. Such a shift is manifested not only substantively but formally; to move from consequences to intents is to move from a narrative method that proceeds from the outside in to one that proceeds from the inside out. While *Adam Bede*'s narrator imagines herself as a natural historian or a witness in the witness box, the narrators of *Middlemarch* and *Daniel Deronda* do not assume such roles.

Though I distinguish the internal from the external here, I do recognize that acts and consequences live as much in the mind as outside of it: we can conceive of internal consequences just as we can conceive of internal acts. In *The Principles of Morals and Legislation*, Jeremy Bentham remarks in his chapter "Of Human Actions in General" that "acts may be distinguished into *external* and *internal*. By external, are meant corporal acts; acts of the body: by internal, mental acts; acts of the mind. Thus, to strike is an external or exterior act: to intend to strike, an internal or interior one."[5] But this terminology did not suit John Austin in the nineteenth century. While first accepting this terminology, Austin later repudiated it:

> I am convinced, on reflection, that the terms are needless, and tend to darken their subjects. . . . And it is utterly absurd (unless we are talking in metaphor) to apply such terms as 'act' and 'movement' to *mental* phenomena. I therefore repudiate the term '*internal* acts'; I hastily borrowed the distinction from the works of Mr. Bentham: A writer, whom I much revere, and whom I am prone to follow, though I will not receive his dogmas with blind and servile submission.[6]

What I register in this repudiation is some discomfort with the relation that the "metaphor" (as Austin calls it here) creates. If we apply the same terminology to what goes on in the mind and what goes on outside of the mind, the distinction becomes clouded. If we speak of internal acts, can an internal act be deemed a part of an *actus reus* for the purpose of defining a crime? Austin's rejection of Bentham indicates how much was at stake here. In looking

at paired terms—internal/external, subjective/objective, moral/legal, intent/
act—I will explore the *relations* between such terms, and not the one absent
the other. It is in part because we cannot equate acts and consequences with
the external alone that Dickens and Eliot can challenge the boundaries between the act and the intent. As I have argued in my analysis of *Oliver Twist*,
the idea of an "internal act" is very much alive in Dickens's novel. Dickens
produces in Fagin the activity of thought that very soon thereafter is manifested in Sikes's murder of Nancy. When Gwendolen wills the death of her
husband in *Daniel Deronda*, her guilt arises out of her perception of her own
internal act against him. More self-consciously and more philosophically than
Dickens, Eliot interrogates these relations. Where is the distinction between
the internal (intents, motives, desires) and the external (act, consequences)
contested? Where is it reaffirmed? Eliot's art shapes and is shaped by the relations between these elements.

As part of this undertaking, I consider Eliot's work in the context of certain legal developments of the nineteenth century, and more particularly the
developments of and in what has come to be known as analytical jurisprudence. Eliot owned a copy of Austin's *Lectures on Jurisprudence*, dated 1875,
and she included maxims from the works of Austin and Bentham in her notebooks.[7] For example, Eliot paraphrases Austin's attempt in *Lectures on Jurisprudence* to distinguish the Science of Jurisprudence from Positive Morality
and the Science of Ethics:

> The *Science of Jurisprudence* is concerned with *positive laws*, without re-
> gard to their goodness or badness. *Positive Morality*, laws of opinion or
> sentiment, whether right or wrong. *Science of Ethics (or Deontology)* af-
> fects to determine the test of positive law & morality — to expound
> them as they ought to be. It consists of two departments: the one af-
> fects to determine the test of positive law & is styled the Science of
> *legislation*; the other affects to determine the test of positive morality,
> & is styled the science of *morals*.[8]

The distinctions to be made between law and morality and Austin's considerations of them are on her mind in 1875 (as evidenced by this notation), but I
would argue that these considerations are germane to her earlier work as well.
Eliot and G. H. Lewes traveled in the circles in which it would have been difficult not to have been knowledgeable about the study of *mens rea* and *actus
reus* pursued by the analytical jurisprudential writers. I am struck by how
often and how centrally questions of criminal responsibility and of the external and internal elements of crime are presented in Eliot's novels—and presented in a specifically criminal law context. We know that Eliot used Henry
Maine's *Ancient Law* when she was composing *Middlemarch*, and if she was
aware of Maine during the composition of *Middlemarch*, she was also aware of
Austin, as Maine's work was so often set against Austin's.[9] James Fitzjames
Stephen had himself paired these works in a 1861 *Edinburgh Review* article entitled "English Jurisprudence."[10] And G. H. Lewes had reviewed a work of

Sarah Austin (John Austin's wife and editor) entitled *Germany, from 1760 to 1814; or, Sketches of German Life, from the Decay of the Empire to the Expulsion of the French* (1854).[11] So too the influence of Austin's work would have been apparent in other materials with which Eliot would probably have been familiar through other relationships. She was, for example, a good friend of the philosopher Henry Sidgwick, who turned his mind to questions about intention and knowledge in relation to moral and legal responsibility. Her reading on free will and determinism would have brought her into contact with detailed analyses of desire, motive, intention, act, and consequence, the terms being handled in the jurisprudential writing on criminal law as well as in the decisions of judges reported in newspapers and other periodicals. Evidence of Eliot's reading in the analytical jurisprudence might be found, for example, in a scene from *The Mill on the Floss* in which questions of intent, act, and consequences are at issue. Turned aside by Tom in favor of Lucy, Maggie pushes the favored Lucy into the mud. The narrator then attends to the distinction between Maggie's passions, which have all the intensity of a heroically tragic struggle, and her action, which does not. The narrator names the action a "rash deed."[12] The vocabulary Eliot attributes both to Tom and to the servant Sally in response to Maggie's crime situates the scene in a legal (albeit a comically legal) context. First there is this from Tom:

> It was not Tom's practice to "tell," but here justice clearly demanded that Maggie should be visited with the utmost punishment: not that Tom had learnt to put his views in that abstract form; he had never mentioned "justice," and had no idea that his desire to punish might be called by that fine name.[13]

The ironic tone masterfully undermines Tom's self-righteousness, but the thinking Tom does is in touch with questions about acts, consequences, and punishments, indeed about justice itself. Shortly thereafter, Sally must intervene: "'But Lors ha' mussy, how did you get near such mud as that?' said Sally, making a wry face, as she stooped down and examined the *corpus delicti*."[14] Tom is left to reassess the situation: his "imagination had not been rapid and capacious enough to include this question among the foreseen consequences."[15] A. S. Byatt, the editor of the Penguin edition of *The Mill on the Floss*, glosses "corpus delicti" using a definition from Austin's *Lectures on Jurisprudence*, but since those lectures weren't published until 1863, it is unlikely Eliot herself had access to that work.[16] It is more likely that she has in mind Bentham's work in *The Principles of Morals and Legislation* that takes up the relations of passions to acts, of rash deed to foreseen consequences, all of which turn up in this scene from Eliot's early novel.

Eliot's first major full-length work, *Adam Bede* (1859), generates not conflict but rather a marked harmony of legal and moral principles of responsibility (though, as I will argue, the fissures between the legal and the moral emerge the more Eliot weights interiority and destabilizes consequences). A central moral guide of the novel—the affable though not infallible Augustus

Irwine—is both a cleric and a magistrate, a fact that Eliot makes clear the very first time Irwine appears in the book. And when Hetty goes on trial for infanticide (*Adam Bede* is one of the two Eliot novels that contains a formal trial; the other is *Felix Holt*), that trial invokes both the moral and the legal in its judgment of responsibility, which is itself securely anchored to the consequences of Hetty's act. The first order of business for both moral and legal judgment in *Adam Bede* is an examination of consequences. Nowhere are the consequences of Hetty's infanticide more upsettingly represented than in the testimony of John Olding, the laborer, who recalls hearing a strange cry, and then, "just as I was stooping and laying down the stakes, I saw something odd and round and whitish lying on the ground under a nut-bush by the side of me. And I stooped down on hands and knees to pick it up. And I saw it was a little baby's hand" (436). The "And . . . And" here calls to mind a biblical syntax; the biblical comes to permeate this legal tribunal. Olding's legal testimony penetrates the character Adam Bede and creates in him the suffering that, as the narrator tells us earlier in the chapter, is a kind of "baptism" (427). When the moment of judgment comes, it is shared not just by judge and jury but by the whole of the community:

> It is sublime—that sudden pause of a great multitude, which tells that one soul moves in them all. Deeper and deeper the silence seemed to become, like the deepening night, while the jurymen's names were called over, and the prisoner was made to hold up her hand, and the jury were asked for their verdict.
> "Guilty." (437)

There is both legal and moral justice in the requirement that Hetty hold up her hand, as if she must physically reenact the child's own suffering (one of the most powerful moments in the whole of the novel is when Olding recounts seeing the little hand of the half-buried child). As I will argue hereafter, often *in Adam Bede* the horror and the materiality of consequences overpower ambiguous states of mind through which we often admit excuse. The narrative method of this early novel turns the question of responsibility on the consequences of actions. They can be known. But what can be known of desires, intentions, knowledge? The narrator herself on occasion names the limits of her own power to see into and through her characters, likening herself to both natural historian and legal witness giving testimony under oath. As natural historian or legal witness, the narrator must infer those elements that are not visible—states of mind among them—from those that are visible, from acts and consequences. Yet the narrator does not, in point of fact, limit herself to the external. Her explorations of state of mind destabilize the novel. Eliot exercises her novel prerogative by fully entering into the minds of her characters, and she brings us with her. Having done so, the basis for our judgment and hers is altered; we are moved to want the subjective state to play a larger part in the assessment of responsibility. Should a subjective test of criminality replace objective tests? Criminal law was itself asking whether knowledge and intentions could be presumed from the natural consequences of acts or whether evidence of *actual* knowledge and intention needed to be introduced. What begins to develop in *Adam Bede* is a tension between the internal (desires, motives, intents, knowledge) and the external (act and consequences), a tension that the novel cannot resolve but rather suspends. Nor does it need to resolve the tension it produces, since unlike a legal case it issues no verdict or sentence. The tension remains.

Tensions between the subjective and the objective in Eliot's work are not only thematized but formalized. Certainly in *Adam Bede*, Eliot thematizes the relation between character and environment, and in the most famous passage from the novel the narrator cautions us not to pass too harsh a judgment on the weakened Arthur Donnithorne for (like Dr. Lydgate in *Middlemarch*) Arthur is forever changed by his own deeds. The narrator concludes: "Our deeds determine us, as much as we determine our deeds; and until we know what has been or will be the peculiar combination of outward with inward facts, which constitutes a man's critical actions, it will be better not to think ourselves wise about his character" (315). *Adam Bede* is concerned not only with the judgment of character but with the assessment of responsibility for the critical actions themselves and "the peculiar combination of outward and inward facts."

As we move from *Adam Bede* to *Felix Holt*, Eliot's fourth novel, the friction between inward and outward becomes more marked and more troublesome for Eliot, who raises and dispatches the questions broached more quickly and in a more contained section of her narrative. My own treatment of these relations in the novel *Felix Holt* is necessarily brief since I think they cluster in and around one section of the novel: the section in which Felix Holt is drawn into the riot that follows the local elections, gets into an altercation with a constable, and unintentionally kills him. He is subsequently tried and convicted for leading a riot, as well as for assault and, most signficantly, manslaughter, only to be immediately pardoned. What Eliot produces in *Felix Holt* is a quite simplistic conflict between legal and moral bases of judgment, as she herself shifts her focus from the external to the internal, from a consequence to an intention and a motive. She lines up the external with the legal and the internal with the moral; and here the moral and the legal are at odds, as the criminal law refuses to account for the real desires and intentions of the hero, Felix Holt. Though the legal proceedings exclude the more subtle questions that the relations between motive, desire, intention, and knowledge provoke, outside the courtroom, such questions are framed nonetheless. Felix has not intentionally killed the constable; however, Eliot leaves us to wonder about the recklessness of his act. Should Felix bear the responsibility for an act done to avert a greater evil but, after all, rashly committed? Eliot does not explore this question in any detail, and at the end of this section of the novel, she contents her reader with Felix's pardon, brought about in no small measure by the testimony of Esther Lyon, whose struggle to suppress her own egoism has long been of deep interest to Felix, who has himself a romantic attachment to her. Esther's testimony evokes sympathy from the jurymen, but more than this, she testifies to Felix's state of mind just before he enters the rioting mob. Like sympathy itself—Eliot's highest moral virtue—the testimony as to state of mind is pushed aside in the courtroom to make room for what Eliot calls the "facts" of the case—a man is dead by Felix's hand. No more need be known. Esther's testimony only reenters when the concerns become not those of justice but of mercy. After an adjudication of guilt and a sentencing, the moral considerations are brought to bear on Felix's case, and he is pardoned.

But the relative simplicity of the conflict offered in *Felix Holt* does not survive in Eliot's latest and greatest works, *Middlemarch* and *Daniel Deronda*. Although Eliot eschews any formal legal judgments in either work, I would argue that these works engage the most legally charged questions: what is the relation of a criminal state of mind to a criminal act? When does a criminal intent become a criminal act? The distinction between act and intent was itself being renegotiated in light of the developments in physiology and psychology that G. H. Lewes took up so passionately in *The Physiology of Common Life* (1859) and *Problems of Life and Mind* (1874–79); Lewes died during the composition of the third series of *Problems of Life and Mind*, which Eliot herself completed and saw through to publication.[17] These questions engage both the relations of the internal and external elements of crime and the relations of the legal to the moral. The possibility of representing a murderous thought as a murderous action in a realist novel—a novel that rejected idealized and overly didactic writing and was more markedly in touch with the complexities and contradictions of daily life—is an opportunity to expand moral censure well beyond the law's reach—but with opportunity comes risk.[18] Moving in and among the inner lives of the characters they present, Eliot's novels have the power to erase distinctions between the internal and the external, and it is Eliot's rich representation of the possibility of this erasure that my investigation will, in part, explore.

To work out this relation novelistically is a radically different undertaking from what a trial or judicial opinion or legal treatise might produce for many reasons, not the least of which is that the novel gives us imaginative access to another person's mind. Eliot's psychological realism demanded no less than that we experience the inner lives of these characters and, in certain key instances, the crime in mind. Through *Middlemarch*'s Nicholas Bulstrode, Eliot offers an anatomy of a potentially ambiguously criminal state of mind that precedes the commission of a crime. The vividness of Bulstrode's death wish—to the reader as well as to the character—complicates the relations between desire and intent, intent and act, act and consequence. Some critics may read Eliot as herself equating a murderous desire with the act of murder, but she never gives us a desire or an intent without some overt act, and the subtle and ambiguous relations among motive, desire, intent, act, and consequence generate some of her most distinctive and memorable writing. While Eliot keeps the formalities of criminal law out of *Middlemarch* and *Daniel*

Deronda, the criminal law reenters to recall into moral thinking the necessity of an external act, though Eliot further tests the boundaries of the external act by representing omissions and situating those omissions in potentially criminal contexts. The legal and the moral negotiate the internal and the external, as the passages with which I began—from H. L. A. Hart's *Concept of the Law* and from James Fitzjames Stephen's *History of the Criminal Law of England*—intimate. So must the novel. Eliot's realist novels represent—sometimes ambivalently and inconsistently but never uninterestingly—not only the vexed relations between the mind and the act but, by extension, the vexed relations among the legal, the moral, and the novel in questions of responsibility.

⊰ TWO ⊱

"To Fix Our Minds on That Certainty"

Minding Consequences

in *Adam Bede* and *Felix Holt*

Consequences": "a round game, in which a narrative of the meeting of a
lady and gentleman, their conversation, and the ensuing 'consequences'
is concocted by the contribution of a name or fact by each of the players, in ignorance of what has been contributed by others" (*OED*).[1] *Adam Bede* is no
game, but Eliot's narrative of the meeting of Hetty Sorrel and Arthur Donnithorne is importantly a narrative of consequences, and it is a narrative
in which ignorance (sometimes willful) produces not amusement, or even
ridicule, but catastrophe. It is the romance between Hetty Sorrel, the vain and
naive milkmaid, and Arthur Donnithorne, young squire and grandson of the
landlord, that brings forth such consequences. The result of their secret
union is a pregnancy that leads to the great tragedy of the book. Without
knowing that Hetty is pregnant, Arthur breaks off the relationship and leaves
Hayslope, their village. Later, the pregnant Hetty quits the village and her life
with the Poysers in search of him, has the baby en route, and buries it alive.
The dead child is later exhumed by a traveling laborer. Hetty is tried for the
crime of murder, convicted, and sentenced to be hanged. At the last minute
Arthur (who has returned to Hayslope and learned of Hetty's fate) gets a re-
prieve for Hetty in the form of a partial pardon. The pardon reduces Hetty's
sentence from hanging to transportation for life. In addition, and less cata-
strophically, Arthur destroys the hopes of the straight-as-an-arrow carpenter
Adam Bede, who, ignorant of the sexual relationship between Hetty and
Arthur and believing that Hetty had grown to love him, had planned to wed
Hetty. Adam is both damaged and regenerated by the incident. Arthur also
brings scandal to the home of Poysers, a home whose very foundation is its

good, honest, unsullied name. In short, consequences abound in *Adam Bede*, and out of such consequences arise questions of responsibility.

It is a simple truth that the consequences we intend are not always the consequences that occur. More troublingly, we may not intend any consequences at all, yet despite our best un-intentions, there are still consequences to our actions, for good or ill. Consequences are not always under the control of intents; if they were, what would it mean to have an accident? It was with the analytical jurisprudence of Jeremy Bentham and John Austin in the late eighteenth and early nineteenth centuries that these relations were being so fully interrogated. While much of John Austin's work was published early in the nineteenth century, it was not until after his death in 1859 (at the age of 69) that his work, particularly his *Lectures on Jurisprudence*, was read and acclaimed. But J. S. Mill attended the lectures Austin gave at the University of London, where in 1826 he had been appointed to the Chair in Jurisprudence and the Law of Nations.[2] He prepared the lectures for the course that would become his *Lectures on Jurisprudence* in Bonn, Germany and, as others have noted, was influenced by the more systematic legal codes then in place on the continent, as was Bentham. Some of the lectures he delivered during his term at the University of London were printed as *The Province of Jurisprudence Determined* in 1832. It was a book that found something of an audience but that did not, according to Wilfred E. Rumble, "receive the attention that [Austin] felt it merited."[3] Not until a second edition of *The Province of Jurisprudence Determined* was issued in 1861 and the whole of the lectures (edited under the acknowledged expert hand of his widow, Sarah Austin, herself an important writer and thinker, more famous than her husband) were published in 1863 did Austin attain special status in the newly emerging field of jurisprudence that he had, to a large extent, inaugurated.[4] Austin's work was being reissued just at the time that James Fitzjames Stephen had begun his own career as a barrister and journalist, and in 1861 he reviewed Austin's *Province of Jurisprudence Determined* along with Henry Maine's *Ancient Law* for the *Edinburgh Review*.[5]

Austin was, to say the least, tuned into the difficulties of defining acts and consequences. In *The Lectures on Jurisprudence* he parces out the elements of firing a gun:

> Most of the names which seem to be names of acts, are names of acts, coupled with certain of their consequences. For example, If I kill you with a gun or pistol, I shoot you: and the long train of incidents which are denoted by that brief expression, are considered (or spoken of) as if they constituted an act, perpetrated by me. In truth, the only parts of the train which are my act or acts, are the muscular motions by which I raise the weapon; point it at your head or body, and pull the trigger. These I will. The contact of the flint and steel; the ignition of the powder, the flight of the ball toward your body, the wound and subsequent death, with the numberless incidents included in these, are conse-

quences of the act which I will. I will not those consequences, although I may intend them.[6]

The scrupulous detailing of those elements that comprise parts of the act and those that comprise the consequences serves Austin's larger purpose, for Austin argues that while it is appropriate to say that one wills an act, one cannot 'will' a consequence. But it also needs to be said that moral philosophers might dispute Austin's classification, since the distinction between acts and consequences is not as clear as Austin would have it.[7] In Austin's exposition on intention, his analysis also modifies and remodifies the way we name a consequence. So, for example, an intended consequence may not be a wished consequence. Or a consequence may not be intended at all. Imagine, he suggests, that

> My yard or garden is divided from a road by a high paling. I aim with a pistol at a mark chalked upon the paling. A passenger then on the road, but whom the fence intercepts from my sight, is wounded by one of the shots. For the shot pierces the paling; passes to the road; and hits the passenger.
>
> Now, when I aim at the mark, and pull the trigger, I may not intend to hurt the passenger. I may not contemplate the hurt of a passenger as a contingent consequence of the act. For though the hurt of the passenger be a probable consequence, I may not think of it, or advert to it, as a consequence. Or, though I may advert to it as a possible consequence, I may think that the fence will intercept the shot, and prevent it from passing to the road. Or the road may be one which is seldom travelled, and I may think the presence of a stranger at that place and time extremely improbable.[8]

The modifiers attached here to consequence — contingent, probable, possible — readjust our attitudes toward the agent. Austin takes care with his modifiers and their connections to the state of mind of the agent as he analyzes responsibility for this act.

This is a complicated business, and one in which the stakes are high, since questions of moral and criminal responsibility depend in no small part on how we conceive of the consequences of an act. In *Adam Bede*, Arthur Donnithorne intends to have sexual relations with the innocent Hetty Sorrel, surely, but does he intend to get her pregnant? It is a probable result. Does he foresee that pregnancy or her desperate actions with respect to it? What did women in her position do with a child? Will it make a difference if those consequences, though in fact unforeseen (however foolishly), were not unforeseeable (yet another differentiation in moral and legal debate on responsibility)? Consequences both do and do not have a life of their own, whatever the state of our intentions and desires with respect to them, and nineteenth-century jurists, particularly Austin, took up the task of making explicit the possible disjunctions between intents and consequences, desires and consequences, knowledge and consequences. Having taken up such disjunctions, though, how would responsibility be assigned for those consequences? Would the test of criminal responsibility be objective—based on consequences from which intention and knowledge are presumed—or subjective, based on actual knowledge and intents? Henry Sidgwick's 1874 book *The Methods of Ethics* attends to the same issues, and I turn here briefly to Sidgwick, since this work represents what Eliot might have known about these issues through moral philosophy. Six years before the publication of *The Methods of Ethics*, in 1868, Sidgwick, a fellow of Trinity College, had become a good friend of Eliot and G. H. Lewes.[9] Though Sidgwick's book was published fifteen years after *Adam Bede*, it illuminates the questions that were then much discussed in legal and moral philosophical circles. Sidgwick construes the relation between intention and consequence such that intention includes foreseen consequences:

> when we speak of the intention of an act we usually, no doubt, have desired consequences in view. I think, however, that for the purposes of exact moral and jural discussion, it is best to include under the term 'intention' all the consequences of an act that are foreseen as certain or probable, since we cannot evade responsibility for any foreseen bad consequences of our acts by the plea that we felt no desire for them, either for their own sake or as means to ulterior ends: such undesired accompaniments of the desired results of our volitions are clearly chosen or willed by us.[10]

In short, Sidgwick deems that an accused intends, even wills, the consequences that he foresaw as certain or probable, whether or not they are desired. Sidgwick's separation of knowledge from desire owes much to John Austin's work on the mental element of crime, and in my later discussion I will take up this distinction in some detail. Moreover, in the preceding passage, Sidgwick attends to specific foreseen consequences, but what about the unforeseen but foreseeable consequence? A moral and legal conflict was developing in the nineteenth century concerning such consequences. Some nineteenth-century courts held that knowledge and intent could be imputed to an accused on the basis of the "natural" consequences of his act, without any further evidentiary showing. So too courts held that even if an accused did not in fact foresee the consequences of his action, he might be held responsible if he *should* have foreseen those consequences. In such cases, consequences define, perhaps even create a state of mind.

Once understood, this business makes the oft-heard excuse "I didn't mean to . . ." sound quite a hollow note, a note hollow enough that when Arthur Donnithorne pathetically gives this explanation to Adam Bede, it distances us from him. At the end of *Adam Bede*, after Hetty Sorrel has been transported and Arthur must face the jilted Adam, the most he can say of Hetty and for himself is "I never meant to injure her" (470), and Eliot does not allow either Adam or the reader to exonerate Arthur on such insufficient grounds. The excuse echoes the thought with which Arthur has earlier consoled himself, the thought that "He had said no word with the purpose of deceiving her, her vision was all spun by her own childish fancy," yet he also feels "obliged to confess to himself that it was spun half out of his own actions" (314)—but not his own desires or intentions. His obligation is to recognize the consequences of his acts even in the absence of bad "purpose." After the great tragic events have come to light, Arthur rejects his own excuses even as he feels the need to tell Adam that he "did struggle" before ruining her, that "it would never have happened, if I'd known you loved her" (470), that the letter he sent to Hetty breaking off their affair "was the best thing I could do," that "in that letter, I told her to let me know if she were in any trouble" (470).[11] Still, he ends with the simplest of statements about intentions, acts, and consequences: "I was all wrong from the very first, and horrible wrong has come of it" (470). For all his talk of intents and struggles, Arthur does not palliate either the wrongfulness of the act or its tragic consequences. The novel stands behind this terse statement of responsibility, attempting to leave behind the potential complications his excuses introduce. This newly matured Arthur initiates a sympathetic response from the newly matured Adam (who might otherwise respond by hitting him) and Eliot lets Arthur finally get it right: what are struggles in the face of consequences? If he did not in fact intend them, he might as well have. It is the same principle that earlier on in the novel the narrator must announce because Arthur cannot or will not face it himself. After Adam catches Hetty and Arthur in a compromising position, Adam forces Arthur to break off their relations lest something more serious should happen (little knowing that something more serious has already happened). Contemplating the letter he must write, Arthur rationalizes his behavior, believing that no harm has come to Hetty and that by his actions he can right his wrong by facilitating a marriage between Hetty and Adam. He derides himself for deceiving Adam about the seriousness of his affair with Hetty (Hetty and Arthur have already had sex), while consoling himself with the thought that "if ever a man had excuses, he had" (317). But after the fact, the narrator has no patience with Arthur's self-serving logic and laments tersely and unsympathetically, "Pity that consequences are determined not by excuses but by actions!" (317)

The excuses to which Arthur alludes and that the narrator delegitimizes (even as Arthur concocts them) bring us back to the complications of his intentions, since in the privacy of his own mind he insists to himself that he had no control over either his desires or his intentions, that he couldn't help what had happened. On the verge of writing this unpleasant letter to Hetty, he dodges responsibility by concluding: "At all events, he couldn't help what would come now" (317). But what good, the novel asks, is all this thinking about excuses when we have these consequences right in front of us?

My argument about *Adam Bede* is that the novel produces inconsistent attitudes toward consequences in the assignation of responsibility for our acts, including the act of writing a novel. Such inconsistencies resonate with those developing in the criminal law itself. Consequences assume a primacy in *Adam Bede*; they determine guilt. Yet the inconsistencies in Eliot's treatment of consequences introduce questions about whether states of mind in the novel (and in life) can and should be defined by consequences: are we to judge intentions through consequences? Do consequences define blame? Attempts to legitimate a purely consequentialist view of responsibility, like that which had already been articulated by utilitarians like James Mill and would later be espoused in a revised form by the philosopher G. E. Moore, are not consistently maintained in *Adam Bede*; what one finds in the novel and in the criminal law of the period is hard thinking and continuous modification of a consequentialist view. In these modifications—modifications that nineteenth-century criminal law was itself explicitly working through—Eliot negotiates the territory between the external (consequences, acts) and the internal (desires, motives, intents) and between the objective and the subjective bases of responsibility. These negotiations allow her to explore the possibilities and contingencies of moral and legal responsibility, but as a novelist she is not required to reduce her narrative to a position. While no one would accuse Eliot of promoting a morally relativisitic world in which questions of duty and responsibility are up for grabs, in *Adam Bede* she incorporates the inconsistencies in nineteenth-century conceptions of responsibility and exposes the contested space between subjective and objective visions and versions of blame.

In the first part of my argument on *Adam Bede*, I will demonstrate the inconsistencies at work in the novel's conception of consequences; inconsistencies with which the nineteenth-century the criminal law was itself grappling (and with which the twentieth century continues to grapple). The truth is that consequences at once do and do not define a crime. In the nineteenth century, criminal law imputed intents from consequences: a defendant was deemed to intend the natural consequences of his acts. Although not a rule of law, it was often treated as such, so much so that Stephen in his *History of the Criminal Law of England* has to remind his readers that it was a logical but not a legal rule. The maxim, says Stephen, "is sometimes stated as if it were a positive rule of law, that a man must be held to intend the natural consequences of his act. I do not think the rule in question is really a rule of law, further or otherwise than as it is a rule of common sense."[12] Defendants were presumed to have intended the natural consequences of their acts, and such a presumption was treated as close to irrebuttable by some,[13] though certainly the defense of insanity, for example, would rebut the presumption, since insanity negates *mens rea* entirely. Not much is said in Stephen's discussion about the use of the word "natural," but J. W. C. Turner—in his oft-cited edition of *Kenny's Outlines of Criminal Law*—remarks that "This use of the word 'natural,' although hallowed by tradition, is not happy; for all consequences must be 'natural.' What is really meant is consequences which an average man would be expected to foresee."[14] Edward Griew notes some ambiguity in nineteenth-century applications of the term "natural," asserting that "'natural' sometimes meant 'which must necessarily follow' and more often 'which was probable' (whence the customary pleonasm, 'natural and probable')."[15] Later I will work through the complications and contradictions that arose out of the interpretation and application of this proposition in the nineteenth century. It is a proposition from which the criminal law of England in the twentieth century has attempted, with some success, to distance itself.[16]

Notwithstanding the substantive rule that makes an accused presumptively responsible for the natural consequences of his acts, the state of mind of an accused did then and does now have much to do with the definition of crime and the assignation of legal and moral blame. Nowhere was this more at issue in the nineteenth century than in attempts both at common law and in draft statutory provisions to distinguish murder from manslaughter and to distinguish manslaughter from an accidental killing that did not amount to a culpable homicide at all. Felix Holt is charged with manslaughter; the chapters that follow the riot ask us to consider whether Felix should be responsible for the consequence of his attack on the hapless constable or not. Though the formal trial of Felix Holt marginalizes testimony about Felix's state of mind (an issue that I consider later in this chapter), the narrator's representation of Felix's state of mind during the riot and at the moment he strikes the constable cannot and will not be marginalized. The state of mind accompanying a homicide changes the very nature of the crime, and the question of how far a man was to be held responsible for the unforeseen consequences of his act—the very question that Augustus Irwine raises on Arthur Donnithorne's behalf—vexed judges and writers on criminal law as it must have Eliot and as it still vexes her readers.

The first part of my argument focuses on two overtly contrasted scenes from *Adam Bede*: one before the infanticide and one after. I then read these scenes with and against the inconsistencies at work in the theories of criminal responsibility developing in nineteenth-century criminal law. In the first of these scenes, the cleric Augustus Irwine makes a particular case to Arthur Donnithorne about responsibility for consequences. Whatever our state of mind may be before we act, Irwine maintains, we are on notice that our bad acts might produce bad consequences. Irwine's speech implies that since bad consequences take no notice of our mental state, we should not expect our "fluctuations" (171), as he calls them, to be relevant when responsibility is assessed. Our mental fluctuations will have nothing to do with responsibility. Irwine concentrates on the external in this first passage—on the act and its consequences. By contrast, in the later scene that I will analyze, Irwine appears to stand his earlier principle on its head. Now he makes the case that it matters that an accused has not foreseen the consequences of his act. Suddenly, specific knowledge about consequences becomes an element of responsibility, while he makes us see how insufficient consequences themselves are as a way of assessing blame. In short, Irwine brings us back into the mind of the accused. In this new context, with the consequences very much before us, Irwine revises his consequentialist views, and in so doing Eliot imagines how our own judgment of consequences might be revisited, particularly in the face of the actual intents of an accused and the consequences of those intents.

I next consider Eliot's experimentation with a modified consequentialist view and the complications that emerge from her representations of the inner lives of her characters. The immediate representations of the desires, motives, intentions, knowledge to which she would turn her mind so fully in *Middlemarch* and *Daniel Deronda* shape our attitudes toward moral and legal responsibility even in her early work. Eliot at times uses consequences to determine intents, but the relation is not so easily described or circumscribed. The mental elements at work in the novel destabilize if not the consequences themselves then (as importantly) our relations to them. Arthur Donnithorne's weak and ambiguous intentionality modifies our judgment of his responsibility for the acts and consequences that follow from his irresolution. Even if the "fluctuations" of the mind cannot actually alter a consequence (the book reminds us over and over again that what's done cannot be undone), they matter. It is often the case that the writing in *Adam Bede* about mental states is most in touch with the novel's realist ambitions—that is, the writing that tries to avoid the overtly didactic, that imagines the complexities of character, as against the idealistic writing that Eliot produces in this novel, particularly in the representations of Dinah Morris.

In the third part of my argument, I will take up the way bad consequences themselves are not fixed in the manner that the narrator sometimes contends that they are. Even as the narrator censures any attempt to make good come of evil, the plot of the novel as a whole produces that very outcome. This last claim leads me into an examination of the novel's use of allusion and its own power to generate unforeseen consequences. Allusions work both to shape and to unsettle our expectations about plot and character: we are invited to read one story through another so that we may foresee some promised end. But by incorporating another's narrative into her own, Eliot inevitably alters the prior text; and the consequences of her use of that text cannot be fixed.

After this extensive discussion of consequences and *Adam Bede*, I turn briefly to *Felix Holt*, where, as I note in my prologue to this chapter, Eliot offers a straightforward conflict between the legal and the moral. My analysis of certain scenes from *Felix Holt* identifies the instances in which Eliot shifts her focus from the external to the internal, from consequences to intents, motives, and desires. Although the criminal law refuses to take into full account the desires of our hero Felix Holt (to which we get access through the third person narration), eventually the ad hoc pardoning process that follows Felix's trial uses motive to—if not exonerate—at least liberate Felix. But it is unnerving that the novel will not exonerate its hero. Though Felix has not intentionally killed the constable, Eliot leaves us to wonder about the recklessness of his act. Should Felix bear the responsibility for a rash act done to avert a greater evil?

⊰ Consequentialism and *Adam Bede* ⊱

Consequentialism is a moral theory—or, as James Griffin articulates it, is a part of a moral theory generally labeled utilitarian.[17] James Mill, for example, promoted utilitarianism's explicit concern with consequences as part of an ethical education. Martin Weiner reports that Mill believed that utilitarianism "would encourage, and, if necessary, compel men to focus their minds on the long-run consequences of their acts and in the process come to defer gratification. Consequentialism would build character."[18] Consequentialism wants acts judged not in themselves but by their consequences, and the utilitarian position (too simply put) is that an action is right when it produces more happiness than unhappiness and wrong when it produces more unhappiness than happiness. The backbone of consequentialism is, as G. E. Moore succinctly renders it, "that the question whether an action is right or wrong always depends upon its total consequences."[19] Moore entitles chapter 5 of his *Ethics* "Results the Test of Right and Wrong," and he uses the chapter to respond to serious objections leveled against the theory. But serious objections remain. The first is that it is not so easy as John Austin might have us think to draw a line between an act and its consequences. An act, explains Griffin, "may be fixed at a number of different points along a number of different dimensions."[20] Though what consequentialists want to resist is the conclusion that acts are intrinsically good or bad, it is sometimes the case that they do acknowledge that this conclusion follows logically from their premises. In *Principia Ethica*, Moore concedes that the judgment of acts depends not just on consequences but also on an evaluation of an act and its consequences.[21] For objectors like Griffin, this concedes quite a lot, for in it is tucked the concession that while we still want to judge right and wrong by the claim that happiness is desirable and unhappiness undesirable, it does not necessarily follow that we need to look at consequences at all in order to make a moral judgment:

> The utilitarians who revise their consequentialism are right. The focus of interest in moral judgments is not consequences alone but a whole consisting at least of act and consequences. Any decision to act based on the benefit of the act itself is open to revision if harm is discovered in the consequences; any such decision based on the desirability of the consequences is open to revision if harm is discovered in the act itself. But they are wrong to think that we must always consider the whole; as we have seen, moral judgments may be made considering only the act. And to say that any judgment about an act is open to revision if there is substantial benefit or hurt in the consequences is quite different from saying that the original judgment could never even have taken place without considering the consequences.[22]

This discussion seems at first glance very far from the mind or world of George Eliot. Would Eliot affirm the law of the greatest happiness for the greatest number that one locates in the work of Bentham and Mill? Probably not, but one might still be mindful of William Butler Yeats's passing remarks, in his essay "At Stratford-on-Avon," that Eliot, like the Shakespearian critics of her day, "grew up in a century of utilitarianism, when nothing about a man seemed important except his utility to the State."[23] Indeed, Eliot edited articles with John Chapman for the *Westminster Review*, once edited by John Stuart Mill, and she contributed several articles to that periodical, including her review of Mackay's book *The Progress of the Intellect*, which articulates a form of consequentialism that I discuss hereafter. Moreover, at least one aspect of utilitarianism seems very much in line with one of Eliot's highest virtues: self-sacrifice. For, as one critic put it, "it seems to require that one neglect or abandon one's own pursuits whenever one could produce even slightly more good some other way. Nor, it seems, is this an empty demand, for in a world as full of human suffering and misery as this one, only those with an extraordinary degree of moral self-confidence will be prepared to claim that there is no possible way they could do any more good for the world than by doing exactly what they are already doing."[24] There is much that is Eliotic in such a principle, and while Eliot would never accommodate utilitarian principles as a whole, in *Adam Bede* she manifests an unexpected affinity with utilitarian consequentialism.

Consequence is a word that appears with provocative frequency in *Adam Bede*, but not, as I suggested earlier, unmodified, for consequences in and out of *Adam Bede* can be desired or undesired, intended or unintended, foreseen or unforeseen. These differences make a difference in the novel, in law, and in life; to bring in the actual intentions and knowledge of the accused is to invoke the importance of the relation between a mental state and a consequence, to concede that while attention to the mental state of an actor might not change the nature of the consequence, it may indeed change our attitude toward the responsibility assigned to the actor for the consequence. Impelled by analytic jurisprudence, nineteenth-century jurists were taking a long hard look at the place of both the unintended and the unforeseen (or the unforeseeable) consequence in the criminal law. Jurists were also considering the problem of the unforeseen consequence as against the unforeseen but foreseeable consequence. Would an objective test of criminality be applied?

"Pity that consequences are determined not by excuses but by actions!" (317) exclaims Eliot's narrator, and her exclamation calls up in the reader an unsympathetic response to the excuses Arthur mounts in his defense. Note the centrality of consequences: what we understand is not so much that acts determine consequences but rather that consequences determine our judgment of acts. Eliot's use of the passive voice makes the agent in the sentence appear to be the "consequences" themselves and not the "acts." We all know, the narrator insists, that this is how the world works no matter what we tell ourselves. In fact, Arthur has already been warned about the consequences of his actions, a warning he does not heed. Like the narrator, Mr. Irwine cautions Arthur Donnithorne about consequences.

Eliot begins the sequence of events that ends with Irwine's warning with a telling encounter between Arthur and Adam Bede. Feeling guilty about his intimate exchanges with Hetty, Arthur has resolved to speak to his friend and advisor Mr. Irwine. By confessing to Irwine his meetings with Hetty, Arthur hopes to "secure himself" (119) against any future indiscretion. On the way, Arthur meets Adam Bede (his childhood friend). In the course of their conversation, Adam manifests a certain attitude toward consequences that Irwine will shortly reiterate. This emphasis is impossible to ignore:

> I've seen pretty clear, ever since I could cast up a sum, as you can never
> do what's wrong without breeding sin and trouble more than you can
> ever see. It's like a bit o' bad workmanship—you never see th' end o'
> the mischief it'll do. And it's a poor look out to come into the world to
> make your fellow-creatures worse off instead o' better. (166)

Adam turns a consequence into an object—the bit o' bad workmanship, like an ill-made chair—and judges his acts by it. The wrong is wrong not solely but here primarily because of the sin and trouble it breeds. "Breeds" is, of course, a loaded word in the context of this novel, since what is bred is not an object but a child.

In the scene with Irwine that follows, Eliot invests more and more in questions of Arthur's responsibility for the consequences of his acts. By the time Arthur actually arrives at Irwine's, his shame has got the better of him and he is less inclined to tell Irwine of his as yet small indiscretions with Hetty. On the morning Arthur arrives, it happens that Irwine is thinking about his duties as a magistrate: "presently Dent brings up a poor fellow who has killed a hare" (168), so questions of responsibility are much on Irwine's mind. Though wanting to confess, Arthur finds himself once again in the position of doing "the very opposite of what he intended." Nevertheless, he determines to raise the question of his responsibility, if only hypothetically. Each hypothetical situation Arthur poses to Irwine imagines some element of excuse, and excuse in *Adam Bede* is often linked to the instability of a mental state. Arthur asks Irwine to imagine a hypothetical man who is not in control of his own desires because a woman has bewitched him; he asks Irwine to affirm that man is "ruled by moods that one can't calculate on beforehand" (170), moods that conflict with and in the end overpower the man's intentions. Finally, he asks Irwine to affirm that a man "who struggles against a temptation into which he finally falls at last" (171) is not as bad as and should not be judged like "the man who never struggles at all" (171). The hypothetical situations Arthur constructs frame the problem as one that makes the internal state the key element in passing judgment. Certainly these hypotheticals call agency into question. The hypothetical man Arthur produces is not the agent of his own acts, and that strategic move more often than not depends on Arthur's introducing questions about states of mind.

Irwine's response to Arthur's hypotheticals uses consequences to displace the instabilities of mental states. Irwine reshapes Arthur's examples so that they are controlled not by internal states of thinking or feeling but by the consequences of those states of thinking or feeling. A man should always keep "unpleasant consequences before his mind" (170), instructs Irwine, and in so doing the mind will become fixed on such consequences. This, Irwine suggests, is what man can and should do. And when Arthur insists that a man who struggles should be judged differently from the man who never struggles at all, Irwine delivers one of the novel's more memorable speeches and gives Arthur what seems like fair warning. Of such a man, Irwine remarks,

> I pity him, in proportion to his struggles, for they foreshadow the in-ward suffering which is the worst form of Nemesis. Consequences are unpitying. Our deeds carry their terrible consequences, quite apart from any fluctuations that went before—consequences that are hardly ever confined to ourselves. And it is best to fix our minds on that certainty, instead of considering what may be the elements of ex-cuse for us. (171)

In this emphatic statement of principle in which the word "consequences" appears no less than three times, there is an attempt to fix responsibility, to detach it from what is named first "struggles" and then "fluctuations." Indeed, movements of mind are set "apart" from deeds and, more specifically, the con-sequences that those deeds carry.[25] Here is Irwine giving as a "certainty" that which has not yet happened as against the mere possibility of excuse. Conse-quences have a more material existence here, even though they have not yet occurred. While the fluctuations of mind are figured in the past, conse-quences are situated not in the future tense but in the present. The proleptic pressure Irwine exerts is to recognize consequences in the here and now, to read in the present what will happen in the future. Whatever pity the sympa-thetic Irwine may feel individually, he affirms that judgments can and should be based on consequences. The hypothetical man can and should fix his mind on such consequences. By extending Irwine's logic, we are led to see that knowledge and intent can always be read in consequences.

No less emphatic but to a very different effect is Irwine's later defense of Arthur. Speaking with the distraught Adam Bede after his beloved Hetty is ar-rested, Irwine has the unenviable job of trying to calm him down. Adam can-not believe that Hetty has killed the child or, if he does, he must believe that Arthur should bear the guilt for the crime. What seems a given but unspoken assumption is that Hetty is less autonomous actor than victim. Eliot shows herself as, perhaps, more interested in thinking through the complexities of Arthur Donnithorne's moral and legal responsibility than she is in Hetty's, whose infanticide raised and continues to raise questions of responsibility that admitted (and continue to admit) inconsistent answers.[26] Though Hetty is tried and convicted of murder, very few women who killed their newborns were treated as murderers. In his review of the Minutes of Evidence attached to the Report of the Capital Punishment Commission of 1866, D. Seaborne Davis records the Commission participants as all giving evidence not only that women charged with infanticide were more often convicted of the lesser charge of concealment, but also that they were being acquitted altogether. Further, "[s]ince 1849, no woman had been executed for infanticide."[27] While *Adam Bede* is set in 1799, juries did mitigate the sanctions for infanticide—a capital crime—in the eighteenth century, as they did for other crimes as well, most notably theft.[28] Sentencing Hetty to death makes questions about Arthur's responsibility all the more acute.[29]

Having to confront Hetty's catastrophe not in the abstract (as before when Arthur posed the problem as hypothetical) but in the actual, Irwine rewrites his earlier moral principle:

> In these cases we sometimes form our judgment on what seems to us strong evidence, and yet, for want of knowing some small fact, our judgment is wrong. But suppose the worst: you have no right to say that the guilt of her crime lies with him, and that he ought to bear the punishment. It is not for us men to apportion the shares of moral guilt and retribution. We find it impossible to avoid mistakes even in determining who has committed a single criminal act, and the problem how far a man is to be held responsible for the unforeseen consequences of his own deed, is one that might well make us tremble to look into it. The evil consequences that may lie folded in a single act of selfish indulgence, is a thought so awful that it ought surely to awaken some feeling less presumptuous than a rash desire to punish. (424)

Part of what is happening in the passage is that Irwine wants to keep Adam from physically assaulting Arthur, and so when he says "it is not for us men to apportion the shares of moral guilt and retribution," he means (I think) that Adam shouldn't take matters into his own hands. Beyond that, however, Irwine wants to make a point about criminal responsibility. First he asserts that the mistakes made in the assignation of criminal responsibility should make us hesitant to assign moral blame. Then he points to a specific problem in criminal law, and a specific term enters his argument: the unforeseen consequence. Having put the unforeseen consequence into play, Irwine destabilizes Adam's certainty about who is responsible for the infant's death. From the very beginning of the passage, Irwine frustrates attempts at a certainty or a fixity, and this instability is immediately at odds with the stability and certainty Irwine's earlier speech to Arthur manifested. Consequences appear to spin out of control into infinity. Not only are we unable to determine who has done a single criminal act, but even when we can determine who has committed what act, we cannot know "how far a man is to be held responsible for the unforeseen consequences of his own deed." It is a central question: how far *is* a man to be held responsible for the unforeseen consequences of his own deed? Now the hypothetical man does not foresee the consequences arising out of his deed, and the fact that they are unforeseen matters. Irwine invokes the limitations of the actual knowledge of the accused as a defense and so introduces a subjective test of criminality. He who does not foresee a consequence perhaps should not be held responsible for it. In the earlier passage, Irwine links some hypothetical man with responsibility for the consequences of his acts, since the consequences themselves were allowed to pass judgment on the wrongdoer, whatever his state of mind. Consequences were an objective certainty. While earlier consequences were carried in acts, now they "lie folded," a locution that registers that which is in a sinister way hidden from us. The syntax of the sentence about "evil consequences" itself seems to immaterialize the consequences. The sentence reads: "The evil consequences that may lie folded in a single act of selfish indulgence, is a thought so awful that it ought surely to awaken some feeling less presumptuous than a rash desire to punish." The subject of the sentence is 'the evil consequences that lie folded in the act' and the main verb is the "is." And what are ("is") the evil consequences? A "thought," a thought so awful we should feel something other than vengeful. It is actually quite hard to tell what the "thought" in Irwine's declaration refers back to. Irwine means to say that thinking about all those unforeseen evil consequences produces a thought so awful that we should be more generous, but the sentence as written appears grammatically to equate those evil consequences and the thought. The contorted grammar of the sentence manifests the work Irwine (and perhaps Eliot herself) has to do to dematerialize the consequences. Notice, too, what sounds like an agreement error in this sentence: "evil consequences" are plural and disagree with the sentence's singular verb. In fact, there is an agreement error here: consequences in this case are not thoughts, no matter how Irwine states the case. When Irwine problematizes consequences first by calling into question the way we interpret objective evidence and second by dematerializing them, he effectively turns us back to *mens rea*. This shift imposes a limit on the consequences for which Arthur might be held responsible. What he asserts is that the consequences of Arthur's act were in fact unforeseen and that his act was motivated by what he calls selfish indulgence. As readers, we concur with Irwine's assessment because we have special access to Arthur's mind. We have read Arthur's mind (as Irwine has not, since he cannot) and the novel invites us to affirm Irwine's judgment—at least for the moment, for the novel does not allow the matter to rest there.

In response to Irwine, Adam voices the objection that calls Irwine's use of the unforeseen into question: "What if he didn't foresee what's happened? He foresaw enough; he'd no right t'expect anything but harm and shame to her" (425), insists Adam. While Irwine names the consequences of Arthur's acts unforeseen, he does not name them as unforeseeable, and Adam counters Irwine's argument by introducing foreseeability. Adam moves from the subjective point of view—"What if he didn't foresee what's happened?"—to the objective: "he'd no right t'expect anything but harm and shame to her." "Expect" shows up in a telling way in Adam's retort since it suggests that which Arthur should have expected: that his seduction of Hetty would mean that her own expectations would be tragically ruined. The complications of this scene speak not only to the complexity of Irwine and Adam as developing characters but also to the difficulties of applying consequentialism to the specific case. As the novel unfolds, so does our relation (like Irwine's) to the questions of responsibility that are raised. The consequentialist impulse remains, and Adam voices it, but it is challenged by the representations of the interior life that Eliot generates.

The tension this dialogue creates also plays out in Victorian criminal law, but as is not possible with a case before a court, Eliot can move on and away from the conflict she so powerfully represents. At this moment of crisis, the novel suddenly backs away from this conflict and offers a temporary resolution that is, perhaps, less than satisfying. Irwine does not answer Adam's objection; instead, he reassures Adam with the very Eliotic thought that since we all live in the social medium, Arthur will share Hetty's punishment: "Men's lives," says Irwine, "are as thoroughly blended with each other as the air they breathe" (425). The danger now, as Irwine presents it, is that Adam contemplates Arthur's punishment, and to do so is wrong. So, says Irwine, "as long as you do not see that to fix your mind on Arthur's punishment is revenge, and not justice, you are in danger of being led on to the commission of some great wrong" (425). Oddly, in Irwine's first lecture to Arthur about consequences, he advises him to "fix our minds on that certainty," the certainty that acts lead to consequences. Now the fixing of the mind turns out to lead to revenge and not justice. What Irwine encourages Adam to feel is sympathy, no matter what the consequences of Arthur's actions. And this, as the narrator has already instructed us, is Adam's least developed impulse, as he himself knows:

> he had too little fellow-feeling with the weakness that errs in spite of foreseen consequences. Without this fellow-feeling, how are we to get enough patience and charity toward our stumbling, falling companions in the long and changeful journey? And there is but one way in which a strong determined soul can learn it—by getting his heartstrings bound round the weak and erring, so that he must share not only the outward consequence of their error, but their inward suffering. (210)

The "weakness that errs in spite of foreseen consequences" refers both to the weakness of Adam's father (who has accidentally drowned himself attempting to return home in a drunken stupor) and also to Arthur. The naming of the (soon-to-be) consequences as foreseen here resituates responsibility more clearly on Arthur's shoulders, yet the invocation of sympathy makes the question of responsibility and of consequences less central. More central is that Adam feel sympathy for those who err.

Yet the novel's promotion of the sympathetic response does not displace its interest in the questions of responsibility it also explores, and particularly the way consequences do and do not determine responsibility. Eliot's own ideas about the relations of knowledge and intentions to consequences might have found their shape in Charles Bray's 1841 work *The Philosophy of Necessity or, The Law of Consequences; as Applicable to Mental, Moral, and Social Science.*

Bray, whom Eliot met in the same year as the book's publication, became one of Eliot's closest friends. In *The Philosophy of Necessity*, Bray (under the section heading "The Application of Philosophical Necessity to Responsibility, Praise and Blame, Reward and Punishment, Virtue and Vice") remarks,

> if a man commit an act of injustice or treachery, he suffers its conse-
> quences in the distrust and resentment of his fellow-men, though his
> evil action be the result of bad education and temptation; because the
> certain connexion of such conduct with such consequences, is neces-
> sary to make men attach importance to good education and the avoid-
> ance of temptation. We are thus accountable to our Maker for the
> breaking of his laws, whether such breach proceed from our igno-
> rance, our convictions, or our feelings.[30]

Some of George Eliot's earliest and most significant book reviews register her commitment to the study of consequences, a commitment that had once seemed unshakable. Defending R. W. Mackay's investigation of Greek and Hebraic religious practices against those who dismissed such labors as point-less, Eliot, in her January 1851 review of Mackay's book *The Progress of the Intellect*, argued that Mackay's work was of very great significance. One can un-derstand, announced Eliot, "divine revelation" only by understanding "the presence of undeviating law in the material and moral world—of that invari-ability of sequence which is acknowledged to be the basis of physical science, but which is perversely ignored in our social organization, our ethics and our religion."[31] More than invariability of sequence, Eliot pushes on toward an "inexorable law of consequences":

> The divine yea and nay, the seal of prohibition and of sanction, are ef-
> fectually impressed on human deeds and aspirations, not by means of
> Greek and Hebrew, but by that inexorable law of consequences,
> whose evidence is confirmed instead of weakened as the ages advance;
> and human duty is comprised in the earnest study of this law and pa-
> tient obedience to its teaching.[32]

The shifting in this abstract passage from sequence to consequence and the linking of these terms to law, duty, evidence, sanction, and deed is suggestive not only of natural laws and divine laws but also of positive laws, of the rules by which men and women are imprisoned or even executed.[33] Even the trope of the impressed seal evokes the legal world. Mackay himself had been a lawyer, as Eliot no doubt knew. Eliot bases her judgments of deeds and aspi-rations on consequences. We work backward from consequences to acts and intents. In this sure-footed passage, there is a marked and remarkable confi-dence in what can be known, in the belief that sequences and consequences can be and are recognizable and should be studied.

Eliot introduces these concerns not only in her writing but about her writing, and about writing more generally. One can see, first of all, an attrac-tion to consequences for one who, as the narrator remarks in *Adam Bede*, is

"obliged to creep servilely after nature and fact" instead of allowing herself
"to represent things as they never have been and never will be" (177). Critics of
Adam Bede have very usefully identified the ways in which Eliot's own reading
in natural histories and her emerging views of the role of the natural historian
influenced her story. Reading *Adam Bede* together with Eliot's review of *The
Natural History of German Life* leads Sally Shuttleworth to conclude that Eliot
reconceives of the role of writer as one who works "simply to reflect, or objectively record, an unchanging external realm."[34] There is much to this, since
in *Adam Bede* itself the narrator pledges "to give no more than a faithful account of men and things as they have mirrored themselves in my mind. . . . I
feel as much bound to tell you, as precisely as I can, what that reflection is, as
if I were in the witness-box narrating my experience on oath" (177). While
Shuttleworth frames this as of a piece with Eliot's interest in natural history,
she does not account for Eliot's move from natural history to the positive law.
What makes Eliot think here of the legal situation—of the witness in the witness box—is not only the safeguards against perjury that the legal oath erects
(including the punishments decreed for perjury) but the limitations of the
witness's testimony. Witnesses may testify only to their own (relevant) experiences to those external matters of which they have knowledge. What wit-
nessses "know" about another's state of mind they infer from external circumstances. Indeed, the limitation on our ability to see into another person's
mind means that we must look (not only but importantly) to acts and consequences to understand intent. Making herself a witness in a witness box requires the narrator to read mental states in acts and consequences. And up to
a point, this is sufficient to the world of *Adam Bede*, at least as that world appears at the beginning of the novel. There is in the novel a great faith in the
objective signs that can be read and measured. The opening chapters of the
novel give a powerful sense of the cyclical, the security of being able to foresee events from the tableau Eliot presents.

But what might seem possible in the abstract of the Mackay review and
from the perspective of that review gets very difficult in the particular. When
Irwine considers the problem of unforeseen consequences, he does so in the
context of criminal and moral responsibility. It was a problem in criminal law
(as well as in ethical debates) to decide how far a man ought to be held responsible for the unforeseen consequences of his own deed, because unforeseen consequences are not always unforeseeable consequences. Taking up
the problems of the particular case, criminal law jurisprudence rejects in part
the powerful emphasis on consequences at work in the passage from Eliot's
Mackay review. Victorian criminal law jurisprudence engages in its own hard
abstract thinking and also in analyses of particular cases not unlike those with
which George Eliot is so often associated. But unlike Eliot, who can defer
judgment, the law must judge, and sentence, and punish.

How far would consequences determine guilt? An accused, writes Austin,
cannot be said to intend unforeseen consequences (and would not be held
criminally responsible for them) if, because of a missupposition, he does not

believe the consequence will follow. So too, just at the time that Eliot was composing *Adam Bede*, the presumption that a man was deemed to have intended the natural consequences of his act was coming under serious attack. In *R v. Cox*, decided in 1859, the same year *Adam Bede* was published, Justice Bramwell instructed a jury that "a man is generally supposed, by law, to intend the natural consequence of his act, but, in this case, it is not so, and to find the prisoner guilty of a felony, you must be satisfied of the existence of actual intent to wound, as charged in the indictment."[35] The defendant in *Cox*, a gipsy, had been charged with wounding with intent. Here are the facts as the report so effectively gives them:

> The prisoner, with two other women and three men, were encamped as gipsies on a common. The prosecutor and another policeman were directed by the owner of a neighboring plantation (not the lord of the manor), who had sustained damage from the tribe, to remove them. The police ordered the gipsies to remove, who refused to do so, and one of the men assaulted one of the police, who thereupon proceeded to take him into custody. The other policeman (the prosecutor) took hold of two of the women, and while holding them, the prisoner struck him on the back with a scythe, the edge of which was fenced, with the exception of two inches at the end, inflicting a wound half an inch in depth, and an inch in length.[36]

Surprisingly, Bramwell's first holding was that the police "had no right to interfere with the gipsies, except at the order of the owner of the land, and their resistance, without the use of weapons, would have been justifiable." But as weapons were used, Bramwell had to take up whether the jury could presume from the natural consequences of the act of resisting arrest that the defendant intended the injury to the policeman. Bramwell answered with a decisive no. They could not so presume. Some other evidence of actual intent had to be offered. In order to find her guilty of the lesser charge of unlawful wounding, Bramwell held that the jury had to decide whether the defendant knew "that the end of the scythe was uncovered, and therefore likely to wound." Again the jury was required to find actual knowledge instead of being allowed to presume that knowledge from the consequences of the acts or even the acts themselves.

What the nineteenth-century criminal law plays out are conflicting ideas about how much can be presumed from consequences. In his 1991 philosophical account of knowledge and intent in the criminal law, Alan White offers two competing lines of nineteenth-century cases that demonstrate Victorian disagreement about this essential issue. He begins in 1811,[37] with a case (*R. v. Farrington*) that invokes consequences as a way of determining both knowledge and intent.[38] The line of cases following *Farrington* created a legal fiction about knowledge and intent: if certain consequences were deemed the natural consequences of a given act, then an accused could be deemed both to have known them and to have intended them. The objective fact of consequences creates knowledge and intent, and no showing of actual intent or knowledge would be necessary. A defendant could attempt to rebut the presumption by introducing competing evidence, but the presumption—that a man is deemed to intend the natural consequences of his acts—was very powerful; the Criminal Justice Act of 1967 specifically abolished it. Observe, though, another line of cases offered by White beginning in 1841, cases that held that the accused had to have actually foreseen a consequence in order to be held responsible for it as an intentional offense, whether or not such a consequence could be adjudged natural or probable. So even if consequences were deemed to be those that a reasonable man would expect, that showing would not be enough to demonstrate that the defendant foresaw those consequences or intended them. These courts required additional evidence of actual knowledge, more than the claim that a reasonable man must have foreseen such consequences. A prosecutor could not simply rely on consequences or acts to tell the story about intention and knowledge. He had to build a more extensive case about the mental state of the accused to get a guilty verdict.

These cases locate a conflict in Victorian thinking about how to assess criminal responsibility. Were consequences enough to determine an accused's guilt, or did some actual and specific subjective state have to be proved, beyond the presumption that a man intends the natural consequences of his act? How much did the individual's mind matter? In his earlier work *A General View of the Criminal Law*, published in 1863, four years after *Adam Bede*, James Fitzjames Stephen himself interrogates the legal principle that "a man intends the natural consequences of his actions" by asking his readers to consider the man who neither intends nor foresees those consequences. Stephen gives the poor soul a voice in a fictional dialogue between accused and judge: "'I did not mean any harm,'" says the prisoner [a phrase eerily reminiscent of Arthur Donnithorne's excuse in his last scene with Adam]. "'In my own mind,'" says the judge, "'I do not care whether you did or not, but as against you I have the right to say that you meant to do what you really did.'" Of such a scenario Stephen concludes:

> Legal fictions are always a matter of regret. Even if they are practically convenient, they have a strong tendency to make men indifferent to the truth; and if the intention of prisoners really were irrelevant, it would be better to throw the law into a different shape, and to enact specifically that persons who do acts, of which the natural consequence is to kill, etc. shall be punished, instead of introducing the question of intent at all.[39]

Stephen resists such a result, just as he resists certain applications of the felony murder rule. In *A History of the Criminal Law of England*, Stephen reports unhappily on a case he himself tried in which thieves were charged with murder because a man they robbed had a heart attack and died.[40] More compellingly, Victorian judges were faced with whether or not to find those who performed illegal abortions guilty of murder if the woman subsequently died.[41] Such cases persistently (and perennially) ask us to consider what are the natural consequences of acts. As Irwine's second speech suggests, consequences begin to look as unstable and unpredictable as states of mind themselves.

In his edition of *Russell on Crime*, J. W. C. Turner takes Fitzjames Stephen to task for the sections on murder and manslaughter that he composed for the 1874 *Bill for the Codification of the Law of Homicide* because they combine a subjective and an objective test of criminality. While some sections require a showing of actual knowledge and intent, others require only implied malice (implied from the consequences of the act) or that the accused "ought to have known" that his acts would cause certain consequences.[42] Of the contradictions in the sections, Turner surmises that they are the "result of a conflict between two incompatible views, stubbornly maintained by two opposed groups of Commissioners, which has emerged as an illogical compromise."[43] Turner, by contrast, applauds the efforts of the *Reports of the Royal Commission of 1833*, where "the need of a subjective test of criminal liability is emphasized." To shore up support for his position, Turner adduces this passage from the *Seventh Report of the Commissioners* (dated 1843) in which the Commissioners declared:

> If all consequences (or even the proximate ones) of a voluntary act were at the time of the act present to the mind of the doer, he could justly be liable for all those consequences, for he would be the voluntary author of all. The case, however, is far from otherwise: consequences, the most disastrous, often result inevitably from acts done with the best intentions and are such as could not have been guarded against by any previous exertion of caution. In other instances evil consequences, although remote and unexpected, are still such as might have been avoided by care. In others the consequence may be more or less likely or probable, and the degree of likelihood or probability may be extended till it amount to moral certainty. The degrees of likelihood or probability being in truth infinite, it is clear that no assigned degree of likelihood or probability that an injurious consequence will result from any act can serve as a test of criminal responsibility. Such a degree of likelihood or probability admits of no legal mode of ascertainment, and it would, if capable of being ascertained, afford no proper test of guilt, for it is not the precise degree of likelihood or probability in such cases, but the knowledge or belief that the thing is likely or probable which constitutes mens rea. The proper test of guilt in such cases is that of knowledge and consciousness on the part of the malefactor that hurt or damage is likely to result or will probably result from what he does: his criminality consists in the wilfully incurring the risk of causing loss or suffering to others.[44]

Turner pressures us to feel the injustice and impracticality of anything but a subjective standard, given how many stories we can tell about consequences. We cannot, insists Turner, assume that the doer is "the voluntary author of all."

Arthur Donnithorne's mind matters to *Adam Bede*'s thinking about his moral and even, perhaps, his legal responsibility, and, moreover, our access to his mind invites us to apply a subjective standard of liability to him, though that access does not in any way simplify the task of judgment before us. On the eve of sending Hetty the letter that ends their relationship and announces his plan to leave the village without her, something crosses Arthur's mind, a thought that is quickly deferred:

> A sudden dread here fell like a shadow across his imagination—the dread lest she should do something violent in her grief; and close upon that dread came another, which deepened the shadow. But he shook them off with the force of youth and hope. What was the ground for painting the future in that dark way? It was just as likely to be the reverse. (316–7)

But is it just as likely to be the reverse? That they must be shaken off "with the force of youth and hope" suggests not. Possibilities are introduced and rejected, and though "it was an unfortunate business altogether . . . there was no use in making it worse than it was, by imaginary exaggerations and forebodings of evil that might never come. The temporary sadness for Hetty was the worst consequence: he resolutely turned away his eyes from any bad consequence that was not demonstrably inevitable" (314). We judge Arthur harshly here because his rationalizations deny the inevitability of the bad consequences of his acts that he himself imagines, and his imagined consequences are not exaggerations. But these passages are ambiguous enough so that it is hard to say what he foresees and what he refuses to foresee. The novel introduces a subjective test of liability, and then it provides us access to a mind that does and does not foresee the consequences of its acts. The different kinds of narration of consciousness—from the narrator's description of Arthur's thoughts to the presentation of those thoughts in Arthur's own voice—put us in touch with the mind's movement from partial recognition to insistent denial.

In Arthur Donnithorne Eliot takes up the hard case. How is it that Arthur, whose intents are so benevolent, who is so keen to gain and maintain the esteem of his future tenantry and so squeamish about causing harm to anyone other than himself, should find that he has destroyed not one life but two? How is it that he has irreparably damaged his friendship with the boy scout Adam Bede and finally has lost the respect of those from whom he most craved approval, including Mr. Irwine? Introduced to us first in his dressing room, Arthur looks the part of a young squire, issuing orders to his servant and admiring his figure in the mirror, a figure attractive enough to distract the figures depicted in his dressing-room tapestry—Pharaoh's daughter and her maidens—from their duty to their infant charge, Moses. Though mirrors, with the suggestion of egoism (one of the most terrible of Eliotic sins), signify moral corruption in Eliot's world, the narrator treats Arthur gently here, mocking him, but not bitterly, as he turns his faults into virtues:

> His own approbation was necessary to him, and it was not an approbation to be enjoyed quite gratuitously; it must be won by a fair amount of merit. He had never yet forfeited that approbation, and he had considerable reliance on his own virtues. No young man could confess his faults more candidly; candor was one of his favourite virtues; and how can a man's candor be seen in all its lustre unless he has a few failings to talk of? But he had an agreeable confidence that his faults were all of a generous kind—impetuous, warm-blooded, leonine; never crawling, crafty, reptilian. It was not possible for Arthur Donnithorne to do anything mean, dastardly, or cruel. "No! I'm a devil of a fellow for getting myself into a hobble, but I always take care the load shall fall on my shoulders." Unhappily there is no inherent poetical justice in hobbles, and they will sometimes obstinately refuse to inflict their worst consequences on the prime offender, in spite of his loudly-expressed wish. It was entirely owing to this deficiency in the scheme of things that Arthur had ever brought any one into trouble besides himself. (123–4)

The passage begins with Arthur imagining a happy economy of merit and approval, virtue and flaw guiding his life and world. Moreover, the system he imagines is self-enclosed. He provides both the virtue and the vice here, the transgression and the redemption, since what is the virtue of candor without the vice to confess? He himself offers judgment of the good-natured character deficiencies he notes, for his actions, to the extent they are ill considered, are not intentional. Impetuosity—the fault of a mammal such as himself—is set against the intentional deceptiveness, the intentional cruelty of the reptile. Turning difficulties into "hobbles"—a word that in its slight and almost comic unsteadiness attempts to make inconsequential the injuries it signifies—deflates a potentially judgmental response that Arthur might invite of himself. But the ironic tone with which the narrative voice takes up Arthur's hobbles keeps us from feeling too comfortable with his fictional scheme of things, since poetical justice may belong more to the poetical mind that figures difficulties as hobbles than to the hobbles themselves. The narrative generates a gap between the internal wish and the external consequence, and the narrative irony pushes us to feel that what matters is not the wish but the consequence.

Which makes one wonder what to do with the representation of Arthur's state of mind in *Adam Bede*, since Eliot invests in its complications both before and after the tragic consequences have occurred. After we experience all the irony directed toward Arthur, it comes as some surprise to us when the narrator criticizes Adam for his one-sidedness, and gestures toward something the narrator knows about Arthur's state of mind that Adam does not. In a late scene (after Hetty has been arrested), Adam attempts to shift blame from Hetty to Arthur, but the narrator intervenes on Arthur's behalf:

> How busy his thoughts were, as he walked home, in devising pitying excuses for her folly; in referring all her weakness to the sweet loving-ness of her nature; in blaming Arthur, with less and less inclination to admit that his conduct might be extenuated too! His exasperation at Hetty's suffering—and also at the sense that she was possibly thrust for ever out of his own reach—deafened him to any plea for the mis-called friend who had wrought this misery. (326)

The concurrence of "excuses," "extenuated," and "plea" invokes criminal law and the complications of state of mind. While Adam cannot see the extenua-tions and excuses that apply both to Hetty and to Arthur (though the narrator calls Adam "just," he is too jealous to be fair), with the help of the narrator we can. With Arthur, Adam can only notice that which has been "wrought": his misery, her suffering. He sees only the consequences of the conduct, while the narrator turns our attention from consequences to excuses. The narrator calls on Adam (and on us) not just to sympathize with Arthur (however he might have erred) but to extenuate his guilt.

What are Arthur's excuses, and how does Eliot guide us in our judgment of them? He is weak, to be sure; he succumbs, no doubt. But it is not merely to this that Eliot adverts. Through Arthur, Eliot begins to explore the com-plexities of intention. John Blackwood, on reading the first chapters of *Adam Bede* in manuscript, wrote to Lewes that Hetty "is painted in such irresistible colours that I am very sorry for the well-intentioned Arthur."[45] Blackwood may here be echoing Boswell from the *Life of Johnson*, where Boswell ob-serves to Johnson that "the great defect of the tragedy of *Othello* was that it had not a moral; for no man could resist the circumstances of suspicion which were artfully suggested to Othello's mind," an observation that John-son himself resists, as we, I think, resist Blackwood's attempt at exculpation here.[46] Eliot handles the situation in a more sophisticated way than Black-wood articulates. When Arthur resolves to confess to Irwine near the begin-ning of the novel as a way "to secure himself against any more of this folly," he believes that "the mere act of telling it would make it seem trivial" (119). Yet when the time comes, he does not confess, and the narrator is left to explain this omission:

> Was there a motive at work under this strange reluctance of Arthur's which had a sort of backstairs influence, not admitted to himself? Our mental business is carried on much in the same way as the business of State: a great deal of hard work is done by agents who are not ac-knowledged. In a piece of machinery, too, I believe there is often a small, unnoticeable wheel which has a great deal to do with the mo-tion of the large obvious ones. Possibly, there was some such unrecog-

nized agent secretly busy in Arthur's mind at this moment — possibly it was the fear lest he might hereafter find the fact of having made a confession to the Rector a serious annoyance, in case he should not be able quite to carry out his good resolutions? I dare not assert that it was not so. The human soul is a very complex thing. (172)

The narrator is unwilling either to attribute conscious deviousness to Arthur or to exonerate him. A state of mind moves her to think of the affairs of state that are tangled enough to make us feel that the right hand does not know what the left hand is doing. Still, if the agents of the state who exert their backstairs influence are unacknowledged, they are not unpaid. The analogy to machinery appears to let Arthur off the hook altogether, since it makes the movements of the mind agentless. But Eliot brings agency — albeit "unrecognized" — immediately back into the picture. Negations do important work in this passage: the agent not acknowledged or unrecognized, the wheel unnoticed. But is the wheel unnoticeable? Is the agent unacknowledgeable? Or do we choose not to acknowledge, not to recognize? It is hard enough to work out the double negative of "I dare not assert that it was not so." The passage is difficult tonally as well, since there seems a tongue-in-cheek quality to the whole of it and particularly to its last understatement, but what is being said feels nonetheless true. "Possibly" not once but twice connotes the narrator's sudden distance from Arthur's mind, in which she has already roamed quite freely. This speculative note suggests the difficulty of understanding the "agents" of minds, even if one had the access of a third person narrator. The human soul is a "very complex thing," and given that, how are we to judge Arthur Donnithorne's responsibility for the consequences of ensuing acts? Not, then, by intentions but rather by acts and consequences, which can be known. The generalities this passage invokes — the move from Arthur's mind to all minds — takes us out of his mind and suggests that the narrator herself does not know everything about the workings of the mind, though she also gives her last line the kind of ironic bite that comes only with a very special knowledge of the mind in question. Eliot's exploration of the ambiguous world of the interior is of a piece with her realist principles, but at the same time the complexities of Arthur's turns of mind here underline the brutal straightforwardness of the consequences upon which his mind is supposed to be fixed.[47]

The making and unmaking of a mind is what, at least in one passage of the 1863 edition of *A General View of the Criminal Law*, leads Fitzjames Stephen to defend what he calls "the rule" that "the law presumes that a man intends the natural consequences of his actions."[48] Although he questions the rule, he also reiterates its soundness:

> For what is the meaning of intent? It means the end contemplated at the moment of action, and by reference to which the visible parts of the action are combined. This intent is seldom permanent for any very considerable time, and often varies from moment to moment, espe-

cially in people who are either weak or wicked. A man meditating a crime may be, and probably often is, in twenty minds (to use a common and most expressive phrase) about it up to the very moment of execution. How, then, can it be known which particular intent was present at that moment? Perhaps he himself was not then distinctly conscious of it, and probably his subsequent recollections would be treacherous. The way in which, in fact, he did move is the only trustworthy evidence on the subject, and consequently is the evidence to which, and to which alone (in all common cases), the jury ought to direct their attention.[49]

While Stephen in the same paragraph in which this passage appears has rejected the "legal fiction" that allows judges to disregard a defendant's intentions in the name of the rule that a man is presumed to intend the natural consequence of his acts, he also recognizes the fictionality of the idea of a single intent. He brings to life here—not as vividly as Eliot, but still vividly—the temporal play of one thought with another and the difficulties of knowing another's (or even one's own) intentions at any given moment. This brings Stephen back to the rule about intents, acts, and consequences. Stephen's "consequently" appears at a significant moment, for it joins the act and consequence to the evidence that will tell on the defendant. The plurality and impermanence of intents is set against the solidity of acts and consequences.

The tonal ambiguity of Eliot's "The human soul is a very complex thing" and the passage on Arthur's "motives" as a whole simultaneously move us to base our judgment on acts and consequences and to consider how deeply actual knowledge and actual intentions matter in the question of responsibility. Unlike the witness in the witness box or Stephen's jury, the narrator of *Adam Bede* has special access to Arthur's state of mind, access that gives her an unchallenged authority to produce at once a mind made up and then unmade and undone, a mind not in control of itself but also in control of itself. Eliot gives a lot of room to Arthur's mind as it tries to get free of the desire for Hetty and is once again taken over by it:

> When Arthur went up to his dressing-room again after luncheon, it was inevitable that the debate he had had with himself there earlier in the day should flash across his mind; but it was impossible for him now to dwell on the remembrance—impossible to recall the feelings and reflections which had been decisive with him then, any more than to recall the peculiar scent of the air that had freshened him when he first opened his window. The desire to see Hetty had rushed back like an ill-stemmed current; he was amazed himself at the force with which this trivial fancy seemed to grasp him; he was even rather tremulous as he brushed his hair—pooh! it was riding in that break-neck way. It was because he had made a serious affair of an idle matter, by thinking of it as if it were of any consequence. (128)

The inevitability of the flash that recalls his decision not to see Hetty comes up against the impossibility of dwelling on the memory of that decision. This is the mind working against itself in ways it does not or will not recognize.

So the instability of the inner life returns us to consequences. The universal law at work in *Adam Bede* is simply this: if wrong is done, wrong will come of it. But more than this, we know wrong from its bad consequences. The universal law gives us both sequence and consequence. The novel's plot is invested in this premise, and Eliot makes explicit her disapproval of Arthur's attempts to rewrite the law so that right can result from wrong. If right comes from wrong, it becomes much harder to classify the wrong act as wrong. Eliot's irritation at the idea that right should come from wrong informs much of the novel, and particularly her attack on Arthur Donnithorne. Bitterly ironic is the narrator's tone when she describes the way the gentleman converts consequences into compensatory damages, the way Arthur as a young gentleman is entitled to feel that if "he should unfortunately break a man's legs in his rash driving, [he] will be able to pension him handsomely; or if he should happen to spoil a women's existence for her, [he] will make it up to her with expensive bon-bons, packed up and directed by his own hand" (124). Most bitter is this last part—"by his own hand"—if we imagine it anticipates the little hand of the dying child, or Hetty's hand held up at the moment of judgment. Arthur has earlier behaved as if he could compensate for the consequences of his acts, a kind of behavior that elicits from the narrator a multilayered response:

> Arthur's, as you know, was a loving nature. Deeds of kindness were as easy to him as a bad habit: they were the common issue of his weaknesses and good qualities, of his egoism and his sympathy. He didn't like to witness pain, and he liked to have grateful eyes beaming on him as the giver of pleasure. When he was a lad of seven, he one day kicked down an old gardener's pitcher of broth, from no motive but a kicking impulse, not reflecting that it was the old man's dinner; but on learning that sad fact, he took his favourite pencil-case and a silver-hafted knife out of his pocket and offered them as compensation. He had been the same Arthur ever since, trying to make all offences forgotten in benefits. (312–3)

"Deeds of kindness were as easy to him as a bad habit": the ease of the deeds does not exactly negate them, but the narrator does make it close to impossible to appreciate the deeds, given the simile she presents here. As with *Middlemarch*'s Dorothea Brooke, Arthur's idealism and fellow-feeling are also bound up with his egoism. Though Arthur may console himself with the thought of a self-contained world of injuries, when the unthinkable happens and consequences do reach outside of him, he trusts to a system of compensatory damages to set the world aright. The relation between offender and complainant here is explicitly compensatory—a civil offense against a specific

individual and not a criminal offense the harm of which is social as well as individual. As it turns out, the consequences of his actions are neither self-contained nor compensable. So, for example, the narrator figures Hetty's actions
after she has been deserted by Arthur as

> the motions of a little vessel without ballast tossed about on a stormy
> sea. How pretty it looked with its particoloured sail in the sunlight,
> moored in the quiet bay!
> "Let that man bear the loss who loosed it from its moorings."
> But that will not save the vessel—the pretty thing that might have
> been a life-long joy. (340)

"Let that man bear the loss" invokes the language of civil tort, in which private
individuals can sort out the compensatory damages due (or not) to a plaintiff.
However, the next line of the passage makes plain that the loss remains. The
language of compensation is insufficient. Arthur's is not tortious but criminal
conduct. "[C]riminality consists in the wilfully incurring the risk of causing
loss or suffering of others," remarked the Royal Commission of 1843.[50] Is this
what Arthur does? Worse is Arthur's own rewriting of the consequences of
his actions:

> Hetty might have had the trouble in some other way if not in this. And
> perhaps hereafter he might be able to do a great deal for her, and make
> up to her for all the tears she would shed about him. She would owe
> the advantage of his care for her in future years to the sorrow she had
> incurred now. So good comes out of evil. Such is the beautiful
> arrangement of things! (314)

This arrangement echoes in the one that *Daniel Deronda*'s Gwendolen once
saw for herself, until she is brought to see the error of her ways: "I wanted to
make my gain out of another's loss—you remember?—it was like roulette—
and the money burnt into me."[51] Arthur does not yet understand how his system allows his gain at the expense of another—though he will. Writing about
Arthur's economy of loss in his Marxist reading of the novel, John Goode also
sees Arthur's view as compensatory. Attending to the scene in which Arthur
intentionally knocks over the gardener's broth and attempts to offer compensation in the form of a pencil case, Goode notes that "Compensation creates a
safe distance between offender and victim because it easily merges into another class notion, 'liberality.' . . . [Arthur] makes retribution [*sic*] for an offence against human relations with a thing; the thing has no relevance for the
old man's needs, and its value is defined entirely by Arthur."[52] I agree that the
compensation Arthur offers here and conceives of elsewhere in *Adam Bede*
falls short of being fairly compensatory and that his class status allows him to
define the terms of that compensation. Yet, while I take Goode's point that
Eliot is denouncing the social order that at best turns a blind eye to such behavior (behavior that leads to Hetty's ultimate tragedy), Goode's odd (though
correct) use of retribution when I think he means restitution is more telling,

for it is exactly retribution that the civil law cannot exact. Compensation falls woefully short in a criminal case, which explains Adam Bede's own desire for retribution and not restitution.

Adam Bede is himself the first to suggest that Arthur is criminally responsible for the death of the child. Enraged by Arthur's behavior, Adam proclaims, "I only want justice. I want him to feel what she feels. It's his work . . . it was him brought her to it" (423). Adam's language reconstructs Arthur as an accessory before the fact to Hetty's crime, though it is easy to see at once that the novel itself does not offer Arthur as a figure who encourages or advises Hetty to commit murder. Arthur is no Fagin. Moreover, Arthur's connection to the crime itself is remote. As Turner reports, the civil law handles such issues by posing an objective test of liability that seeks to discover whether a "reasonable man" in the defendant's situation would have foreseen the consequences of his action. Tellingly, Turner remarks in his very next paragraph that

> There is no such 'reasonable man' test of remoteness for criminal liability in common law offences: but it is not so much needed since . . . the doctrine of *mens rea* has come to operate as a limitation, constituting as it does a subjective test in the rule that the prosecution must establish beyond a reasonable doubt that the accused man foresaw that certain harmful consequences would or might result from his conduct.[53]

Where the civil law limits responsibility by imposing an objective test, criminal law uses *mens rea* to define the consequences for which an accused might be held responsible. In *Adam Bede*, Eliot begins to realize a shift from an objective test for criminal responsibility—what is foreseeable to a reasonable man—to a subjective test that looks to actual knowledge, a test that makes responsibility much harder to affix because it is difficult to judge what someone else knew and when he knew it—both in the novel and out of it. Nowhere is that shift more evident than in Irwine's responses to Adam's accusations against Arthur.

Mr. Irwine is quick to expose the foolishness of Adam's impulse to convict Arthur, for, as he says, "No amount of torture that you could inflict on him could benefit her" (424). We are clearly out of the compensatory world in which spilled broth can be made up for with a sacrificed pencil case. Eliot makes no bones about this at the end of the novel in the scene in which Arthur confesses his transgressions to Adam and announces that he will leave the village so that Adam and the Poysers may remain. Arthur's plan offends Adam because it assumes restitution, and more than restitution. In Arthur's pleas, Adam thinks "he perceived in them that notion of compensation for irretrievable wrong, that self-soothing attempt to make evil bear the same fruits as good" (467).

But, problematically, though the novel itself censures attempts to make good come from bad—or at least to erase bad by doing good—the novel does, in the end, allow good to arise out of bad. So even consequences themselves are not fixed in the manner Irwine imagines, and this state of affairs makes trouble both in and out of the novel, since the novel depends on the stability of consequences. If good comes from bad, what of the "inexorable law of consequences"? The sequencing of Hetty's crime seems to produce a right from a wrong. Her confession to Dinah brings her closer to repentance and maturity. Adam too gains as a result of what has happened. He gets the right girl in the end, and he has learned the lesson of sympathy.

There is obvious anxiety in the novel about such a reading, so much so that very near its end, Eliot has the narrator confront the issue head on. Looking back on "the story of the painful past," the narrator realizes that the story Adam tells himself after Hetty is transported is not quite the same story that we have read: "no story is the same to us after a lapse of time; or rather, we who read it are no longer the same interpreters; and Adam this morning brought with him new thoughts through that grey country—thoughts which gave an altered significance to its story of the past" (529).[54] I note, first, something rather straightforward and commonsensical about such a statement. While a story may remain the same, our relation to it and interpretation of it change. Readers alter stories, as they themselves are altered by them—a point I shall return to shortly when I consider the way allusion operates in *Adam Bede*. How are we to accommodate a narrative that makes good come from bad? The narrator anticipates our objection:

> That is a bad and selfish, even a blasphemous spirit, which rejoices and is thankful over the past evil that has blighted or crushed another, because it has been made a source of unforeseen good to ourselves: Adam could never cease to mourn over that mystery of human sorrow which had been brought so close to him: he could never thank God for another's misery. And if I were capable of that narrow-sighted joy on Adam's behalf, I should still know he was not the man to feel it for himself: he would have shaken his head at such a sentiment, and said, "Evil's evil, and sorrow's sorrow, and you can't alter its nature by wrapping it up in other words. Other folks were not created for my sake, that I should think all square when things turn out well for me. (529)

One might recognize here Eliot's resistance to the very foundations of Christian theology from which she is distancing herself. The unforeseen consequences of Arthur's act have turned into an unforeseen good (again the "unforeseen" appears here), and the narrator attempts to cut readers off at a reasonable conclusion they are likely to reach—that a good consequence can come from a bad act. The narrator also calls readers to account for the "narrow-sighted joy" they might feel "on Adam's behalf" (because he has found Dinah). New ways of telling the story—ways of "wrapping it up in other words"—do not change what cannot be altered. Adam defeats the idea that we should rejoice that good has come from bad, but the narrator does not allow the simplicity of this interpretation. She, in her turn, creates a recognizable and quite moving figure to demonstrate the decency of Adam's happiness:

> it is not ignoble to feel that the fuller life which a sad experience has brought us is worth our own personal share of pain: surely it is not possible to feel otherwise, any more than it would be possible for a man with a cataract to regret the painful process by which his dim blurred sight of men as trees walking had been exchanged for clear outline and effulgent day. (529–30)

Rather than being blotted out here, as happens in *Middlemarch*, sight is restored, as is our contact with humanity: trees miraculously become men. The commitment to making the joy that comes out of sorrow a sign of decency is itself evidence of Eliot's decency. But the phrasing of this passage makes the exchange of joy for pain rather too self-contained to be true to the story of Adam Bede, for Adam's joy has come at the cost of the suffering of others as well as his own. Even the figure of the man with a cataract who regains his sight assumes that he who now experiences the joy has experienced all the pain. In the end, the narrator does not reconcile the inexorable law of consequences with the unforeseen good.

Here the novel undermines the inexorable law of consequences—the pattern Mackay laid bare in *The Progress of the Intellect*—even as it at times suggests that the right kind of novel might write that law for a patient reader to see. Both impulses—the impulse to assert the law and the impulse to question it—are at work in *Adam Bede*. The novel is itself put forward as a form that might teach us that law, and Eliot thematizes the novel's potential in her treatment of Hetty Sorrel, who has no capacity to foresee a probable future. This incapacity is explicitly related to her never having read a novel. An early encounter with Arthur leads her into a daydream about a love affair that has no connection to the world in which she lives. She sees Arthur in the grove and "behind it lay a bright hazy something—days that were not to be as the other days of her life had been. It was as if she had been wooed by a river-god" (135). Lacking any specific language of projection, she lapses into the vagueness of the "bright hazy something" and the days that can only be described as somehow different from those she knows (135). And her vision is of romance, or jewels. The narrator explains,

> Hetty had never read a novel: if she had ever seen one, I think the words would have been too hard for her: how then could she find a shape for her expectations? They were as formless as the sweet languid odors of the garden at the Chase, which had floated past her as she walked by the gate. (135)

The coincidence here of shape and expectation gestures toward the shape Hetty's expectations ultimately take: the shape of an unborn child. But since she cannot shape her expectations, she is left at their mercy. There is, more-over, the sense here that so common a plot is this that any novel reader would recognize it.

⊰ The Consequences of Allusion ⊱

In "The Plot of Tom Jones," R. S. Crane argues that plot is not action alone but the synthesis of character, thought, and action, which has "a certain power to affect our opinions and emotions. We are bound, as we read or lis-ten, to form expectations. At the very least, if we are interested at all, we desire to know what is going to happen or how the problems faced by the characters are going to be solved."[55] Crane suggests what we readily agree with: most readers get the most pleasure out of plots that provoke "a superior kind of in-ferential activity."[56] As many critics have noted, in *Adam Bede* Eliot writes within the tradition of classical tragedy but about low rather than high fig-ures—not kings or gods but milkmaids and carpenters. The form of tragedy suits her consequentialism, since it invites us to feel that consequences are present before they have happened. If it is our duty to fix our mind on that certainty, then we need to have the certainty put before us.

That Arthur Donnithorne is not only a Donnithorne but a Tradgett (on his mother's side) prepares us for what is to come. In the chapter provocatively entitled "Links," we are linked to the world of Greek tragedy through Irwine, who has with him "the first volume of the Foulis Aeschylus, which Arthur knew well by sight" (167).[57] More specifically, since old Mrs. Irwine, also on the scene here, has been talking of getting young Arthur married and married well, Irwine is put in mind of "the warning given him by the chorus in the *Prometheus*" (170). And what is that warning?

> It's best
> to marry in one's own rank. May no one
> who works with her hands long for marriage
> to those puffed up by riches, or deemed great
> because of the ancestry they come from.[58]

Notwithstanding Irwine's good-natured banter about that warning, it remains a sobering piece of business. We know, after all, what Irwine doesn't—that Arthur is worried about his passion for Hetty. So the novel allows us to expect the tragedy of the highborn interfering in the life of the low. Later references to *Medea* gesture toward a more specific tragic consequence: infanticide.

So too the fact that Arthur is reading *Zeluco: Various Views of Human Nature Taken from Life and Manners, Foreign and Domestic* by John Moore, M.D.,[59] gives us more information than we may want. This is also the novel that Arthur takes with him to his forest cottage—the Hermitage—as he watches and waits for Hetty to appear on her way home to the Poysers. Eliot's readers might well have been more knowledgeable about the heavy-handedly moral

Zeluco than about *Medea* or *Prometheus*. Zeluco, young, wealthy, and ruthless, ruins young women unlucky enough to cross his path and ends his life in misery. Though Zeluco never sees the light, Bertram, another young man of position, fortunately does. In his full examination of the relations between *Zeluco* and *Adam Bede*, Irving Buchen takes us through the ways that Arthur's reading of *Zeluco* would tell on him. When the reprobate Zeluco inquires of Bertram about the nature of good and evil, Bertram's answer, "Whatever a man soweth that he shall reap," is echoed in Irwine's moral statements.[60] Though Arthur plans to finish *Zeluco* while waiting for Hetty, he ends up throwing "the book into the most distant corner" (132). If Eliot's readers had themselves managed to finish *Zeluco*, they would know with some certainty what Arthur does not: that the affair will have a tragic and not just an inconvenient outcome. One might be tempted, then, to see this as an unusual instance of dramatic irony in Eliot if one did not feel that Arthur too knows how the book will end, else why has he pitched it across the room?

So the story of *Adam Bede* would be all but written through allusion—if allusions were as stable and two-dimensional as the preceding analysis suggests. They are not. The story of Prometheus is, after all, susceptible to more than one interpretation. Indeed, *Prometheus Bound* reappears as the epigraph to chapter 16 of *Daniel Deronda* in a way that provokes a reinterpretation of the story and a reinterpretation of all story in terms of feeling and action:

> Men, like planets, have both a visible and an invisible history. The astronomer threads the darkness with strict deduction, accounting so for every visible arc in the wanderer's orbit; and the narrator of human actions, if he did his work with the same completeness, would have to thread the hidden pathways of feeling and thought which lead up to every moment of action, and to those moments of intense suffering which take the quality of action—like the cry of Prometheus, whose chained anguish seems a greater energy than the sea and sky he invokes and the deity he defies. (149)

This is a complicated passage, moving as it does from the astronomical to the historical and then the psychological. It is characteristic of *Daniel Deronda* that a mental state should "take the quality of action" and that this passage from Eliot's last novel should be deeply interested in the relations among feeling, thought, and action, between the invisible and the visible, between that which the narrator of the novel can see (and then report) as against the work of the scientist. What I want to bring out as most relevant to my discussion of allusion in *Adam Bede*, however, is a bit more straightforward. The story of Prometheus becomes not one of tragedy but of triumph. The epigraph to chapter 38 of *Daniel Deronda* deepens the contradiction:

> There be who hold that the deeper tragedy were a Prometheus Bound not *after* but *before* he had well got the celestial fire into the νάρθηξ whereby it might be conveyed to mortals: thrust by the Kratos and Bia

of instituted methods into a solitude of despised ideas, fastened in
throbbing helplessness by the fatal pressure of poverty and disease—
a solitude where many pass by, but none regard. (439)

A like complexity arises out of Eliot's ungainly allusion to Coleridge's *Lyrical
Ballads*. One can see her working hard to get *Lyrical Ballads* into Arthur's discussion with Irwine, but her efforts are all too visible. This effort makes evident the significance of that work to her story. Arthur recommends the book
to Irwine and his mother as a volume full of "queer, wizard-like stories . . .
most of them seem to be twaddling stuff; but the first is in a different style—
"The Ancient Mariner" is the title. I can hardly make head or tail of it as a
story, but it's a strange, striking thing" (66). As the editor of the Penguin *Adam
Bede* notes, "'The Ancient Mariner' by Coleridge is, significantly, about a man
who commits a crime with Nature" (551–2). Yet it is also a story in which the
consequences of an act seem far out of proportion to the act itself. Note Coleridge's own assessment of the poem. When told by Mrs. Barbauld that the
poem had no moral, he rejoined:

> in my own judgment the poem had too much; and that the only, or
> chief fault, if I might say so, was the obtrusion of the moral sentiment
> so openly on the reader as a principle or cause of action in a work of
> such pure imagination. It ought to have had no more moral than the
> Arabian Nights' tale of the merchant's sitting down to eat dates by the
> side of a well, and throwing the shells aside, and lo! a genie starts up,
> and says he must kill the aforesaid merchant, because one of the date
> shells had, it seems, put out the eye of the genie's son.[61]

To juxtapose the crime of the mariner to the crime of the merchant is to suggest the barbarism of judging a man by the consequences of his act. Whether
or not Eliot had Coleridge's response in mind, and it is certainly possible
that she did, she would have had in mind the ambiguities of the mariner's
crime.

Allusions, then, work both to shape and to complicate our expectations.
Even as they foretell the plot—allowing us to foresee consequences—they
also revise it. As much as *Adam Bede* is committed to the fixing of our minds
on the inexorable law of consequences, Eliot resisted John Blackwood's attempts to get her to sketch out the whole of the story for him after he had read
the opening chapters. In fact, Blackwood had already told himself the story.
He remarks in a letter of March 31, 1858, "The Captain's unfortunate attachment to Hetty will, I suppose, form a main element in the Tragic part of the
story . . . I hope things will not come to the usual sad catastrophe."[62] Moreover,
she was justly peeved at the book's reviewers who spoiled the story by giving
away the plot, and she toyed with the idea of getting published a "Remon-
strance" that would say that "As the story of *Adam Bede* will lose much of its
effect if the development is foreseen, the author requests those critics who
may honour him with a notice to abstain from telling the story."[63] That "fore-

seen" should turn up here is striking. The aesthetic pleasure that Eliot wants us to feel in unfolding her plot is in conflict with her didactic purposes.

"Who shall tell," the narrator asks directly in *Middlemarch*,

> what may be the effects of writing? . . . As the stone which has been kicked by generations of clowns may come by curious little links of effect under the eyes of a scholar, through whose labours it may at last fix the date of invasions and unlock religions, so a bit of ink and paper which has long been an innocent wrapping or stop-gap may at last be laid open under the one pair of eyes which have knowledge enough to turn it into the opening of a catastrophe.[64]

The use of "catastrophe" here recalls an earlier use in *Middlemarch*, when Lydgate's would-be wife, Madame Laure, stabs her husband during a performance of a play. The narrator summarizes the evening as one in which "the old drama had a new catastrophe" (148). What we later learn of Laure (on which more later when I take up *Middlemarch* in full) is that her act is the result of both accident and design, as the coming to another's work and its incorporation into one's own can be both accident and design. In his chapter on chance in George Eliot's novels, Leland Monk persuasively reveals Eliot's ambivalence toward the role of chance in her novels: it is at once a necessary part of her commitment to realism and a threat to a morally ordered world. Once introduced, chance is hard to contain and makes trouble for the author's "ability to exercise a concerted will. . . . The disparity between the intentions and the outcomes of the two documentary wills read in *Middlemarch* demonstrates in general that when the will is expressed in and as writing it can generate unforeseeable effects."[65] Monk lights particularly on the letter of Bulstrode that Raffles chances to find and then turns against him. Monk uses Bulstrode's lost-and-found letter as evidence that in Eliot's novel "a text becomes legible in ways the authorial will could never predict or foresee."[66] It is Dinah's letter to Hetty that serves as a "pretext" (366) for her traveling away from the Poyser home and that ultimately ends in the murder of the infant, a consequence that, needless to say, the writer of the letter—the Methodist preacher Dinah Morris—would never have intended, predicted, or foreseen. So too Hetty uses Arthur's letter on the journey to find him. As Monk's argument suggests, chance problematizes prediction and foreseeability for both the characters in and the writer of the novel. Chance, then, makes the staunchest consequentialist view even less appealing.

The turn in *Adam Bede* from a consequentialist view foretells a shift that Eliot would play out in her later novels. Whereas in *Adam Bede*, the best Irwine can do is avert his eyes from the problem of responsibility for unforeseen consequences, Eliot dramatizes this specific legal knot of issues in her fourth novel, *Felix Holt*, to which I will now briefly turn. Felix is quite obviously another version of Adam Bede; these are Eliot's workingmen. And neither seems to know his own strength. But where chance or fate saves Adam from actually killing Arthur during their fight in the wood after Adam discovers Arthur and Hetty together, Felix does in fact kill an officer who (like Felix, ironically enough) is attempting to control rioting townspeople.

How different in feeling is *Adam Bede* from *Felix Holt,* not only because the former is a pastoral and the latter an industrial novel but in their representations of responsibility for the criminal act. In *Felix Holt,* the novel preceding *Middlemarch,* Eliot explicitly imagines a conflict of intents and consequences. What occasions this conflict is a riot that occurs during Treby's election day. It is this kind of violence Felix has long feared, and as soon as he hears that a mob is gathering in the town, he sets out to help control the escalating tensions. After he observes that the local constables have control over the crowds, Felix ventures to the home of Esther Lyon, whom he loves but on principle has already renounced. The sequence is relevant here, since Eliot first introduces the possibility of a riot, then diverts our attention to the squelched romance between Felix and Esther, and then puts Felix back into the growing violence of the election-day mob. The meeting with Esther discombobulates, and "For the first time [he] . . . had lost his self-possession."[67] Upset, he returns not home but to the town, for he concludes: "it would be better for him to look at the busy doings of men than to listen in solitude to the voices within him; and he wished to know how things were going on" (263). So Felix enters the scene not composedly but rather discomposedly. What he finds in town is a drunken crowd ready to do its worst.

Eliot drops Felix into a violent scene just at the moment that he is feeling the least in control, when he feels, as the narrator says, "at variance with himself" (262). When he throws himself into the violence of the crowd, it is in part to escape from the confusion of mind he is experiencing for the first time. Seeing the riot, he quickly forms a plan to keep the mob from destroying property and injuring people, and the plan that he imagines makes him a part of the violent mood: he decides that he will enact the role of mob leader in order to divert and contain the mob. The narrator gives us access to his intentions in a most unambiguous way: he was "determined, if he could, to rescue both assailers and assaulted from the worst consequences. His mind was busy with possible devices" (266–7). Attempting to save the innkeeper Spratt, Felix positions himself in the center of the mob, but he is perceived by Officer Tucker, the constable, to be what he, in fact, is pretending to be: the leader of the insurrection. When Tucker lunges for Felix,

> he discerned the situation; he chose between two evils. Quick as lightning he frustrated the constable, fell upon him, and tried to master his weapon. In the struggle, which was watched without interference, the constable fell undermost, and Felix got his weapon. He started up with the bare sabre in his hand.... Tucker did not rise immediately; but Felix did not imagine that he was much hurt. (267)

The language of deliberation is very much in play here as Felix sizes up the situation and out of necessity decides to fend off the constable. The narrator carefully moves us from the deliberations in Felix's mind to the image he projects to those who "watched without interference" (267). There is a special terseness in "He started up with the bare sabre in his hand" that manifests quite powerfully what Felix looks like to those who are doing the watching. The bad omen at work in "Tucker did not rise immediately" is not dispelled by Felix's own sense of what has happened ("Felix did not imagine that he was much hurt"). What has happened is that, intending only to knock Tucker down, Felix has killed him. As events unfold, what Eliot puts us in touch with are Felix's motives: "he had chiefly before his imagination the horrors that might come if the mass of wild chaotic desires and impulses around him were not diverted from any further attack on places where they would get in the midst of intoxicating and inflammable materials" (268). Following closely on the heels of his altercation with Tucker, the narrator explains Felix's inability to foresee the disaster to come, and she does so not only by invoking human nature more generally but also by telling us what Felix believed he was doing. She gives us access (again) to his good intentions:

> It was not a moment in which a spirit like his could calculate the effect of misunderstanding as to himself: nature never makes men who are at once energetically sympathetic and minutely calculating. He believed he had the power, and he was resolved to try, to carry the dangerous mass out of mischief till the military came to awe them. (268)

Readers of *Adam Bede* might be surprised to find the narrator announcing here that "nature never makes men who are at one energetically sympathetic and minutely calculating." At the end of *Adam Bede*, the eponymous hero is importantly both. His calculations and his ability to foresee consequences distinguish him from Arthur Donnithorne. His are the calculations of the craftsman, and the vocabulary of workmanship—of leveling and making square, for instance—is also a moral vocabulary. By the last chapter of the novel, Adam has also developed a sympathetic understanding of Hetty and Arthur. In making Felix "energetically sympathetic" and not "minutely calculating," Eliot invites us to invest in Felix's good motives and intentions as against the bad consequences of his actions. Moreover, while the narrator explicitly notes that what Felix fails to calculate is the impression he gives to the scene's witnesses, the ominous last line about Tucker implies that Felix is equally incapable of calculating the effect of the blow he has delivered.

The mob itself seems devoid of motive or intent, as the narrator makes clear. So confused are they that they eagerly follow Felix when he holds himself out as a leader. When Felix instructs them in their carrying of Spratt the innkeeper (Felix wants him held up high on their shoulders so that he is not dragged), the crowd simply believes "that he had some design worth knowing, while those in front were urged along partly by the same notion, partly by the sense that there was a motive in those behind them, not knowing what the motive was" (268). The crowd is a "medley of appetites and confused impressions," but Felix has clear intentions: "What Felix really intended to do," the narrator announces, " was to get the crowd by the nearest way out of the town" (268). Beyond defense attorney or judge or jury, the narrator can tell us what Felix "really intended." These "real" intentions are never subject to question or argument by an authority equal to the third person narrator. Such is the power of the novel.

But Felix's own power falls noticeably short. He does not foresee that there are others in the vicinity whose purposes are in direct opposition to his. Among the crowd are, as the narrator describes them, "some sharp-visaged men who loved the irrationality of riots for something else than in its own sake" (270). These men seek plunder, and so they redirect the crowd to Treby Manor. Felix fails because "While [he] was entertaining his ardent purpose, these other sons of Adam were entertaining another ardent purpose of their peculiar sort" (270). After the fact and only after, Felix has the knowledge of the consequences his acts have wrought. Once Felix registers this, he is brought up short by the "the sense that his plan might turn out to be as mad as all bold projects are seen to be when they have failed" (270). Having been carried along by his own purpose, Felix cannot see other possibilities until after the fact. Hindsight is, after all, twenty-twenty.

Felix's diversionary plan fails. The mob heads to Treby Manor to do its worst, and it does so. As the crowd heads for the Manor, Felix has time to reflect on whether he should continue with the crowd or send word for military reinforcements. He stays with the crowd, not only because he imagines that others were in a better position to deliver that information, but also because "Felix Holt's conscience was alive to the accusation that any danger they might be in now was brought on by a deed of his" (270). This is not the end he desired, of course, but this is nevertheless a consequence, one brought about by his "deed." And the narrator introduces a blackly comic bit of understatement when we find that it "did occur to him that very unpleasant consequences might be hanging over him of a kind quite different from inward dissatisfaction" (270). At the end of the day, he is arrested for manslaughter, for assaulting an officer, and for leading a riot.

Throughout chapter 33—the riot chapter—we are being prepared for the trial to come. Eliot persistently puts before us that which witnesses observe Felix Holt doing. The narrative juxtaposes the externality of acts and consequences—all of which are catastrophic—with the internality of Felix's motives and intents, to which we alone have special access. But the catastrophic consequences do not blot out Felix's heroic state of mind. Mr. Lyon, a moral guide on the order of *Adam Bede*'s Mr. Irwine—a choric figure with whom we are invited to agree—may see "no clear explanation of Felix Holt's conduct" (296) (he does not know what we know), but he feels that "Felix was innocent of any wish to abet a riot or the infliction of injuries; what he chiefly feared was that in the fatal encounter with Tucker he had been moved by a rash temper, not sufficiently guarded against by a prayerful and humble spirit" (296). Mr. Lyon sees Felix's act as a function of immodesty, a "too confident self-reliance" (296), as he describes it to Esther. But in "rash temper" we register more than overconfidence; "rash temper" suggests the possibility of passion and recklessness, a disregard of consequences. Though Felix may not have wished to injure anyone, should we not find him responsible for the natural consequences of his own acts? Even in Mr. Lyon's consideration of the case the subjective comes up against the objective. While Felix may not have desired or intended to abet the riot or inflict injuries, he should have seen both results as probable.

However, the ambivalence in Lyon's appraisal of the case does not inform the whole of the treatment of it in the novel. In *Felix Holt*, Eliot moves further in the direction of making moral responsibility depend not on consequences but on a state of mind. The moral and legal separate at this moment. State of mind redefines the moral judgment of consequences. Preparing for trial, Mr. Lyon assesses the chances of success before the law:

> though he were pronounced guilty in regard to this deed whereinto he hath calamitously fallen, yet that a judge mildly disposed, and with a due sense of that invisible activity of the soul whereby the deeds which are the same in the outward appearance and effect, yet differ as the knife-stroke of the surgeon, even though it kill, differs from the knife-stroke of a wanton mutilator, might use his discretion in tempering the punishment, so that it would not be very evil to bear. (358)

Felix will be found guilty in a court of law, but at his sentencing the elements of moral judgment might reenter (as indeed they do during the meetings that happen after the trial). Lyon's analysis presses us to classify a deed not by its consequences—the surgeon and the mutilator perform the same physical act that brings about the same consequence—but by the intent behind it. Note that Eliot gives the same name to the act of the surgeon and the wanton mutilator: the knife stroke. Everything remains the same outwardly. What is left is to look inward. But looking at the act only and its consequences, how would a witness know the difference between "the knife-stroke of the surgeon" and the "knife-stroke of the wanton mutilator"? The novel gives us the difference because it can go into the minds of both surgeon and mutilator.

When Felix pleads his own case before the judge at his trial for manslaughter, he defends himself by explaining what he foresaw and what he intended. He pleads "not guilty" to the charge of manslaughter because, as he says before the court, "I know that word may carry a meaning which would not fairly apply to my act" (370). Here Felix gives his own "concise narrative of his motives and conduct":

> When I threw Tucker down, I did not see the possibility that he would die from a sort of attack which ordinarily occurs in fighting without any fatal effect . . . he attacked me under a mistake about my intentions. . . . I should hold myself the worst sort of traitor if I put my hand either to fighting or disorder—which must mean injury to somebody—if I were not urged to it by what I hold to be sacred feelings, making a sacred duty either to my own manhood or to my fellow-man. (370)

Note the care with which Felix says what he did and did not foresee. About the legal issues in *Felix Holt*, Eliot had consulted an acquaintance, Frederic Harrison, who was, among other things, a lawyer. Harrison gave her extensive advice both on the questions of inheritance law that turn up in *Felix Holt* and on the trial scene in the novel.[68] Harrison might well have helped her think through Felix's defense, in which he would assert that he did not foresee the consequences of his actions. The basis of Felix's defense is not only that he did not foresee the consequences (because he reasonably concluded that such a blow does not ordinarily cause death) but also that his intentions were of the highest order. The other witnesses presented at trial have little left to do than present evidence to support Felix's claim that the consequences of his acts "were due to the calamitous failure of a bold but good purpose" (372). Even Harold Transome gives evidence that "Holt's sole motive was the prevention of disorder . . . the anxiety thus manifested by Holt was a guarantee of the statement he had made as to his motives on the day of the riot" (373). Esther Lyon's decision to testify and her testimony—both of which form the central moral action of these chapters—arises out of her sense that the legal proceeding has not brought forth for consideration the essential elements of Felix Holt. She is the last witness, and she gives voice to what we take as the final word on this business: "he could never have had any intention that was not brave and good" (376).

The narrator characterizes the effect Esther has on the judge, jury, and audience as momentary and unrecognizable by the criminal law: "the effect was not visible in the rigid necessities of legal procedure. The counsel's duty of restoring all unfavourable facts to due prominence in the minds of the jurors, had its effect altogether reinforced by the summing up of the judge" (366-7). Then, unexpectedly, Eliot puts us in the mind of the judge himself, as well as those attending the trial, and this move reinforces the divisions between moral (and novel) possibilities and legal procedures that the chapter as a whole has been inscribing. "It was not," comments the narrator,

> that the judge had severe intentions; it was only that he saw with severity. The conduct of Felix was not such as inclined him to indulgent consideration. . . . Even to many in the court who were not constrained by judicial duty, it seemed that though this high regard felt for the prisoner by his friends, and especially by a generous-hearted woman, was very pretty, such conduct as his was not the less dangerous and foolish, and assaulting and killing a constable was not the less an offence to be regarded without leniency. (377)

Here the testimony as to mental state appears to be reduced to that which might incline a judge to indulgence, or that which might be characterized as "pretty." The offense remains the offense.

The emphasis on "conduct" in the passage just quoted suggests that what is under consideration is only external consequences: the assault and the killing. The scene renders a simplification of the legal treatment of intent, which might explain the not very convincing writing here. The effect of Esther's testimony becomes "visible" (378) only outside of the courtroom, in a meeting that takes place the next day. Outside the halls of justice, the questions of motive and intent become once again discernible. The meeting of magistrates and country gentlemen to discuss the possibility of making an appeal for a pardon on Felix Holt's behalf refigures Felix's offense. All are influenced by Esther's testimony—her "maidenly fervour" (378)—and the main substance of that testimony concerned Felix's intentions ("he could never have had any intention that was not brave and good"). Unexpectedly, too, another figure (briefly) enters this scene—Philip Debarry, the son of Sir Maximus Debarry. Of this father and son, the narrator remarks:

> Among these one of the foremost was Sir Maximus Debarry, who had come to the assizes with a mind, as usual, slightly rebellious under an influence which he never ultimately resisted—the influence of his son. Philip Debarry himself was detained in London, but in his correspondence with his father he had urged him, as well as his uncle Augustus, to keep eyes and interest awake on the subject of Felix Holt, whom, from all the knowledge of the case he had been able to obtain, he was inclined to believe peculiarly unfortunate rather than guilty. (378)

"Peculiarly unfortunate rather than guilty": in "unfortunate" we register consequences as accidental and not intentional, as "guilty" suggests. More than Esther's sympathy is at work in the meeting that follows the trial. This extralegal and ad hoc pardoning process admits all of the vibrations that the legal process had sought to suppress. Felix is no longer presumed to have intended the natural consequences of his actions. Instead, something more subjective enters this informal proceeding. The men are swayed by the absent son (who is himself swayed by his regard for Mr. Lyon, to whom he feels "obliged" for some unnamed reason) and by the ardour of Esther's testimony. The subjectivity tucked into the juxtaposition of the "unfortunate" as against the "guilty" pushes the men finally to file their memorandum on Felix's behalf. Still, Felix is not exonerated. Though Felix's crime is pardoned, he continues to bear the legal judgment of guilt, a judgment based on the consequence of his act.

How much more complex this judgment will become in *Middlemarch* and *Daniel Deronda*.

⊰ THREE ⊱

Middlemarch, Daniel Deronda, and the Crime in Mind

Working out the relations between the interior life and the external acts and consequences of characters in the late novels of George Eliot is a humbling enterprise. One is tempted to simplify, to suggest that the internal displaces the external in these great and complicated texts. But the novels resist this reductive analysis. The relation is not, as Henry Alley describes it at one point in his essay on murder in Eliot's novels, a clear "versus." Of *Daniel Deronda*, Alley comments that "Foremost is the problem of murderous intent versus murderous action."[1] Later in the essay he makes the difference between them irrelevant: "As a moralist," he remarks, "Eliot certainly wanted to show how culpability extends to those who have killed in their thoughts, no matter what the outcome."[2] It is true that Eliot holds her characters accountable for murderous thoughts, and yet she also tests the limits of that accountability, which is why in these late novels acts and consequences remain important factors in judgment. Nor is the relation between thought and act a straightforward "either/or." In his discussion of blackmail in *Middlemarch*, Alexander Welsh concludes that the blackmailer Raffles "has either died or been killed by Bulstrode—and it may not matter which, since Bulstrode has prayed for his death as well as given him the brandy."[3] Welsh is right that Bulstrode has prayed for Raffles's death and has allowed Mrs. Abel to give Raffles the brandy, but the conclusion Welsh implicitly draws from these facts—that culpability would attach even if Bulstrode had not given Raffles the brandy—assumes too much. It makes a difference that Eliot gives us both a state of mind and an act, that Bulstrode's prayer has become an intention and that his intention turns into an attempt.

Relations between thoughts and acts are neither oppositional nor interchangeable. When Carol Christ calls attention, in passing, to "Eliot's constant preoccupation with the relationship between intention and action," she neglects a necessary question: what persistently draws George Eliot to that relationship?[4] The answer is a matter of both form and substance. Representing the mind in action came to mean in Eliot's novels—as it would later and more fully and extremely in the novels of Henry James—representing the action in mind. Even the early novel *Adam Bede* is deeply invested in the activity of the mind. Adam at his workbench transforms the passion he feels for Hetty into his labor, but the narrator reminds us that the transformation of passion does not find expression only in the external act. Such passion might find "An outlet from the narrow limits of our personal lot in . . . the still, creative activity of our thought" (212). Eliot's "our" generously includes her audience in the possibilities of thought. We are provoked, too, by the stillness of the activity here. Eliot sets off the activity of the mind from the activity of the arm, without denying creativity to either "outlet."

Eliot's formal experiments both influence and are influenced by the introduction of criminal acts into her narrative. While we may take heart in the "still, creative activity of our thought," Eliot's novels on occasion deal in the kind of thought that creates to destroy. When in *Middlemarch* Nicholas Bulstrode imagines the death of Raffles, his thought produces a murderous impulse. By manifesting so vividly the activity of thought—by internalizing the act—Eliot introduces the possibility that thought has an active power, but what are the ramifications of such a possibility? And if thoughts are as powerful as acts, why are acts so central to Eliot's novels? When Carol Christ claims that Eliot allows certain characters—Gwendolen Harleth of *Daniel Deronda* and Caterina Sarti of "Mr. Gilfil's Love-Story" among them—to imagine aggressive acts while saving them from actually committing any acts of aggression, her argument depends on our allowing that the thought is as bad (or good) as the act, and, further, that the thought of evil is enough to create the reformative guilt needed to light the way toward spiritual salvation; however, in both cases Eliot provides more than the thought. After all, in the two cases Carol Christ cites, knives are involved. It is indeed a dagger that Caterina sees before her, and it is a dagger that Gwendolen hides in the drawer of her dressing case. A dagger is more material than a thought, and it matters. Carol Christ's argument makes the problem of act and thought in Eliot a means to an end—the end being the reformative guilt experienced by the repentant chosen. But this reduction does not account for the interest that *Middlemarch*, for example, takes in working through relations among desires, impulses, motives, and intentions. Moreover, Carol Christ cannot, finally, account for *Felix Holt*, where Felix, a character Eliot obviously favors, is not saved from an act of aggression, an act that, as Mr. Lyon nervously surmises, is done not intentionally but perhaps recklessly ("by a rash temper" [296] is the way he actually puts it). Nor does Eliot save Adam Bede from attacking Arthur Donnithorne and nearly killing him. It is too easy to say that Eliot's novels imagine that an intent is as bad as (or the same as) an act. Yet Eliot was investigating the representational possibilities of intent as act.

Nineteenth-century analytic jurisprudential thinkers were very much involved in distinguishing internal from external activity and in discriminating among different kinds of mental activity as they related to criminal responsibility. In his lecture 21, "Intention Further Considered," John Austin attends to the problem of present intentions to do a future act. In looking at such a problem, he endeavors to distinguish a bare wish or desire from an intention: "for example, if I wish for a watch hanging in a watch-maker's window, but without believing that I shall try to take it from the owner, I am perfectly clear of *intending* to steal the watch, though I am guilty of coveting my neighbor's goods (provided that the wish recur frequently)."[5] While an intent may form the basis of a sin and a crime, coveting the goods constitutes a sin only. We register Austin's distinction as reasonable, since to intend or to will is different from merely wishing. As in his lecture on will and motive, Austin is here indebted to Hobbes's *Leviathan*, but the Hobbesian analysis is subtler and more provocative:

> To be delighted in the Imagination onley, of being possessed of another mans goods, servants, or wife, without any intention to take them from him by force, or fraud, is not breach of the Law, that sayeth, *Thou shalt not covet*: nor is the pleasure a man may have in imagining or dreaming of the death of him, from whose life he expecteth nothing but dammage, and displeasure, a Sinne; but the resolving to put some Act in execution, that tendeth thereto. For to be pleased in the fiction of that, which would please a man if it were reall, is a Passion so adherent to the Nature both of man, and every other living creature, as to make it a Sinne, were to make Sinne of being a man. The consideration of this, has made me think them too severe, both to themselves, and others, that maintain, that the First motions of the mind, (though checked with the fear of God) be Sinnes. But I confess it is safer to erre on that hand, than on the other.[6]

"Imagining or dreaming of the death of him whose life he expecteth nothing but dammage, and displeasure": how close this is to Gwendolen's imagining the death of Grandcourt, or Bulstrode's imagining the death of Raffles, though Eliot takes both Gwendolen and Bulstrode past the dream to the resolution. We mark Hobbes's humanity here, the sense that we cannot stop ourselves from imagining such things or from taking pleasure in the fictions we create. But then there is a difference between "imagining or dreaming" (with the latter suggesting that such thoughts are both less than conscious and further away from an act) and resolving. The resolution is the sin, and, as Hobbes notes in his next paragraph, the overt act becomes the crime. To fiction and imagination, Hobbes gives the widest latitude. What of Eliot?

"How you do paint and dissect Bulstrode's feelings," John Blackwood wrote to Eliot on September 7, 1872. "It is a terrible picture of the attempt to love God and Mammon, for you throw in a touch of reality in the wretch's religion which removes him from the ordinary religious hypocrite of his school. In the struggle that night he, as it were, hardly knew himself that he was committing murder when he gave the brandy. That is the impression you have left I think."[7] As an early, perhaps the first, response to Book 7 of *Middlemarch*, it is telling that Blackwood's letter gets right into the thick of things. He and his family were fortunate enough to get the pages before they were offered to the public, and Blackwood remarks in the same letter that as he and his wife and daughter are reading Book 7, they feel "ahead of the rest of the world." Blackwood's letter draws my attention because of the centrality and conjunction of "paint and dissect" in his response to Bulstrode.[8] One might argue that the pairing reflects Blackwood's recognition of the conjoining of the aesthetic and the scientific in *Middlemarch*, Eliot's most scientifically informed novel. Such a reading would suffice, had Bulstrode not put Blackwood in mind of a story of his own, which he is moved to produce in the same September 7 letter. Having praised the section of *Middlemarch* after Bulstrode's exposure and in which we see "the harpies gathering to their prey," Blackwood digresses into his own anecdote:

> A humorous old bachelor, relative of mine, had retired from business to live about 20 miles from Edinburgh, and one Sunday had out a batch of his Lawyer cronies. Late at night when they had ably dissected their various acquaintances, the liquor in the dining room ran short. My friend said, "Gentlemen, there is the key of the cellar and any of you may go and get up whatever you like, but damn me if I'll leave my character in your hands for five minutes."[9]

Blackwood makes no comment on this story, not even to reflect on its being another story about a key to a liquor cabinet and some odd fear that one's character might be in trouble, and in trouble in some faintly legal way. The harpies have become cronies, and decidedly legal ones. Now the dissection is not so much scientifically but legally informed. What Blackwood might be responding to here is the anatomizing of Bulstrode's state of mind that Eliot presents. The coming back to dissection tells on Blackwood; it is much on his mind.

The legal carries some importance in these observations, since the charge Blackwood brings against Bulstrode is murder; however, the charge is itself in need of some dissection: "In his struggle that night he, as it were, hardly knew himself that he was committing murder when he gave the brandy." The syntax produces a momentary uncertainty in meaning that arises out of the placement of the reflexive pronoun. As one reads the sentence, what it at first evokes is "he, as it were, hardly knew himself." The use of "himself" is in itself curious since the pronoun is not quite needed. Take it out and the obvious meaning—that Bulstrode did not know he was committing murder—remains the same. But there is a distinctly different emphasis when the pronoun is included and when it is placed after "knew" and not, say, after "he" (as in "he

himself hardly knew"). Blackwood's syntax generates an uncertainty that
gives us a murder committed by a man out of contact with his own mind,
though Blackwood's "hardly" leaves him room to go back on his own words.
The murder is committed without knowledge that it is actually being committed; it is committed during an absence of mind. As Blackwood struggles
with Eliot's dissection of character, he finds himself imagining a murder that
is not a murder, for murder cannot be committed without knowledge of its
commission. The impression Eliot leaves is as complicated as Blackwood's
letter suggests.[10]

While Blackwood offers praise for the complexities that Eliot's dissection
produces, Yeats in his commentary on some of the same effects at work in
Eliot's *Romola* displays his disgust. Yeats begins by praising Balzac, who understands that "behind the momentary self, which acts and lives in the world,
and is subject to the judgment of the world, there is that which cannot be
called before any mortal Judgment seat, even though a great poet, or novelist,
or philosopher be sitting upon it."[11] From there, Yeats compares Balzac's
withholding of judgment—even his forgiveness of sin—with Eliot's very different enterprise:

> Great literature has always been written in a like spirit, and is, indeed,
> the Forgiveness of Sin, and when we find it becoming the Accusation
> of Sin, as in George Eliot, who plucks her Tito in pieces with as much
> assurance as if he had been clockwork, literature has begun to change
> into something else. George Eliot had a fierceness one hardly finds
> but in a woman turned argumentative, but the habit of mind her
> fierceness gave its life to was characteristic of her century."[12]

The obvious misogyny of the last sentence of this passage, along with the
slight sloppiness of syntax (evidenced by the confusing "but . . . but" construction) undermines the claim Yeats makes, yet the main idea has a certain
aptness. Yeats's language reveals much about Eliot's treatment of Tito as well
as her treatment of Bulstrode. She does pluck her Bulstrode in pieces, and
perhaps he is dissected like clockwork, since we are invited to know so much
about what makes him tick. That dissection, among other things, backs our
accusations against him, but those accusations are not so simple as Yeats's
formula would have us believe.

Middlemarch contains its fair share of deaths—not only of Raffles but of
Casaubon and Peter Featherstone, as well as the ill-fated husband of
Madame Laure, who makes a brief but memorable appearance before he is
killed (murdered?) by his wife. The deaths of both Raffles and the husband of
Laure, as he is called in the novel, involve Lydgate, though he is implicated in
the second as he is not in the first. As a young doctor studying in Paris, Lydgate puts himself under the romantic spell of the actress Laure, who, with
her husband, act the parts of lovers in an unremarkable and unnamed melodrama. The climax of said play is the mistress's stabbing of the male lover,
and climax it is, as when in one performance the stabbing is performed actu-

ally and theatrically. Though witnessed by a theatre full of spectators, still the act is not easily classified: "was it a murder?" That is the question rippling through Paris (150).

What is obvious is that through Laure's story Eliot reveals Lydgate's "spots of commonness": his vanity and egoism. Laure is a lesson that Lydgate never quite learns well enough. But if Laure serves Eliot's purpose in this way, she also does something more, and to that something more I now turn, for Laure's name calls up not only the law itself but also the intersection of story and the law (lore/law). Of all the possible stories Eliot might have told to reveal Lydgate, it is provocative that this is the story she invents, and its sensationalism—more Dickensian than Eliotic—seems out of place in this greatest of realist achievements.

The drama Laure enacts is framed by "some galvanic experiments" (148) Lydgate is performing on living frogs and rabbits, experiments that involve making an animal's muscle move by applying an electric shock to it. Before going to the theatre, Lydgate attends to this work, and after the unhappy events, he returns to these experiments, as if to immerse himself yet again in a world where one can understand an act. Such experiments yield the simplest kind of action—a simple stimulus and response. Neither frog nor rabbit can be said to intend the act, but are instead left to wonder over "their trying and mysterious dispensation of unexplained shocks" (148). Against such an action, we juxtapose the act that Laure performs on stage, a most public of acts in which nothing is hidden—nothing except the intent with which the act is done, which is to say that quite a lot is hidden.

It is the "hidden fact" of intent to which the narrator alludes when, a propos of Lydgate's search for Laure, who disappears from the Paris scene, she says rather cryptically, "Hidden actresses, however, are not so difficult to find as some other hidden facts" (150). Eliot does not allow us access to Laure. Like Lydgate, we size up the crime from the outside. It is on the question of intent that the judgment of the act turns. The killing done, "Paris rang with the story of this death:—was it a murder?" (150). In the face of such accusations Lydgate "vehemently contended for her innocence. . . . The notion of murder was absurd; no motive was discoverable, the young couple being understood to dote on each other; and it was not unprecedented that an accidental slip of the foot should have brought these grave consequences. The legal investigation ended in Madame Laure's release" (150). The passage folds Lydgate's point of view into the narrator's; both read the situation from the outside. The terseness of "The legal investigation ended in Madame Laure's release" gives us not so much a clearing of Laure as the law's giving up the possibility of proving its case, a note sounded also in "no motive was discoverable" (150), which leaves the possibility of a motive undiscovered, as distinct from "there was no motive." Undaunted by any such doubts, Lydgate follows Laure. Faced with his undeterrable attentions and insistent proposals, Laure gives Lydgate what the law could not procure. Yet her disclosure does not have the openness or emotional charge of a confession:

"I will tell you something," she said, in her cooing way, keeping her arms folded. "My foot really slipped."

"I know, I know," said Lydgate, deprecatingly. "It was a fatal accident—a dreadful stroke of calamity that bound me to you the more."

Again Laure paused a little and then said, slowly, "*I meant to do it.*"

Lydgate, strong man as he was, turned pale and trembled: moments seemed to pass before he rose and stood at a distance from her.

"There was a secret, then," he said at last, even vehemently. "He was brutal to you: you hated him."

"No! he wearied me; he was too fond: he would live in Paris, and not in my country; that was not agreeable to me."

"Great God!" said Lydgate, in a groan of horror. "And you planned to murder him?"

"I did not plan: it came to me in the play—*I meant to do it.*" (151)

I am interested here in the way Laure stages her disclosure, with its pauses, its pacing, its changes in tone. The italics are Eliot's, not once but twice, and they give us the definitive line-reading of this performance. Consider, then, that Eliot first introduces the puzzle of an intentional accident in a theatrical space, a space in which we have no access to the inner lives of the players, except through action and voiced speech. More puzzling still is the way the tenses work in Laure's admission. When she says "'*I meant to do it*,'" her use of the past tense is equivocal. We cannot know what period in the past she means to identify. The plan came to her in the play, but had she meant to do it before? Like the law (at least as Eliot represents it), Lydgate can only admit of two explanations—accident or premeditation with motive ("It was a fatal accident. . . . He was brutal to you. . . . You planned to murder him"), and, faced with the complication Laure presents, he can only stand "mute," while instantaneously reimagining Laure not as the distressed damsel he had mooned over moments before but "amid the throng of stupid criminals" (151). But Laure, as if anticipating Freud, conceives of an intentional accident, a site where a desire becomes an accident. The most obvious onomastic pun here—Laure/law—connects the ambiguity Laure's action generates to the ambiguities the law itself lives in and with, though ultimately the law must decide whether an act is intentional or accidental.

One question to ask here is why this sequence in the novel is imagined dramatically. Like Lydgate, we remain outside of Laure—one never gets access to her inner life, as one might not in a drama, or at least not the access one expects to get in a George Eliot novel—and Laure remains unfathomable, arms folded: "'I will tell you something,' she said, in her cooing way, keeping her arms folded. 'My foot really slipped.'" The passage masterfully juxtaposes the intent to reveal ("I will tell you something") against the refusal to disclose ("arms folded"), and Eliot's use of "folded" implicates the refusal to reveal her state of mind since, as the *OED* annotations suggest, to "unfold"

is to give up what is in the mind.[13] We are left, then, to reconcile the two explanations of the act that Laure provides, without any clue as to how to make
a judgment.

But what is closed off in a dramatic scene might be opened up novelistically. When Lydgate first meets Rosamond, he misjudges her badly and sadly,
for his misjudgment creates the circumstances through which he ties his own
hands. The first time Lydgate gets a good look at Rosamond, she appears to
him "as if the petals of some gigantic flower had just opened and disclosed
her" (156). Though Lydgate determines that Rosamond is Laure's "very opposite" (156), the narrator's description of her maneuverings suggests otherwise;
though an amateur, Rosamond is as gifted an actress as her predecessor. On
leaving the Vincy house, the narrator opens Lydgate to us further. Lydgate,
turning back to "Louis' new book on fever" (161), reengages his active imagination, and the narrator takes the opportunity to contrast the stringency with
which Lydgate studies science to the laxness with which he ponders romance
and marriage. The narrator's descriptions of Lydgate's scientific aspirations
make clear that Lydgate identifies imagination as the central impulse and
guiding force of his undertaking. The terms Eliot chooses to represent that
undertaking reveal how closely Eliot associated the artistic and the scientific.
As George Levine remarks in his chapter on Eliot in *The Realistic Imagination*,
critics reasonably consider this passage to be Eliot's metaphoric description
of her own novelistic practices.[14] In his analysis of the passage, Levine
plumbs the depth of Eliot's thinking about complex scientific writing, which
was itself making the imagination central to scientific research. What makes
the passage germane to my arguments about Eliot's novel is the way it joins an
implicit statement about narrative strategies with observations about the desire to reveal the inner life and to understand madness and crime: "he wanted
to pierce the obscurity of those minute processes which prepare human misery and joy, those invisible thorough-fares which are the first lurking-places
of anguish, mania, and crime, that delicate poise and transition which determine the growth of happy or unhappy consciousness" (162). It is not surprising that Lydgate names crime and mania as subjects of scientific study; nor is
it surprising that Eliot compares scientific and novelistic practices. At the
core of her comparison is the shared ambition to gain access to the "invisible
thorough-fares." That this passage occurs between other passages in which
Lydgate misreads Rosamond's inner life illuminates Lydgate's more limited
capacity as against the narrator's powers. Where Lydgate fails to pierce those
lurking places, the narrator succeeds. She has the power to inhabit the interior life.

Though Lydgate does not learn from Laure, we register the complexities
of criminal intention that she represents. The critic Simon During reads
Laure's case (and Dorothea Casaubon's and Gwendolen Harleth's) as Eliot's
literary interpolation of monomania, a condition named by Etienne Esquirol
and first recognized in France in 1825 as a "break between faculties" that

might manifest itself as a sudden and unexplained violent act. The most salient feature of the monomaniacal act, according to During's research, is its motivelessness and also its frequent manifestation as an imitation of someone else's monomaniacal act (one monomaniac imitated another), "for to detach one's will from one's understanding, to have no motive, is to become vulnerable to repeating an act under the guidance of some external representation [i.e., newspaper reports of monomania cases]."[15] During contends that Laure is "a victim of the epidemic of monomania," vulnerable to the "guidance of some external representation."[16] So too he argues that the so-called motivelessness of her act, like most acts labeled monomaniacal, attempts to deprive the act of meaning. During assumes the "entry of monomania into this scene" from the narrator's remark that "no motive was discoverable" and from the likely date of the incident—the late 1820s—and its location (Paris) and from the similarity between the words spoken by France's most famous monomaniac, Henriette Cornier, and Laure. Cornier, a servant, for no apparent reason killed her employer's nineteen-month-old daughter by cutting off her head. But, argues During, Cornier had a motive: she had been mistreated by other employers, and so to call her crime "motiveless" was to deprive it of its political meaning. In short, monomania as a diagnosis denied meaning to acts that might expose cultural oppression.

What During leaves out of his suggestive analysis is that no one in the novel *Middlemarch*—not the French gossips or the law itself—suggests the possibility of madness as an explanation for Laure's crime, though it was much at issue in Cornier's case. If madness enters the scene at all, it is only through Lydgate's sense of his own madness in pursuing Laure ("He knew that this was like the sudden impulse of a madman" [150]). His impulsiveness stands in contrast to Laure's unimpulsiveness. The competing explanation is not madness but chance—the slipping of the foot. Moreover, in During's argument, Laure has to be imitating Henriette (without knowing it, victim that she is) while having the presence of mind to create a fictional motive (an unsatisfying marriage) to serve as actual motive. Where Henriette could not articulate a motive for her crime, Laure clearly does. She no longer wishes to be married. There is something remarkable about the parallels During adduces (time, place), and Eliot may indeed have been aware of Henriette's case through her reading for and with Lewes of certain texts on psychology that Lewes was interested in as he was preparing his *Problems of Life and Mind*, but it is difficult to imagine Laure as a victim. During wants to have it both ways, arguing at once that Laure's is a monomaniacal act inspired by Henriette's case and that Eliot must conceal its monomaniacal status because of its threat to "narrative sequence" and to patriarchy more generally. According to During, monomania

> is concealed. Why? No doubt because Eliot's fiction cannot cope with the decay of psychic structuration or narrative sequence that the condition imposes: after all, as a monomaniac's, Laure's act would be

strictly meaningless. But it is also concealed for something like the opposite reason: because Laure comes closer to Henriette she also
comes closer to Dorothea, and the distinctions upon which the
novel's ostensible moral message hangs begin to fail. With monomania, a more dangerous meaning looms: murder is no longer a matter of
conscious motives; rather, motives can be given problematic sense by
that larger pattern "patriarchy" that covers all women—from Laure to
Dorothea—who are objects of proprietorial sexual desire.[17]

That During makes Eliot's concealed introduction of monomania mean
something (that the act is meaningless) and then "its opposite" gives one
pause. In short, Eliot very deliberately introduces monomania only to conceal
it. What this leads to is that "the startling and bleak message that *Middlemarch*
takes from monomania can be spelled out: in freeing themselves from male
sexual domination, women commit murder."[18] So (argues During), Dorothea
thinks of herself as having murdered Casaubon, though I think he could not
really show (nor does he attempt to show) that Casaubon's relation to
Dorothea is one defined by male sexual desire.

I take this time to work through During's argument because it is attending
to a potent cluster of ideas. In looking to monomania as his subtext, During
has to fill in gaps and contort the novels to support his claims. Still, he focuses
on the problem of an act that seems to be two things at once. During says that
monomania breaks down "the distinction between a motivated and an unmo-
tivated killing."[19] But the distinctions *Middlemarch* and *Daniel Deronda* investigate more compellingly are the distinctions between a desire and an intention, between an intentional killing and a desired but unintentional killing.
Wisely, During does not mention the most complicated death in *Middlemarch*—that of Raffles—because it simply will not accommodate the structure
he imposes on the novel. When During gets to Gwendolen and *Daniel
Deronda*, he has an even harder path to clear, since who has a better motive for
murder than Gwendolen? Yet the drowning scene in *Daniel Deronda*, as I will
discuss later, explores the relations between a desire, an intent, and an act in
the assignation of moral and legal responsibility. While During struggles to
make monomania relevant to the novels, he misses the opportunity to consider the novels in the context of a more pertinent (but perhaps less sensa-
tional) set of legal and philosophical ideas.

Writing on such ideas in the 1830s is John Austin, who so persistently
prosecuted questions about the relations between intention, act, and consequence. While much of Austin's undertaking in his account of criminal law is
to distinguish intention from negligence, his focus is clearly on intention; it is
the term that "meets us at *every* step, in *every* department of Jurisprudence."[20]
In large part, Austin's enterprise in his *Lectures on Jurisprudence* is defini-
tional. His own stated intention is to rescue certain key terms—*will, motive,
intention*, and *negligence* among them—from "philosophical and popular jar-
gon."[21] Tellingly, Austin attempts to justify what, judging from his explana-

tion, some of his nineteenth-century students might have registered as need-less: "Nor is this incidental excursion into the Philosophy of mind a wanton digression from the path which is marked out for my subject [that is, the analysis of the terms right and duty]."[22] I include this apology to suggest that Austin's analysis of these terms would not have been anticipated as part of legal study. Austin's justification for this undertaking indicates that he took up the terms used to describe state of mind—*motive*, *will*, and *intent*—not as the exclusive property of those writing about the philosophy of mind but as the foundational concepts of all law and of life, since all duties are backed by sanctions and sanctions influence the will either to do the act or to not do the act, as the case may be. Moreover, since duties require either an act or a for-bearance, and every act or forbearance "is the consequence of a volition, or of a determination of the will,"[23] then we can understand duty only by under-standing will. Finally, since injuries give rise to certain rights (the right to compensation, for example) and since injuries can be intentional or negligent (or reckless) or accidental, we cannot understand the nature of an injury (or of the rights to which it may give rise) without understanding intention and neg-ligence. As part of this exploration, Austin takes up with both hands the diffi-culties of defining states of mind:

> The state of a man's mind can only be known by others through his acts: through his own declarations, or through other conduct of his own. Consequently it must often be difficult to determine whether a party *intended*, or whether he was merely negligent, heedless, rash. The acts to which we must resort as evidence of the state of his mind, may be *ambiguous*: insomuch that they lead us to one conclusion natu-rally as to the other. Judging from his conduct, the man may have *in-tended*, or he may have been negligent, heedless, or rash. Either hy-pothesis would fit the appearances which are open to our observation.
>
> But the difficulty which belongs to the *evidence* is transferred to the *subject of the inquiry*. Because we are unable to determine what was the state of his mind, we fancy that the state of his mind was itself *indeter-minate*: that it lay between the confines of consciousness and uncon-sciousness, without belonging exactly to either. We forget that these are antagonist notions, incapable of blending.[24]

A few paragraphs earlier, he asserts more vehemently, a

> state of mind between consciousness and unconsciousness—between intention on the one side and negligence and heedlessness on the other—seems to be impossible. The party thinks or the party does *not* think, of the act or consequence. If he thinks of it, he *intends*. If he do not think of it, he is *negligent* or *heedless*. To say that negligence or heedlessness may run into intention, is to say that a thought may be *absent* from the mind, and yet (after a fashion) *present* to the mind. Nor is it possible to conceive that supposed mongrel or monster, that

which is *neither* temerity *nor* intention, but partakes of both:—A state of mind lying on the confines of each, without belonging precisely to the territory of either.[25]

But this is the territory in which Eliot's *Middlemarch* moves; this the mongrel or monster that Eliot creates:

A man vows, and yet will not cast away the means of breaking his vow. Is it that he distinctly means to break it? Not at all; but the desires which tend to break it are at work in him dimly, and make their way into his imagination, and relax his muscles in the very moments when he is telling himself over again the reasons for his vow. (695–6)

Here we are in the tortured mind of Nicholas Bulstrode, but we are also in every mind that has vowed and not vowed. Consider the simultaneity of the conscious reaffirmation of the vow and the not-conscious workings of the desires on the muscles themselves; the desires look like independent contractors. We have a state of mind that feels both intentional and unintentional: he means to break the vow but indistinctly. Can we say that he is conscious of the desires at work on his imagination and his muscles? The passage invites us to think not.

Conceiving of something like the same problem, Wittgenstein remarked on the oddity of the law's assuming that we can understand our own actions:

In a law-court you are asked the motive of your action and you are supposed to know it. Unless you lie you are supposed to be able to tell the motive of your action. You are not supposed to know the laws by which your body and mind are governed. Why do they suppose you know it? Because you've had such a lot of experience with yourself? People sometimes say: "No-one can see inside you, but you can see inside yourself," as though being so near yourself, being yourself, you know your own mechanism. But is it like that? "Surely he must know why he did or why he said such and such."[26]

Wittgenstein brings us back to Blackwood: "he, as it were, hardly knew himself that he was committing murder when he gave the brandy." When Nicholas Bulstrode gives John Raffles another hundred pounds, a bribe to buy his silence, Eliot puts this problem to us yet again. The narrator discloses that "Various motives urged Bulstrode to this open-handedness, but he did not himself inquire closely into all of them. As he had stood watching Raffles in his uneasy sleep, it had certainly entered his mind that the man had been much shattered since the first gift of two hundred pounds" (676). Motives enter Bulstrode's mind as do intentions, but does he know why he is doing what he is doing or that he intends to do it? Note the intelligence of the writing here. Eliot syntactically separates Bulstrode from his motives, as if mirroring his own attempts to elude responsibility for his actions. He is the object to their subject. Or is she, rather, mirroring syntactically the way motives sometimes work in and on us? Bulstrode's openhandedness is set off against the closedness of the inquiries into motive. Bulstrode opens his hand but closes off inquiry even as the shattered image of Raffles enters his mind. The mind seems to close and open to certain possibilities for the future.

What is introduced theatrically with Madame Laure gets unfolded novel-istically only when Eliot brings Raffles to Nicholas Bulstrode, and it is just after the Laure episode—in the very next chapter—that Eliot focuses on Bul-strode. When George Eliot turns her full attention to Bulstrode and the con-flicts and crises of mind he experiences at the sickbed of Raffles, she becomes involved fully in investigating the continuum of states of and in the mind that situate it within or keep it without the reach of moral or legal blame. I find these Bulstrode chapters utterly absorbing in their movements inside the mind of this character. Eliot often makes use of interior monologue in these chapters. We usually (though certainly not always) find ourselves in the most direct contact with Bulstrode's mind: what we get is not a narrative descrip-tion of his thoughts but the thoughts in his own idiom. The power of Bul-strode's desire for Raffles's death leads him to an "apology" (692) for that de-sire, which his words of prayer cannot squelch. In this apology, he catalogues sin as a function of the external: "Should Providence in this case award death, there was no sin in contemplating death as the desirable issue—if he kept his hands from hastening it—if he scrupulously did what was prescribed" (692). Bulstrode legalizes the intervention of Providence, conceiving of the situation as a "case," imagining the act of Providence as an "award" and the conse-quence as an "issue." He goes further still by putting himself in the moral and legal clear as long as he does that which Lydgate instructs him to do. He thinks hopefully of the possibility that such treatment might itself lead to death, ending with the knowledge that even acts themselves will not be judged in and of themselves, for "intention was everything in the question of right and wrong" (692).

Bulstrode's statement of this key principle—"intention was everything in the question of right and wrong"—is necessarily tainted, since it comes as part of his larger apology for his actions. But that taint does not undermine the principle itself, which Eliot had earlier allowed *Felix Holt*'s Mr. Lyon—a character beyond reproach—to espouse ("deeds which are the same in the outward appearance and effect, yet differ as the knife-stroke of the surgeon, even though it kill, differs from the knife-stroke of the wanton mutilator" [358]). Moreover, Bulstrode follows a specific definition of intention, and this is no simple hypocrisy: "Bulstrode set himself to keep his intention separate from his desire. He inwardly declared that he intended to obey orders" (693). The distinction Bulstrode invokes is an important one—one that signaled a significant development in Austinian jurisprudence, for, as the twentieth-cen-tury jurist George Fletcher explains,

> The central issue in the debate about the nature of intentionally com-
> mitting an offense turns on the relationship between intending and

desiring. In German and Soviet law, it is generally assumed that an actor intends a result only if he desires to bring about that result. There is considerable support for an analogous account of intending in the common law. Yet, an influential analysis beginning with John Austin in the nineteenth century holds that intending should be considered apart from the issue of desiring.[27]

If intent is considered apart from desire, what matters is not the desired outcome (Raffles's death) but the intended act (giving Raffles the medicine and not the liquor). Austin notes that desired consequences are usually but not always intended, and intended consequences are not always desired.[28] By way of example, Austin offers this:

> You shoot at Sempronius or Styles, at Titius or Nokes, desiring and intending to kill him. . . . Your desire of his death, is the *ultimate motive* to the volition. You contemplate his death, as the probable consequence of the act.
>
>   But when you shoot at Styles, I am talking with him, and am standing close by him. And, from the position which I stand with regard to the person you aim at, you think it not unlikely that you kill *me* in your attempt to kill *him*. You fire, and kill me accordingly. Now here you *intend* my death, without *desiring* it. . . . [S]ince you contemplate my death as a probable consequence of your act, you intend my death although you *desire* it not.[29]

While in the criminal law of the nineteenth century jurists applied this analysis to attach responsibility to those who undertook reckless acts knowing but not desiring that injuries or fatalities might result, Bulstrode calls on intention to protect him from moral and legal liability. Intention (he hopes) shields him from responsibility.

Intention, then, performs a function that words alone cannot. All Bulstrode's efforts to convert words into desires fail him: "through all this effort to condense words into a solid mental state, there pierced and spread with irresistible vividness the images of the events he desired" (692). The images have a vividness that the actual words lack. Words are no match for the power of the imagination coupled with desire, for the images arise out of the desire. His prayers echo the substance of his desires even as he may resist them: he "mentally lifted up this vow as if it would urge the result he longed for—he tried to believe in the potency of that prayerful resolution—its potency to determine death. He knew that he ought to say, 'Thy will be done'; and he said it often. But the intense desire remained that the will of God might be the death of that hated man" (685). Images of Raffles's death themselves become a kind of nonverbal language, "a language to his hopes and fears, just as we hear tones from the vibrations which shake our whole system" (685).

In these chapters, the narrator explores the separation of the desire from the intent and complicates our moral judgments of Bulstrode. After Bulstrode delivers what we recognize as a bribe to the ignorant Lydgate, the narrator intercedes to modify what otherwise might be a hasty judgment. I have quoted the following passage previously, but it is worth restating here. Of Bulstrode, she remarks:

> He did not measure the quantity of diseased motive which had made him wish for Lydgate's goodwill, but the quantity was none the less actively there, like an irritating agent in his blood. A man vows, and yet will not cast away the means of breaking his vow. Is it that he distinctly means to break it? Not at all; but the desires which tend to break it are at work in him dimly, and make their way into his imagination, and relax his muscles in the very moments when he is telling himself over again the reasons for his vow. (695–6)

"Is it that he distinctly means to break it? Not at all." Here again the narrator disconnects the desire from the intention. Compare this passage to the one I considered earlier in my discussion of *Adam Bede*, in which the narrator imagines the reasons why Arthur does not tell Irwine of his budding romance with Hetty. That passage, too, considers the problems of motives and the unacknowledged and unrecognized agents "secretly busy" and ends with the tonally enigmatic statement that "The human soul is a very complex thing" (172). Indeed it is, and this later *Middlemarch* passage on motive and intents is richer and more complex; it exposes Bulstrode's state of mind, and it suggests something about Eliot's as well. Eliot made several changes to the passage in manuscript, and her changes indicate second and third thoughts. In manuscript, what follows the sentence ending with "like an irritating agent in his blood" are these stops and starts: "A Neapolitan made a vow to the Virgin never to use his stiletto, and thought of casting it into the sea, but ended by locking it in a box which he buried, putting the key" (695, n.3) and then "When a man has resolved to break the law no more yet" (695, n. 3). The sentence that now reads "A man vows and yet will not cast away the means of breaking his vow" had once read "A man vows and yet provides an escape for himself in case he should break" (695, n. 3). Eliot breaks off at "break," not pursuing this analogy. But she actualizes the story of the stiletto, the sea, and the locked box in *Daniel Deronda*, where Gwendolen has possession of a dagger and, afraid of the use she might make of it, locks it in a box and casts the key into the sea. Soon thereafter, she puzzles over how to get the box open without the key. As I will argue later, the fact that Eliot turns what in *Middlemarch* is an internal crisis into an external act in *Daniel Deronda* is of some importance to the later novel, but what I want to highlight about the revised and final text of *Middlemarch* is how, having cut out these potentially diverting analogies, Eliot gets us to focus on the difference between intent and desire— of "meaning to" and desiring—and the physiology of desire. Desire works through the blood and then on the imagination and the muscles. Two chapters earlier, the narrator makes use of the same kind of simile. Speaking of Bulstrode's more indirect misdeeds, the narrator likens them to "the subtle muscular movements which are not taken account of in the consciousness, though they bring about the end that we fix our mind on and desire" (675). Another manuscript revision bespeaks the care Eliot took to represent the differences between different states of mind. She registered, for instance, a difference between "a murderous feeling" and a "murderous impulse." In her manuscript, she offers this version of yet another passage in which the narrator lays open Bulstrode's mind: "Bulstrode felt himself getting irritated at the persistent life in this man, whom he would fain have seen sinking into the silence of death: imperious will had a murderous feeling toward this brute life, over which will, by itself, had no power" (696). The final version substitutes "stirred murderous impulses" for the vaguer "had a murderous feeling" (686, n. 7) I note too that Eliot distinguishes between will and impulse in the final version. The will stirs the impulse. In these passages, the impulses Bulstrode feels begin to appear uncontrollable as does his imagining of the death itself. The narrator has already asserted that Bulstrode "could not but see the death of Raffles, and see in it his own deliverance" (692), and in this we may recall Hobbes's humane claim that it may not be a sin to imagine the death "of him, from whose life he expecteth nothing but dammage and displeasure." The longer Bulstrode imagines and desires Raffles's death, the more his mind and body appear to act of their own accord. So when he forgets to tell Mrs. Abel to stop giving Raffles the opium, the text raises the obvious question: did he mean to forget—to break his vow? Not at all. But when, remembering, he walks not to the patient's room but into his own, he crosses a threshold (figuratively and literally), and what follows closely on the heels of this now intended omission (for which Bulstrode tellingly makes an excuse: "it was excusable in him, that he should forget part of the order, in his present wearied condition" [697]) is an act.

In Bulstrode Eliot gives us an intention that is and is not separated from or under the control of a desire and a state of mind in which a person might simultaneously mean and not mean to do a given act. Eliot appears to choose her terms carefully later as well, in the passages in which Lydgate must consider whether the now-exposed Bulstrode had tried to bribe him and whether Raffles was treated improperly. In the final text, the relevant passage reads: "He now felt the conviction that this man who was leaning tremblingly on his arm, had given him the thousand pounds as a bribe, and that somehow the treatment of Raffles had been tampered with from an evil motive" (718). An earlier draft had considered "for an evil purpose" or "from an evil intent" as possible alternatives to "from an evil motive" (718, n. 9). Eliot does not use the vocabulary of state of mind with complete consistency. In dramatizing Bulstrode's state of mind, she does not produce the kind of document that sets out definitions and labors to put all these matters straight, as John Austin was doing. Yet she is in touch with the differences among an intent and a motive and a desire, differences to which both Austin and later James Fitzjames Stephen had persistently returned.[30] Stephen saw the confusion between motive and intent as characteristic of the eighteenth century and pushed hard to clarify the difference in the nineteenth. Intention is an element of a crime, Stephen argues. Motive may be evidence that a crime has been committed but is not necessary for a finding of guilt or innocence. Whether or not an accused desired the death of his alleged victim, what has to be proved is that he intended to do the act that caused that death. The distinction itself is hard to maintain. In his essay "Act, Intention, and Motive in the Criminal Law," Walter Wheeler Cox questions the discriminations made between these terms: "Is the difference fundamental or is *motive* merely a name for a certain kind of intention?"[31] But both "purpose" and "intent" impute to Bulstrode an intentionality that the more distant "motive" avoids. When Eliot exchanges purpose and intent for motive, she makes room for the possibility of a mind that both intends and does not intend. Whereas before, with Madame Laure, Eliot represented this paradox theatrically, now she plays this possibility out not theatrically but novelistically, through the narrative voice, and we see it suddenly not only as a paradox but as a function of the way minds work. The narrative turns an anomalous event into a function of the human mind. Her knowledge extends to all minds, and she posits her specific and special knowledge to make a general statement. Yet the difficulties of understanding state of mind are such that at the decisive moment in the scene, the moment at which Bulstrode hands over the key to the wine cabinet, she closes off our access to his thoughts. Like the key to the locked box that the Neapolitan considers throwing into the sea but ends up keeping, this key seems to emerge quite on its own through Bulstrode's door. I have long been struck by Eliot's use of the passive voice at the crucial moment: "Here a key was thrust through the inch of doorway" (698). Eliot shifts point of view from Bulstrode to Mrs. Abel, and the most we get to know of Bulstrode at this juncture is the cryptic "A struggle was going on within him" (698), a struggle that Eliot does not represent. By making use of the passive voice, the novel dramatizes Bulstrode's own turning away from responsibility—the key appears as if from out of nowhere, not by his own hand. But I think too that by keeping us outside of Bulstrode at this moment, Eliot renders that which Blackwood and Wittgenstein both gesture toward. Her shifting to Mrs. Abel's point of view does not suggest her shiftiness but rather a recognition that there is a great deal about *mens rea* that cannot be known, either by the actor himself or even by the narrator who has such special access to his mind. The human soul *is* a very complex thing. Finally, though, there is not just a desire or an intention or even an omission, but an act—"Here a key was thrust through the inch of doorway"— and the act makes a significant difference to both a moral and a legal judgment of Bulstrode. True, Eliot complicates the act by making its consequences ambiguous, but the conjunction of the mind and the act determines his legal and moral responsibility. Desiring Raffles's death is not enough. The activity of the mind in itself—with all its struggles and its complex turns—does not on its own bring onto Bulstrode moral or legal opprobrium, for, as Hobbes remarked, to take pleasure in the imagining of the death of one's enemy is "a Passion so adherent to the Nature both of man, and every other creature, as to

make it a Sinne, were to make Sinne of being a man." Moreover, by not representing Bulstrode's intention to kill Raffles (except as such an intention manifests itself in the act of handing over the key to Mrs. Abel or in the omission
to tell her about when to stop administering the opium), Eliot effectively couples the intention with the act: they emerge (albeit passively) at the same time.
As a result, it becomes more difficult to say that moral culpability inheres in
an intention to kill since Eliot does not give the intention absent the act (or
omission). Without collapsing the distinction between an intention and an
act, Eliot attaches responsibility to an intention coupled with an act.

Writing to Alexander Main in December of 1872, G. H. Lewes entertained
this family friend with "a rare sample of moral judgment" in the form of a response to Bulstrode's treatment of Raffles:

> A lady known to Mrs. Lewes declared to another lady that she couldn't
> get to sleep at night thinking of "poor Bulstrode and all that had fallen
> on him after sitting up to tend to that wretch. . . . and *I don't believe* it
> was the Brandy that killed him. . . . Well, now Bulstrode has *nothing left*
> *but Christ!*" Isn't this just the sort of touch George Eliot would have in-
> vented? To me it is strangely significant. 1st of the profoundly real im-
> pression the book makes. 2nd of the profoundly immoral teaching
> that passes for religious. Here is a pious woman so utterly blinded by
> the fact of Bulstrode's piety that it prevents her from seeing what Bul-
> strode himself sees, the guilt which that piety has not prevented. In
> real life where motives are hidden and deeds admit of many explana-
> tions, we would expect the mere fact of piety to lead judgment astray,
> and make people seek for any but a criminal explanation; but there we
> see that in the face of the clearest evidence in the sinner's own con-
> fession, the guilt is not believed in![32]

Lewes is right to take the unnamed lady to task for her blinding piety, but he
himself takes some liberties with the text, blinded perhaps by the impression
the book has made on him and by his own pieties, for while Bulstrode makes
something that is called a confession to his wife, it is, after all, a silent one
("His confession was silent, and her promise of faithfulness was silent" [741]),
and, more tellingly, eleven chapters later we have Bulstrode imagining his
wife as "a tribunal before which he shrank from confession and desired advocacy" (811). What becomes clear is that Bulstrode has *not* fully confessed — either to God or to his wife:

> His equivocations with himself about the death of Raffles had sus-
> tained the conception of an Omniscience whom he prayed to, yet he
> had a terror upon him which would not let him expose them to judg-
> ment by a full confession to his wife: the acts which he had washed
> and diluted with inward argument and motive, and for which it
> seemed comparatively easy to win invisible pardon — what name
> would she call them by? That she should ever silently call his acts

Murder was what he could not bear. He felt shrouded by her doubt: he got strength to face her from the sense that she could not yet feel warranted in pronouncing that worst condemnation on him. Some time, perhaps—when he was dying—he would tell her all: in the deep shadow of that time, when she held his hand in the gathering darkness, she might listen without recoiling from his touch. Perhaps: but concealment had been the habit of his life, and the impulse to confession had no power against the dread of a deeper humiliation. (811)

Lewes's mocking of the lady reader makes clear what the novel does not make quite so clear. There is the ambiguity of "yet" here (he clears himself with God, "yet he had a terror upon him which would not let him expose [his equivocations] to judgment . . . to his wife," "she could not yet feel warranted in pronouncing the worst condemnation on him") that shows up elsewhere in connection with Bulstrode and his guilt: just before Raffles's death, we have Bulstrode in prayer again, but he "had not yet unravelled in his thought the confused promptings of the last four-and-twenty hours" (698); after Raffles's death, as he rides past the Green Dragon (where the Raffles story has already leaked out), the narrator intercedes to tell us that "He had not confessed to himself yet that he had done anything in the way of contrivance to this end; he had accepted what seemed to have been offered" (706). "Yet" obviously gives us the promise of a full confession to come. "Yet" leaves room in Bulstrode for a sense that he still does not recognize his own acts and intentions. Would Lewes have likewise mocked Blackwood when he remarked of Bulstrode that "In the struggle that night he, as it were, hardly knew himself that he was committing murder when he gave the brandy"? Oddly, Lewes gives the ambiguity of the deed as against the clarity of the feeling, as if in contradiction to the sense in *Daniel Deronda* of the simplicity of act as against the complexity of feeling. Why does Lewes believe we see more than we do and that we see it more clearly than we do? In large part what Lewes calls up in his letter is the access we have in the novel (as we do not have in what he names "real life") to the state of mind of the actor.

"He went through a great deal of spiritual conflict and inward argument to adjust his motives, and make clear to himself what God's glory required" (698), we are told. "Adjust" is the key word for Bulstrode, deflating the high spiritual tone with which he goes about his business, and gestures toward Bulstrode's hypocrisy—the sham of his piety. One complication here, though, is that Bulstrode (as Blackwood himself suggests in his letter) is not the usual religious hypocrite. Hypocrisy requires an intent to sham, a pretense of being what one is not. Bulstrode's hypocrisy is instead of a piece with his hypochondria: there is an element of genuine (if self-serving) belief in that which is not so. Even as the story of Bulstrode's past is fully unfolded before us, the narrator softens her judgment of him in terms like those Blackwood introduces in his letter:

There may be coarse hypocrites, who consciously affect belief and emotions for the sake of gulling the world, but Bulstrode was not one of them. He was simply a man whose desires had been stronger than his theoretic beliefs, and who had gradually explained the gratification of his desires into satisfactory agreement with those beliefs. If this be hypocrisy, it is a process which shows itself occasionally in us all, to whatever confession we belong, and whether we believe in the future perfection of our race or in the nearest date fixed for the end of the world; whether we regard earth as a putrefying nidus for a saved remnant, including ourselves, or have a passionate belief in the solidarity of mankind. (606)

The power of this passage arises out of its ability to step back from its subject and give us a more profound sense of what Bulstrode is and is not. The narrator assumes the right to judge and the readiness to be judged, since what else does *Middlemarch* often produce if not a passionate belief in the solidarity of mankind? That there should be more than one kind of hypocrisy (and maybe this is not even the right word, as her "if this be hypocrisy" suggests) — a conscious gulling and something less intentional — means that Bulstrode's way of moving through his desires to his resolutions and to his actions should not be simplified. Whatever we call this "process," it means that Bulstrode's later dealings with Raffles cannot be easily marginalized as the workings of the hypocritical mind. What Eliot reveals in Bulstrode is no conscious shamming — which makes judgment of him all the more difficult.

Tellingly, Eliot engineers the circumstances of the case so that Bulstrode cannot be held legally responsible for Raffles's death. While there are metaphoric trials in *Middlemarch*, the novel contains no formally legal trials, as there are in *Adam Bede* and *Felix Holt*.[33] Eliot's interest in *Middlemarch* is in the power of public opinion as the arbiter of guilt and innocence: the legal is taken up into the social. In George Eliot's *Quarry for Middlemarch* — the notebook in which she sketched out her plans for chapters and ideas for scenes in the novel — she makes clear to herself that she needed to be careful in her Bulstrode sections to elude the law's reach: "The idea which governs the plot about Bulstrode is, that there is nothing which the law can lay hold of to make him responsible for; the Nemesis is wrought out by the public opinion determined against him."[34] This particular Greek figure has appeared before, in Irwine's sermonizing to Arthur Donnithorne on unpitying consequences. In Bulstrode's case, the divine retribution arises out of the public opinion of Middlemarch society and is decidedly extralegal. Public opinion, though on a smaller scale, is also Arthur Donnithorne's Nemesis. The significant matter in both cases is that both become cases for some other kind of justice. "That there is nothing that the law can lay hold of to make him responsible for" does not necessarily mean that Bulstrode should not be held legally responsible for Raffles's death or would not be held legally responsible for that death if the law had access to his interior life the way we do. In the novel itself, the lawyer Hawley (exchange the *H* for an *R* and you have an anagram for "lawyer") reaches the same conclusion after he has done a quick bit of private eye work: "Mr. Hawley was not slow to perceive that there was no handle for the law either in the revelations made by Raffles or in the circumstances of his death" (707). So too when Raffles threatens Bulstrode, Bulstrode replies contemptuously, "the law has no hold on me either through your agency or any other" (519). In the same scene, the law itself becomes difficult to grasp. Trying to come up with the last name of Ladislaw, Raffles ruminates, "'It began with L; it was almost all l's" and as he gets closer he has "a sense that he was getting hold of the slippery name. But the hold was too slight, and he soon got tired of this mental chase" (520). Since Ladislaw's name actually proffers the law as its suffix, one wonders whether Eliot imagines not only that the law cannot lay hold of Bulstrode, but also that it cannot be laid hold of (I note that "laid" and "law" are tucked into "Ladislaw"), that is, that the ambiguities and complications in the law itself make it difficult to pin down. What makes Bulstrode so slippery that the law cannot get hold of him, and what makes the law so elusive that *we* cannot lay hold of it? Why might this be of such importance to Eliot that she calls it "The idea which governs the plot about Bulstrode"? The controlling feature of this plot is that it eludes the legal process. But the novel can do what the law cannot. Though the law cannot lay its hands on Bulstrode, the novel can, and though we may find the law elusive, we can lay our hands on the novel.

One obvious answer to the first question—why can't the law get its hands on Bulstrode—is that there are evidentiary difficulties here, alluded to in the novel but never worked out in any detail. None of the evidence that Hawley the lawyer gathers from his interviews with Mrs. Abel, Bulstrode's servant and the figure who actually administers opium and brandy, or any of the information he gleans from the impromptu medical inquiry he convenes appears (according to the novel) to amount to a legally cognizable case. One supposes that these are the kind of "real life" problems to which Lewes refers when he considers the cases in which "motives are hidden and deeds admit of many explanations," though in this case the people who investigate are not at all blinded by Bulstrode's piety; instead his piety makes them more eager to find him guilty. Their efforts, however, prove fruitless. "Nothing could be legally proven" (707) is the conclusion Farebrother reports. There are references throughout to a lack of evidence. The work Eliot does through Hawley to convince us that the law cannot get a handle on Bulstrode makes one feel how hard she labors to put Bulstrode out of the law's reach. The purposive references to the interviews with Mrs. Abel and the medical experts demonstrate that the external facts of Bulstrode's conduct have been exposed but the law can go no further, and, as with Madame Laure, it is left without a handle. The medical experts Hawley calls on—a Monsieurs Toller and Wrench—review "all the particulars which had been gathered from Mrs Abel in connexion with Lydgate's certificate, that the death was due to *delirium tremens*; and the medical gentlemen, who all stood undisturbedly on the old paths in relation to this disease, declared that they could see nothing in these particulars which could be transformed into a positive ground of suspicion. But the moral grounds of suspicion remained" (709). Though the treatment Raffles received goes on record—both the brandy and the opium—neither overt act can be seen as hastening the death of Raffles, since old-style medical men perceive that treatment as correct. The difficulty in no small part arises out of problems of causation. Since Raffles got the treatment others would have prescribed, how can it be said to have caused his death, any more than Toller and Wrench have caused the death of other patients similarly treated? What remain hidden are not Bulstrode's acts but his intents.[35]

The juxtaposition of the positive and the moral ("they could see nothing in these particulars which could be transformed into a positive ground of suspicion. But the moral grounds of suspicion remained") is the juxtaposition of the legal and the moral, as the tag 'positive' had come to be associated with the legal, and particularly with the work of Bentham and Austin. On this distinction the criminal jurisprudential writers are clear: "Sinful thoughts," writes Fitzjames Stephen, "and dispositions of mind might be the subject of confession and of penance, but they were never punished in this country by ecclesiastical criminal proceedings."[36] The reasons for such a limitation on even the ecclesiastical criminal law's reach are, as Stephen remarks, "obvious," for

> If it were not so restricted it would be utterly intolerable; all mankind would be criminals, and most of their lives would be passed in trying and punishing each other for offences which could never be proved.
>
> Criminal law, then, must be confined within narrow limits, and can be applied only to definite overt acts or omissions capable of being proved, which acts or omissions inflict definite evils, either on specific persons or on the community at large.[37]

The postmortem chapters in *Middlemarch* invite readers to register a difference between the moral and the legal bases of judgment. So immersed have we been in Bulstrode's desire for and imagination of Raffles's death that when it finally comes, we might well conclude that we are to judge him based on thoughts inaccessible to legal investigation, and that judgment must be moral and not legal. The novel provides what all the legal investigation humanly imaginable cannot provide. Eliot, then, exposes the law's limits in *Middlemarch* but not in the service of an agenda that would insist that states of mind should determine questions of responsibility, whether moral or legal. Though she separates the moral from the legal, she still asserts the importance of the act to moral and legal judgments and to the judgments of the novel itself. While Hawley's investigations are introduced to assert a distinction between the legal and the moral, in reasserting this distinction through Hawley, Eliot does not base judgment of Bulstrode on the immorality of his thought alone. If we convict him, we do so based on a conjunction of an act and a state of mind. The profound complexities we experience in and through Bulstrode's mind make us uncomfortable with a judgment based on thought in and of it-self. Eliot is not satisfied—and does not satisfy us—with Bulstrode's prayers for death. Nor is she satisfied with Bulstrode's decision to withhold Lydgate's instructions from Mrs. Abel. She moves from the prayer to the omission and ultimately to an overt act. We still need the act. Why? Because the state of mind is so complex? Because even when we are given access to that mind, am-biguity remains? I think so. True, difficulties arise out of the ambiguity of the status of the act as well. According to Lydgate, the administration of brandy and opium would constitute a bad act; according to Toller and Wrench, it would not. Eliot crafts this case so that she can exclude the necessity of bring-ing Bulstrode before a formal legal tribunal (as she had done with Hetty Sor-rel in *Adam Bede* and Felix Holt), but it is still the conjunction of a state of mind and an overt act that she puts before us for judgment. The moral judg-ment, as Eliot represents it, is still in touch with the necessities of an act, and so too is her own narrative. The unfolding of Bulstrode's mind in these chap-ters allows Eliot to explore fully the possibilities of the mind's activity, and that extraordinary exploration returns her to the very limits the law lives by. Responsibility—legal, moral, and novel—needs an act.

⚔ Attempts and Temptations ⚔

Eliot calls Book 7 of *Middlemarch* "Two Temptations" and so sets up the crises that both Lydgate and Bulstrode endure. Chapter 66 of Book 7 be-gins with one of two epigraphs from *Measure for Measure*: "'Tis one thing to be tempted, Escalus, / Another thing to fall" (656)[38] and thus prepares us for the temptations of Lydgate first, as he wanders into the Green Dragon and con-siders gambling as a means of escape from the financial hardships into which he has already fallen. Fred Vincy also finds his way to the gaming tables at the Green Dragon, and his way of justifying his return to the tables (following so closely on the heels of his promises to Mary Garth) is revealing: "Fred did not enter into formal reasons. . . . It is in such indefinable movements that action often begins" (660). The movements the narrator has in mind here are them-selves movements of mind, figurations of the activity of the mind that turn into action.

The indefinable movements of mind spurred on by temptation and trans-formed into action put us in mind not just of one meaning of temptation but of another as well. For while the "Two Temptations" may be those associated with Lydgate and (a bit later) with Bulstrode, Eliot may also be thinking of two senses of temptation itself: of temptation and attempt. After all, the tempta-tion the key to the wine cabinet holds for Bulstrode is more than a temptation. If the brandy hasn't killed Raffles, Bulstrode may still have attempted to mur-der him. But even before Eliot conceived of Bulstrode, she imagined another case of what might be classified as attempted murder: Caterina Sarti's thwarted attack on Captain Wybrow in "Mr. Gilfil's Love-Story." Caterina's is a case Eliot would rewrite more thrillingly in her last great work, *Daniel Deronda*. In rewriting Caterina's murderous scenes, Eliot makes evident her sustained interest in this knot of issues that concern the relations between the internal and external elements of crime, for the scenes once again require us to confront the boundaries of criminal responsibility and the novel's power to challenge those boundaries.

The *OED* lists "temptation" as a meaning of *attempt*, which falls out of use after the seventeenth century. And the two citations given in support are to the Bible and *Paradise Lost*. The connection between a temptation and an attempt is, above all, Miltonic. Adam to Eve in Book 9 wants both senses. Why, asks Adam, do I want you to stay with me? Not because I do not trust you on your own,

> but to avoid
> Th' attempt itself, intended by our Foe.
> For he who tempts, though in vain, at least
>   asperses
> The tempted with dishonour foul.[39]

There are shifts from subject to verb and back to subject as the attempt becomes "tempts" and creates "the tempted." Attempts move the tempted to attempts of their own. Adam's logic enacts the closeness of the temptation and the attempt. Making "intended" the third term shows *attempt* as primarily a crime of intent, though when the attempt becomes the temptation in *Paradise Lost*, it becomes an action—an aspersion that fouls the tempted. Milton is everywhere in Eliot, as is Shakespeare, so this constellation may have been in her mind. We should consider further that *attempt* (meaning both "attempt" and "temptation") works its way into *Measure for Measure*, an important source for Book 7 of *Middlemarch*, and quite in touch itself with the relations of intention and action, temptations and attempts. In the first scene of act 3, the duke, disguised as the friar, introduces Isabella to his plan to snare Angelo for Mariana: "The maid will I frame, and make fit for his attempt" (3.1.255–6). Posing as Isabella, Mariana is the temptation provoking Angelo's attempt. Paradoxically, Angelo's attempt at deflowering Isabella remains only an attempt, even though he completes the act. There remains something curious, however, in the way Isabella grandly excuses Angelo by turning his attempt back into an intent:

> My brother had but justice,
> In that he did the thing for which he died;
> For Angelo,
> His act did not o'ertake his bad intent,
> And must be buried but as an intent
> That perish'd by the way. Thoughts are no
>   subjects,
> Intents but merely thoughts. (5.1.447–53)

Isabella moves from act to intent to thought—indeed, "merely thoughts"—as she attempts to deactivate Angelo's attempts. But attempts are not so easily dismissed.

In his version of *Kenny's Outlines of Criminal Law*, J. W. C. Turner explains that "the essence of attempt lies in the intention and not in the acts done in furtherance thereof. In other words the criminality is constituted more by the *mens rea* than by the *actus reus*."[40] However, all crimes require an *actus reus*, and attempts are no exception: "Since," Turner continues, "*mens rea* alone is not a crime the courts required a physical element also; but in this case only as much was necessary as could establish the *mens rea*."[41] The overt act becomes, then, nothing more than an evidentiary requirement, and even an innocent act (one not forbidden by law—for example, giving an opium addict brandy) could be construed as evidence of a criminal attempt. Significantly, it was not until 1801 that attempts became crimes recognized at common law.[42] By midcentury, Victorian jurists were working out definitions of *attempt* in earnest. Writing of such efforts, Fitzjames Stephen notes that "The law as to what amounts to an attempt is of necessity vague. It has been said in various forms that the act must be closely connected with the actual commission of the offence, but no distinct line on the subject has been or as I should suppose can be drawn."[43] Holdings were challenged as casting the crime of attempt too broadly or too narrowly. *R v. Eagleton* (1855)[44] was attacked as providing too confined a definition. Others criticized *R. v. Chapman* (1849)[45] and *R. v. Dugdale* (1853)[46] as producing a definition that might capture the morally questionable but not the legally culpable.[47] Attempts became sites at which the disputed boundaries of criminal responsibility shifted one way and then another.

The confessional scene between Caterina Sarti and Maynard Gilfil in the anticlimactic scenes near the end of "Mr. Gilfil's Love-Story" from *Scenes of Clerical Life* (1858)—a collection of three stories and Eliot's first published work of fiction—was not the finest Eliot ever wrote. It is instead a mechanical and overemphatic early version of one of the last scenes she would write—that between Gwendolen and Daniel Deronda in which Gwendolen confesses her own wish to murder Grandcourt. "Mr. Gilfil's Love-Story" concerns the unhappy life of Mr. Gilfil, the hapless parson who falls for Caterina Sarti, the adopted daughter of Sir Christopher Cheverel and his wife. Gilfil's love is unrequited, for Caterina has eyes for the more attractive but less morally upright Captain Wybrow. Wybrow recklessly woos Caterina but engages himself to the more suitable Miss Assher. The scenes following Caterina's betrayal are the ones on which I will focus. I briefly turn to this early story not only as evidence that in one of her first pieces of fiction Eliot engaged questions of act and state of mind but also to explore how she engaged them, or, as happens in the story, backed off from engagement. Provoked by Miss Assher's cruelty and feeling utterly deceived and exposed by Wybrow, Caterina heads for her appointed meeting with him (where he intends to persuade her to marry Mr. Gilfil), and in her hand is a weapon—a dagger, in fact.

Her act—the taking up of the weapon—transforms her, but Eliot allows us to witness the transformation only in its external manifestations: "See how she rushes noiselessly, like a pale meteor, along the passages and up the gallery stairs! Those gleaming eyes, those bloodless lips, that swift silent tread, make her look like the incarnation of a fierce purpose, rather than a woman."[48] The gothic melodrama here keeps us at a distance from this woman scorned—how close could one get, after all, to a pale meteor?—until Caterina is no longer woman but Purpose. Eliot turns a mental state into a physical one: purpose becomes Purpose. The description itself is told from the point of view of an outsider. We are to observe what she looks like, how she rushes noiselessly; we are commanded to see the eyes, the lips, to listen for the silent tread. Eliot does not create or invite us into Caterina's inner life at this moment. There is an emphatic and dramatized deliberateness represented, even in the syntax: "she darts to the cabinet, takes out the dagger, and thrusts it into her pocket. In three minutes more she is out, in hat and cloak. . . . Her hand is in her pocket, clenching the handle of the dagger, which she holds half out of its sheath" (155). We do not have access to her thoughts, so we infer her purpose from her action. That we are on the verge of a murder seems all but assured.[49] Then, finally, we are for a moment in her mind as she imagines confronting Wybrow:

> Wait, wait, O heart!–till she has done this one deed. He will be there–he will be before her in a moment. He will come back towards her with that false smile, thinking she does not know his baseness–she will plunge that dagger into his heart. (155)

The deliberateness of her actions preceding this description coupled with this clear statement of intent ("she will plunge that dagger into his heart") certainly lead us to believe that the intents will become acts—that the purpose will be carried out—which makes the narrative intervention at the scene's end all the more unexpected: "Poor child! poor child! she who used to cry to have fish put back into the water—who never willingly killed the smallest living thing—dreams now, in the madness of her passion, that she can kill the man whose very voice unnerves her" (156). The renaming of purpose as dream is less than persuasive, as if to take what has been moved from imagination to a determined purpose back into imagination. To invoke "the madness of passion" is to invalidate the intention itself, since madness calls intent into question. The narrator's intervention annuls it. Moreover, there is no danger that Caterina will actually murder Wybrow since, alas, he is already dead. Not only is purpose nullified, but the attempt itself is made impossible. A dead man cannot be murdered.

That Caterina's crime is impossible (Wybrow has been struck down by undiagnosed heart disease before she arrives) makes the scene even more complex (verging, perhaps, on the preposterous). The Victorian criminal case law on impossible attempts was inconsistent. Following *R. v. Collins*,[50] a case in which a defendant was acquitted of the charge of attempted theft because the pocket he tried to pick was empty, Fitzjames Stephen takes up this problem in *A History of the Criminal Law of England*:

> The most curious point on this subject is the question whether, if a man attempts to commit a crime in a manner in which success is physically impossible, as for instance if he shoots at a figure which he falsely supposes to be a man with intent to murder a man, or puts into a cup pounded sugar which he believes to be arsenic, or attempts to pick an empty pocket, he has committed an attempt to murder or to steal. By the existing law he has committed no offence at all, and this is also the law of France, and I believe of other countries, the theory being that in such cases the act done merely displays a criminal intention.[51]

But the holding in *Collins* conflicted with that of an earlier case, *R. v. Goodchild*,[52] in which the accused who had helped a nonpregnant woman induce a miscarriage was found guilty of the statutory offense of administering medicine with intent to procure a miscarriage. Finally, *Collins* was explicitly overruled in *R. v. Ring* in 1892.[53] What should the law do with an intent that cannot be fulfilled? Should such an accused be held responsible for such an intent?

When Caterina faints in Gilfil's arms, having run from the sight of the dead body, he finds the dagger in her pocket. His first thought is that she intended suicide, but then it occurs to him that she might have had another use for the weapon in mind. He examines the weapon and seeing no trace of blood takes it from her. Finally, though, Caterina must answer to Gilfil for the dagger, and she confesses all. When Gilfil asks, "'Did you mean to kill yourself, Tina?'" (178), she replies simply, "'To kill *him*'" (178). But Gilfil knows her real intentions, apparently, and knows them in a way that echoes the narrator's own earlier interventions. "Tina, my loved one, you would never have done it," Gilfil explains to Caterina. "God saw your whole heart: He knows you would never harm a living thing. He watches over His children, and will not let them do things they would pray with their whole hearts not to do. It was the angry thought of a moment, and He forgives you" (178). An angry thought, yes, but not an intention to kill. Indeed, it is not God but the narrator who has interceded on Caterina's behalf and who knows enough to instruct us as to what could and could not be done (note that Gilfil all but echoes the narrator in his invocation of the "living thing"), but even that intervention cannot keep us from voicing an objection or two, and Eliot allows those objections to be voiced through Caterina. She is quick to correct him, quick to point out that she "had had such wicked feelings for a long while" (178), and then, in words that will later find their way into *Daniel Deronda*, "'when I meant to do it . . . it was as bad as if I had done it'" (179). What follows is Gilfil's pressuring Caterina to see it his way, but it is also the narrator's way, and Caterina is not the only one feeling the pressure. We notice the accretion of Gilfil's explanations. Caterina is exonerated first because thoughts are not deeds ("we mean to do wicked things that we never could do,"179), then Gilfil concedes that she has done something but pleads mental incapacity ("you hardly knew what you did" [179], Gilfil claims, echoing the narrator's assertion of Caterina's madness earlier), and then finally he invokes a provocation defense ("he gave you provocation. . . . When people use us ill, we can hardly help having ill feeling toward them. But that second wrong is more excusable" [179]).

Like the Victorian cases on impossible attempts, Eliot's early story produces some ambivalence about the responsibility that should attach to Caterina based on a bad intent coupled with an act that cannot be carried out. The story tries to nullify intent by giving Gilfil the right excuses: Caterina was temporarily insane, or she never really did intend to kill Wybrow. More pressing still is the fact that her intents had and could have no consequences. Gilfil sermonizes:

> "Our thoughts are often worse than we are, just as they are often better than we are. And God sees us as we are altogether, and not in separate feelings or actions, as our fellow-man sees us. We are always doing each other injustice, and thinking better or worse of each other than we deserve, because we only hear and see separate words and actions. We don't see each other's whole nature. But God sees that you could not have committed that crime." (179)

Here he takes the pressure off intents—they can be bad, but they do not make us bad—and considers that God is the best judge because he alone knows all our feelings and conduct (our "whole nature")—though I note here that like God, the narrator too sees inside Caterina and has told us that she could not and did not do this act. Gilfil will not fully absolve her of guilt, nor does the story as a whole, but he and it go a very long way toward recognizing that intentions alone may not make us even morally responsible. However intense, they are not acts. Although Eliot allows her Caterina to act, in the end she, like Isabella in *Measure for Measure*, turns the attempt back into an intent, and then all but voids the intent itself.

When Eliot rewrites this scene at the end of *Daniel Deronda*, the statements of the earlier story have turned into the questions Deronda poses to himself: "Was she seeing the whole event—her own acts included—through an exaggerating medium of excitement and horror? Was she in a state of delirium into which there entered a sense of concealment and necessity for self-repression?" (642). And then aloud to Gwendolen: "And it has all remained in your imagination. It has gone on only in your thought. To the last the evil temptation has been resisted?" (644). Deronda finds this ambiguity too painful to bear, and when Gwendolen names herself as a murderess, he insists on the exonerating narrative: "Don't torture me needlessly. You have not murdered him. You threw yourself into the water with the impulse to save him. Tell me the rest afterwards. This death was an accident that you could not have hindered" (642–3). Though Deronda presses Gwendolen to accept this version, she is not so easily silenced as is Caterina by the resistance of her father confessor. Gwendolen will tell her story to Deronda.

What is fascinating about the playing out of this scene between Gwendolen and Deronda is the way it does and does not replay in dramatic form what has already been presented as part of an interiorized narrative two chapters earlier. Why two versions? Are we invited to compare the narrative to the dramatic versions of the scene to confirm the truthfulness of Gwendolen's confession to Deronda? This is partially right, since Gwendolen shapes the story she tells Deronda in ways that have as much to do with her relation to him as with the truth of what actually happened on the yacht. She depends on him to guide her spiritually, and he is oppressed by the weight of her conscience. What Deronda fears most is that Gwendolen is too truthful, that she tells him more than he wants to know. Beyond these considerations, I think the two chapters manifest a formal ambivalence that itself may demonstrate Eliot's ambivalence about the consequences of the imaginative work of the inner life and its representation in a specifically criminal context. In chapter 54, we are commanded to "enter into the soul of this young creature as she found herself . . . on the tiny plank-island of a yacht" (623). Right from the start of the chapter, Eliot attends to an inner/outer distinction, as in the first paragraph when she notes that we find Gwendolen "at the very height of her entanglement in those fatal meshes which are woven within more closely than without, and often make the inward torture disproportionate to what is discernible as outward cause" (622)—a sentiment that is all but repeated a few paragraphs later ("The embitterment of hatred is often as unaccountable to onlookers as the growth of devoted love, and it not only seems but is really out of direct relation with any outward causes to be alleged," 626). These proto-Jamesian sentences set us up for the turbulence of the inner as against the relative stability of the outer. Moreover, as the earlier chapter brings us into Gwendolen's murderous thoughts it invites us to take the thoughts for real action. Yet at the crucial moments the narrator turns us away from Gwendolen. Eliot goes very far here, but she also pulls us up short. Something isn't safe. What is safer is the representation of the scene as confession—as testimony—because it preserves the ambiguity of what actually passed through Gwendolen's mind in those moments. When in her confession Gwendolen pronounces herself guilty as charged, Deronda feels relief that "the word 'guilty' had held a possibility of interpretations worse than the fact" (648). This is a strange reaction. Because the word is necessarily ambiguous, Deronda takes comfort in that ambiguity. In the word "guilty" spoken by Gwendolen, Eliot moves us out of the purely internal. To turn thoughts into speech is to reintroduce a relation between internal and external that requires interpretation. We are called on to look again, as is Deronda, not for the evil thought but for the evil deed.

Chapter 54 of the novel begins with an epigraph from Shelley's tragedy *The Cenci*:

> The unwilling brain
> Feigns often what it would not; and we trust
> Imagination with such phantasies
> As the tongue dares not fashion into words;
> Which have no words, their horror makes them dim
> To the mind's eye.[54]

In Shelley's poem these lines are spoken by the son of Count Cenci, a tyrant who has murdered his other sons and committed incest with his daughter, only to be purged of his crimes by a corrupt, bribe-accepting pope. Here Giacomo is imagining a parricide but refusing to speak the word. A few lines later, he teeters on the edge of thinking himself a murderer already, since his thoughts have made him so ("I am as one lost in a midnight wood, / Who dares not ask some harmless passenger / The path across the wilderness, lest he, / As my thoughts are, should be—a murderer").[55] The odd use of "trust" in the earlier passage probably attracted Eliot. Thoughts can be trusted because they embody that which might never actually be done, and yet in the later passage, which she does not quote, thoughts are not so trustworthy. Still in these lines Shelley gives the imagination a freedom not allotted to speech. So too does Eliot, for early on in the novel we get to know of Gwendolen that

> those who feared her were also fond of her; the fear and fondness being perhaps both heightened by what may be called the iridescence of her character—the *play* of various, nay, contrary tendencies. For Macbeth's rhetoric about the impossibility of being many opposite things in the same moment, referred to the clumsy necessities of action and not to the subtler possibilities of feeling. We cannot speak a loyal word and be meanly silent, we cannot kill and not kill in the same moment; but a moment is room enough for the loyal and the mean desire, for the outlash of murderous thought and the sharp backward stroke of repentance. (72)

The allusion is to Macbeth: "Who can be wise, amazed, temp'rate and furious, / Loyal and neutral in a moment?" (2.3.123–4). The contraries at work in this passage are potent—fear and fondness, loyalty and enmity, attack and repentance. Perhaps the most powerful opposition in play here is that of action (including speech) to feeling and thought, the former having to conform itself to "clumsy necessities" while the latter moves between and among "subtler possibilities." Eliot's reference to *Macbeth* performs many functions, not only to evoke a murder in mind but also to suggest, perhaps, her belief in the superiority of the novel to the drama, since the novel's third person narrative can represent feeling in language without requiring a character to express through voiced speech his or her own feelings. Here too imagination is "trusted" in ways that speech and action are not. Eliot promotes the freedom and possibilities of feeling and thought over the limitations of speech and action, and in so doing she creates not simply an opposition but a hierarchy.

Where in *Adam Bede* the narrator compares the "narrow limits of our personal lot" and the "still, creative activity of our thought," in this passage from *Daniel Deronda* the narrator, by invoking the clumsiness of action as against the subtleties of feeling, represents a more detailed relation between the inner world of possibility and the outer world of necessity. As much as this relation takes in, it does not take up the ambiguities of language itself. When Eliot insists, reasonably enough, "We cannot speak a loyal word and be meanly silent," she performs an adverbial sleight of hand, for while it is true that we cannot speak and be silent in the same moment, we can speak a word that is both loyal and mean and we can be loyally or meanly silent. In short, the line between thought and action is not so easily drawn. The contradictions of a thought complicate our relations to the ensuing action. Consider how at the end of this passage the thoughts take on the attributes of the acts themselves ("the outlash" and the "backward stroke"). What is at stake are the relations of the one to the other.

"A moment is room enough for the loyal and the mean desire, for the outlash of murderous thought and the sharp backward stroke of repentance": certainly Eliot works to create this tension in Gwendolen floating around in the Mediterranean with Grandcourt. Eliot explicitly figures these two battling impulses as Temptation and Dread: "In Gwendolen's consciousness Temptation and Dread met and stared like two pale phantoms, each seeing itself in the other—each obstructed by its own image; and all the while her fuller self beheld the apparitions and sobbed for deliverance from them" (628). Help is figured in "the form of Deronda's presence and words" doing battle against "the form of some fiercely impulsive deed" (628). The center of interest in this chapter is clearly the activity of Gwendolen's mind. Thought is so active that we can well imagine this thought outside of Gwendolen. It has all the violence of an act. But at the moment that Grandcourt actually falls into the water, the narrator averts her eyes. At the crucial juncture, when Gwendolen's mind is working at its most fevered pitch, the narrative focus abruptly shifts. We get, suddenly, a very beautiful passage from a travelogue:

> They were taken out of the port and carried eastward by a gentle breeze. Some clouds tempered the sunlight, and the hour was always deepening toward the supreme beauty of evening. Sails larger and smaller changed their aspect like sensitive things, and made a cheerful companionship, alternately near and far. The grand city shone more vaguely, the mountains looked out above it, and there was stillness as in an island sanctuary. Yet suddenly Gwendolen let her hands fall, and said in a scarcely audible tone, "God help me!" (635)

It is not until Gwendolen's confession to Deronda that we get her description of her own thoughts in vivid detail:

> "And because I felt more helpless than ever, my thoughts went out over worse things—I longed for worse things—I had cruel wishes—I

fancied impossible ways of—I did not want to die myself; I was afraid of our being drowned together. If it had been any use I should have prayed—I should have prayed that something might befall him. I should have prayed he might sink out of my sight and leave me alone. I knew no way of killing him there, but I did, I did kill him in my thoughts."

She sank into silence for a minute, submerged by the weight of memory which no words could represent.

"But yet all the while I felt that I was getting more wicked. And what had been with me so much, came to me just then—what you once said—about dreading to increase my wrong-doing and my remorse—I should hope for nothing then. It was all like a writing of fire within me. Getting wicked was misery—being shut out for ever from knowing what you—what better lives were. That had always been coming back to me in the midst of bad thoughts—it came back to me then—but yet with a despair—a feeling that it was no use—evil wishes were too strong. I remember then letting go the tiller and saying "God help me!" But then I was forced to take it again and go on; and the evil longings, the evil prayers came again and blotted everything else dim, till, in the midst of them—I don't know how it was—he was turning the sail—there was a gust—he was struck—I know nothing—I only know that I saw my wish outside me." (647–8)

Eliot gives us Gwendolen's own representation of the vigorous activity of the thoughts "as they went out over worse things," but there are gaps here too in this dash-heavy passage. Deronda notices but does not press Gwendolen to fill in such gaps: "She unconsciously left intervals in her retrospect, not clearly distinguishing between what she said and what she had only an inward vision of" (645). It is as if she assumes Deronda has access to her interior life as we, with the narrator, have had access to that life, and yet, at the very moment Gwendolen exclaims "God help me!" we are outside of her, as we are outside of her here as well, listening with Deronda to the narrative she tells of the moments just before Grandcourt's death. She calls up the "evil prayers" and the "bad thoughts," but they are not presented to us here as acts. They remain internalized and partially hidden, as does "the weight of memory which no words could represent." By putting us outside of her at the crucial moment, Eliot begins to reaffirm both the distinction and the necessity of the distinction between a thought and a deed.

Unlike Captain Wybrow, Caterina Sarti's betrayer in "Mr. Gilfil's Love-Story," Grandcourt is very much alive when Gwendolen is imagining his death. She has willed his death, and then it has happened. Yet Gwendolen's dramatic telling of the story to Deronda reinscribes a distinction between a thought and a deed. To distinguish the thought from the deed, Eliot produces an act: Gwendolen, we suddenly learn, has been carrying a dagger around with her. She reports to Deronda:

"It had all been in my mind when I first spoke to you—when we were at the Abbey. I had done something then. I could not tell you that. It was the only thing I did toward carrying out my thoughts. They went about over everything; but they all remained like dreadful dreams—all but one. I did one act—and I never undid it—it is there still—as long ago as when we were at Ryelands. There it was—something my fingers longed for among the beautiful toys in the cabinet in my boudoir— small and sharp, like a long willow leaf in a silver sheath. I locked it in the drawer of my dressing-case. I was continually haunted with it, and how I should use it. I fancied myself putting it under my pillow. But I never did. I never looked at it again. I dared not unlock the drawer: it had a key all to itself; and not long ago, when we were in the yacht, I dropped the key into the deep water. It was my wish to drop it and de- liver myself. After that I began to think how I could open the drawer without the key; and when I found we were to stay in Genoa, it came into my mind that I could get it opened privately at the hotel." (644)

Confessing to Deronda, she wants to tell all, to reveal finally every incriminat- ing fact, and it is telling that this fact—that she hid a dagger—is the one she has kept from him for so long. She is weighted by this act, and is much at- tuned to the difference between what had been in her thoughts only and what she did ("I had done something then," "it was the only thing I did," "I did one act—and I never undid it"). Of this unexpectedly disclosed fact, Carol Christ remarks, "the revelation that Gwendolyn [*sic*] has been carrying a dagger with her to murder her husband is a unique instance in Eliot's fiction of withhold- ing information central to our understanding of the heroine's predica- ment."[56] Carol Christ calls the disclosure an "afterthought, a rationalization for the intense revulsion Gwendolyn experiences."[57] For Carol Christ, the late revelation "by particularizing that fear [that Gwendolen may do something impulsive] after Grandcourt's death by informing us that Gwendolyn actually had been tempted to murder her husband, Eliot associates Gwendolyn with a new and much more serious potential for evil."[58] I agree, and Carol Christ's use of "tempted" calls up the more serious "attempt" that the dagger mani- fests, but though Carol Christ mentions Eliot's interest in the relation be- tween intention and act, that concern drops out so that she can make a larger point—not unlike that which During makes in his analysis of the case of Madame Laure—that Eliot censures the aggression Gwendolen feels toward Grandcourt. But moving beyond the censuring of that aggression, there is the question of the act itself against the thoughts that produced it. By calling at- tention to Gwendolen's statement that she kept the knife in her possession (even if under lock and key), Eliot reasserts the necessity of an act in appor- tioning responsibility. She *has* done something. The "one act," as Gwendolen calls is, reinscribes the line between thought and act. Gwendolen had taken a step toward murdering her husband, the first step in an attempt to kill him, though she desists. Still, her nascent attempt is important since it distinguishes thought from act.

But no sooner does Eliot draw that line then she contests it again. After learning of Grandcourt's death, the very first thing Deronda does on Gwendolen's behalf is to get "a formal, legally-recognized statement from the fishermen who had rescued Gwendolen" (641). That statement confirms the accident and the probability that Grandcourt had not known how to swim. The legal formalities are quickly set aside, but not the legal questions, for Deronda enacts the roles of priest, defense attorney, and judge. If, as Henry Alley proposes, it does not matter whether there was a murderous desire or a murderous act, why does Deronda predicate the question of Gwendolen's guilt on whether her desire begot an act? Deronda works hard to prove beyond a reasonable doubt that Gwendolen's evil thoughts remained thoughts:

> It seemed almost certain that her murderous thought had had no outward effect—that quite apart from it, the death was inevitable. Still, a question as to the outward effectiveness of a criminal desire dominant enough to impel even a momentary act, cannot alter our judgment of the desire; and Deronda shrank from putting that question forward in the first instance. He held it likely that Gwendolen's remorse aggravated her inward guilt, and that she gave the character of decisive action to what had been an inappreciably instantaneous glance of desire. (648–9)

The ambiguity of the "outward effect" makes Deronda's meaning hard to decipher here. Does he mean that it seemed almost certain that Gwendolen never acted on her murderous thought or that the murderous thought itself did not somehow will the boat to turn against Grandcourt? Note, too, the uncomfortableness of the "seemed almost," where there is a world of difference between almost certain and certain. The "almost" opens up a question for Deronda, "a question as to the outward effectiveness of a criminal desire dominant enough to impel even a momentary act." This is a weird and weirdly awkward sentence, since it raises a question only to say that such a question is morally irrelevant since, whatever the answer, it "cannot alter our judgment of the desire." Then the sentence turns back on itself: "and Deronda shrank from putting that question forward in the first instance." We move from a question about an act to a statement that judgment depends on desire and then back to a question about an act that is never raised. Instead, Deronda makes a quasi-judicial holding, which produces a definitive gap between decisive action and an "inappreciably instantaneous glance of desire." Whatever the nature of Gwendolen's desire, it is neither inappreciably instantaneous nor a glance. The fear that Gwendolen's thought was as powerful as an act remains very much alive here.

Then, as if to contain the tension just created, in the very next chapter Deronda gives a version of the events that the novel does not challenge. When

Gwendolen raises the question that Deronda refuses to raise himself, Deronda's answer puts the matter to rest, though not with the kind of defini- tive language one might expect:

> If it were true that he could swim, he must have been seized with cramp. With your quickest, utmost effort, it seems impossible that you could have done anything to save him. That momentary murderous will cannot, I think, have altered the course of events. Its effect is con- fined to the motives in your own breast. Within ourselves our evil will is momentous, and sooner or later it works its way outside us—it may be in the vitiation that breeds evil acts, but also it may be in the self- abhorrence that stings us into better striving. (650–1)

There are reservations—in the "seems," "I think," and "may be"s—that reflect the limitations of Deronda's exculpation. The "I think" of "That momentary murderous will cannot, I think, have altered the course of events" destabilizes this pronouncement. She is acquitted not beyond a shadow of a doubt but be- yond a reasonable one. Even though an evil will is still attributed to Gwen- dolen, it is attributed to all of us as well, even Deronda himself. The move from her motives to the motives within "your own breast" to that "within our- selves" sounds rather a false note with respect to Deronda (an evil will in Deronda seems unlikely), yet the voice we register at the end of the passage is not Deronda's but the narrator's. This version gets its authority from the closeness of Deronda's voice to the narrative voice, a voice we hear in the shift from "your" to "our." I am interested, too, in the use of "vitiation" in this sen- tence, since the word and its cognates appear elsewhere in Eliot's works but always through the voice of the narrator. Of the fallen Arthur Donnithorne in *Adam Bede*, the narrator insists: "No man can escape this vitiating effect of an offence against his own sentiment of right" (315), then twice in *Romola*: first of Savonarola: "No man ever struggled to retain power over a mixed multitude without suffering vitiations."[59] and then of Tito's need for Tessa's company, compared to "the oncoming of a malady that has permanently vitiated the sight and hearing."[60] In each passage, vitiating or vitiation or being vitiated is a corrupting or corruption that the narrator imagines, and imagines as hap- pening without exception, as the similar syntax suggests: "No man can es- cape" and "No man ever struggled." Deronda speaks with the voice of the nar- rator, but, unusually, he offers arguments in the alternative. The evil will produces either the vitiation that breeds evil or the self-abhorrence that brings at least the possibility of good.

In third and final series of G. H. Lewes's *Problems of Life and Mind*, which Eliot prepared for publication after his death, he writes:

> To imagine an act is to rehearse it mentally. . . . Hence it is that a long- meditated crime becomes at last an irresistible criminal impulse. In- dulgence in the imagination of the act has grooved a pathway of dis- charge, and set up an abnormal excitability in this direction, which,

like a neuralgia, is for ever irritating by its restless impulses, and can only be quieted by discharge on the motor organs.[61]

Lewes, like his more famous friend Herbert Spencer, makes a case for the relations and at times the identicality of the psychological and the physiological. The idea that the psychological could have a profound impact on the physiologic was not new. Reviewing the works of Alexander Bain, John Stuart Mill remarked, "when we consider, for example, the case of all our stronger emotions, and the disturbance of almost every part of our physical frame, which is occasioned in these cases by a mere mental idea, no rational person can doubt the closeness of the connexion between the functions of the nervous system and the phenomena of the mind."[62] But of special interest to me is the way the psychological has become physiological, as if the act has already happened in the thought, such that the act itself is finally anticlimactic. When "to imagine" reemerges as "to rehearse," we have moved from the preactual to the actual. Lewes names the rehearsal as the crime itself: the "long mediated crime" that turns back into a criminal impulse. "Indulgence" introduces a moral element recalling *Adam Bede* and Irwine's naming of Arthur Donnithorne's "single act of selfish-indulgence" (his seduction of Hetty) so that we know that the imagination of this act is wrong, but wrong as a bad act in itself as it "has grooved a pathway of discharge" until the discharge itself is inevitable.

All of this should put us in mind of Gwendolen and her long-meditated crime, her rehearsal of the crime in her mind, and then the possibility of discharge. But Eliot makes matters even more complex by putting at least one of the "acts" in question in the form of an omission and in so doing makes the boundary between thought and act even harder to identify. How, after all, can we use the language of act—of "outward effect" (to use Deronda's words) or of "discharge" (to use Lewes's)—when what is at issue is a forbearance:

> "I saw him sink, and my heart gave a leap as if it were going out of me. I think I did not move. I kept my hands tight. It was long enough for me to be glad, and yet to think it was no use—he would come up again. And he *was* come—farther off—the boat had moved. It was all like lightning. 'The rope!' he called out in a voice—not his own—I hear it now—and I stooped for the rope—I felt I must—I felt sure he could swim, and he would come back whether or not, and I dreaded him. That was in my mind—he would come back. But he was gone down again, and I had the rope in my hand—no, there he was again—his face above the water—and he cried again—and I held my hand, and my heart said, "Die!"—and he sank; and I felt "It is done—I am wicked, I am lost!" (648)

By coupling a bad intention with an omission, Eliot actualizes the intent and deactualizes the 'act' (since it is an omission to act). Why this coupling? Again Eliot pushes up against the limits of moral and legal responsibility. Indeed,

the moral and legal ramifications of omissions interested Eliot, for she introduces them in both *Daniel Deronda* and in *Middlemarch*. Eliot would have
been well informed about the distinction between acts and omissions under
law, having been sent Macaulay's "Notes to the Indian Penal Code" by James
Fitzjames Stephen during the composition of *Middlemarch*. In his discussion
of crimes by omission in the second edition of *A General View of the Criminal
Law*, Fitzjames Stephen reports that "Lord Macaulay has some curious remarks on this in his notes on the Indian Penal Code. I lent the book to Mrs.
Cross (George Eliot) for her novel of *Middlemarch*. It approaches the subject,
but in *Daniel Deronda* a much more striking illustration of the principle is
given."[63] The principle given is this: "that the omission must be an omission
to discharge a legal duty. An omission to do what it is not a legal duty to do is
not crime at all, even if the omission causes, and is intended to cause death.
It is not a criminal offence to refuse to throw a rope to a drowning man, or to
allow a man to walk over a cliff, or into a quicksand when a word of advice
would save him."[64] "Notes to the Indian Penal Code" was returned to Fitzjames Stephen in November 1872 not by Eliot herself but by G. H. Lewes. The
letter that accompanied the returned book describes the pleasure with which
Lewes apparently read both the Code and Macaulay's notes on the Code, and
Lewes refers in particular to Macaulay's notes about crimes of omission.[65] In
note M of Macaulay's *Notes* — "Offences Against the Body" — Macaulay attends
to the problem of the "evil effects" produced by omissions rather than by
acts. Macaulay distinguishes omissions that should be punished as acts and
those that should not be by concluding that one can be punished only for
omitting to do an act that one has a legal (and not a moral) duty to perform; so
a parent has a duty to a child, a doctor to a patient, even a jailer to a prisoner.
But then, as there often is in the criminal law, we come up against problem of
line-drawing:

> It will hardly be maintained that a man should be punished as a mur-
> derer because he omitted to relieve a beggar, even though there might
> be the clearest proof that the death of the beggar was the effect of this
> omission, and that the man who omitted to give the alms knew that
> the death of the beggar was likely to be the effect of the omission. . . .
> It is difficult to say whether a penal code which should put no omis-
> sions on the same footing with acts, would produce consequences
> more absurd or revolting. There is no country in which either of these
> principles is adopted. Indeed, it is hard to conceive how, if either were
> adopted, society could be held together.
>
> It is plain, therefore, that a middle course must be taken; but it is
> not easy to determine what that middle course ought to be. The ab-
> surdity of the two extremes is obvious. But there are innumerable in-
> termediate points; and wherever the line of demarcation may be
> drawn, it will, we fear, include some cases which we might wish to ex-
> empt, and will exempt some which we wish to include.[66]

How and whether society "could be held together": here is one of Eliot's deepest concerns, and what is at stake for Eliot is her ability to convince her reader of the absolutely essential part that duty plays in the functioning of any society. Should society find a negligent parent who fails to feed his child as re-pugnant as the tight-fisted man? Both cause the death at issue. Eliot herself gets into the thick of this dilemma in her handling not only of Gwendolen and Bulstrode but, surprisingly, of Dorothea Brooke's uncle as well. Mr. Brooke is well beyond the reach of the criminal law, and his omissions are eas-ily distinguishable from those of Bulstrode and Gwendolen, but Bulstrode strangely haunts Brooke. By all accounts, Brooke is a negligent landlord, and his refusal to revalue his properties and to undertake repairs means that his tenants suffer terrible hardships. In an attempt to push her uncle into action, Dorothea speaks passionately to him about the condition of his farmers: "Think of Kit Downes, uncle, who lives with his wife and seven children in a house with one sitting-room and one bedroom hardly larger than this table! — and those poor Dagleys, in their tumble-down farmhouse, where they live in the back-kitchen and leave the other rooms to the rats" (379). What makes Brooke's stinginess and hypocrisy different from Bulstrode's or less open to the kind of social judgment and punishment that Bulstrode endures? The difference is framed primarily in terms of intent. As Sir James says, "'Brooke doesn't mean badly by his tenants or any one else, but he has got that way of paring and clipping at expenses'" (373). That the law cannot reach Brooke frustrates no one, except perhaps Dorothea and the drunken Dagley. That Brooke should have to suffer Dagley's unpleasant attacks or those of oth-ers (and be humiliated by them) is justified, but he will never be exiled. Bul-strode's, is of course, another story. As is Gwendolen's.

Acts emerge in George Eliot's texts in ways that suggest that Eliot affirms the necessity of an act in assigning moral and legal responsibility, though she also submerges acts in ways that turn all our attention back to intention. Gwendolen eludes the law's grasp, to be sure, but Eliot puts Deronda and her readers in the position of figuring out whether she has committed a legally cognizable crime in not helping her drowning husband. And yet, bad inten-tions do not stand entirely on their own in Eliot's world. By dramatizing the manner in which desires become temptations while intentions become at-tempts, Eliot makes the act not only evidence of but also that which solidifies a very unstable mental state; the act, then, remains important to questions of legal as well as moral culpability. So where does this leave us? In *The Real Life of Mary Ann Evans*, Rosemarie Bodenheimer observes of Eliot that her "narra-tive strategies were determined by the desire to achieve an interpretive justice and flexibility that she knew to be unavailable in life. It is a kind of justice in which verdicts are endlessly deferred, their outlines blurred and complicated by further twists of perspective, further bits of evidence, further explana-tions."[67] What Bodenheimer persuasively calls up here is the openness of Eliot's fiction, and, tellingly, Bodenheimer situates that openness in the con-text of evidence and verdicts and justice. While I agree with Bodenheimer that Eliot's justice has a flexibility that the law itself cannot afford, Eliot does not offer judgment without bounds. Although not limited by the boundaries of the criminal law, Eliot respects them. Her cases remain connected to the criminal law's requirement of an act (or omission). That she complicates those acts so thrillingly as she intertwines them with her narrative representations of desire and intent shows how invested she is in these relations. But as she illuminates the complications the criminal law must handle in negotiating between acts and intents, so too is her writing illuminated by them.

⚛ FOUR ⚛

James Fitzjames Stephen and the
Responsibilities of Narrative

Writing to his friend Lord Lytton in September 1884, Fitzjames Stephen described his current enterprise, a book on one of the best-known stories of English imperialistic tyranny in the eighteenth century. What was absorbing Stephen were the events surrounding the execution of the Maharajah Nuncomar on August 5, 1775, and the participation in those events of Warren Hastings, the then governor-general of Bengal for the East India Company (he presided from 1772 to 1781), and Sir Elijah Impey, the first chief justice of the newly formed Supreme Court of Calcutta and chief justice at the trial of Nuncomar.[1] Here is how Stephen reports those events to Lytton:

> It is a most curious story with some of the characteristics of a legal novel about it. First Nuncomar accuses Hastings of bribery, then Hastings accuses Nuncomar of conspiracy. Then a native, one Mohun Persaud, accuses Nuncomar of forgery who is hanged on this accusation and acquitted on the one charge by Hastings. Then Impey is accused of judicial murder before the House of Commons, which after hearing evidence throws out the bills against him. By arrangement I hope to make the whole thing as clear as glass, and in particular to throw light on [illegible] false and ignorant accusations.[2]

Stephen gives a characteristically efficient summary of these complicated legal proceedings, of which I will give a fuller account in the second half of this chapter, though a few more details might prove useful here. Nuncomar—a wealthy and powerful Brahmin, who took advantage of and was taken advantage of by East India Company officials—brought corruption charges against Governor-General Hastings, one of Nuncomar's longtime enemies.

Hastings, in effect, countersued. While neither the charges Nuncomar leveled against Hastings nor Hastings's against Nuncomar issued in a conviction, these accusations arguably gave rise to a case that ended in Nuncomar's execution. A third and seemingly unconnected party, Mohun Persaud, charged Nuncomar with forgery in connection with an amazingly convoluted probate matter. Persaud, as a representative of the estate of a man named Bollakey Doss, claimed that Nuncomar had bilked the estate out of some assets by forging a bond that gave him (Nuncomar) title to certain East India Company bonds. The criminal case against Nuncomar was the result of Persaud's civil suit. Nuncomar was tried as a forger, found guilty, and executed by hanging. One of the judges who heard Nuncomar's case was Sir Elijah Impey, a schoolmate of Hastings. When Hastings and Impey returned to England some years later, Nuncomar's execution became the centerpiece of Edmund Burke's attack on the Company's pattern of corrupt (even murderous) governing practices and on Hastings and Impey in particular. Having sentenced Nuncomar to death, Impey was then tried in Parliament as a judicial murderer. He was ultimately acquitted—as was Hastings. Though acquitted in the eighteenth century, Impey was convicted in the nineteenth, not by a court but by the widely read and broadly influential 1841 *Edinburgh Review* essay by Thomas Macaulay entitled simply "Warren Hastings." By his own account, this story and Macaulay's retelling of it took hold of Stephen and provoked him to write *The Story of Nuncomar and the Impeachment of Sir Elijah Impey*.

Writing *The Story of Nuncomar* was a different kind of undertaking than anything Stephen had yet attempted. While not wholly distinguishable from other texts he had already written, including *A History of the Criminal Law of England*, it was unique in its focus on a single historical event and its breadth and depth of analysis. The case also had, as Stephen suggests in his letter to Lytton, a certain shape that readers would recognize as novelistic. Stephen moves with caution around the idea of this "story" as a novel (it contains "some of the characteristics of the legal novel," not all), but he registers the "characteristics" nonetheless. What those characteristics are we must infer from the story Stephen tells, one that offers a complex plot, multiple accusations and suspects, and the thrill of both an execution and an attack on and later acquittal of the reputed executioners—executioners who happened to be the chief justice and the governor-general themselves. The story offered the attractions of conspiracy and dirty dealings. Central to this story is the unexpected twist that transforms Impey from judge to suspected murderer.

I pause here on the word "story" because it is the word Stephen uses not only in his epistolary description but also, more emphatically, in the title of what was his last major work: *The Story of Nuncomar and the Impeachment of Sir Elijah Impey*. In his biography of his older brother, Leslie Stephen finds evidence that Fitzjames Stephen had reported his intention to write "a monograph upon "'Impey's Trial of Nuncomar.'"[3] At some point, the "trial" became a story. The parallel structure of the titular phrases leads us to expect *The Trial of Nuncomar and the Impeachment of Sir Elijah Impey* (setting off the earlier formal procedure against the later one); instead Stephen presents the first part of his work as a story. The breadth and intrigue of the plot that the history presented invite Stephen to imagine the novel possibilities of the story he is himself telling.

But Stephen was no novelist, a fact he announced without hesitation to Lord Lytton in a letter six months later: "Your poem to you is exactly what my Impey has been to me. I have no doubt it must be an absorbing thing to make poems and novels. I never at any time in my life had the least humour for either pursuit."[4] Yet in an April 29 letter to Lady Egerton, with whom he was also corresponding about his "Impey," he more readily imagines, at her suggestion, himself as a legal novelist:

> You suggest that I should write a novel. I should like some parts of it well enough, but the young women, and the love making, and the social scenes would completely beat me, and I am afraid that my criminal trial, and the murder, and the detectives, and the historical personages would be so much too much like the real things, that nobody would read them. I have sometimes thought, in reading a novel, that it would be amusing to try to write a scene or two in one's own words. I am sure, for instance, I could make the conversations in Scott's novels, those, I mean which are not written in broad Scotch—infinitely more like real conversations than they are at present, but I do not think that I should get further than that in the way of novel writing.[5]

Strikingly, it is during the period in which Stephen composes *The Story of Nuncomar and the Impeachment of Sir Elijah Impey* that this nexus of talk about novel-writing occurs. That Stephen should be thinking about novel-writing just as he is putting together his *Story of Nuncomar* is evidence that the relations between facts and fictions were much on his mind. His own aesthetic preference for what he calls in his letter the "real" aligns him with George Eliot. Eliot achieves what Stephen knows he cannot: a realistic treatment in a novel of "the young women, and the love making, and the social scenes," a treatment producing a true representation that is not merely a mimetic representation. Leaving aside the condescension one registers in this characterization of novel-writing (reminding us, by the way, of Eliot's own attack on such work in "Silly Novels by Lady Novelists"), Stephen sees a tension between a representation that wants to recreate reality and one that is interesting or entertaining—readable, in fact. His "novel" would not be read. Nor was *The Story of Nuncomar* much read, while Macaulay's "Warren Hastings" maintained a substantial readership.

In this chapter I explore Stephen's attacks on the novels of Dickens and Charles Reade—novels that openly promoted social reform—as well his attacks on the literary-historical essays of his friend and mentor Thomas Macaulay, essays that claim the authority of a fact-based narrative but also take advantage of the license allowed to fictional narratives, the license to enter into the interior life directly. This exploration forms the basis of my reading of Stephen's *The Story of Nuncomar and the Impeachment of Sir Elijah Impey*. In his own narrative, Stephen specifically identifies Macaulay's essay "Warren Hastings" as the work that defined opinion on the participants and events surrounding Nuncomar's trial, and Stephen criticizes Macaulay's historico-fictional versions of Hastings, Impey, and Nuncomar. His criticisms expose what Leslie Stephen also saw as a typical strategy of Macaulay, one that converted "conjectures into irresistible illusions."[6] Part of this critique necessarily attends to the way Macaulay's essay, as well as other treatments of Hastings, Impey, and Nuncomar, represent mental states. Stephen assesses the narrative movement from external acts and circumstances to the interior life to reveal how freely these had been (and continued to be) manipulated by those who had created the myth of Hastings and Impey. The stated assumption behind Macaulay's influential essay on Warren Hastings is that Chief Justice Elijah Impey conceived of himself and behaved as Hastings's ever-loyal friend—a friend who was also Hastings's toady. In short, Macaulay avers that in all that Impey did with respect to the trial and execution of Nuncomar he was motivated by his desire to please Hastings. Having made that assumption, Macaulay fictively enters Impey's mind to show his readers that these were his desires and that those desires became legal actions. A finding of guilt, then, against Impey is (as a result) close to irresistible, because we have not only his actions but, seemingly, direct access to his state of mind. With these consequences in front of him, Stephen tries to set out the responsibilities and the limits of crime narratives, whether fictional or nonfictional. Yet even in so doing he implicitly challenges them. He himself slides into the minds of the figures he represents, showing by example how readily narrative takes liberties with and in the minds of others. This slippage does not make Stephen's text indistinguishable from the others he critiques, but it does expose points of contact between these texts, and it suggests the difficulties in and the dangers of the representation of the interior life in narratives about criminal responsibility.

In our own century, we take for granted that writers of nonfiction will make use of fictional privileges, and particularly the privilege of narrating the thoughts of another. Gerard Genette notes this state of affairs without much ado, citing as evidence a 1988 article from the *New Yorker* in which the narrator blithely enters the mind of a would-be purchaser of Van Gogh's *Irises*. Genette names both the "New Journalism" (which the *New Yorker* article represents) and the "nonfiction novel" as prime examples of types of nonfiction writing that use the apparatus of fiction.[7] Genette's observation is in service of an analysis that considers whether one can legitimately distinguish between fiction and nonfiction as narrative genres, and on what grounds. Central to Genette's discussion is the claim that "fictional narrative alone can give us direct access to the subjectivity of another."[8] But when nonfictional texts "borrow" (Genette's word) such a mode—what then? While I do not seek in this study to enter into the debate about whether one can speak of distinctions between fictional and nonfictional discourse, I do wish to consider the consequences of nonfiction's "borrowing" from fiction—or at least the consequences as Stephen saw them—when questions of criminal responsibility are at issue.

That factual and fictional elements might be combined in a single text would be nothing new to nineteenth-century readers. In his study of the origins of the English novel, Lennard Davis considers the protonovelistic forms that combined facts and fictions, particularly in the telling of stories about criminals.[9] That such hybrid forms as novels would grow to have significant social power made them a different kind of force to be reckoned with. Macaulay's essays, for instance, combine what Macaulay himself in his "History" names as the "art of narrative" and historical fact; they assume the license of the novel's third person narrator to go directly into the interior lives of the figures presented. More often than not, Macaulay obscures the fact that he is either creating the details of the story he tells or is inferring them from a specific piece of evidence. The inferences from act and circumstances to intent that Macaulay necessarily makes are, after all, matters of conjecture in Macaulay's narrative—as they are for the rest of us. But Macaulay on occasion operates like the third person narrator of *Middlemarch*, articulating his story as if he has access that we do not have; he articulates the story with what Stephen calls, generously, his "characteristic vigour" (2:43). Looking specifically at Macaulay's conclusion that Impey refused to commute Nuncomar's capital sentence "in order to gratify the Governor-General,"[10] Stephen says with uncharacteristic lenience, "It is to be regretted that Macaulay did not add a little skepticism to his other accomplishments, but his faith was great, and throve at times on what seems very insufficient food" (2:43)—faith, one surmises from the context of this example, in his ability to see into the figures he described and name with certainty their intentions. Much emphasis is placed on "in order to" in Macaulay's conclusion, so that the audience is left to understand that this author can know with certainty why Impey did what he did. Tellingly, Stephen objects to this strategy, not only in the historical work of Macaulay but also in the work of contemporary novelists who fictionalized actual criminal cases. Novels that assumed the authority of fact but took the license of fiction were as troubling to him as Macaulay's histories.

I do not seek, as Stephen did, to vindicate Impey or Hastings, nor do I make any claims about the accuracy of Stephen's description of the events he presents. I also recognize how deeply embedded the policies of British colonialism are in the rhetoric of *The Story of Nuncomar and the Impeachment of Sir Elijah Impey*. As evidence of Fitzjames Stephen's admiration for the colonial enterprise in India, his biographer brother Leslie Stephen reports that Fitzjames often turned to the Indian Empire as an example of England's excellence: "The 'whole fabric' of the Indian Empire, he says, is a monument of energy, 'skill and courage, and on the whole, of justice, and energy, such as the world never saw before.'"[11] Moreover, Stephen's work is sometimes racist. He was a man of his time, no doubt, and he shared the limitations of the time in which he lived, as we share the different limitations of the time in which we live.

I take up these limitations later, but I would note here that they do not invalidate the contributions Stephen's work does make. First, Stephen could not be counted on to defend the empire's officials under any and all circumstances. Stephen appeared as counsel for John Stuart Mill's Jamaica Committee, a group dedicated to prosecuting Governor Edward Eyre and General Nelson of Jamaica for the murder of George Gordon, a Jamaican of color who occupied a seat on the Jamaican legislature. Following an armed insurrection, Governor Eyre had Gordon arrested for his alleged participation in that insurrection. General Nelson then ordered Gordon's court-martial and authorized his subsequent execution.[12] Weighing in against the Jamaica Committee was the Eyre Defence Committee, which could boast Dickens, Tennyson, and Carlyle among its members. Though a friend and admirer of Carlyle (he was later an executor of Carlyle's will), Stephen argued that Eyre's conduct had been "violent, tyrannical and imprudent to a degree which I hardly imagined possible"[13] and that Eyre had hanged Gordon "not because it was necessary to keep the peace, but because it seemed to be expedient on general political grounds. This was what the law called murder, whatever the propriety of the name."[14] When Nelson alone was tried, Stephen attempted to convince the court before which he appeared (on the Committee's behalf) that Eyre should also be indicted.

But it is not only evidence of Stephen's criticism of the empire that makes his work on *The Story of Nuncomar* relevant. Stephen's response to Macaulay and to the authority Macaulay appropriated when he began to assume the license of novelists in his historical narratives illuminates the representational practices of legal, historical, and fictional texts in the nineteenth century. Moreover, the subject of the narrative Stephen examines—judicial murder—raises the stakes significantly, not only for Stephen, himself a high court judge, but for his audience. Stephen had long been interested in the representation of judicial murder, and particularly in its fictionalized representation, which he comments on in his 1859 review of *A Tale of Two Cities*. In this early review, he objects to Dickens's trial of Charles Darnay. After summarizing the trial as Dickens presents it, a trial in which "the judge shows great reluctance to allow any circumstance to come out which would be favourable to [Darnay], and does all in his power to get him hung, though the evidence against him is weak in the extreme,"[15] Stephen introduces a report of a trial of a French spy that appeared in the *State Trials* for 1780. So close are the trials that Stephen asserts that "it is difficult to doubt that one trial is merely a fictitious 'rendering' of the other." In quite a straightforward way, Stephen argues (in brief) that the reported trial was fairly conducted. "It is surely a very disgraceful thing," Stephen concludes, "to represent such a transaction as an attempt to commit judicial murder."[16] What are the responsibilities attendant on the representation of "such a transaction as an attempt to commit judicial murder"? I concede immediately that the historian and the novelist have different responsibilities, but what of the historical novelist? Has he no responsibilities? Or the novelist who explicitly seeks through his fictions to reform institutions by means of his fictions? What of Macaulay? As we ourselves debate the responsibilities of journalists who take such liberties, so too did Stephen consider the responsibilities of the powerful voices in his own time.

When Stephen censures Macaulay (and others) for producing his irresistible illusions in the course of his narrative on Hastings, Impey, and Nuncomar, he challenges the representational practices of these writers. But Stephen was not content with exposing the fictionalized work of Macaulay. As his friend Alfred Lyall reports in his 1889 book *Warren Hastings*, Stephen "undertakes to establish, by argument drawn from the general motives of human action, the moral certainty that Hastings was totally unconnected with the business and that the popular impression against him is utterly wrong."[17] Lyall views this strategy as ill-judged since Stephen's "demonstration is necessarily less conclusive, and we may reasonably hesitate about standing surety to this extent for the undiscoverable motives and behavior of a man in the situation of Hastings."[18] I will return to this passage when I take up Stephen's attempt to demonstrate "the moral certainty" that both Hastings and Impey were innocent of the charges made against them, but for now I want to note, as Lyall does, the shift in Stephen's argument. Stephen turns from arguing that Hastings and Impey could not be proved guilty to arguing that they were in fact innocent.

The attempt not only to correct but also to replace earlier versions of the story reveals the power and the limits of narratives (Stephen's narrative included) that call on external facts to read internal states. In "The Relation of Novels to Life" (1855), an early essay published in *Cambridge Essays*, Stephen found himself thinking about the limits of the novelist's capacities in representing his hero and, in particular, "the furniture of his mind":

> The hero of a novel may not be like the author. He may be ludicrously unlike; but it is hardly possible that the furniture of his mind should not have been supplied by the author from his own mental stores, although its arrangement in the two men may differ. The reason is, that we know our own feelings, but we only know other men's actions, and infer from them that they feel as we should feel if we were to act in the same manner. Therefore, when we are to describe feelings as they present themselves to us upon introspection, and not as we view them in, or infer them from, other people's acts, we must necessarily draw from ourselves, as we have no other models. I know that when A. was angry he spoke harshly, that B. imputed ungenerous motives, that C. misrepresented, and so on but I can only infer the feelings of A., B., and C., when they so acted, from my own experience of my own feelings when I acted in the same way. But though a writer cannot but invest characters with many of his own feelings, he by no means identifies himself with all or any of them.[19]

The distinction Stephen draws our attention to here is not a distinction between the novel and life, as the title of the essay promises; rather, it is between
thought and action. Although the idea (asserted again in this passage) that we
can infer conclusions about state of mind only from acts and circumstances is
a familiar one, I now need to attend to Stephen's supplement to that principle: "we only know other men's actions, and infer from them that they feel as
we should feel if we were to act in the same manner." We infer feelings from
actions, and the feelings we infer are those "we should feel if we were to act in
the same manner." The novelist's representation of his character's interiority
can come only from his experience of his own interiority, just as Stephen's attribution of interiority to his hypothetical acquaintances A., B., and C. must
arise out of his own experiences. But, I would add, our experiences of interiority are also shaped by vivid, detailed representations of the inner self, and in
the nineteenth century, the novel could disseminate its fully realized versions
of the inner life quite widely. The novel's representation of interiority becomes part of one's own experience of the inner self. So, I argue, the textual
evidence in *The Story of Nuncomar and the Impeachment of Sir Elijah Impey* suggests that Stephen furnishes the minds of Hastings and Impey with the impulses of his own mind, shaped by his own reading and other experiences. As
much as he seeks to make acts and circumstances deliver an impartial representation of this story—and particularly the story of motives and intents on
which so much hinges—they do not.

   We who live in an age in which objectivity is at best under suspicion and
at worst dismissed as a fantasy will not be surprised that Stephen's narrative
reveals as much about the objects under investigation as about the subject
who tells the story. Stephen's narrative raises questions both about how his
own relation to Impey and Hastings inflects his reading of motives and intents
and also about the complications of bringing fictional practices into nonfictional representations of interiority. Such questions engage critics in other
ways—ways that will for the moment take us away from Stephen and *The Story
of Nuncomar*. In their introduction to the collection of essays entitled *Questions of Evidence*, James Chandler, Arnold I. Davidson, and Harry Harootunian
consider issues surrounding interpretation more generally as they attend to
the "modern critical tradition . . . that grounds interpretation in *Einfuhlung*,"[20]
that is to say, in empathy. Using the thesis of Stephen Greenblatt's *Renaissance
Self-Fashioning*, Chandler, Davidson, and Harootunian imagine the ways the
empathetic feelings of the critic shape the representation of the object. In
short, the inner life of the critic determines the inner life of the object[21] Although the brief argument that the editors of *Questions of Evidence* mount is
inadequate to support the suggestion in their introduction that empathy con-
taminates "the motives underlying the critical tradition that has defended itself under the banner of interpretive empathy,"[22] their observations are germane to my own exploration of the way Stephen's narrative, particularly his
narrative of the desires and intentions of Hastings and Impey, at some moments turns their story into his own. Stephen imagines what a reasonable

man might have intended when faced with the choices Impey and Hastings were making, but the reasonable man looks more and more like Stephen himself. This result may indicate the particular limits of the representation of interiority, limits that it seems to me Stephen himself recognized and tried to illuminate. All representations are limited in one way or another. Yet so much turns on the stories we tell about interiority (in criminal law, this is often a matter of life and death), and so much is assumed in narratives about what can be known, particularly in the nineteenth century, that those stories warrant special attention.

Clearly these questions are relevant to many different undertakings, and one might explore the ways that different thinkers in different disciplines must take for granted the inferential nature of their findings. How do historians, philosophers, psychologists, or, for that matter, literary critics know what they know about the way people think? How do their own nonfictional narratives present this material? How do their narratives represent the limits of what can be represented? Each of these disciplines considers what its own responsibilities will be to the bases and limitations of speculation. In "Checking the Evidence: The Judge and the Historian," for example, Carlo Ginzburg asserts that the classification of Michelet's *La Sorcière* (noted by Ginzburg as a work "dismissed as a sort of novel at the time of its publication") as "one of the masterworks of nineteenth-century historiography" signals a "shift" that "has brought that peripheral, blurred area between history and fiction close to the center of contemporary historiographical debate."[23] Ginzburg analyzes different kinds of conjectures in different historiographical texts, and states simply and without paltering that "not all conjectures are equally acceptable."[24] My own investigation into Stephen's response to Macaulay overlaps with (though is not the same as) Ginzburg's treatment of what he calls the "blurred area." I pursue here questions about how representations of interiority have been challenged in legal and literary narratives of the Victorian period.

The interdisciplinary study of law and literature is itself beginning to attend to such questions more broadly. A panel entitled "Ways of Telling Legal Events," held at the 1998 meeting of the Working Group on Law, Culture, and the Humanities, provides a provocative example. As part of this panel three speakers delivered presentations arguing that the way law and legal events are told shapes what can be told about them. One of the panelists, the literary critic Peter Brooks, examined criminal confessions and the United States Supreme Court's attempts to make decisions about the admissibility of confessions hinge on whether or not such confessions could be deemed voluntary.[25] Brooks argued that the Supreme Court creates a story about voluntary and involuntary confessions by invoking a context within which the confession takes place. Certain external circumstances make the confession voluntary (reading a suspect his rights, access to an attorney) while certain other circumstances (closed room, absence of attorney, hot lights) mean that the confession has been coerced. But, argued Brooks, really all confessions are coerced, reflecting not acts of will but signs of shame and abjection. Brooks took the Court to task for its often naive attempts to read voluntariness through external circumstances. Commenting on Brooks's critique of the Supreme Court's opinions on the admissibility of confessions, Austin Sarat, the panel moderator, gave the following rejoinder:

> Brooks's paper makes a wonderful contribution in suggesting the limits of law's ability to read those interior states. Law does so, when it does so, by deducing them from the context in which particular tellings occur. The criminal confession is treated as voluntary if certain external attributes are present, and others are absent. And, far from indicating voluntariness and free will, confessions, Brooks argues, are indications of dependency, shame, and abjection. Here Brooks makes a point about the nature of a particular genre of telling. As important as that is, one might ask whether Brooks is any better at reading the inner life of the speaking subject than any other external observer would be. Applying Ewick and Silbey's rich analysis of categories of resistance, as well as Natalie Zemon Davis's writings on confessions in an earlier era, one might identify a whole range of interior states which might accompany such speech acts, from abjection to empty ritual, from voluntariness to a distanced performance.[26]

Sarat might have gone a bit farther with his argument here. As a skillful reader of and writer on Dostoevsky and Freud, Brooks has experienced *these* powerful representations of confession and of the inner lives of those who confess. These narratives shape his own narrative of the inner life of the confessant. Sarat's response to Brooks importantly brings to the fore not only the law's limited capacity to infer mental states, but the limitations with which all interpreters must contend.

These limits do not invalidate the stories about legal events that Brooks or Sarat or James Fitzjames Stephen tell, but they do provoke us to be more engaged in the multiplicity of possibilities, the shaping of those possibilities, and the limitations of what can be told. They also invite us to think more specifically about the different narrative strategies for representing the interior life, particularly since so much turns on those representations and the uses to which those representations are put. Does an author describe, relate, judge, characterize, or narrate a story of the interior life? What makes Stephen's work on *Nuncomar* relevant to work being done more recently is that it challenges us to ask a difficult question: how do we, how should we, weigh narratives of the interior life? In a courtroom, narratives representing states of mind rely on inferences from external acts and circumstances admitted into evidence. What makes one narrative any more or less accurate than another? I am not suggesting here that there are not some adequate principles on which we might, in comparing one narrative to another, decide that one was more believable than another. This kind of comparison happens practically every day of the year, as we decide (on and off the jury panel) between two (or more) versions of events, versions that very often (particularly in a criminal context) hangs on whether an act was or was not intentional, whether a party did or did not know some fact, whether a motive did or did not exist, and if so, whether it did or did not motivate the actor to do what he is alleged to have done. My goal in this chapter is not to set out those principles but to suggest that Stephen's narratives sometimes illuminate and sometimes mask how far narratives can and should allow us to make judgments about the interior life. The ways that narrative confers authority on the stories of the interior life are complex and require close attention.

The criminal law of the Victorian period was particularly attuned to such complexities. As the new Victorian disciplines of psychology and psychiatry intersected with the criminal law, judges and other jurisprudential thinkers had to cope with the stories medical experts told that claimed to see into the minds of men. But no one can see into the mind of man, as Justice Coleridge reminded his jury in *R. v. Monkhouse* (1849),[27] a case in which the defendant pleaded that at the time of the shooting at issue, he was intoxicated and therefore did not intend to murder the deceased, John Farmer Monkhouse. Coleridge remarked to his jury: "The inquiry as to intent is far less simple than that as to whether an act has been committed, because you cannot look into a man's mind to see what was passing there at any given time. What he intends can only be judged by what he does and says, and if he says nothing, then his acts alone must guide you to your decision."[28] Juries, like the rest of us must be 'guided' by external circumstances to some belief about the interior life. So too medical doctors. Denman's instructions to his jury in the case of Martha Prior, who was tried for infanticide and who mounted an insanity defense (claiming that she had been under the sway of an irresistible impulse) make clear his own resistance to the medical expert's testimony: "The judgment of the medical gentleman had been very rashly formed. How could one person dive into the mind of another, and express an opinion with regard to its being in an unsound state when there was no evidence of any alteration of conduct, or any circumstances in the case to show alienation of mind?"[29]

"The question as to the prisoner's state of mind," Stephen asserts in *A History of the Criminal Law of England*, "is frequently the question in the case, and no class of questions involves more difficult inquiries." These "difficult inquiries" may entail a set of narrative responsibilities, responsibilities like and unlike those that pertain when narrators make use, as they always must, of facts in their fictions.

⊰ Facts, Fictions, and James Fitzjames Stephen ⊱

The relations and responsibilities of fiction to fact had long been of interest to James Fitzjames Stephen, first as a reviewer of novels and, more specifically, of fact-based novels that sometimes manipulated facts in ways Stephen thought irresponsible. In one of his earliest reviews, "The License of Modern Novelists," Stephen takes on and up Dickens, Charles Reade, and

Elizabeth Gaskell, each identified as a novelist-reformer who believed that it was "part of the high commission of literature to try offences which elude the repression of the law, and to denounce with hyperbolic violence actions which may not have been committed at all, or which may have been committed from very different motives."[30] These novelists, claims Stephen, misunderstand both their "duties and their rights" as novelists, and while novelists have different duties to their public than, say, a judge or a legislator, the power these novelists in particular wield and their desire to engage in public discourse about particular social, legal, political controversies means that they have acquired not only rights but duties to their reading public.[31] Stephen's rhetoric indicates that he recognizes the power of novels that promote social reform, and he makes his concern explicit in the review's first pages, where he calls novelists of his time "the most influential of all indirect moral teachers." Citing the sales data for the novelists he reviews, he concludes his first paragraph by noting that "Upwards of a million cheap shilling volumes which ornament railway book-stalls are disposed of annually, and the effect of these publications on the whole mind of the community can hardly be exaggerated."[32] Stephen's tone here is unmistakably hostile, and he makes no secret of his hostility throughout. In an article for the *Saturday Review,* written as, it seems, a kind of sequel to this *Edinburgh Review* piece (and entitled "The *Edinburgh Review* and Modern Novelists"), Stephen says of Reade and Dickens: "These gentlemen seriously mean to be listened to as practical teachers; and it is the boast of those who admire their method of instruction, that their romances are more influential than fifty Blue-books."[33]

Though the earlier review begins with an attack on Dickens's *Little Dorrit* and what Stephen identifies as Dickens's ignorant representation of administrative government, the bulk of the review is devoted to an analysis of Charles Reade's novel *It Is Never Too Late to Mend.* Of interest to Stephen in this novel is Reade's treatment of the mismanagement and horrific practices, which had recently come to light, of the Birmingham Gaol. Government officials investigated the prison and its administrators in 1853 after a prisoner—identified as "a boy named Andrews"—hanged himself. On completion of the investigation, the governor of the prison, Lieutenant Austin, was tried for the infliction of illegal punishments and convicted. He served three months in prison.

As Stephen notes, Reade makes little effort to pretend that the characters in his story do not represent their actual counterparts, and there are indeed striking similarities between the names of the actual prison officials and prisoners and the characters in Reade's novel. Having exposed Reade's not-so-brilliant disguises, Stephen proceeds to compare the facts of the case to Reade's fictional representation of those facts and gives a partial list of the exaggerations and misrepresentations in Reade's novel. He attends in particular to the misrepresentations that put questions of intent beyond doubt. For example, in the actual case, the court conjectured but could not be sure that the prisoner Andrews had intended to commit suicide, since he hanged himself just at the time when the warder brought him his bed, and he was in fact "not quite dead when he was cut down."[34] Reade, by contrast, alters the time of the incident "so as to put beyond all doubt an intention which, on the evidence before the Commissioners, was only a matter of conjecture."[35] But why should this matter so much to Stephen? There is even something blackly comic in Stephen's wanting to correct Reade here by asserting that the boy was not quite dead when found—almost, but not quite. What matters to Stephen is not only the ease with which such writers distort the facts to reach an audience but also the way they pervert the audience itself. Reading such literature, says Stephen, "has so depraved some of the most necessary faculties of the reading public as to render it almost incapable of applying the laws of inference to the generalizations of novelists."[36] While Reade puts the motives of the governor of Birmingham Gaol before his readership in no uncertain terms—"What more natural than that such a nature should find its excitement in tormenting; and that by degrees this excitement should become, first a habit, and then a need? Torture had grown upon stupid, earnest Hawes as it seasoned the white of egg, a mindless existence"—Stephen responds, "Considering this is a mere matter of inference, it is rather strong language, even for a novelist."[37]

Worse still, Stephen reports, is the way Reade distorts fact to create "a corrupt conspiracy between a great variety of persons to pervert the course of justice; and inasmuch as the description of Lieutenant Austin's misdeed affords the principal foundation for these attacks, it is obvious that by exaggerating the facts, additional weight is given to these inferences."[38] In the course of his review, Stephen himself presents evidence of the misconduct of prison officials and magistrates; so too he agrees that the sentence pronounced on Austin was much too lenient, but he cannot abide the creation of the narrative that Reade constructs out of these facts. Such authority had the novel that the facts as Reade represented them (including claims about intent) became the facts on which the public based its own opinion. Faced with the novel as a medium through which legal, political, and social issues might be most forcefully imagined, Stephen finds himself powerless against its methods of representing intent and its ability to make itself immune to criticisms aimed at such misrepresentation. Of this writing, Stephen remarks (in a later review of a forgettable book called *Novels and Novelists*): "The fundamental vice of novels, considered as works of instruction, lies in the circumstance that the novelist makes his facts, and that, if he is charged with inaccuracy, he can always plead that he is writing a novel, and not a political treatise."[39] Pleading fiction, novelists distort fact, Stephen claims, and the "great dexterity of the novelist is proved by the fact, that he inclines his readers to dispense with evidence the study of which would supersede his unsupported assertions."[40] If we are willing to turn over policy-making to novelists without requiring the evidentiary rigor imposed on other decision-making bodies, "why not," asks Stephen,

write a striking tale in a magazine or a newspaper, to establish before
trial, the guilt or innocence of Palmer or Bernard? It would of course
be a monstrous absurdity and a gross wrong to an accused person to
do anything of the kind. But why is it less unjust in principle to act in
a similar way toward bodies of men, and to prejudge questions of
great depth and intricacy, by excited, noisy, and constantly reiterated
assertions?[41]

That the "striking tale" becomes by the end of the passage the "excited,
noisy, and constantly reiterated assertions" attests to Stephen's intensified
opposition to the kinds of fictions that operated as media of reform but dis-
pensed with the evidentiary process necessary to support the assertions
made. Stephen remarks of the "literary mind" that it is "apt to give itself up to
foregone conclusions, and illustrates the distinction—a distinction implied in
the difference between imagination and reason—which exists between the
skill in the production of literary effects, and skill in the verification and em-
ployment of alleged evidence."[42] Stephen goes too far in suggesting that novelists skilled in producing literary effects are not also skilled in applying reason to those effects; however, more important is the idea of a leap to a
foregone conclusion, the confidence with which hard-to-prove matters can
be asserted in a "striking tale" in a manner that leaves nothing but an assur-
ance that something doubtful or probable has become a sure thing. Stephen
had early on stumbled through an insufficient analysis of the difference between the way character is known in life and the way it is known in the novel:

> Men whose opinion is worth anything upon such matters are very cau-
> tious indeed in describing characters by a few broad phrases; for no
> lesson is sooner learnt than that such general language requires to be
> modified in innumerable ways before it can, with any kind of correct-
> ness, be applied to any individual case. In life character is inferred
> from actions, in most novels actions are ascribed to particular people
> in order to illustrate the author's conceptions respecting character.
> Language therefore is inadequate, when applied to real persons, as it
> is adequate and exhaustive when applied to the common run of ficti-
> tious ones.[43]

The shift from "in life" to "in most novels" depends on the difference between
an inference from conduct to character and a rhetorical move from character
to conduct. In novels, claims Stephen, the author predetermines a character
and uses action as illustration, while in life our opinions about character
evolve as we observe more about an individual's conduct. Tucked into this
contrast is also the assumption that the novel can give us direct access to character while in life we must infer character from action. What is inadequate
about this analysis is that it unfairly simplifies the representations of characters in novels. Stephen's assumptions about an author's relation to character
are unjust to the more complex ideas about character that George Eliot, for

instance, imagined: "character too is a process and an unfolding" (146), the narrator of *Middlemarch* famously asserts, and is not something fixed or easily illustrated. In *Middlemarch*, and in other Eliot novels, we both interpret character from action and action from character. But it is not Eliot whom Stephen challenges in the passage just quoted: it is Dickens.

When Stephen says of Dickens that he has "almost completely debauched our sympathies and understandings on the subject of the relation which opinions should bear to facts,"[44] we register both Dickens's power and Stephen's sense of Dickens's abuse of such power. Stephen rightly understood Dickens to be both a major figure in public debate, key to the formation of public opinion, and a figure protected from attack, notwithstanding Stephen's ongoing attacks on him. In "Mr. Dickens as a Politician," Stephen laments:

> A novelist has no responsibility. He can always discover his own meaning. To the world at large, *Jarndyce v. Jarndyce* represents the Court of Chancery. To any one who taxes the writer with unfairness, it is merely, he is told, a playful exaggeration. . . . To the thousands of feverish artisans who read *Little Dorrit*, the Circumlocution Office is a *bona fide* representation of Downing-street. To any one who remonstrates it is nothing but a fair representation of what exists, just exaggerated enough to make the subject entertaining.[45]

It is telling, I think, that in considering these matters, the terms "represents" and "representing" should play such prominent roles. It is telling too that Stephen should imagine the horror we should feel if a fiction writer composed a story exonerating or condemning an alleged criminal before trial ("Why not write a striking tale in a magazine or a newspaper, to establish before trial, the guilt or innocence of Palmer or Bernard?"). That fiction should displace trial by jury is unthinkable to Stephen, yet he wonders aloud whether fiction was already replacing other kinds of policy-making processes.

Faults in Stephen's attacks on Dickens and on Victorian novels more generally there certainly are. Stephen's own "rules of literary composition"[46] are notably limited. He wants the "skillfully constructed plot" and a certain "careful and moderate delineation of character; and neither of these are to be found in Mr. Dickens's works."[47] At least half of his review of *Little Dorrit* takes up the complexities and inadequacies of the novel's plot, and while readers of *Little Dorrit* may agree with Stephen's critique, the review itself is unjust to the novel as a whole. Stephen could not recognize, as Ruskin — for instance — could, that there was truth in the caricatures Dickens presented. Note this from Ruskin's commentary on *Hard Times*: "The essential value and truth of Dickens's writings have been unwisely lost sight of by many thoughtful persons merely because he presents his truth with some colour of caricature. Unwisely, because Dickens's caricature, though often gross, is never mistaken. Allowing for his manner of telling them, the things he tells us are always true."[48] Stephen, by contrast, can only say of *Little Dorrit*'s characters that they "remind us of the cheap theatrical prints of our schoolboy days, and of the inartificial way in which boys used to act a play in the nursery."[49]

So it is not for the purpose of promoting Stephen as a gifted literary critic that I produce the passages from his reviews. My focus is narrow. While Stephen may not have been a subtle reader, what he brings to our attention vividly and provocatively is that particular obligations pertain when novels, or indeed any other texts, enter into questions of law, politics, administration or other public issues and proffer facts about such matters on which readers draw conclusions. Reade subtitled *It Is Never Too Late to Mend* a "matter-of-fact romance," openly joining the factual and the fictional. The novel's title not only takes a cliché applied to individuals (it is never too late to mend) and applies it to a society but also signals that this novel has different responsibilities to its readership. Victorian novels that took up such questions were of particular concern because, like, television programs or films in our own time, these novels reached the largest audiences.

⚜ Macaulay, Stephen, and "The Story of Nuncomar" ⚜

After quoting a passage from Macaulay's 1828 *Edinburgh Review* essay entitled simply "History," George Levine remarks, in his seminal work *The Boundaries of Fiction*, that "Macaulay was attracted to fiction; and it is no accident that his thoughts about history were bound up with thoughts about fiction."[50] Levine persuasively argues that for Macaulay the writing of history enabled him to exercise his imaginative powers and produce a body of work more useful (so he asserted) to the world than a collection of novels but also very like novels. Levine summarizes Macaulay's ambitions using these large terms: "Great history is alone among the literary arts in at once creating an imaginative world and remaining faithful to the real and the responsibility of knowledge."[51] Macaulay's "History" has itself much to say about the responsibilities of the historian: "A perfect historian," declares Macaulay," must possess an imagination sufficiently powerful to make his narrative affecting and picturesque. Yet he must control it so absolutely as to content himself with the materials which he finds, and to refrain from supplying deficiencies of his own."[52] Macaulay maintains this position throughout "History," and many other passages could be adduced in which he both authorizes the historian's imaginative powers and rejects any fact not supported by "sufficient testimony."[53]

Macaulay announces in no uncertain terms that the historian should incorporate into his narrative the characteristics that readers would expect to find in novels: "A truly great historian," claims Macaulay, "would reclaim those materials which the novelist has appropriated."[54] As Levine notes, Macaulay argued that history should approach both the great and the small, both the large events of a period and its seemingly trivial activities. Following what he identifies as Walter Scott's lead, Macaulay sees the future of history in the past of "ordinary men as they appear in their ordinary business and in their ordinary pleasures."[55] While Macaulay identifies the ordinary as having been "usurped" by the novel, he also announces his intention of expropriating the subject for history itself. If ordinary man and his pleasures might be an apt subject for treatment, how might the historian treat that subject? Macaulay looks to the legal trial and to imaginative literature (novel, biography, autobiography, memoir) as models. He rebukes Herodotus, who "tells his story like a slovenly witness."[56] Herodotus, claims Macaulay, "unacquainted with the established rules of evidence, and uninstructed as to the obligations of his oath, confounds what he imagines with what he has seen and heard, and brings out facts, reports, conjectures, and fancies in one mass."[57] Hume, Gibbon, and Mitford also come in for censure as historians whose "own witnesses are applauded and encouraged; the statements which seem to throw discredit on them are controverted."[58] Still, Macaulay rejects histories that proceed more fully like our own trials, where two sides battle it out before an audience. Of such histories, Macaulay concludes: "While our historians are practicing the arts of controversy, they miserably neglect the art of narration, the art of interesting the affections and presenting pictures to the imaginations."[59] Not unreasonably, Macaulay promotes both the picturesque and the truthful, the narrative impulse and a fidelity to evidence. The two combined produce something more than facts and circumstances; the resulting narrative gives us access to more than the externals of historical figures. We should see

> Elizabeth in all her weakness and strength . . . uniting in herself the most contradictory qualities of both her parents, — the coquetry, the caprice, the petty malice of Anne, — the haughty and the resolute spirit of Henry. We have no hesitation in saying that a great artist might produce a portrait of this remarkable woman at least as striking as that in the novel of Kenilworth, without employing a single trait not authenticated by ample testimony.[60]

That Macaulay compares the work of his hypothetical historian — the "great artist" — with Scott's novel *Kenilworth* illuminates Macaulay's belief that history was superior to the historical novel. Where Scott could not claim the authority of authenticated testimony, the historian could. Here was the best of both worlds. The historian could go where the novelist had gone, backed by the authority of fact. And the historian should want, in particular, to reach into character. Macaulay's praise of Tacitus focuses on "the delineation of character," a talent for which he has, according to Macaulay, "very few superiors among dramatists and novelists."[61] Macaulay demonstrates the way Tacitus produces "an individuality of character which seems to pervade all their words and actions. We know them as if we had lived with them."[62] In his analysis, Levine rightly calls attention to the way Macaulay's narratives put readers in the skins of the historical subjects described, allowing readers to "see and hear and feel what people of the past experienced." [63]

Of Macaulay's *History*, Levine writes: "With his *History* Macaulay consciously challenged comparison with the great historians and the most successful of contemporary novelists. He was attempting what he regarded as the most difficult of intellectual labors. But he managed to suppress all signs of labor so that the *History* remains a startlingly readable and exciting narrative, with all the fascination of a good Victorian novel."[64] Though Levine considers only the *History of England* here, the same observations, as he himself remarks in a footnote, could be made about Macaulay's *Essays* as well. The density of detail and the vividness of description, the interest in character and plot development, signal the influence the novel exercised over Macaulay, as (indeed) histories themselves and Macaulay's *History of England* in particular exercised its influence over the novel. Historiography and novel-writing have long influenced each other, as Defoe's *Journal of the Plague Year* (and many other texts) attests. Whatever research Macaulay did in support of his claims in the *History*, the "signs of labor," as Levine calls them, were erased. Erased was the evidence on which his inferences were based. What was left? The third-person narrative itself, which owed much to what Levine calls "the realistic aesthetic of the midcentury novel."[65] So close to the novel was Macaulay's narrative that Levine goes so far as to say that a reader, not knowing that Macaulay was a historian, could not distinguish his history from a novel. But while Levine offers claims about the similarities between Macaulay's *History* and the nineteenth-century novel, he does not consider the role of the third person narrator, or the ways that narrator may have influenced Macaulay's art as it imagined the inner life for its readers.

While Stephen may not have been introduced to the story of Nuncomar, Impey, and Hastings by Macaulay's astonishingly influential essay on Hastings, he was at the very least captivated by it through Macaulay's provocative retelling. On the eve of Macaulay's burial in Westminster Abbey, Stephen published his tribute to Macaulay, noting in particular that "There are probably no finer compositions of their kind in the language than the Essays on Lord Clive and Warren Hastings. The founders of our Indian Empire stand out before us as they fought and conquered, with the radiance of victory and patriotism shining through the blemishes and crimes by which they were stained."[66] In a later *Saturday Review* piece on Macaulay's works, Stephen reiterated his praise of Macaulay: "His best essays, those on Clive and Hastings, are as good as anything in the *History of England*."[67] And in one of his earliest essays, "The Characteristics of the English Criminal Law" (1857), he is apparently so at ease with the evil-doing of Hastings and Impey that he can make an example of them in passing. Noting his objections to the vague common law definitions of certain crimes (as distinct from the definitions found in statutes), Stephen casually provides this illustration:

> It must also be remembered that, in unquiet times, a loose definition
> of crime may shake the foundations of society. When Hastings hung
> Nuncomar, he used the law for a purpose for which it was never de-

signed. Cases might well be imagined in which a partial jury and a vindictive Government might hang an innocent man for murder without departing in the least degree from the law. Coroners' juries have more than once found verdicts of wilful murder against soldiers or policemen in times of popular excitement.[68]

Stephen's early impression of the story of Nuncomar expressively demonstrates Macaulay's success in doing with his historical narratives what he said he hoped to do with them: "The instruction derived from history thus written would be of a vivid and practical character. It would be received by the imagination as well as by the reason. It would be not merely traced on the mind, but branded on it."[69] In the penultimate paragraph of *The Story of Nuncomar*, Stephen recalls again the impression Macaulay's essays had made on him:

> I do not think any one can have a stronger admiration than myself for
> Macaulay's *Essays*. Their manly sense, their freedom from every sort of
> mysticism, their courage and directness, their sympathy with all that is
> good and honourable, untainted by the very faintest touch of senti-
> mentality, made them in my boyhood my favourite book. I knew them
> almost by heart at one time, and the essays on Hastings and Clive were
> the writings which upwards of forty years ago gave me a feeling about
> India not unlike that which Marryat's novels are said to have given to
> many lads about the sea. (2:271)

The passage produces Stephen's affection for Macaulay's work in a way that feels entirely genuine, notwithstanding the fact that it turns up at the end of a book that takes Macaulay so much to task. But one registers Stephen's view of these essays as experiences of his youth, works that he associated with the adventure novels of Marryat. The comparison again locates Macaulay's work with and not against the novel. The principles at stake for Stephen were important enough for him to launch an attack on this central figure in his life. As curious as the story of Nuncomar and Impey is ("It is a most curious story," Stephen had written Lord Lytton), more curious still is the fact that when Stephen came to write *The Story of Nuncomar and the Impeachment of Sir Elijah Impey*, he would refute Macaulay and even rebuke him.

   While Stephen gives a thumbnail sketch of the events surrounding Nuncomar's trial in his September 1884 letter to Lytton, they are complicated enough to require a more detailed summary. One needs to know something more about the major figures in Stephen's narrative and some dates and points of orientation. Still, I cannot hope to do justice to the complexity of even this relatively small slice of colonial history.

   Warren Hastings was born in December 1732. He met Sir Elijah Impey when they were both schoolboys at Westminster School (Hastings had been sent by his uncle after his father had all but abandoned him), and Impey's son, E. B. Impey, who published a life of his father, reported that Impey and

Hastings were "bosom friends" (2:23). Hastings' patron/uncle died in 1749, and Hastings, as a biographer reports, "finished a regular course of merchants' accounts under Mr. Thomas Smith at Christ's Hospital, and his guardian [Joseph Creswicke] got his nomination as a writer"[70] for the East India Company. He left for Bengal in January 1750. Hastings was moved around within Bengal and held various Company positions. Upon the death of the "old Nawab of Bengal," Aliverdi Khan, Indian rule of the area became destabilized, and Sujah-ud-Daula, the grandson of Aliverdi Khan, came to power. In this year, Nuncomar, a Brahmin, became a high official of Hughli and thereafter replaced Hastings in his position as collector of revenue in various areas of the region. After a series of complicated events, Sujah-ud-Daula had all Company employees imprisoned, and Hastings was taken into custody in a region then known as Kasimbazaar (an important trading post). Following the incident, which came to be associated with that of the infamous "Black Hole of Calcutta," and during the period when Lord Clive was waging his war against Sujah-ud-Daula, Hastings was released from custody. Hastings joined Clive as a volunteer when Clive reclaimed Calcutta and was with Clive at the Battle of Plassy, though there is no evidence that Hastings had any part in the conspiracy headed by Clive that ultimately saw the demise of Sujah-ud-Daula, murdered by the son of Mir Jaffir. It was Mir Jaffir who, after cutting deals with Clive, became the new ruler.[71] Thereafter Hastings began to move up the ranks, as did Nuncomar. It was also during this time that Hastings made contact with Nuncomar. Lyall reports that in Hastings's letters to Clive, mention is made of that fact that "Nuncomar, who was already figuring as an important agent of the English, had been sent up to collect revenue within his jurisdiction without formal notice to himself; and Clive replied briefly that no slight was intended."[72] In 1762, Hastings investigated Nuncomar for producing forged letters used to incriminate another Indian. According to one source, Nuncomar was put under house arrest for "acting as a go-between" for an Indian official and the French.[73]

Hastings returned to England in 1765 and then sailed back to India in 1769 when he was appointed to the presidency of Madras. In 1772 he became the East India Company's governor-general of Bengal.[74] In this year too, Hastings was asked by the Company to make use of Nuncomar to gather information about another Indian, Mahomed Rheza Khan. Stephen quotes the following letter from Company officials to Hastings:

> We cannot forbear recommending you to avail yourself of the intelligence which Nuncomar may be able to give respecting the Naib's administration; and while the envy which Nuncomar is supposed to bear this minister may prompt him to a ready communication of all proceedings which have come to his knowledge, we are persuaded that no scrutable part of the Naib's conduct can have escaped the watchful eye of his jealous and penetrating rival. (2:39, n. 2)

And a bit later:

we have the satisfaction to reflect that you are too well apprised of the subtlety and disposition of Nuncomar to yield him any post of author-ity which may be turned to his own advantage, or prove detrimental to the Company's interest. Though we have thought it necessary to inti-mate to you how little we are disposed to delegate any power or influ-ence to Nuncomar, yet, should his information and assistance be serv-iceable to you in your investigation of the conduct of Mahomed Rheza Khan, you will yield him such encouragement and reward as his trou-ble and the extent of his services may deserve. (1:39, n. 2)

This letter goes far toward defining the relationship between Nuncomar and the Company. He was used but not trusted—rewarded but not empowered. Eventually, Hastings did arrest Mahomed Rheza Khan for alleged abuses con-nected to the latter's duties as a collector of native revenues (through a com-plicated set of arrangements, Indians and Company agents had shared this right). Notwithstanding Nuncomar's information, Mahomed Rheza Khan was acquitted, though he was not to reclaim his appointment since the position he held as collector no longer existed; it had been absorbed by the Company it-self. Thereafter, Nuncomar's son was given a high office and an income.

In 1773, Parliament passed one of the first and most significant acts re-garding the Company's activities in India. The Regulating Act of 1773 repre-sented a concerted effort to correct, stabilize, and control the exercise of power in India. The act created a council made up of the governor-general and four other council members. In addition, the Supreme Court of Judica-ture was established, of which Sir Elijah Impey was named as the first chief judge. Impey was appointed with three other judges, Sir Robert Chambers, and justices Stephen Lemaistre and John Hyde. Impey, as I noted earlier, was a longtime friend of Hastings and was born in the same year as his friend, 1732. Unlike Hastings, he attended university—Trinity College, Cambridge—and became a student at Lincoln's Inn. In 1756 he was called to the bar, and in 1757 he earned a fellowship at Trinity. He practiced law until he was appointed to the Supreme Court of Calcutta. Impey and the other judges arrived in Cal-cutta in 1774 with three members of the newly appointed Council, Philip Francis, Colonel John Clavering, and Colonel George Monson. (Richard Bar-well, the other member, was already in India.)[75]

Led by Francis, who was to be Hastings's most ardent adversary, the coun-cil of Francis, Clavering, and Monson began to investigate Hastings, whom they suspected of corruption. On March 11, 1775, Francis introduced to the Council a letter from Nuncomar accusing Hastings of various illegal acts, in-cluding extortion. Nuncomar appeared before the Council on the same day to present his charges, though Hastings was not present, having dissolved the Council in the face of Francis's declared intention to read the charges. Dis-solving the Council did not, as it turns out, end the meeting, since the other Council members remained to hear Nuncomar. In April, another figure ap-peared on the scene—Commaul O Deen—who, according to Hastings, reported to him that he had "escaped" from the custody of Nuncomar and a man named Fowke. Commaul O Deen claimed that Nuncomar and Fowke attempted to force him to sign a petition accusing Hastings and Barwell of bribery. On April 23, Hastings and Barwell brought conspiracy charges against Nuncomar and two others. Nuncomar and the others were released on bail. Then, on May 6, approximately eight weeks after Nuncomar had initially approached the Council with his claims against Hastings, an Indian named Mohun Persaud charged Nuncomar with forgery, a charge that arose out of a then pending and longstanding civil case against Nuncomar, the complexity of which makes Dickens's *Jarndyce v. Jarndyce* look like a simple dispute. The civil case, which had been brought eight years earlier, involved a claim made by the estate of Bollakey Doss for money owed by Nuncomar as a result of an allegedly forged bond Nuncomar had allegedly passed off in order to collect valuable East India Company bonds from the estate. Here are the facts. At the death of Bollakey Doss, Nuncomar had in his possession bonds that showed that the late Bollakey Doss owed him money. One of the bonds claimed that Nuncomar was owed money because some jewels he had given to Bollakey Doss to hold for sale had been stolen when Bollakey Doss's house had been plundered by the English in 1758. After Bollakey Doss's will was probated, the estate paid to Nuncomar some East India Company bonds in exchange for the bonds that Nuncomar claimed Bollakey Doss had given to him. One of the returned bonds was a suspected forgery, though the estate made the exchange in any event. After the exchange, a civil suit was brought by Mohun Persaud, to whom Bollakey Doss had given power of attorney in his will, on behalf of one of the estate's trustees (Gungabissen). The criminal suit arose out of this civil suit. That the suit was brought eight weeks after Nuncumar made his charges against Hastings became a key fact in the impeachment trials of Impey and Hastings, and so deserves emphasis here. Though acquitted of the charge of conspiracy against Hastings (the counterclaim Hastings had asserted against him), Nuncomar was tried for forgery—a capital offense—before an all-English jury and convicted. Sir Elijah Impey was the chief justice of the court (along with Chambers, Hyde, and LeMaistre) that convicted and sentenced Nuncomar. Nuncomar's sentence was death by hanging.[76] The court did not commute his sentence, and Nuncomar was hanged on August 5, 1775.

On December 3, 1782, Impey left India, having been recalled by the Crown to answer charges of corruption unrelated to Nuncomar's execution. It appears that when he returned to England, he was not required to answer to those charges, and he was not dismissed from office, though he resigned in November 1787. Almost ten years after the hanging of Nuncomar, in February 1785, Warren Hastings left India and returned to England. In June 1786 the House of Commons voted that there were sufficient grounds for impeachment of Hastings, and in May of that year articles of impeachment were approved. The charge of conspiracy with Impey for the murder of Nuncomar was not among them. However, in 1787, articles of impeachment against

Impey were approved, with the first charge against him being the judicial murder of Nuncomar, a charge that, as Stephen reports, "was regarded as so much the most important of [all the charges] that Impey begged to be heard upon that first" (2:7). His petition was granted, and his case began on February 4, 1788. Impey was acquitted of all charges. In April 1789 Edmund Burke made his famous speech charging Hastings and Impey with the murder of Nuncomar.[77] Hastings was acquitted of all charges in 1795.

After a short introduction and description of the origins and the make up of the Supreme Council and Supreme Court in Bengal, Stephen produces brief biographies of these figures. In his biographical sketch of Hastings, Stephen makes a courteous but rather grudging bow to Macaulay and to the essay on Hastings from which he borrows in this chapter, since that essay, "though imperfect, and, I think in some particulars unjust, has told the main features of his career in a way which supersedes the possibility of competition, and inclines me to content myself with a simple reference to it" (2:21). Yet the criticisms of Macaulay's rhetoric shape the chapter as a whole. Of Macaulay's description of Nuncomar, Stephen asserts: "Nuncomar's character is described by Macaulay in terms in which I think his rhetorical power greatly overcame the discriminating good sense shown in so many of his descriptions of character" (1:41). Stephen also objects to Macaulay's "super-superlatives" (1:41, n.1), and in a footnote even takes the opportunity to mock the claims of Macaulay when pushed to their logical conclusion.[78] For Macaulay, Nuncomar lacks all moral sense, but Stephen introduces two other voices, that of Sir Gilbert Elliot (who helped prosecute Impey) and that of Barwell (an ally of Hastings and another Council member), both of whom contradict Macaulay's conclusion.

More than exaggeration is under attack. Take, for example, Macaulay on Nuncomar's behavior after the arrival of Francis: "That bad man was stimulated at once by malignity, by avarice, and by ambition. Now was the time to be avenged on his old enemy, to wreak a grudge of seventeen years, to establish himself in the favour of the majority of the Council, to become the greatest native in Bengal."[79] Stephen turns from Macaulay's third person narrative, a narrative that claims to have knowledge that only a divine power would have, to give instead a more general—though still vivid in its use of superlatives—description of the environment within which Nuncomar thrived: "It may be doubted whether any human being has ever passed his life under greater moral disadvantages. The decay of the Mogul Empire constitutes one of the blackest scenes in human history—a scene of reckless and brutal violence, bloody but indecisive war, endless intrigues and frauds" (1:41). When Stephen finally draws his conclusion about Nuncomar's character, he remains outside it, explicitly inferring his reading of Nuncomar from the circumstances in which he lived: "Of all the provinces of the Empire none was so degraded as Bengal, and till he was nearly sixty years old Nuncomar lived in the worst and most degraded part of that unhappy province. A pushing, active, prominent successful ma⸗ in such circumstances could hardly be

other than Nuncomar actually was, false all through, and dead to every sentiment except pride, hatred, and revenge" (1:42). Here Stephen proceeds from
the general to the particular: given what the state of Bengal then was, Nuncomar could hardly have been other than what he was in order to succeed.
I note the echo of Macaulay in the recitation of Nuncomar's deadly sins:
where Macaulay gives us Nuncomar stimulated "by malignity, by avarice, and
by ambition," Stephen provides "pride, hatred, and revenge." But note that
the form of the narrative is different. "Now was the time to be avenged on his
old enemy, to wreak a grudge of seventeen years, to establish himself in the
favour of the majority of the Council, to become the greatest native in Bengal" assumes a special authority by taking on, in essence, the voice of Nuncomar. Macaulay invites us to experience Nuncomar's state of mind as Nuncomar was himself experiencing it. The narrative offers an unmediated
experience of Nuncomar's interior life. As extreme as the conclusions
Stephen presents are (and in part it is itself Macaulayesque and attests to
Macaulay's remarkable influence), he premises them in an explicit way on the
circumstances of Nuncomar's life. He infers character from circumstance,
and while he pressures us to draw the same inference (when Stephen says
that Nuncomar "could hardly be other than" he was, we recognize his own
rhetorical move), they are inferences outright.

The voice of a powerful third person narration is registered throughout
Macaulay's essay. The usually silent conversion of documents—whether they
be letters or eyewitness reports or earlier historical works—into Macaulay's
narrative leaves little trace of the evidence on which his facts are based. Consider this passage:

> It was not safe to drive to despair a man of such resource and of such
> determination as Hastings. Nuncomar, with all his acuteness, did not
> understand the nature of the institutions under which he lived. He
> saw that he had with him the majority of the body which made
> treaties, gave places, raised taxes. The separation between political
> and judicial functions was a thing of which he had no conception. It
> had probably never occurred to him that there was in Bengal an au-
> thority perfectly independent of the council, an authority which could
> protect one whom the council wished to protect. Yet such was the fact.
> The Supreme Court was, within the sphere of its own duties, al-
> together independent of the Government. Hastings, with his usual
> sagacity, had seen how much advantage he might derive from possess-
> ing himself of this stronghold; and he had acted accordingly.[80]

It is not only that Macaulay may be filling in gaps with details culled from his
imagination but also that the passage proceeds without recourse to outside
authority. The only authority is that of the speaker, and he seems to know
quite a lot, including the state of Nuncomar's knowledge about the nature of
political and judicial power in Calcutta. True, Macaulay inserts a "probably"
into his description that defuses the vigor of these assertions. But this is not

much of a concession. The relations between those powers is presented as "a thing of which he had no conception." It is not possible, according to this telling, that he weighed the gains and losses of going before the Council. The only possibility is that he had no conception of the separation of powers. In short, this passage reads like a passage from a nineteenth-century novel.

One could adduce more examples from Macaulay's essay on Hastings and from his other essays and from the *History of England* (all works Stephen knew well) in which Macaulay proceeds with the authority of a speaker empowered to see more, to see into the figures presented:

> Nuncomar, stimulated at once by cupidity and malice, had been con-stantly attempting to undermine his successful rival.[81]

> Hastings thought it a masterstroke of policy to reward the able and unprincipled parent by promoting the inoffensive child.[82]

> Nuncomar had purposed to destroy the Mussulman administration, and to rise on its ruin. Both his malevolence and his cupidity had been disappointed. Hastings had made him a tool, had used him for the purpose of accomplishing the transfer of government from Moor-shedabad to Calcutta, from native to European. The rival, the enemy, so long envied, so implacably persecuted, had been dismissed unhurt. The situation so long and ardently desired had been abolished. It was natural that the Governor should be from that time an object of the most intense hatred to the vindictive Brahmin. As yet, however, it was necessary to suppress such feelings.[83]

Having erased, as Levine notes the "signs of his labor" and having put his re-search into this form of narrative, Macaulay obscures the inferential nature of his own narrative. He tells the facts of the case not only as if he were present but as if he were present in the minds of his characters. Indeed, the license Macaulay takes is the license that other historiographers had taken. Samuel Rogers's *Recollections* records Henry Grattan's criticism of those who took such liberties: "Historians," remarks Grattan, "are not contented with telling us what was done, but they pretend to enter into the secret motives of men."[84]

The first mention of Impey in Macaulay's "Warren Hastings" appears in Macaulay's description of Hastings's early years at Westminster. Of this rela-tion, Macaulay speculates: "we may safely venture that, whenever Hastings wished to play any trick more than usually naughty, he hired Impey with a tart or a ball to act as fag in the worst part of the prank."[85] When Macaulay gets to Nuncomar's trial, he is moving full throttle. To the Indians, "The counterfeit-ing of a seal was, in their estimation, a common act of swindling; nor had it ever crossed their minds that it was to be punished as severely as gang-rob-bery or assassination. A just judge would, beyond all doubt, have reserved the case for the consideration of the sovereign. But Impey would not hear of mercy or delay" (403). The difference between "did not hear of mercy or delay" and "would not hear of mercy or delay" suggests something of the way Macaulay operates throughout. In "would not," Macaulay goes beyond a fact. He provides instead special access to Impey, and the way the paragraph unfolds suggests that the narrator knows rather than infers. Like the hypothetical judge whom Macaulay imagines — the "just judge" — Macaulay can imagine Impey's state of mind as well. Moreover, the recourse to "beyond all doubt" asserts a divine knowledge. Macaulay has access to a world beyond doubt.

Macaulay's world was not to be Stephen's. In his biography of Fitzjames Stephen, Leslie Stephen includes a letter from Fitzjames Stephen's father, James Stephen, in which the elder Stephen compares Macaulay's skills with those of his eldest son and takes the opportunity to advise Fitzjames (though indirectly) to forego attempts to imitate his friend and mentor. The paternal advice comes as a response to the first article Fitzjames Stephen wrote for the *Edinburgh Review*, an 1856 piece on Cavallier, who, as Leslie Stephen reports, was "the leader of the Protestant revolt in the Cevennes."[86] Leslie Stephen recalls:

> He had selected a picturesque bit of history, capable of treatment after the manner of Macaulay. "I have read it," says my father, in words meant to be read to Fitzjames, "with the pleasure which it always gives me to read his vigorous sense, clear and manly style, right-minded and substantially kind-hearted writings. My respect for his understanding has been for a long time steadily increasing, and is very unlikely to be ever diminished. . . . But I shall best prove that respect by saying plainly that I do not like this paper as well as those in which he writes argumentatively, speculatively, and from the resources of his own mind. His power consists in reasoning, in the exposition of truth and fallacies. I will not say, for I do not know, that he wants the art of story-telling, but, taking this as a specimen, it seems to me deficient in the great art of linking together a series of facts in such a manner that the connection between them shall be at once perceptible to the most ignorant and inattentive reader, and shall take easy and irresistible possession of the mind. That is Macaulay's pre-eminent gift.[87]

"Argumentatively, speculatively, and from the resources of his own mind," as set against a narrative mode in which the story "shall be at once perceptible to the most ignorant and inattentive reader, and shall take easy and irresistible possession of the mind": the contrast is substantial. One is tempted to reduce the contrast to the analytic as against the poetic, but that reduction does an injustice to the analytic and the poetic. In "Milton," Macaulay himself makes such a distinction. "Analysis is not the business of the poet" (13), Macaulay explains, and he generates an illustration that turns on motives:

> If Shakespeare had written a book on the motives, it is by no means certain that it would have been a good one. It is extremely improbable that it would have contained half so much able reasoning on the sub-

ject as is to be found in the "Fable of the Bees." But could Mandeville have created Iago? Well as he knows how to resolve characters into their elements, would he have been able to combine those elements in such a manner as to make up a man—real, living, individual man?[88]

The argument Macaulay makes here—that Shakespeare's plays, including *Othello*, do not produce compelling moments of analysis—is wrong, though such analytic moments are dramatically and not discursively realized. But beyond this misrepresentation, both Macaulay and James Stephen mark out a distinction between speculation and "the art of story-telling" that gives one pause. There is surely a difference between an analysis of motive in Mandeville and the dramatic presentation of Iago; one could understand that the responsibilities of the former would be different from those of the latter, but both invite judgment. In the case of Macaulay, James Stephen articulates the aspects of Macaulay's works that made them so formidable. Macaulay assumes the authority of fact ("the great art of linking together a series of facts") and the form of narrative that appears to close down the reader's own powers of analysis ("in such a manner that the connection between them shall be at once perceptible to the most ignorant and inattentive reader, and shall take easy and irresistible possession of the mind"). The essays assert the authority of an analysis, and yet they shut down an analytic response.

Whether or not Fitzjames Stephen had such a gift, he could see the danger in the narratives Macaulay produced. Their irresistibility gave them their power, and part of that power came not from the presentation of an analysis of motive but from a creation of character. So Macaulay can write of Hastings: "The motive of Hastings was misdirected and ill-regulated public spirit,"[89] while Impey becomes worse than impish; he is "a fiend in human shape, and a very contemptible one."[90] Having created this fiendish character, Macaulay assigns him clear intentions. Attending to the events surrounding another accusation against Impey, unrelated to the trial of Nuncomar, Macaulay asserts: "It was not easy for him to intrude himself into a business so entirely alien from all his official duties. But there was something inexpressibly alluring, we must suppose, in the peculiar rankness of the infamy which was then to be got at Lucknow."[91] And a bit later: "With what object, then, did he undertake so long a journey? Evidently in order that he might give, in an irregular manner, that sanction which in a regular manner he could not give, to the crimes of those who had recently hired him; and in order that a confused mass of testimony which he did not sift, which he did not even read, might acquire an authority not properly belonging to it, from the signature of the highest judicial functionary in India."[92] When he sums up Impey's sentencing of Nuncomar, the narrative strategy is very like: "No rational man can doubt that he took this course in order to gratify the Governor-General."[93] Macaulay makes good use of "in order to" in two of these three passages, and its frequency suggests how much hinges on intention. The concessions made in "we must suppose" and "Evidently" make some small gesture toward something conjectured but not known, yet note that Macaulay invokes the "rational man" here not as a way of inferring Impey's intentions from some standard of reasonableness. He is not saying that any rational man might have been motivated by loyalty to Hastings, as was Impey. Instead Macaulay introduces the rational man as a man like himself—the man who knows that Impey intended to murder Nuncomar. No rational man can doubt Impey's intentions, because Macaulay has given us access to Impey's mind. Macaulay puts "Evidently" to use, and yet even with its suggestion of "evidence," "Evidently" gives us something that is obvious and irrefutable and not something inferred. The weight of the narrative buries the inferential cues.

Stephen's answer to Macaulay is to turn from a way of thinking that makes free use of the adverb "Evidently" to one that more overtly separates evidence from such assertions of knowledge. If Macaulay erases the signs of his labor, they are writ large in Stephen's *Nuncomar*. Here is Stephen introducing Impey to his readers after quoting passages from Macaulay's account:

> I have not, in my own experience of persons holding conspicuous positions in life, met with any of the fiends in human shape, or even with any of those parti-coloured monsters with characters like the pattern of a shepherd's plaid, half black, half white, which abound in Macaulay's histories, and form one of the principal defects in those most delightful books. I have read everything I could find throwing light on Impey's character, and it appears to me that he was neither much blacker nor much whiter, in whole or in part, than his neighbours. He seems to me to have resembled closely many other judges whom I have known. He was by no means a specially interesting person, and was in all ways a far smaller man than Hastings. He seems to have had an excellent education both legal and general, to have been a man of remarkable energy and courage, and a great deal of rather common-place ability. I have read through all his letters and private papers, and I can discover in them no trace of corruption. Though he had a strong avowed and perfectly natural anxiety about his own interests, he seems to have had a considerable share of public spirit. . . . When his conduct in the different matters objected to is fully examined, I think it will appear that if the whole of his conduct is not fully justified, he ought at least to be honourably acquitted of the tremendous charges which Macaulay has brought against him. (1:34–5)

Stephen's recourse to "it appears to me," "He seems to me," "He seems to have had" (twice) registers the speculativeness of his narrative procedures. The first-person narrative makes its responsibility to the evidence paramount, as Stephen's claims to research make clear ("I have read everything I could find throwing light on Impey's character," "I have read through all his letters and private papers"), and what is required is a full examination. His explicit references to evidence—letters and private papers—mark his work as openly inferential. This narrative will tell a story, but it will be a story that proceeds from conduct and circumstance to character.

Comparing his brother's treatment of Nuncomar, Hastings, and Impey to that of his family friend Macaulay, Leslie Stephen creates a seemingly perfect equation: "Fitzjames's mental excellencies and defects exactly invert Macaulay's."[94] The criticisms Leslie Stephen launches against Macaulay are both substantial and persuasive. Like his brother, Leslie Stephen recognizes Macaulay's "Warren Hastings" as the work in which he "reached the very culminating point of his surpassing literary skill."[95] And like his brother, he could see the uselessness of trying to unseat Macaulay. Macaulay's opponents "may disprove his statements; they can hardly hope to displace his versions of fact from their hold upon popular belief."[96] As an opinion-maker, Macaulay was beyond refutation. More than this, Macaulay's essays slipped from fact to fancy: "His imagination undoubtedly worked upon a great mass of knowledge; but the very nature of the imaginative process was to weave all the materials into a picture, and therefore to fill up gaps by conjecture. He often unconsciously makes fancy do the work of logic."[97] And later:

> We can never be certain whether one of Macaulay's brilliant pictures is—as it sometimes certainly is—a fair representation of a vast quantity of evidence or an audacious inference from a few hints and indications. It represents, in either case, the effect upon his mind; but the effect, if lively enough, is taken to prove itself. He will not condescend to the prosaic consideration of evidence, or to inserting the necessary "if's" and "perhapses" which disturb so painfully the impressions of a vivid narrative.[98]

The distance between the fair representation and the audacious inference is wide, but as Leslie Stephen suggests, the vividness of the narrative makes the representation not fair but irresistible, and the sense that Macaulay is inferring is lost in the vivacity and momentum of the prose. Leslie Stephen calls attention to Macaulay's conjectures and inferences, but as Stephen himself notes, Macaulay leaves out most of the verbal cues—the necessary *ifs* and *perhapses*—that would invite us to register his picture as conjectural, and the cues that are present are barely audible. Without the necessary cues, we are to assume that Macaulay is a special seer. Special seers do not require the *ifs* and *perhapses*. T. S. Eliot's Tiresias in *The Waste Land* should not have said (as he does in a manuscript of *The Waste Land*) "She turns and looks a moment in the glass, / Hardly aware of her departed lover; / Across her brain one half-formed thought may pass"; to which Ezra Pound, having crossed out the "may," responded in his marginal commentary on the manuscript, "make up yr. mind you Tiresias if you know know damn well or else you don't."[99] Macaulay knows.

While Leslie Stephen all too easily absolves Macaulay of responsibility for the slipperiness of his essays by invoking the unconscious ("He often unconsciously makes fancy do the work of logic"), he also absolves the reader of his responsibility for becoming engrossed in them. Such was Macaulay's power, and it was a power Fitzjames Stephen did not claim to have and was not recognized as having. His "imagination did not clothe the evidence with brilliant colours; and, on the other hand, did not convert conjectures into irresistible illusions."[100] Here Leslie Stephen articulates with striking clarity Macaulay's practice, for it is the conversion of conjecture into illusion (whether resistible or not) that the essays demonstrate, and he praises his brother for not imitating Macaulay's conversion acts, but the compliment does not have much punch, for it is preceded by critique. The nakedness of the evidence Fitzjames Stephen presents has no appeal for Leslie Stephen. We watch Leslie Stephen move from one hand to the other as he attempts to fix the positions of both Macaulay and Fitzjames. Of his brother's narrative practice in *The Story of Nuncomar and the Impeachment of Sir Elijah Impey*, Leslie Stephen declares: "He is applying to an historical question the methods learnt in the practice of the courts of law. The book is both in form and substance the careful summing up of a judge in a complicated criminal case. The disadvantage, from a literary point of view, is obvious."[101] By implication, the literary point of view is not Fitzjames Stephen's point of view, and so the contrast Leslie Stephen builds is between the literary practices of Macaulay and the legal (and nonliterary) practices of Fitzjames Stephen. A few pages later, Leslie Stephen gives a name to his brother's mode: it is, for Leslie Stephen, "the purely judicial method,"[102] a method disadvantaged because of what it must exclude. The method "tends to the exclusion of considerations which, though rightly excluded from a criminal inquiry, cannot be neglected by an historian."[103] What, in particular, Leslie Stephen thinks was excluded from Fitzjames's Stephen's legal narrative is the "impression" that Hastings must have had a hand in Nuncomar's prosecution:

> A jury would be properly directed to acquit Hastings upon the charge of having instigated the prosecution of Nuncomar. Yet, after all, it is very hard to resist the impression that he must have had some share, more or less direct, in producing an event which occurred just at the right moment and had such fortunate results for him. It would be very wrong to hang a man upon such presumptions; but it is impossible to deny that they have a logical bearing upon the facts.[104]

If Macaulay represents the power of irresistible illusion and Fitzjames Stephen the judicial method, then Leslie Stephen tries to occupy a middle position. He is the historian who cannot neglect what the judge excludes but who will not convert conjecture into illusion. I am, however, interested in the way the irresistible, and in particular the irresistible impression ("it is very hard to resist the impression") resurfaces here. Even as Leslie Stephen distances himself from Macaulay, the passage bears Macaulay's mark. The picture Leslie Stephen produces—of a coincidence that is no coincidence— makes an impression on the mind. Is this not like what Leslie Stephen, just a few paragraphs earlier, describes as what happens to and in Macaulay, where a picture that represents "the effect upon his mind" becomes an effect that "if lively enough, is taken to prove itself"? Although Leslie Stephen argues that a capital sentence should not be based on the "presumptions" he names, why would any judge exclude them (unless they were deemed prejudicial) if they had "a logical bearing on the facts"? If it would be wrong to hang a man based on such presumptions, would it also be wrong to imprison him? The passage is surprisingly slippery (unrepresentative of the rest of the biography) as Leslie Stephen shifts from the pressure of "it is very hard to resist the impression that he must have" to the looseness of "some share, more or less direct" and the pejoratively critical "presumptions" (suggesting them as misleading as against the "facts" at the end of the passage) but finally to the insistence of "it is impossible to deny" and the recourse to the "logical." Perhaps Stephen is registering the slipperiness of the problem itself. The passage at once denies that these presumptions provide sufficient proof of the accusation and then immediately asserts that it must be the case that the presumptions have the force of logic that lead us to a certain conclusion. By the end of the passage, one feels that it would not be proper for a jury to acquit Hastings. Instead of occupying a middle position between his brother and Macaulay, Leslie Stephen is unable to negotiate the middle space.

Curiously enough, Fitzjames Stephen does not (as Leslie Stephen appears to claim) exclude as irrelevant the fact of the coincidence of the two events at issue (Nuncomar's accusations against Hastings and Mohun Persaud's accusations against Nuncomar) that Leslie Stephen highlights. Whether one agrees or disagrees with the specific observations Fitzjames Stephen makes about this evidence—and it would not be unreasonable to disagree with his findings—one should recognize the fullness with which Fitzjames Stephen handles the accusation. What Fitzjames Stephen asserts is that the coincidence is not sufficient proof of guilt though it rightly raises a suspicion of guilt. Working out the problem, Fitzjames Stephen conceives hypotheticals in support of this analysis. That Hastings had an interest in Nuncomar's arrest and that Nuncomar was arrested

> can be accepted as proof of a conspiracy between Hastings and Impey only by a person who is prepared to assume in general terms that whenever any one in whose death A has an interest dies under such circumstances that B, a friend of A's, may possibly have caused that death by criminal means, A and B must be presumed to have conspired to have murdered the deceased. One consequence of such a rule would be that if a doctor were the friend of the heir to a large fortune, and the medical attendant of the owner, and if the owner died whilst the doctor was in attendance on him, the doctor must be presumed to have poisoned him. (2:39–40)

The analogy Stephen creates between this hypothetical and the case against Hastings is not entirely persuasive: Stephen's fictive doctor has no pressing interest in the death of the patient, since he is not in debt or in any way an enemy of the victim. By framing the account in this way, Stephen implicitly downplays the threat Nuncomar posed to Hastings. But more provocative is the consideration that the story Stephen tells is one we have heard before. The hypothetical Stephen produces is not very far from one of the crucial subplots of George Eliot's *Middlemarch* that I have examined in detail in chapter 3.[105] Recall that Raffles, under the care of Dr. Lydgate and Bulstrode, dies. Bulstrode, it is soon discovered by the town, has a large interest in the blackmailer Raffles's death, and Lydgate is indebted to Bulstrode, who has recently provided him with a large loan. We know that there is no conspiracy between Bulstrode and Lydgate, both because we have witnessed the scenes between them and because we have special access to the interior lives of both Bulstrode and Lydgate. Middlemarchers (aside from Dorothea and perhaps Farebrother) are quick to presume that such a conspiracy exists, and Eliot is not uncritical of their willingness to move from presumption to conviction, at least in their minds if not in a court of law. One observation to make, then, is that Eliot rejects the presumptions this stock novel plot raises. More than this, the access Eliot gives us to Lydgate and Bulstrode makes a difference to the reader's experience of the events. So too does Macaulay's own narrative authority make a difference to the reader's experience of Hastings. What makes the impression of Hastings's guilt irresistible to Leslie Stephen is the power of this stock story and the way Macaulay has already told it. Combining the authority of history and the license of fiction, Macaulay turns a presumption into a proof. It is this move that Fitzjames Stephen's legal historical narrative attempts to reverse. But, as even Leslie Stephen himself admits, Macaulay's critics "may disprove his statements; they can hardly hope to displace his versions of fact from their hold upon popular belief."[106]

The "judicial method," as practiced by Fitzjames Stephen, resists with some success the pressure of the fictionalized historical narrative Macaulay creates, a narrative that (as George Levine has shown) itself owes its shape to the nineteenth-century novel, as the novel was itself influenced by the historical narrative. With its "characteristics of a legal novel," Stephen's *Nuncomar* attempts to produce a responsible narrative that combines elements of the novel, history, and legal procedure. Stephen frames his own narrative as an attempt to correct what he believed to be Macaulay's injustice to Impey, though Stephen is quick to add that it was not an injustice that Macaulay committed intentionally. After listing the reasons why he remains Macaulay's great admirer, including the work Macaulay did on the Indian Penal Code, which Stephen elsewhere praises, Stephen offers what is at once an excuse for Macaulay and a foundation for his own book. The work and life of Macaulay as a whole "make me anxious if I can to repair a wrong done by him, not intentionally, for there never was a kinder-hearted man, but because he adopted on insufficient grounds the traditional hatred which the Whigs bore to Impey, and also because his marvellous power of style blinded him to the effect which his language produced" (1:3). Stephen here extenuates Macaulay's guilt by alleging that the wrong done was unintentional, ready as he is to infer intention from the circumstances within which Macaulay lived and from the style of the writing itself. Stephen adduces a state of mind that is negligent (and not intentional), and he bases his conclusion on his own personal knowledge of Macaulay (which he openly acknowledges) as well as from the intensity of the rhetoric itself.

Yet by the end of *The Story of Nuncomar and the Impeachment of Sir Elijah Impey*, Stephen has implicitly reconsidered his earlier judgment. Though the last paragraph of the book begins by offering Macaulay protection from accusation, it ends with its own accusation against him. Having cleared Impey of judicial murder, Stephen accuses Macaulay of literary murder, an accusation that radically revises Stephen's earlier claims about Macaulay's good intentions. *The Story of Nuncomar and the Impeachment of Sir Elijah Impey* begins and ends with claims about Macaulay's intentions. Whereas at the beginning of the work Stephen says that Macaulay's wrong was committed unintentionally, by the end Stephen has turned Macaulay's negligent act into a murder. To make this claim, Stephen calls, quite unexpectedly, on Thomas De Quincey to illuminate his final analysis. Of Macaulay's essay Stephen concludes: "To the memory of Impey it was a gibbet. To the whole English nation it has become the one popular account of the early stages of the Indian Empire—the accepted myth. Slightly to adapt the famous remark of De Quincey in his essay on *Murder as a Fine Art*, Impey has owed his moral ruin to a literary murder of which Macaulay probably thought but little when he committed it" (2:272). The "remark" of De Quincey that Stephen has in mind is from De Quincey's second essay in the series grouped together as *On Murder Considered as One of the Fine Arts*, and the remark itself is not as famous as the observations that immediately precede it. Even John Bartlett's *Familiar Quotations* (fourteenth edition) includes the following passage:

> For, if once a man indulges himself in murder, very soon he comes to think little of robbing, and from robbing he comes next to drinking and Sabbath-breaking, and from that to incivility and procrastination. Once begin upon this downward path, you never know where you are to stop.[107]

What Bartlett does not include is the next sentence, to which Stephen alludes: "Many a man dated his ruin from some murder or other that perhaps he thought little of at the time." Stephen's adaptation is more than slight and it places responsibility for Impey's ruin on Macaulay. In De Quincey's passage, the ruined man is the murderer. In Stephen's adaptation, the ruined man is the victim. Impey does not merely date his ruin from his murder; he owes his ruin—his moral ruin—to Macaulay's literary murder, and while Stephen cannot know what Macaulay thought at the time, the probability, claims Stephen, is that he was not thinking about the consequences of his act.

Why does Stephen bring De Quincey in at this crucial moment, in the last sentence of his work? After all, Stephen needs to do quite a bit of adapting to make De Quincey's sentence apt to his own narrative. The tone is also markedly distinct. Where De Quincey's "some murder or other," as well as the sentences that precede this bit (on the degenerative influences of murder), make the satire unmistakable, Stephen's accusation is without irony. What De Quincey's essay delights in is the connection between murder and art.[108] By naming Macaulay's act as a literary murder and invoking De Quincey's essay, Stephen allows us to consider Macaulay's representational methods as not just culpable but homicidal. That Stephen should convert a story about a judicial murder — Impey's alleged murder by trial of Nuncomar — into a literary murder gives us pause, since Stephen shifts attention from the violence of a judicial act to the violence of a literary narrative.[109] Without calling into question the brutality of a judicial murder, had such been proved, Stephen takes seriously the violence of Macaulay's own telling.

Much depends on Stephen's representations of intent throughout the narrative. Such questions occur even on the margins of the text, where footnotes, particularly at the beginning of the work, invoke matters of intent with some frequency.[110] And when Stephen himself comes to handling the states of mind of the accused — Hastings and Impey — he offers up a narrative method markedly distinct from that of Macaulay. First and foremost, Stephen presents a detailed account of the trial of Nuncomar, including transcripts of the examination of witnesses and of Impey's summing up at the end of the trial. Stephen sorts through the evidence introduced at trial (by the prosecution and the defense), the objections to such evidence, and rulings on the evidence issued by the panel of judges. Stephen explicitly works from the transcript to discover Impey's intentions. More than once in the work, he reminds his audience that he is one of the first writers to analyze in detail the transcript ("I think I may claim to be the first writer [except Mr. Adolphus] who has really studied the matter fully. Most of those who have written upon it have not, as I believe, ever read the trial at all" [1:106]). Having examined the transcript in such detail, Stephen declares in no uncertain terms that "no man ever had, or could have, a fairer trial than Nuncomar, and that Impey in particular behaved with absolute fairness and as much indulgence as was compatible with his duty" (1:186). Macaulay's essay takes up none of the details of Impey's conduct at the trial, which fact Stephen tacitly notices when he makes this telling observation about the difference between his own narrative, which he associates with the trial stories presented in the *State Trials*, and Macaulay's essay: "the first matter which directed my attention to the subject was the glaring contrast between Impey's conduct as described in the *State Trials* and his character as described by Lord Macaulay" (1:186). Though Macaulay makes reference to Impey's conduct in his essay ("Of Impey's conduct it is impossible to speak too severely," "But we must not forget to do justice to Sir Elijah Impey's conduct on this occasion"[111]), he moves not from conduct to inferences about character but rather from character to conduct. Impey's conduct is determined by what Macaulay already imagines him to be like as a young student with Hastings at Westminster; for Macaulay, Impey's habit of mind was always to serve Hastings. The shift from conduct to character in the preceding passage reveals the different discursive practices, as Stephen sees them, in the *State Trials* (and Stephen's own narrative) and in Macaulay's essay.[112]

The trial transcript defines the limits of Stephen's inferences about Impey's intentions. Each question asked, each ruling, each detail mentioned in Impey's summing up becomes the alleged criminal act—the external element—through which the internal element is inferred. Once Stephen establishes in his own mind the fairness of the trial, questions about motives—about what interests moved Impey—become irrelevant. So, for example, Stephen takes Impey's eighteenth-century accusers to task for making motive an element of a crime. In Impey's impeachment trial the lead counsel, Sir Gilbert Elliot, asserted that "unless a corrupt motive could be proved the impeachment ought to fall to the ground," to which Stephen responds that such a remark demonstrates a fundamental confusion between intents and motives. Intents are elements of a crime. Motives are evidence that a crime may have taken place. Moreover, says Stephen,

> If Impey really did conspire with Hastings to destroy Nuncomar, or really did try him unfairly, what did his motives matter? If they were as good as possible he would still be a judicial murderer and an unjust judge. If they were as bad as possible he could be no more. If, on the other hand, Impey tried Nuncomar fairly and did not conspire with Hastings, what did it matter if he had motives for doing the contrary? The existence of a motive for guilt is always an important article of evidence in determining whether the guilt exists, but it can hardly ever form a constituent element in the guilt itself, according to the Whig theory. (2:57, n. 1)

The long and the short of this complicated set of hypotheticals is that if Impey committed the crime, motives are irrelevant, and if Impey didn't commit the crime, then motives are irrelevant. Stephen's logic here is not far from that of Wimsatt and Beardsley in their formulations of the intentional fallacy: "One must ask how a critic expects to get an answer to the question about intention. How is he to find out what the poet tried to do? If the poet succeeded in doing it, then the poem itself shows what he was trying to do."[113] Since Stephen has already determined that the trial was fair (and did not constitute a judicial murder), then nothing more need be said about what may or may not have been in Impey's mind when he presided over the trial. Stephen's logic is not unappealing here, particularly since he admits that "a motive for guilt is always an important article of evidence in determining whether the guilt exists." Yet because Stephen has himself already determined that the trial was fairly conducted in the first volume of work, by the time we get to this passage in this second volume, motives must (following Stephen) be irrelevant. Stephen goes further by saying that even a conspiracy between Hastings and Impey would be irrelevant if the trial was conducted fairly (2:189–90).

As much as Stephen tries to keep motives at bay, they reenter the text in the second volume of the work, and they show up most powerfully after Stephen has declared not only that the accusations against Impey were never proved, but also that Impey was positively innocent of the charges brought against him. In "Warren Hastings," Macaulay exposes Impey's desire to remain utterly loyal to Hastings. Of such a motive, Stephen concludes:

> Impey was no doubt his old friend. They had been school-fellows and had known each other for thirty years, but mere personal friendship is at once too amiable and in common cases too weak a motive to induce a man to commit the foulest of all murders, and it certainly did not prevent Impey from acting afterwards in a way which was in the highest degree unwelcome to Hastings. (2:55–6)

That Stephen adduces evidence of a conflict between Impey and Hastings that arose in the following years to support his conclusion about motive in the trial and execution of Nuncomar suggests that Stephen wants more than his own conjecture about friendship to support his assertions here. But much hangs on the way he imagines this friendship as a motivating impulse. A bit later, he adds: "To suppose [as Macaulay supposes] that out of mere friendship Impey tried to serve a falling man by treacherously murdering his enemy is to ascribe to him on the one hand romantic generosity, and on the other the meanest and most cowardly cruelty" (2:68). The reliance on "mere" in both passages exposes a weakness in his position, for the repetition of the adjective stands in for a more rigorous argument. One question here is whether Stephen himself could imagine being motivated by friendship to commit so heinous a crime. His own narrative gives evidence that he could not. I turn back now to Stephen's comment in his 1859 essay: "we know our own feelings, but we only know other men's actions, and infer from them that they feel as we should feel if we were to act in the same manner." Throughout *The Story of Nuncomar and the Impeachment of Sir Elijah Impey*, Stephen illustrates the truth of his own claim. One is struck by the moments in the narrative in which Stephen speaks in the voice of Hastings or Impey, and Stephen's special connection to Impey is understandable, particularly to Stephen himself. In the second paragraph of the work, Stephen readily discloses his special "interest" in both senses: "The most prominent part too in Nuncomar's story is played by Sir Elijah Impey, and it is natural that a judge who has also held the office of Legal Member of Council in India should feel an interest in the history of a Chief Justice of the Supreme Court of Calcutta charged with judicial murder, alleged to have been committed in order to shield the first Governor-General of Bengal from detection by the majority of his council in corruption" (1:2). Stephen announces this interest without paltering, even though it impugns his own objectivity. In a letter to Lady Grant Duff of October 7, 1883, he goes so far as to refer to "his spiritual brother Chief Justice Impey,"[114] and while the exaggeration of the title "spiritual brother" sharpens the satiric edge, it is not entirely untrue. When faced with the question of whether the trial was fair, given that Impey and the other judges had participated in the cross-examination of Nuncomar's witnesses, Stephen argues: "No one who has not been in that position can understand the difficulty into which a judge is thrown when the counsel do not understand their business" (1:178). And reviewing Impey's summing up to the jury, he observes simply "There is not a word in his summing-up of which I should have been ashamed had I said it myself" (1:186).

The year after *The Story of Nuncomar and the Impeachment of Sir Elijah Impey* was published, Keshub Chandra Acharya published *The Defence of Nundakumar: A Reply to Sir James Stephen's Book*. This short essay, printed by the Sadharani Press in Calcutta, is, I think, remarkable for the way it attends to the limits of Stephen's narrative. Using the facts that Stephen himself presents in his work (and not claiming to have done any independent research), Acharya argues that such facts demonstrate the innocence of Nuncomar (whose name he transliterates as Nundakumar on some occasions and Nunda Coomar on others). Of the guilt of Impey, Acharya is less strident: "As to the question whether Impey deliberately murdered Nundakumar or not; I leave my readers to draw their own conclusions from the facts of the case," though it is clear from the narrative that he thinks both Impey and Hastings guilty.[115] Describing Impey's summing up at the end of Nuncomar's trial, he contends: "Then Sir Elijah Impey sheds crocodiles tears, that he was compelled to make bad observations on the evidence of a man [Kissenjan Dass, a witness for Nuncomar], of whom he entertained so good an opinion."[116] Acharya's narrative of the friendship of Hastings and Impey is discerning:

> Under the circumstances, it was a matter of highest concern to Hastings to bring calumny upon Nundakumar and disgrace him in the estimation of the public, at that moment this could be very easily done by Hastings with a respectable exterior through the instrumentality of Mohun Prosad. Hastings on the other hand, may have encouraged the prosecution, and on the other he may have painted Nundakumar a veritable black devil to his friend Impey. Whether Warren Hastings took Sir Elijah Impey to his confidence, and openly asked him to remove Nundakumar from his way, is a question which cannot be solved now; but looking to the relation which existed between Hastings and Impey, and their conduct throughout and subsequent to the trial, it can be safely asserted that Impey started with the trial of the case with a preconceived idea of the guilt of Nundakumar, and any man having the least experience of the official clique can understand how easy it was for him to bring round the other Judges and the Jury to his opinion, and how Hastings could also influence Impey without making him appear dishonest. Hastings may have adopted the same means, which in the good old days of the indigo Raj, our planters did with district Magistrates against their Zamindar opponents, and prepared the minds of the Judges to believe any story against Nundakumar.[117]

The impulse behind Acharya's narrative of the interior life arises out of his own different set of inferences from the atmosphere in which this trial took place and from the invisible influence exercised among the Europeans in India. "The conspiracy might have been formed without a word being spoken directly on the point," he later asserts, "and both the Judges and the Jury might have been prepared by Hastings to believe everything against Nundaku-mar as gospel truth."[118] Acharya's reading of colonial oppression shapes his narrative of Impey's intents and the intents of the other judges and the jury:

> Sir Elijah Impey, on hearing that Nundakumar was prosecuting his friend in his own council, for corruption and bribery, might have made up his mind to help him without any special request from him for that purpose, and all other judges and members of the jury may have become indignant against Nundakumar for his audacity for bringing charges against the celestial persons of Englishmen in India. It was a duty of the highest concern to all Englishmen not to allow the natives to know, that there was any superior authority over them in England and how they could achieve this, without putting down the first native who ventured to raise his head against them?[119]

Acharya identifies 1775 as a time "when the Europeans in India were looked upon as members of one family,"[120] and in so identifying the period he reads, from the same facts Stephen has presented, the English bias against Nunco-mar. Acharya does not want to claim that Impey deliberately and premeditat-edly murdered Nuncomar ("I am inclined to believe that neither Hastings, nor Sir E. Impey, did think of murdering Nundakumar when the prosecution started"[121]) but that Nuncomar's continued defiance pushed Impey and the other judges to do so.

Acharya's work importantly raises questions about Stephen's own attempts to exonerate Hastings and Impey. When Stephen exposes the dishonesties, exaggerations, and fictionalizations in Macaulay's narrative, he demonstrates the irresponsibility of the highhanded certainty, of omniscience, of the presentation of inferences as known facts, particularly with respect to criminal motive and intent. In his own book on Warren Hastings, Stephen's friend Sir Alfred Lyall praises the work done in *The Story of Nuncomar and the Impeachment of Sir Elijah Impey* for its "method," which laid bare "the loose fabric of assertions, invectives, and ill-woven demonstrations upon which the enemies of Hastings and Impey based and pushed forward their attacks."[122] But even Lyall will not endorse the moments in which "Stephen undertakes to establish, by argument from the general motives of human action, the moral certainty that Hastings was totally unconnected with the business, and that the popular impression against him is utterly wrong.[123] Lyall resists "standing surety to this extent for the undiscoverable motives and behavior of a man in the situation of Hastings."[124] Lyall recognizes the complexity of Hastings "with his reticence, self command, consummate mastery of his instruments, fertility of resource, and firmness of purpose."[125] Not unlike Acharya, Lyall counters Stephen with another possible story about motive and intent: "the fact that Impey tried the man with great patience, forbearance, and exact formality, might prove nothing against an intention to hang him, but only that he was too wise to strain the law superfluously."[126]

What distinguishes Acharya's challenge from Lyall's, quite obviously, is that Acharya's point of view gives his claim about trials of Indians by Europeans in the eighteenth century more authority. Acharya's critique attends particularly to Stephen's representation of the motives and intents of Hastings and Impey. Acharya objects when Stephen interprets the external circumstances of the trial *as if* the trial could be fair, but a trial of an Indian in a colonial territory is necessarily unfair. Acharya's objection to Stephen recalls Peter Brooks's analysis of the Supreme Court's rulings on the admissibility of confessions. Acharya implicitly contests the way Stephen's colonialist discourse tells the legal event—Nuncomar's trial and execution. Brooks argues that the United States Supreme Court creates a story about voluntariness and involuntariness of confessions by invoking a context within which the confession takes place. So too Stephen, like the Supreme Court, invokes legal procedure—the external circumstances—to show that Impey did not commit judicial murder. But for Acharya, these circumstances only confirm Impey's bias against Nuncomar all the more. The very fact of the trial is a sign of that bias. So too for Brooks, all confessions are coerced, always reflect shame and abjection, and never can be deemed voluntary.

To go one step further, I would argue that Acharya's critique of Stephen anticipates the questions Austin Sarat poses about Peter Brooks's work on confession. Sarat asks how Brooks can present such a conclusive rendering of the interior lives—the intentions—of the confessing subjects. Acharya challenges Stephen on the same grounds. And yet, as significant as Acharya's contribution is, one might ask whether Acharya is (in Sarat's words) "any better at reading the inner life of the speaking subject than any other external observer would be." A politically savvy response to this assertion would be that as a colonial subject, Acharya is a de facto better external observer than Stephen is. But is this necessarily so? Mark Kelman, in his contribution to the essays collected in *Questions of Evidence* and entitled "Reasonable Evidence of Reasonableness," asks a related question. Kelman's essay examines the difficulties that pertain when we try to talk about reasonableness in self-defense cases. When is it reasonable to use deadly force against another person? Kelman's essay considers the ways the law evaluates evidence in self-defense cases of claims of "reasonable force," that is, claims that the actor reasonably believed that he or she needed to use deadly force to avoid death or serious injury. To tease out some answers to this question, Kelman presents two hypotheticals to his law school classes. The first involves an abused woman who shoots and kills her sleeping abuser. The second offers a white man on the subway who shoots and kills an African-American youth who might or might not be a threat to him. He asks his students to distinguish these cases. In trying to do so, Kelman reports that his "leftist" students (his name for them) argue that

"Oppressed people . . . have privileged access to both moral truths (like the 'proper' resolution of the question of what sorts of potential suffering ought to justify the use of deadly force) and the facts of social life (for example, how dangerous and abusive men 'really' are)."[127] But, Kelman continues, "The belief that oppression yields knowledge . . . proves difficult to sustain. This is dominantly the case because members of oppressed groups often clash with one another in their vision of moral and factual truths."[128] Acharya's reading of the trial and of the intentions and motivations of Impey and Hastings may be more accurate, but its accuracy does not simply arise out of his status as oppressed. Yet Acharya's essay does suggest the limits of the legal narrative. Focusing on the question of the fairness of the trial itself—the evidence against Nuncomar, the behavior of counsel and judges—Stephen does not account for what Acharya highlights. Was it fair to try an Indian in an English court? Stephen's legal narrative wants to narrow the inquiry to the rights and wrongs of the specific case before him. In response to the assertions that "even if the law of England justified Impey's course, it was so distinctly opposed to natural justice that he was criminal for putting it in force," Stephen gives these familiarly inadequate and self-serving observations: "To admit such a principle would be to destroy the specific character of law, and to throw everything into confusion. To punish a judge for enforcing a bad law implies a right and duty on the part of the judge to decide whether the law is good or not; and this puts the judge above the legislature" (2:17).

Kelman's essay is instructive for another reason as well. An additional problem for law students (and for the rest of us) in evaluating questions about reasonable force when faced with hypothetical situations of the abused woman and the fearful subway rider is that one has to come up with some idea of an objectively reasonable judgment about the use of force. Kelman reports that many of his students consider themselves "hyperskeptics" and actively resist any notion not only of an objectively reasonable judgment about force but also of objective facts more generally: "If asked to state their general, theoretical position on epistemological issues, leftist law students almost invariably enunciate a hyperskeptical multiculturalist position. In this view, there are no transcendent claims to truth at all. The test of the 'veracity' of a proposition is simply its capacity to convince *any* audience that can be identified as forming what might be seen as a subculture."[129] In short, some subcultures would believe the abused woman and others the fearful subway rider. But, as Kelman notes in an aside, such a position not only prevents students from criticizing a racially motivated murder but also might lead to the conclusion that a legal judgment about reasonable force could be based only on "a defendant's 'good faith' in believing that he acted properly."[130] But that proposition leads him to open, if only parenthetically, another philosophic door: "I will set aside," writes Kelman, "the difficult but hardly unrelated question of whether we would have any access to what the defendant genuinely, subjectively believed that was not at least partly mediated by our judgments about what it is 'reasonable' to believe."[131] Kelman does not comment on his parenthetical, but he does suggest that since we are prevented from knowing what a defendant "genuinely, subjectively believed," we have to rely on *our judgments* about what it is "reasonable" to believe. This means that our judgment of another's subjective state, that is, what he actually believed, depends in part on our own subjective judgments about reasonableness—how would we feel in that situation?

From the outset, Stephen must address serious accusations arising out of Hastings's conduct at the time of Nuncomar's accusations against him and in the days following, and he does so in a series of admirably terse sentences. Stephen says of his conduct: "An innocent man would have courted inquiry. Hastings prevented it, and that by an exercise of power which, if not illegal, was questionable and unnecessary [that is, he attempted to dissolve the Council]. An innocent man would at the very least have affirmed his innocence and denied the truth of the accusations made against him. Hastings never did so" (1:69). What Stephen goes on to do is not to outline what Hastings should have done but rather to suggest what Stephen would have done:

> If he had spoken his mind with absolute plainness and without any qualification or reserve I think he would have said: "As to inquiry, inquire if you will as a Committee, but I am a constituent part of the governing body of this country, and I will not accept the position of being at once President of the Court which is to hear and determine and the prisoner brought before it for trial. Besides you, Clavering, Monson and Francis are my real accusers. Nuncomar is acting in concert with you, and as you admit, has been in previous communication with you. You are my bitter enemies, and you shall not be my judges. If I recognised you in that capacity I should merely consent to my own condemnation. I stand on my legal rights and I defy you to do your worst." (1:71)

This is framed as a speculation ("I think he would have said") and the insistently speculative nature of the imagined monologue distinguishes it from Macaulay's practices; still, there is a remarkable sense of detail in this speculation about what Hastings would have said if he had spoken without qualification or reserve. It is impressive, to say the least, that Stephen can present this voice through his own. It seems that it is not Hastings who speaks his mind here but Stephen. What remains is for Stephen to consider why Hastings never denied the truth of Nuncomar's accusations, and his explanation is telling because it openly asserts the limits of his own imagination. "I cannot imagine," Stephen begins, "the state of mind in which a man capable of plotting a judicial murder in order to conceal gross corruption would have had a scruple as to falsely asserting his innocence" (1:72). When Stephen considers why Hastings would not submit to an "instant inquiry," he compares Hastings's situation to that of an accused judge: "If a judge on the bench were accused of partiality or corruption in the course of a trial, he would not consent to an inquiry till the trial was over, and he was accused in due course by a competent authority" (1:70). Is Stephen imagining how he would act, as a judge on the bench, had he been so accused?

Comparing the power and influence of his work on Nuncomar and Impey to that of Macaulay, Stephen remarks in resignation: "this book will be read by hardly any one, and Macaulay's paragraph will be read with delighted conviction by several generations" (2:114). "Conviction" feels particularly apt here, since it is the conviction of Impey as murderer that Macaulay's essay achieves. Stephen was wrong in the short run and right in the long. A collection of reviews of a book entitled *The Private Life of Warren Hastings by Sir Charles Lawson*, published in 1895–96, makes frequent reference to Stephen's work as a successful response to Macaulay's "Warren Hastings." But as an anonymous reviewer of *The Observer* recognizes, in a line that echoes Stephen's, "it is to be feared that when Stephen, Strachey, and Malleson are forgotten, Macaulay will be read by each successive generation with as much eagerness as by his own."[132] The reviewer registers what he sees as the all-too-likely possibility that Macaulay's power will reassert itself, but his "it is to be feared" also calls to mind the nineteenth-century objections to Macaulay. This was the movement of mind that Stephen (and Matthew Arnold) and others represented. Theirs was a turning against Macaulay, and while Macaulay's star has fallen, his "Warren Hastings" remains a work that is read. Stephen's *Nuncomar* is not. But for those who will read the latter, what is gained is an experience of a narrative that sets out to tell a responsibility story responsibly. Stephen's narrative sometimes fails, sometimes frustrates, sometimes exposes its own limitations and biases, but it contests Macaulay's authority and our own to go where he (and we) cannot: into the minds of men.

Conclusion
Modern Responsibilities

When Angel Clare returns to his wife, Tess, near the end of Thomas Hardy's *Tess of the d'Urbervilles*, he recognizes, though imperfectly, a change in her. The meeting is a predictably intense one, since Tess is living with Alec, the man who raped or seduced her (a crux about which many have argued) and who has all but forced her back to him with the promise that he would support her destitute family and by insisting that her husband would never come back to her. Of course, the enlightened Angel does come back to the heartsick Tess. Seeing his wife in tears and hearing her broken explanation and accusation, Angel takes the blame on himself ("'Ah—it is my fault!'"), but Hardy dismisses the attribution of blame as quickly as Angel offers it.[1] The dialogue ends ("he could not get on," 366) and the narrator explains: "Speech was as inexpressive as silence" (366). It is not just that the attribution of fault does no good; it is also that it expresses nothing relevant to the situation in which they find themselves. What follows from Angel's lame assessment of blame is the more potent observation—this time unspoken—which disengages questions of responsibility. Looking at his wife, Angel "had a vague consciousness of one thing, though it was not clear to him till later; that his original Tess had spiritually ceased to recognize the body before him as hers—allowing it to drift, like a corpse upon the current, in a direction dissociated from its living will" (366). This is the penultimate paragraph of the chapter that ends abruptly with Angel suddenly realizing that "Tess was gone" (366)—as indeed she is, in more ways than one. When the next chapter begins, we are unexpectedly in the presence of Mrs. Brooks, the owner of the house in which Tess and Alec are lodged. The sharply ironic tone in which the narrator describes Mrs. Brooks—a woman "too deeply materialized . . . by

213

her long and enforced bondage to that arithmetical demon, profit-and-loss, to retain much curiosity for its own sake" (367)—puts us at a distance from her and from the scene to come. We witness this last scene between Tess and Alec through the eyes and ears of Mrs. Brooks, who, fearing some unprofitable friction between her moneyed tenants, spies on them through a keyhole: not an auspicious vantage point, for she can see only a part of the rooms Tess and Alec occupy, and at best she hears "fragments" (368) of Tess's "murmur of unspeakable despair" (368). Under the best of circumstances, it would be hard to hear "the murmur of unspeakable despair," and listening through a keyhole no doubt makes matters worse. She cannot even hear Alec's response to Tess, which she can describe as only "more and sharper words" (368). Seeing Tess rise, the landlady retreats from the keyhole, returns to her rooms downstairs, hears some shuffling overhead, then notices "the form of Tess passing to the gate on the way into the street" (369). The murder (with a carving knife) remains unrepresented; we discover it with Mrs. Brooks, who chances to look up at her ceiling, where she sees "a spot in the middle of its white surface which she had never noticed there before. It was about the size of a wafer when she first observed it, but it speedily grew as large as the palm of her hand, and then she could perceive that it was red" (369).

I briefly take up Hardy's *Tess* here at the end of my study of Victorian narratives of criminal responsibility because the novel signals for me the beginning of a much more heightened and overt literary modern self-consciousness of and skepticism about the relations between intentions and actions in the context of crime (though not solely in the context of crime) that widens the gap between legal and literary representations of these elements. When Hardy dissociates Tess's body from her living will just moments before she stabs Alec, he makes plain that she is not responsible for the acts her body performs, though the law with its simplistic sense of right and wrong (as Hardy presents it) will hold her accountable for those acts. The body, corpselike and drifting, acts of its own accord. Elsewhere in the novel, Hardy has dissociated Tess's will and body, representing the body's involuntary erotic responses that stimulate often unwelcome male admirers.[2] After the murder, Mrs. Brooks sees "the form of Tess" leaving the house, and Angel—watching something approach him on the road from a distance—can make out only that "the form descending the incline was a woman's" (371) until she is close enough so that he can "believe her to be Tess" (371). The separation of Tess and the form of Tess is striking. Angel's reading of her as the separation of the living will from the dead body gives us a complete disjunction of act from will. When Tess announces to Angel that she has killed Alec (she says first "I have done it—I don't know how" and then "I have killed him!" 372) and Angel responds, "But how do you mean—you have killed him?" (372), his question is provocative, since we and he are not at all sure how or whether that phrase can have meaning when applied to Tess. In the end, it has meaning only in the eyes of the law, an institution that holds onto the very ideas about character that Angel (and the novel itself, which now authorizes Angel's enlightened responses to Tess) has long since abandoned. Tess's strange equivocation, "I have done it–I don't know how," makes sense since her body has nothing to do with her will. These lines echo Tess's earlier exchange with Alec, who—though born again—chucks his newly found evangelical fervor to pursue Tess anew. When she discovers that he has given up preaching, she asks, "'what does this mean—what have I done?'" (313) to which Alec responds prophetically: "'Done?' 'Nothing intentionally. But you have been the means—the innocent means—of my backsliding, as they call it'" (313). When the carving knife later slides into Alec's back, are we to recall this scene and its assertion that she has done "nothing intentionally"? It is not, as it is in Eliot's *Daniel Deronda*, that Hardy imagines the possibility that Tess's will has killed Alec. We have no special access to her inner life before the killing or when she is recounting her last moments with Alec to Angel. Angel sums up his own response to the event with a stunning dismissal of it: "It was very terrible, if true: if a temporary hallucination, sad. But anyhow here was this deserted wife of his" (373) and, finally, "Tenderness was absolutely dominant in Clare at last" (373). The colon that equalizes the truth and the hallucination means that it does not matter which is the case. Clare's "But anyhow" is momentarily startling, though we are asked to accept it. Whether the killing is real or imagined is a question that finds itself beside the point. How far we are from *Daniel Deronda*, where Deronda—also a protector figure—must know what Gwendolen means when she claims to have killed her husband. What hangs in the balance for Hardy in *Tess* is nothing less than character–and, by extension, personality–itself. Throughout *Tess*, Hardy deploys a critique of the idea of a coherent, continuous personality that may be held accountable for its actions. It is an idea Eliot herself was beginning to critique in her last great novel, for as Linda Shires asserts, there are many more "flat" characters in *Daniel Deronda* than we expect in an Eliot novel.[3] Shires builds a strong case for the claim that *Daniel Deronda* questions not only coherence of character but "the very nature of the self,"[4] and while I think Shires says too much when she insists that the novel "commands our attention primarily for a total rewriting of realist character and action," her analysis illuminates the range with which Eliot handles both character and action in *Daniel Deronda*.[5] In *Tess*, Hardy makes Angel Clare champion this notion of a continuous personality—it is this that leads him to desert Tess after she confesses her past to him— until Clare finally lets go of such notions during his miraculous transformation in Brazil. Tess's own memory of her experiences is fragmented, and the third person narrator does not assemble the fragments for us to make a coherent whole. Instead, the narrator encourages us to reject Angel's attempts to create a continuous figure out of the fragments Tess presents.

So it seems we have returned to the beginning of this study—to *Oliver Twist*, where (as I argue) Dickens experiments with the discontinuities between and within conduct and character. But in other ways, we have traveled a fair distance from *Oliver Twist*. Hardy moves us into the self-consciousness of the modern novel by calling attention to Tess as a form, particularly after

Alec's murder. Curiously, both the murder and the figures involved in it begin to look interchangeable. The sign that murder has been committed is the "spot" on the white ceiling that gets larger and larger. Then, when Angel—looking down the road—sees Tess again, he at first notices only that "a moving spot intruded on the white vacuity" (371). The moving spot is Tess. And when the law shows up at Stonehenge to take Tess away, the head of the approaching man is described first as a "mere dot" (381) on the horizon. And finally, at the moment of Tess's execution, Angel and Liza-Lu look down at the prison tower and identify it as "the one blot on the city's beauty" (384). The spots and dot and blot—each associated with the crime and its aftermath—suggest an absence of meaning or a resistance to interpretation. Even Tess's "dirge," which Mrs. Brooks hears just before the murder, offers only an empty form "'O—O—O!'" (367), she repeats.

The question that the preceding analysis of *Tess* raises for me is this: how would one carry forward the work I have done with the internal and external elements of crime beyond the realist novel? In short, I bring this study to a close by suggesting its limits. Moving more fully into modern novels means handling characters overtly presented as fictions. When Winnie Verloc kills her husband near the end of Joseph Conrad's *Secret Agent*—a scene that owes more than a little to Hardy's *Tess*—she assumes the role of both spectator and actor. The heavily ironic descriptions of Mrs. Brooks that begin chapter 56 of *Tess* might well have appealed to Conrad; Winnie Verloc—like Mrs. Brooks—spies (through a keyhole) on her husband and the detective who wants to arrest him. Having learned of the death of her beloved brother, she becomes monomaniacally fixed on the fact that her husband has killed him (Stevie trips while carrying a bomb that Verloc has asked him to carry, an event that also complicates the representation of agency and responsibility). As the scene unfolds, it develops a passionate interiority for this famously outward-looking character who refuses to delve deeply into anything at all, least of all herself. Conrad's murder scene obviously represents a crime, but it also generates questions about whether Winnie acts as an agent of her actions. Though she obsessively imagines herself as a "free woman," a free agent, as it were, the repetition of the phrase only adds to our sense that agency itself is a fiction. She assumes the role of a premeditated murderer:

> She commanded her wits now, her vocal organs; she felt herself to be in an almost preternaturally perfect control of every fibre of her body. It was all her own, because the bargain was at an end. She had become cunning. She chose to answer him so readily for a purpose. She did not wish that man to change his position on the sofa which was very suitable to the circumstances.[6]

Moments before the act, Conrad transforms her into Stevie, who "had flown for shelter straight to the breast of his sister, guardian and protector," and as she approaches Verloc with the carving knife, "the resemblance of her face with that of her brother grew at every step, even to the droop of the lower lip, even to the slight divergence of the eyes."[7] In parodying a revenger's tragedy here, Conrad exposes the fictionality of the moment as he does time and again in this novel. Murder itself is a fiction in *The Secret Agent*, or, as Mr. Vladimir, the ambassadorial polyglot, announces early in the novel, "almost an institution."[8] So is crime. When one of the would-be revolutionaries notes with complacent disgust that someone has tried to blow up the Greenwich Observatory and labels such an act "nothing short of criminal," the Professor—a figure who commands a strange authority in the novel—responds simply but emphatically, "'Criminal! What is that? What *is* crime? What can be the meaning of such an assertion?'"[9]

It is a loaded question, to be sure. Neither Conrad nor Hardy before him rejects in its totality the representation of individual responsibility for a criminal act. Both remain in touch with the questions Dickens and Eliot and Stephen have raised.[10] So, too, although both *Tess* and *The Secret Agent* proceed as third person narratives and give us the access to the interior lives of characters that such narrators can provide, they refuse to assemble the characters or the narratives into a coherent form. *The Secret Agent* produces an overtly nonchronological narrative that involves the literal fragmentation of Stevie. The third person narrator of modern novels either disappears entirely (as in Faulkner's novel *As I Lay Dying*) or is only ambiguously present (as in Joyce's *Portrait of the Artist as a Young Man*) or displays more overtly and consistently his inability to know and to make whole the fragments of the story. One might note here, then, that the novel's loss of what is often called the omniscient narrator makes the novel's narratives more like those of the law or other disciplines in at least one respect, for like a juror, the reader is more insistently called on to make sense of the multiple and often conflicting points of view put into play. But such an analysis does not account for the way modern novels enter and represent the consciousness of their characters. Virginia Woolf's narratives of consciousness, for instance, allow readers direct access to the minds of her characters, access denied to us in law or in our everyday lives. Yet the kind of analysis I have pursued would be unproductive if applied to Woolf's work, not only because she is not a novelist who is deeply interested in the questions about criminal responsibility I pose (notwithstanding her familial tie to the life of the law—she was Fitzjames Stephen's niece) but also because her formal experimentations deny the separation of the internal from the external that plays so central a role in my study.

My analysis also depends on the novel and the law sharing certain assumptions about people, starting with the one that Fitzjames Stephen articulates in *A History of the Criminal Law of England* and with which I began my study: "The general rule is, that people are responsible for their actions." Such a statement has little relevance in the context of, say, Thomas Pynchon's novel *The Crying of Lot 49*. In his investigation of "postmodern fictions of crime," Jon Thompson takes up this novel and sums it up by noting that "it is impossible to tell if there is a crime, who the criminal is (if there is one), what clues there are (if they exist), or even what kind of rationality, or even irrationality, might be applied to the situation in order to resolve the protagonist's doubt."[11] I am not the first (nor will I be the last) to note that postmodernity's radical skepticism about the existence of the individual (or the "subject") empties out the idea of individual responsibility. Postmodern fiction, as Patricia Waugh describes it, "expresses nostalgia for but loss of belief in the concept of the human subject as an agent effectively intervening in history, through its fragmentation of discourses, language games, and decentring of subjectivity."[12] To consider representations of the relations between internal and external elements of crime in such a context would be vexed, at the very least. Once questions of responsibility have been emptied out, what else is there left to say about them?

For its part, however, the criminal law in England, America, and elsewhere continues to make judgments about whether and when people are responsible for their actions. These decisions necessarily entail discussion and judgment about whether a given defendant had the requisite *mens rea* and performed the requisite *actus reus* to be held responsible under the law. Very recent decisions of English courts of appeal demonstrate that the courts continue to face the complexities — however differently realized in the twentieth century — of the relations between the internal and the external elements of crime, and to use the language of individual intentional action to do so. Take the case of *R. v. Dias*, for example, where an English court of appeals found that a defendant who had helped to prepare a syringe for but had not actually injected heroin into a man (who later died from an overdose as a result of that injection) could not be held criminally responsible for his death.[13] Here are the facts of the case as the court reports them:

> The facts of the case are not complicated or, sadly, uncommon. On 27 August 2000, Edward Escott died as a result of an injection of heroin. The only person with him was the appellant. They were both vagrants. They did not know each other well, but in July and August of that year they were living in, or associated with, a night shelter in Northampton. Mr. Escott regularly abused drugs. Drugs other than heroin were found in his body, as was alcohol. However, although he smoked heroin, no one had seen him inject it. The appellant was a heroin addict who did inject the drug. The appellant did not give evidence at trial. When interviewed by the police he had said that he and Escott had agreed to put £5 each into a kitty. The appellant then contacted his dealer and bought a £10 bag of heroin. He and Escott then found a suitable place on the stairway of a block of flats. Using his own "kit", the appellant prepared the heroin injection by putting the powder into a spoon, adding the citric acid and water, heating it up and drawing it into the syringe. He then handed the syringe to Escott. Escott removed the belt from his own trousers, used it as a tourniquet and injected the heroin into himself. The appellant washed the syringe and injected the heroin into himself. By the time the appellant had recov-

ered from the effects of the heroin, Escott was dying. The appellant arranged for a passer-by to call an ambulance and then left the scene. Escott was taken to hospital but died.

This terse and expressive narrative begins the appeals court's discussion of the appellant's responsibility for Escott's death. In some ways, appellant and alleged victim appear indistinguishable—both are drug users and vagrants—and there is the joint enterprise involved in the buying of the drugs (each contributes £5). They live the same life, it seems. But though Escott smoked heroin, he did not inject it, as Dias did: a significant fact for the court, because at the center of the decision is the will of the dead man. The appellant Dias contacts the dealer, uses "his own 'kit,'" and prepares the injection with painstaking deliberation, but when Escott takes "the belt from his own trousers," his will intervenes, and he becomes the intentional, voluntary actor in the narrative. The obvious issue facing the trial court and jury assessing the appellant's criminal responsibility was that the defendant had not himself injected the drug into the deceased. The deceased was at once victim and co-offender. At trial, the judge had directed the jury that the defendant could be found guilty of manslaughter if the prosecution proved that "the defendant assisted and deliberately encouraged Escott to take the heroine." Framed as such, the trial judge imputed the appellant's intent to Escott, in effect displacing Escott's will and substituting in its stead that of the appellant. The appeals court, by contrast, saw the deceased as a voluntary participant. Whatever the appellant's intention, the act itself was performed by an agent who had his own will intact. If, on the other hand, the defendant had injected Escott with the drug, he could indeed have been found guilty. Is there a difference between these cases, asked the appeals judge? Yes. The difference is that where one injects oneself, one acts as a voluntary agent of the harm caused.

Other recent English cases suggest that the boundaries between conduct and character continue to be negotiated. In *R. v. Cerovic*, the appellant had been convicted of making threats to kill his former girlfriend, Marie Stronach, and her sister Sarah Stronach.[14] At issue on appeal was whether or not it was proper for the court to have admitted into evidence facts about a prior incident for which the appellant had been charged with the attempted murder of Sarah Stronach and acquitted. In the prior incident, the defendant, wanting to see the child he had fathered with Marie, brought what he thought was a fake gun to Sarah Stronach's house, claiming that "it was his case that . . . if refused access to his daughter he intended to put the gun to his own head in order to demonstrate how desperate he felt. Unbeknownst to him, the gun was real. A struggle took place during which a round was in fact discharged from the gun, a round which struck Sarah." The jury accepted this version of the events, and the defendant was acquitted. Two years after this incident the defendant was arrested for threatening to kill Marie and Sarah and for harassment. At his trial on these latest charges, the prior shooting was admitted into evidence. The defense objected, and later appealed the conviction, arguing that the evidence of the prior incident (which had not resulted in criminal liability) prejudiced the jury against the appellant. What is clear from the published decision is that the prosecution introduced the shooting into evidence not only to prove that the defendant made the threats at issue but also that he was a dangerous man who would probably carry out those threats. The appeals court made note of the fact that when the appellant was cross-examined by the prosecution, "prosecution counsel suggested to him that he was a man of violence." Notwithstanding such facts, the appeals court rejected the appellant's claim that the evidence prejudiced the jury, arguing instead that such evidence of a prior act was properly admitted because it was "necessary to place before the jury evidence of part of a continual background of history relevant to the offence charged in the indictment" in order to produce a complete account. Without the prior incident, the court concluded, "the account placed before the jury would be incomplete or incomprehensible." The necessity of a complete narrative—a continuous background—that connects character and conduct trumps the appellant's protest against the inclusion of such evidence.

These cases provoke their readers to consider anew how the courts articulate the internal and external elements of crime, what limits they set, how their strategies of argumentation conceal or reveal their own culturally shaped and historically inflected assumptions about the relations between the elements of crime and about criminal responsibility more generally. Is this family of questions still alive in literary narratives of the last century? Yes, but differently. The evolution of the novel as a form makes a difference. It makes a difference, for instance, that the most influential literary narratives about crime written during the last half-century are not novels and not British novels but American nonfiction novels: Truman Capote's novel *In Cold Blood* and Norman Mailer's *Executioner's Song*.

I conclude my study with a brief discussion of Capote's *In Cold Blood* and his later and lesser known nonfiction novella *Handcarved Coffins* because the comparison of these very different texts suggests both the limits of my analytic approach and the depth of the realist novel's representations of criminal responsibility. State of mind is, of course, at the center of Capote's greatest work, *In Cold Blood*. The text's unforgettable monosyllabic title—like a hammer to the head—names intent right from the start. The murders out of which the action of the work springs happen very early on—the bound and battered bodies of the Clutters are described in heartbreaking detail—but the murderous acts themselves are left unrepresented until Perry Smith and Dick Hickock give their confessions in part 3 of the story, the part aptly entitled "Answers." Though Capote makes use of the novelist's license to create a narrator who can offer the thoughts of his characters in free indirect speech, he limits the narrative to direct speech when Perry describes the murders. Capote observes the limits of the genre of nonfiction in these moments: nonfiction must infer its conclusions about the internal life of the figures it presents, as must other disciplines, like law and psychiatry, which also have their say in this section of the work. At the end of Perry's full confession, the lead investigator, Alvin Dewey, articulates his sense that what has been sought remains curiously absent:

> It had been his ambition to learn "exactly what happened in that house that night." Twice now he'd been told, and the two version were very much alike, the only serious discrepancy being that Hickock attributed all four deaths to Smith, while Smith contended that Hickock had killed the two women. But the confessions, though they answered questions of how and why, failed to satisfy his sense of meaningful design. The crime was a psychological accident, virtually an impersonal act; the victims might as well have been killed by lightning.[15]

Coming as it does at the end of Perry's confession from Dewey, a law-and-order figure if ever there was one, these observations carry particular weight. When Dewey conjoins the "impersonal" with the "accident" and finally the bolt of lightning, these accumulated terms work to efface Perry and Dick as agents of the acts. The point is not merely that Perry and Dick acted in cold blood but also that they did not have the capacity to act as persons. In the pages that follow, Capote presents long quotations from the reports of psychiatrists who come to the same conclusion reached by Dewey, and later Perry, and finally by the text itself. The language used by the psychiatrists is discipline-specific ("personality disorganization" (298), "schizophrenic darkness" (302)), but the ideas are consistent with those Dewey and Perry articulate. Capote does not use the license of the novel to create or reconstruct a coherent personality for whom the language of intent makes sense.

Still, if one sets *In Cold Blood* against Capote's later and last work of nonfiction crime narrative–*Handcarved Coffins*, published as part of *Music for Chameleons* in 1980–it is easy to see that the earlier work remains in touch with the traditions of the realist novel and with its representations of criminal responsibility while the latter makes such questions well beside the point.[16] If *In Cold Blood* imagines the murders as impersonal acts, it also sees them as acts for which legal punishment is a rational response. Capote's text invokes a world in which there remains a meaningful connection between the act, the judgment of guilt at trial, and the executions that follow. Though he subtitled *Handcarved Coffins* "A Nonfiction Account of an American Crime," Capote (in his preface to *Music for Chameleons*) labeled the novella "a nonfiction short novel" and so aligned his latest account of crime with his greatest, *In Cold Blood*.[17] *Handcarved Coffins* begins as a diary, then becomes a transcribed interview between a figure named "TC" and Jake Pepper, a detective working for an unnamed state bureau of investigation. Other figures enter the interview as well. These forms–the diary entries, the interviews–attest to the work's authenticity, yet the work as a whole seeks to expose the fictionality of what it offers as real. Where *In Cold Blood* made use of both the mimetic strategies of the realist novel and the forms of nonfiction prose, *Handcarved Coffins* resists novelistic mimesis (including indirect free speech, for example). The work pressures the reader to admit that reality is as constructed and imagined and surreal as the dreams that TC experiences.

Handcarved Coffins has a plot, and the plot involves murders. Jake Pepper is investigating a man named Bob Quinn, whom Pepper believes is guilty of murdering members of a citizens' committee who have voted to divert some of the water from a main river to the other ranches in the community. Such a diversion necessarily reduces the amount of water flowing to the ranch of Bob Quinn. The members are murdered in bizarrely theatrical ways. The first victims are attacked by a nest of imported rattlesnakes that have been drugged into a frenzy and planted in their car. The second victims are incinerated, the third victim is beheaded by a wire, the fourth poisoned by liquid nicotine-tainted Maalox, the last drowned. Before each is murdered, he or she receives a small handcarved coffin in the mail. Pepper cannot prove that Quinn is the murderer, and his failure drives him to a breakdown (the last victim is his fiancée, Addie Mason). TC also self-destructs in the course of the narrative. Pepper finally gives up the case, quits his job, and moves to Oregon. Quinn is never arrested. TC visits him at the end of the account, finding him remarried and happy and fishing in the river.

The combination of drugged rattlesnakes and the little handcarved coffins, whether made-up or not, announces itself as utterly contrived, and that's the point. If tempted by the lure of reality, we are brought up short to face it all as artifice. Addie's river death recalls or even perhaps parodies the destruction of Addie Bundren's body and coffin in Faulkner's *As I Lay Dying*, where Jewel Bundren, Addie's favorite child, becomes Addie Mason's jeweled engagement ring that sticks up out of the water. Even the handcarved coffins recall Faulkner's novel. Unlike *As I Lay Dying*, however, *Handcarved Coffins* includes its author as a character in the narrative. In his preface to *Music for Chameleons*, Capote announces his intention to "set myself center stage" (xviii), an apt metaphor since it again highlights the overt staginess of his undertaking. After Addie Mason is murdered by Quinn—or accidentally drowns in the river—TC imagines in vivid detail the scene in which Quinn murders Addie. Enduring a sleepless night, TC broods over the drowning, and as he does, "Images formed, faded; it was as though I were mentally editing a motion picture" (128). The "motion picture" he edits has Quinn stalking Addie (swimming in the river) until he sees his opportunity to pull her under. What is striking about TC's vision is its sudden use of the novelist's license to imagine the mental activities of his characters:

He hears Addie tell her sister: "I'm going to swim around the bend and sit on the waterfall." Ideal; now Addie will be unprotected, alone, out of her sister's view. Quinn waits until he is certain she is playfully absorbed at the waterfall. Presently, he slides down the embankment (the same embankment the searching Marylee later used). Addie doesn't hear him; the splashing waterfall covers the sound of his movements. But how can he avoid her eyes?" (128–9)

Though the next morning TC rejects his version in favor of the "coroner's common-sense verdict: *Accidental death by drowning*" (129), a later phone call to an acquaintance who also happens to be a retired detective and, it turns out, a friend of Jake's, moves TC to "relate the 'murder' as I had imagined it; the surmises I had rejected at dawn now seemed not only plausible by vividly convincing" (131). But then the friend tells TC that TC's story is also Jake's story: "that is Jake's story. He filed a report, and sent me a copy. And in the report that's how he reconstructed events" (131). Tellingly, TC then feels ashamed, "like a schoolboy caught cheating in an exam," and upset with Jake "for not having produced a solid solution, crestfallen that his conjectures were no better than mine. I trusted Jake, the professional man, and was miserable when I felt that trust seesawing" (132). The narrator is a faker but so too is the "professional man." The professional reconstruction carries no more authenticity than the fiction TC has created, and it is no surprise that Jake is an avid reader of realist novels. Jake, of course, prefers Dickens and Trollope and Melville, which shows what a naif he is; the text catches him acting the part of the fictional detective without knowing it.[18] No wonder he cannot outsmart a postmodern man like Quinn. Reading *Handcarved Coffins*, one notes time and again how insistently and heavy handedly all the elements of the text fold into each other,[19] and this is what (at least for me) makes the work tiresome and ineffectual and at last predictable. But perhaps that is the point as well. After all, crimes–and murders in particular–lend themselves to reproduction. Copycat crimes are common enough so that we are familiar with the idea. *Handcarved Coffins* may aptly be named a postmodern work, but in its obsessive need to expose the artificial and the reproduced, it also seizes on something horribly true about murderers—that they play roles, that they imitate the crimes of others. When Quinn's wife tells TC that Jake Pepper's suspicions about her husband are unfounded, her defense peters out with a world-weary "Ah well, who knows? *Or* cares? Not I. Not I, said the Spider to the Fly. Not I" (113). I suppose we are being nudged to ask who is the spider and who is the fly. No doubt the text at moments parodies the generic conventions of detective fiction. TC is reading a thriller by Eric Ambler when he meets Jake, and he adds that he loves both Agatha Christie and Raymond Chandler. Jake, the hard-boiled detective, dismisses them as fictions, which calls our attention all the more–in a ham-fisted sort of way–to what a fiction he is. The little coffins, the perversely clever murderous set-ups all have the makings of a best-selling detective story, and yet it comes to nothing except Pepper's absence and TC's sense of futility. But more than this is the sense that the how's and why's of the crime are themselves fictions which this true account will not produce. At the end of the text, when TC visits Quinn, Quinn remarks complacently of Addie's death: "'The way I look at it is: it was the hand of God.' He raised his own hand, and the river, viewed between his spread fingers, seemed to weave between them like a dark ribbon. 'God's work. His Will'" (146). This overemphatic writing turns act and intent (work and will) into as much of a fiction as anything else, with the ribbon weaving among Quinn's fingers reminding us (as if we need reminding) that crimes are no more real than anything else. To investigate, then, the representations of internal and external elements of the crimes is as emptily inconsequential an exercise as TC's dreamlike rendering of Addie's drowning.

Victorian legal and literary narratives of criminal responsibility may at moments be evasive, but they do not evade questions of responsibility the way a text like *Handcarved Coffins* licenses itself to do. It is, moreover, difficult to imagine where—through what terms—the criminal law might engage *Hand-carved Coffins*, which explains, perhaps, why the work's law-and-order man, Jake Pepper, throws in the towel at the end and moves out of the picture. But the Victorian texts I have examined could find a common ground, no doubt often as competitors, occasionally as partners, engaging questions of responsibility differently yet in ways that illuminated the gains and losses, justices and injustices of their representation of the elements of crime.

✧ NOTES ✧

INTRODUCTION

1. James Fitzjames Stephen, *A History of the Criminal Law of England*, 2:94.

2. Leon Radzinowicz's five-volume *A History of the Criminal Law and Its Administration from 1750* is also very valuable but does not replace Stephen. Focusing on the administration of criminal law after 1750, Radzinowicz's volumes are most interested in sentencing reform and the institutionalization of the police.

3. M'Carthy, "Novels with a Purpose," 24. Though the article is unsigned, *The Wellesley Index to Victorian Periodicals* attributes the piece to M'Carthy.

4. Ibid. Although M'Carthy argues that such novels — those "with a purpose" — fall short of becoming "successful works of art" (45), nonetheless he registers their power over their large readership.

5. On the crosscultural power of the law and the novel in the nineteenth century, see also Kieran Dolin, *Fiction and the Law: Legal Discourse in Victorian and Modernist Literature*, 31–96.

6. Stephen, "The Relation of Novels to Life," 157. The *Cambridge Essays* was a four-volume series (from 1855 to 1858) that collected essays from members of Cambridge University.

7. Holdsworth, *Charles Dickens as a Legal Historian*, 1.

8. "Judicial Dignity," 450.

9. Stephen, "Mr. Dickens as a Politician," 8.

10. Ibid.

11. Stephen, "Novels and Novelists," 285.

12. Dramas are, of course, involved in representing the inner selves of their characters. In *Theaters of Intention: Drama and the Law in Early Modern England*, Luke Wilson attends to the production of acts and intents in legal and dramatic texts, arguing in particular that the early modern theater was "an institution and mode of representation

profoundly invested in enacting the experience of intentional engagement with the world—an investment matched in many ways by the English common law of the period" (5). What neither the theater or the law can produce in the way that the novel can, however, is access to the invisible world of the mind.

13. In his engaging and suggestive study *The Art of Alibi: English Law Courts and the Novel*, Jonathan Grossman argues that the Newgate novels—and he singles out *Oliver Twist* and Edward Bulwer-Lytton's *Eugene Aram* as prime examples—offered their readers the inner lives of their criminal characters more fully than their predecessors or than other contemporary novels. Grossman puts this observation to good use when he makes his case for distinguishing Newgate novels from their usurpers: detective fiction. Grossman and I part company, however, in his treatment of third person narrators. See note 67, below.

14. In his introduction to *The Cambridge Companion to George Eliot*, 9, George Levine conceives of Eliot's art in these related terms: "George Eliot's realism extends from the external world to the world of individual consciousness—like James and the psychological novelists who followed, she threw the action inside."

15. Thomas, *Cross-Examinations of Law and Literature: Cooper, Hawthorne, Stowe, and Melville*. See also Thomas's "Narratives of Responsibility and Blame in Nineteenth-Century United States Law and Literature," 3–19.

16. In her introduction to *Shifting the Blame*, Nan Goodman makes a powerful case for the claim "that neither literary nor legal narratives in nineteenth-century America can be understood without the other: (10). Citing the work of the great legal thinker and writer Robert Cover, Goodman maintains with Cover that legal and literary narratives "are equally important components for an understanding of the culture as a whole. For it is only in combination with each other that the whole story a culture tells itself about how to act and which patterns of behavior to pursue can be discerned" (Ibid). Likewise, Kieran Dolin in his introduction to *Fiction and the Law* turns to Cover and to Brook Thomas (among others) to support his persuasive assertions about the power of legal and literary narratives to construct culture and about the particular "interfusion of law and novel in the nineteenth and early twentieth centuries" (5). I agree, and such insights inform my own work. I have also benefited from the work of law and literature scholars who have generated analyses of both legal and literary texts that have gone beyond the too-simple premise that literature—whether canonized or not—necessarily improves the moral character of readers. For example, Richard Weisberg notes of his own work (in his response to those who have labeled his readings "sentimental") that "The stress upon literature has little to do with its supposed salutary effect on legal actors." Instead, Weisberg reframes the discussion by thinking about the ways stories "upset the reader" and "make the reader uneasy about the legal assumptions that precede the understanding of the story" ("Literature's Twenty-Year Crossing," 2:57). In this study, I extend Weisberg's analysis to consider how *legal* texts challenge readers' assumptions about literary representations of law.

17. Taylor, *Sources of Self*, 111.

18. In *The Bounds of Agency*, 17, Carol Rovane gives a terrifically clear account of how Locke distinguished personal from animal identity, and maintains that for Locke "personal identity consists in consciousness alone."

19. Maus, *Inwardness and Theatre in the English Renaissance*, 2–3.

20. Shuttleworth, *Charlotte Brontë and Victorian Psychology*, 9. In "The Sovereign Self: Identity and Responsibility in Victorian England," Simon Petch argues that the concept of sovereignty was itself internalized and that "conscience" was elevated as

"the authoritative principle of self-sovereignty throughout Victorian spiritual and moral discourse" (400). Petch's analyses reveal the potency of Victorian conceptions of the inner self.

21. Shuttleworth, *Charlotte Brontë and Victorian Psychology*, 9, 10, 57–70.

22. Unpublished letter, Stephen Papers, Cambridge University Library.

23. For example, Anne Ferry attends to questions of language and the inner self in *The "Inward" Language: Sonnets of Wyatt, Sidney, Shakespeare, and Donne*, where she asks: "How did sixteenth century English poetry develop in ways that enabled Shakespeare and other writers to render a new sense of what is in the heart? How did poets of the sixteenth century come to invent a sense of inward experience reflected in new uses of language in their poetry?" (4).

24. Cohn, *Transparent Minds: Narrative Modes for Presenting Consciousness in Fiction*, 4.

25. Cohn's three types are psycho-narration, quoted monologue, and narrated monologue. Psycho-narration—a term she invents—means, literally, the narration of the psyche. In this type of narration of consciousness, the narrator describes the movements of mind of a character. Quoted monologue, by contrast, is more commonly what we think of as interior monologue, or stream-of-consciousness. The third type Cohn identifies—narrated monologue—straddles the first two types. Critics often refer to this type as free indirect discourse. Cohn provides this succinct description of narrated monologue: "like psycho-narration it maintains the third person reference and the tense of narration, but like the quoted monologue it reproduces verbatim the character's own mental language" (*Transparent Minds*, 14).

26. Ibid.

27. Ibid.

28. *Imagining the Penitentiary: Fiction and the Architecture of the Mind in Eighteenth-Century England*, 203.

29. Ibid., 1.

30. D. A. Miller, *The Novel and the Police*, 23–4.

31. Cohn clarifies the differences between first and third person narration by comparing *David Copperfield* and *What Maisie Knew*. David Copperfield, narrating the story of his own life, is moved "to mention the plausibility of his cognition, particularly when it involves the most inchoate moments of his past. When James tells about Maisie's early childhood feelings, he does not and need not explain how he found out. When David Copperfield does the same, he refers to his source" (*Transparent Minds*, 144).

32. Jaffe, *Vanishing Points: Dickens, Narrative, and the Subject of Omniscience*, 17. George Eliot's gothic novella *The Lifted Veil* is the exception that proves the rule. In *The Lifted Veil*, Eliot conceives of a first person narrator, the doomed Latimer, who is endowed with supernatural powers which enable him both to foresee the future and to read the minds of others. That such a capacity is explicitly marked as supernatural—part of the gothic apparatus of the narrative—separates it from anything readers would expect or accept in a first person narrator not supernaturally endowed. Moreover, it is telling that Latimer loses his powers. He cannot read the mind or know the criminal intentions of his wife Bertha. Those intentions are revealed to him through the intervention of Meunier, the doctor who is willing to attempt a blood transfusion on the dead maid, Mrs Archer, who comes back to life long enough to bear witness to Bertha's evil plan. Sally Shuttleworth takes another view (closer to my own), one which reinscribes the differences between first and third person narration. In *Charlotte Brontë and Victorian Psychology*, Shuttleworth demonstrates the significance of

Bronte's narratorial choices: "In all her works except *Shirley*, Brontë eschews the omniscient third person, with its authoritative claims to lay bare the hidden workings of the inner self" (17).

33. Ibid., 18.

34. Garner, "Fraud as Fact in Melville's *Billy Budd*," 85–90; Stein, "*Billy Budd*: The Nightmare of History," 224, cited in Douglas, "Discursive Limits and Narrative Judgment in *Billy Budd*," 146.

35. Douglas, "Discursive Limits," 147.

36. Ibid., 152.

37. Ibid., 158

38. Eliot, *Adam Bede*, 177. Subsequent citations appear in the text.

39. On Thackeray's narrator, see Ina Ferris, *William Makepeace Thackeray*, 34–5, and George Levine, *The Realistic Imagination: English Fiction from Frankenstein to Lady Chatterley*, 131–44, where Levine explores Thackeray's self-consciousness and his experiments with realistic representation. Dorrit Cohn makes an example of the narrator in *Vanity Fair* in order to show the way Thackeray avoids narrating Becky Sharpe's inner life (*Transparent Minds*, 21). J. Hillis Miller in *The Form of Victorian Fiction*, 71, moves more fully around Thackeray's narrator, seeing him as at once a showman, like Fielding's narrator in *Tom Jones*, and an omniscient teller. However, Miller is quick to add that Thackeray parodies his own omniscience, and in so doing Miller distinguishes Thackeray from Eliot.

40. Thackeray, *Vanity Fair*, 148–9.

41. J. Hillis Miller, *Form of Victorian Fiction*, 63.

42. Ibid.

43. Ibid., 64.

44. Ibid.

45. One needs also to account for the fact that third person narrators do not always speak as figures who necessarily know more than we do. Statements by third person narrators may be offered as generalization or commentary and not as information that the narrator's special power to see into her characters has given her. At these moments, the third person narrator performs a function akin to that of a tragedic chorus.

46. In *Story and Discourse: Narrative Structure in Fiction and Film*, Seymour Chatman attends to the limitations of narrative authority, and in particular to narrators who do not have complete access to the inner lives of characters. Chatham does not qualify omniscience; instead he conceives of omniscience as that which is "opposed to 'limitation' in terms of the capacity to enter characters' consciousnesses" (212).

47. Nussbaum, "The Window: Knowledge of Other Minds in Virginia Woolf's *To the Lighthouse*," 731–53.

48. Ibid., 733.

49. Ibid., 736.

50. Foucault, *Discipline and Punish*, 17–8.

51. Ibid., 18.

52. Sheridan translates Foucault's "*circonstances atténuantes*" as "attentuating circumstances," where we might expect the familiar "extenuating circumstances." When speaking of faults, the verb "*atténuer*" is more usually translated as "to extenuate." In Stephen's *History of the Criminal Law of England*, he gives an account of the special "French system of *circonstances atténuantes*," which suggests that the phrase has a particular legal meaning. In the course of his comparison of French and English criminal law systems, Stephen remarks:

The finding of *circonstances atténuantes* by a French jury ties the hands of the Court and compels them to pass a lighter sentence than they would otherwise be entitled to pass. It appears to me to be as great a blot upon the French system as the way in which that system sets the judge in personal conflict with the prisoner. It gives a permanent legal effect to the first impressions of seven out of twelve altogether irresponsible persons, upon the most delicate of all questions connected with the administration of justice—the amount of punishment which, having regard to its moral enormity and also to its political and social danger, ought to be awarded to a given offence. These are, I think, matters which require mature and deliberate consideration by the persons best qualified by their position and their previous training to decide upon them. In all cases not capital the discretion is by our law vested in the judge.

Stephen, *History of the Criminal Law of England*, 1:560–1.

53. Shuttleworth, *Charlotte Brontë and Victorian Psychology*, 3.

54. Stephen, *History of the Criminal Law of England*, 2:124–5.

55. Stephen, *A General View of the Criminal Law* (1863), 153.

56. Stephen, "The Characteristics of English Criminal Law," 40.

57. Stephen, *A Digest of the Law of Evidence*, 15.

58. Turner, *Russell on Crime*, 737.

59. Stephen, *A Digest of the Law of Evidence*, 20.

60. Ibid. Reviewing the legal history of the use of character evidence, David P. Leonard in "In Defense of the Character Evidence Prohibition: Foundations of the Rule Against Trial by Character" aptly notes that "A satisfactory definition of 'character' is elusive." Interestingly, Leonard offers as one possible definition that of H. Richard Uviller, who (in his 1982 *University of Pennsylvania Law Review* article entitled "Evidence of Character to Prove Conduct: Illusion, Illogic, and Injustice in the Courtroom") maintains that character in the courtroom appears as "a collection of 'traits,' each a self-contained packet of potential conduct consistent with previously observed reactions to events, people, and things" (quoted in Leonard, "In Defense of the Character Evidence Prohibition"). Making character "a self-contained packet of potential conduct" invokes the complexity of the relation between these concepts.

61. Stephen, *A Digest of the Law of Evidence*, 138–9.

62. The term "character" comes with significant literary critical baggage as well. Most obviously, structuralist and poststructuralist critics have sought to expose and demote character. Such critics ask readers not only to resist the temptations to respond to characters as real people but also to recognize them as no more or less than any other device in any given text. In his *A Concise Glossary of Contemporary Literary Theory*, Jeremy Hawthorn quotes passages from an essay by Alan Sinfield ("When Is a Character Not a Character? Desdemona, Olivia, Lady Macbeth and Subjectivity," in Sinfield's *Faultlines: Cultural Materialism and the Politics of Dissident Reading* that offer Desdemona as "a disjointed sequence of positions that women are conventionally supposed to occupy" (Sinfield, *Faultlines*, 53). In Sinfield's eyes, Desdemona "has no character of her own; she is a convenience in the story of Othello, Iago, and Venice" (54). But Hawthorn shrewdly notes that Sinfield's analysis turns back on itself because it "forces the reader to compare [Desdemona] with those others in the play who, he suggests, *are* so possessed of a character" (21). Characters are not real people, of course, but certain characters in Dickens and almost all of the characters in the novels of George Eliot that I examine appear as representations of real people and not as a "sequence of positions." While it is true that the eponymous hero Oliver Twist becomes less of a character and

more of a symbol by the middle of *Oliver Twist* (as I will later discuss), character is alive and well in Dickens's work.

63. Welsh, *Strong Representations: Narrative and Circumstantial Evidence in England*, 83.

64. Ibid., 58.

65. Ibid., 40.

66. Jaffe, *Vanishing Points*, 5–6.

67. Schramm, *Testimony and Advocacy in Victorian Law, Literature, and Theology*. Jonathan Grossman makes similar claims in *The Art of Alibi*, where he asserts that it was the trial (though not solely the trial) that moved authors to create the omniscient narrator: "The imagined spectacle of the newly lawyered criminal courts was, in short, one catalyst in the developing art of narrating other people's minds" (23). In his next paragraph, Grossman quite reasonably qualifies this claim, noting: "This is not to imply that barristers were discoursing in the free indirect style and society, watching them, adopted it. Nor were the new procedures of the courts reconstructing the form of the novel" (23). But he is committed to an argument that poses "the confluence of the procedures of the law court and literary form" (23) and to locating "confluence" or "connection" in the third person narration. Without weighing in on the question of whether advocates in the courtroom were catalysts for third person narration in the novel, the qualification Grossman spells out ("This is not to imply that barristers were discoursing in the free indirect style and society, watching them, adopted it") opens up a space between the legal and the literary that invites examination. Barristers did not and could not structure a narrative the way, say, George Eliot's *Middlemarch* narrator reveals the movements of Bulstrode's mind when he is looking after the dying Raffles. Advocates who attempt to lay bare the minds of their clients work by inference and need to connect the internal to external evidence.

68. Schramm, *Testimony and Advocacy*, 9.

69. Ibid., 10.

70. Ibid., 143.

71. Ibid., 142. Even the fictional lawyers Schramm offers cannot read minds. In the course of her analysis of Anthony Trollope's *Orley Farm*, she notes that Furnival (one of the barristers who represents Lady Mason, on trial for forgery) like the narrator "is able to read her [Lady's Mason's] character" (143). And yet the passage she adduces from the novel ('he felt sure—almost sure, that he could look into her very heart, and read there the whole of her secret') to support her claim does not produce the access Schramm seeks to demonstrate. The move from 'sure' to 'almost sure' marks what Furnival cannot do.

72. Ibid., 10.

73. Ibid., 183.

74. Ibid.

75. Forster, "The Challenge of Our Time," 56.

76. Forster, *Aspects of the Novel*, 71.

77. Ibid.

78. Hart, *Punishment and Responsibility: Essays in the Philosophy of Law*, 114.

79. (1846) 15 M. & W. 404, 153 E.R. 907, cited in Glanville Williams, *Criminal Law: The General Part*, 218.

80. Williams, *Criminal Law*, 31.

81. J. W. C. Turner, *Kenny's Outlines of Criminal Law*, 29. I use this sixteenth edition because this was the first revised and entirely new edition of the *Outlines* published

after those of Courtney Stanhope Kenny. All subsequent editions of Kenny's *Outlines* are also edited by Turner, with few changes significant for my purposes.

82. Anthony Kenny, *Free Will and Responsibility*, 6.

83. *Vide Year Book* (1477) 17 Edw. IV 1.

84. Williams, *Criminal Law*, 1.

85. Stephen, *A General View of the Criminal Law* (1863), 68.

86. Turner, *Kenny's Outlines of Criminal Law*, 24.

87. Stephen, *History of the Criminal Law of England*, 2:95.

88. Hart, *Punishment and Responsibility*, 35, quoting Lord Esher in *Lee v. Dangar* (1892) 2 Q.B. 337.

89. In *Free Will and Responsibility*, Anthony Kenny presents the epistemological objections to this theory of responsibility—the theory on which English and American criminal law is based—which requires a *mens rea* element in crimes. Having accepted Wittgenstein's philosophy of mind, Kenny argues that "there is no epistemological reason to reject the mentalistic concepts which are used in the legal assessment of responsibility, and no reason to think that we are setting judges and juries an impossible task in requiring them to have regard to the state of mind of an accused at the time of the commission of a criminal act" (11).

90. Griew, "States of Mind, Presumptions and Inferences," 67.

91. Pollock and Maitland, *The History of the English Law before the Time of Edward I*, 2:476, n. 5.

92. Coke, *The Third Part of the Institutes of the Laws of England*, 6. Fitzjames Stephen notes that Coke's *Third Institute* "may be regarded as the second source of the criminal law, Bracton being the first." Stephen, *History of the Criminal Law of England*, 3:52.

93. Turner, *Kenny's Outlines of Criminal Law*, 12.

94. Stephen, *History of the Criminal Law of England*, 2:94.

95. Burke, *Report on the Lords Journals 30 April 1794*, vol. 7 of *The Writings and Speeches of Edmund Burke*, 175.

96. Turner, *Kenny's Outlines of Criminal Law*, 32.

97. Boswell, *Life of Johnson*, 4:243–44. Turner misquotes Johnson, giving us instead "'Then he ought to be hanged whenever he acts it'" (*Kenny's Outlines of Criminal Law*, 32). Johnson uses "enthusiasm" here in its less than usual sense. He satirically suggests a religious fervor, or, as the *OED* describes, "possession by a god, supernatural inspiration, prophetic or poetic frenzy."

98. Turner, *Kenny's Outlines of Criminal Law*, 32.

99. Ibid., n. 6.

100. Hart, *Punishment and Responsibility*, 114.

101. Stephen, *History of the Criminal Law*, 2:99.

102. Ibid., 2:101.

103. Though I do not in this study attend to specific legal excuses—the most complex and historically germane of which is insanity—I recognize that the discussions that profoundly shaped Victorian jurisprudential thinking about and judgments of *mens rea* took place in cases where an excuse such as insanity or provocation or mistake was put forward. To defend oneself by pleading insanity is, in effect, to negate *mens rea*, and in order to negate *mens rea*, one has to have in place a conception that can be negated. As Stephen himself explains:

> Matters of excuse are exceptions to the general rule that people are responsible for actions falling within the definition of crimes. The great difficulty of understanding some of these exceptions, and especially of understanding the law re-

lating to madness, is that an exception is necessarily a negation, and that it is practically impossible to understand a negation unless the positive rule of application of which it excludes, is previously understood." *History of the Criminal Law*, 2:99.

In "Judges v. Jurors: Courtroom Tensions in Murder Trials and the Law of Criminal Responsibility in Nineteenth-Century England," Martin J. Weiner painstakingly collects reports of little-known murder trials and adduces persuasive evidence that exposes the conflicts between often lenient juries and tough-minded judges. Of special interest to Weiner is the way nineteenth-century judges and juries handled the terms insanity, provocation, and intention. Weiner notes at the outset of his article that such terms "were in motion during the nineteenth century as part of a broader redefining and reimagining of liability and responsibility."

104. Hart and Honoré, *Causation in the Law*, 325.

105. See Goodman, *Shifting the Blame: Literature, Law, and the Theory of Accidents in Nineteenth Century America*, 65–97.

106. Eliot, *The Mill on the Floss*, 628.

107. Summarizing the potent and widely cited argument of Robert Cover's "Violence and the Word," Lawrence Douglas aptly notes: "The law, in Cover's understanding, remains different from literature in that its capacity to tolerate ambiguity and its ability to articulate common meanings is always limited by its position atop a hierarchy that ultimately relies on physical force, rather than discursive appeal, to enforce its readings on a refractory world" ("Discursive Limits," 144).

108. Leslie Stephen, *The Life of Sir James Fitzjames Stephen*, 146.

109. Ibid.

110. William Palmer, an inveterate gambler often in debt, was tried, convicted, and executed in 1856 for the poisoning of his friend John Parsons Cook. Palmer was also indicted for the murders of his wife and his brother (Palmer was the beneficiary named on both of their insurance policies), but once Palmer was convicted of Cook's murder, the other cases were not pursued. William Dove was also tried and convicted in 1856 for the murder—again, by poison—of his wife. Dove mounted an insanity defense which was rejected by the court. He was hanged in September, 1856. At the end of *A General View of the Criminal Law* (1863), Stephen appends reports of both cases.

111. Radzinowicz, *Sir James Fitzjames Stephen and His Contribution to the Development of the Criminal Law*, 13–4.

112. In 1892, the collection called *Horae Sabbaticae* was published. These three volumes reprint selected articles from the *Saturday Review*. The essays in this collection, and the earlier collection, *Essays by a Barrister* (1862), more often concern the history of ideas and not the questions I raise here. None of the essays from which I quote are included in either of these collections.

113. In his marginalia on Book I of *Paradise Lost*, John Keats remarks that "One of the most mysterious of semi-speculations is, one would suppose, that of one Mind's imagining into Another" (*The Complete Poems*, 518).

1. ORGANIZING CRIME

1. Given how dependent on Foucault's *Discipline and Punish* Miller's book *The Novel and the Police* is, it is unexpected that Miller should argue so readily that Dickens turns to Mademoiselle Hortense and a life of crime as a way of simplifying his great novel. As I suggest in my introduction, part of the undertaking in *Discipline and*

Punish is to suggest how in the eighteenth and nineteenth centuries, law and medicine conspired to reimagine crime not as an act but as a motivation or a perversion. So Victorian disciplinary culture did not fantasize the simplicity of the criminal; instead, what that culture took great pains to engineer was precisely the idea of the criminal and his crime as involving complex psychological impulses that had to be explained and, of course, disciplined. By the nineteenth century, so goes the Foucauldian argument, a crime was no longer the simple matter of who did what to whom, of cause and effect. While Miller reads *Bleak House* as of a piece with the disciplinary technologies Foucault details, the criminal act itself he presents as untouched by such technologies.

2. Sutherland, "Why Is Fagin Hanged and Why Isn't Pip Prosecuted?", 52. So persistent is this question that Sutherland returns to the puzzle Fagin presents in "Does Dickens Lynch Fagin?" an essay in his more recent collection, *Who Betrays Elizabeth Bennet?*, where he includes the responses of several readers to his first attempt to work through the case.

3. But critics have noticed varieties of characterization in Dickens work, to be sure. In *Dickens and Thackeray: Punishment and Forgiveness*, 85, John R. Reed asserts in no uncertain terms that "Dickens goes beyond the merely melodramatic, even in *Oliver Twist*, by a concern for character and individuality. This concern for character will increase in depth and intensity in the novels to follow, but it is already evident in both good and evil characters in *Oliver Twist*." At the end of his expressive early essay "Oliver Twist: 'Things as They Really Are'," 63, John Bayley contends that "what brings Sikes and Nancy to life is the gap between what they look like and what they are like, between their appearance as Dickens insists we should have it, and the speech and manner with which another convention requires him to endow them." Bayley moves towards an argument which proposes that Dickens creates in Nancy and Sikes "a balance . . . between the outward and inward selves that make up a whole person" (64), a balance which Bayley characterizes as "rare" (64) in Dickens's novels. Although Bayley does not develop or clarify the ideas he proposes here (his contrast between appearance and speech/manner suggests not a contrast between outer and inner but rather a contrast between two different external manifestations of character), he begins to identify, albeit ambiguously, what it is about Nancy and Sikes that distinguishes them from other characters. Likewise, William T. Lankford in "'The Parish Boy's Progress': The Evolving Form of *Oliver Twist*" sees Dickens as developing different strategies for representing character in the course of writing the novel. So, argues Lankford, while Dickens begins by producing characters described from the outside, he later locates character internally: "he shifts from one idea of character to another, from the external vision of moralizing principle to internal psychological realism" (29). I agree, though I find these shifts terrifically problematic in the context of a novel that explores criminal responsibility. When Dickens moves from the outside to the inside and so fully represents the conflicts between inner and outer, we are called upon to confront the issues about judgment and responsibility, about the conflicts between conduct and character that he engages.

4. I am indebted to much critical work that has illuminated contradiction and inconsistency in Dickens's work and, more specifically, to William T. Lankford, "'The Parish Boy's Progress': The Evolving Form of *Oliver Twist*," as well as to John Kucich, *Excess and Restraint in the Novels of Charles Dickens*, and *Repression in Victorian Fiction: Charlotte Brontë, George Eliot, and Charles Dickens*. In "Character and Contradiction in Dickens," Brian Rosenberg sees Dickens's characters, specifically those of the late nov-

els, as more elusive and incoherent than we at first recognize, and he values that incoherence outright, saying for the record that "contradiction and uncertainty do not merely color Dickens's characterization but account in large part for its distinctiveness and success" (147). An earlier essay by Rosenberg, "The Language of Doubt in *Oliver Twist*," offers an adroit and persuasive analysis of Dickens's style that demonstrates how style expresses Dickensian doubts about the "ability of the novel and even the language itself to capture and convey truth" (92). Rosenberg locates a conflict between the novel's morally confident assertions and the ambivalence generated in its syntax and diction. These observations are germane to my own argument since they consider the ways Dickens illuminates the novel's power and the limits of that power. Although Rosenberg does not take up the role of the third person narrator, his analysis does raise questions about the limits of what even that narrator can assert.

5. Dickens, *Oliver Twist*, 76. Subsequent citations appear in the text.

6. See Rosenberg, "The Language of Doubt in *Oliver Twist*," 95, where he argues that far from comforting us with the idea that appearance reveals the essence of a character, the novel produces "unreliable connections between appearance and reality." He notes, for example, of the criminal characters—and here his most persuasive evidence is offered in connection with Nancy—that "Appearance . . . tells a cryptic or inconsistent story" (Ibid). While Rosenberg seeks to show how the novel everywhere destabilizes representation, I want to consider the way the novel asserts its power to get behind appearance into the minds of its characters. See also Bayley, "Oliver Twist: 'Things as They Really Are'," 63. In "The Demeanor of Murderers," an article for *Household Words* (June 14, 1856), Dickens asserts in no uncertain terms that he is able to read Palmer's guilt—his "every guilty consciousness" (506)—in his face. Dickens's bravado here is remarkable, but he never pretends that he can actually read Palmer's thoughts directly. That power is vested only in his third person narrators. Dickens's twentieth-century biographer, Edgar Johnson, reports that when a depressed Dickens took a trip with Wilkie Collins together to a horse racing track to do some betting, Dickens suggested that "The men at the race course, the betting stand, and the betting rooms all seemed to him to look like Palmer, the notorious poisoner" (*Charles Dickens: His Tragedy and Triumph*, 2:880). Far from being a face that tells a particular story of guilt, Palmer's is simply the generic face of unsavory men, from which not much can be gleaned.

7. The matter has relevance to not only cultural but theological criticism. See John Milton, *The Doctrine and Discipline of Divorce*, where Milton writes:

The hidden wayes of his providence we adore & search not; but the law is his reveled will, his complete, his evident, and certain will; herein he appears to us as it were in human shape, enters into cov'nant with us, swears to keep it, binds himself like a just lawgiver to his own prescriptions, gives himself to be understood by men, judges and is judged, measures and is commensurat to right reason; cannot require lesse of us in one cantle of his Law then in another, his legall justice cannot be so fickle and so variable, sometimes like a devouring fire, and by and by connivent in embers, or, if I may so say, oscitant and supine.

The Works of John Milton, 3:440.

8. J. L. Austin, "A Plea for Excuses," 179.

9. Duff, *Intention, Agency and Criminal Liability*, 41, quoted in Michael Moore, *Act and Crime*, 61. From this skeptical position Moore himself dissents.

10. Williams, *Criminal Law*, 18.

11. Philosophical analyses of identity continuity have been seriously taken up by philosophers such as David Wiggins and Derek Parfit. See Wiggins, *Identity and Spatio-Temporal Continuity*, and Parfit, *Reason and Persons*. Parfit's work has been the subject of much attention and response (see, for example, *Reading Parfit*).

12. Knapp, *Literary Interest: The Limits of Anti-Formalism*, 123.

13. Ibid.

14. Locke, *An Essay Concerning Human Understanding*, 335.

15. Ibid.

16. Ibid., 346.

17. Ibid. C. S. Greaves' 1865 edition of Sir William Oldnall Russell's *A Treatise on Crimes and Misdemeanors* (known as *Russell on Crime*, the title it later assumes under J. W. C. Turner's authorship) takes up the problem of the defendant accused of a capital offense who loses his mind after his arrest or between conviction and execution. Of such a criminal, Greaves explains,

> If a man in his sound memory commits a capital offence, and before arraignment for it he becomes mad, he ought not to be arraigned for it, because he is not able to plead to it with that advice and caution that he ought. And if, after he has pleaded, the prisoner become [sic] mad, he shall not be tried, as he cannot make his defence. If, after he is tried and found guilty, he loses his senses before judgment, judgment shall not be pronounced; and if after judgment he becomes of nonsane memory, execution shall be stayed; for, per adventure, says the humanity of the English law, had the prisoner been of sound memory, he might have alleged something in stay of judgment or execution. (I:29)

The treatment of the now-insane accused is explained by recourse to claims about the criminal's ability to aid in his own defense (even after judgment), but behind such reasoning stands that which Locke asserts: that the accused is no longer a "forensic person" whom the law may judge and punish. Still, this law appears to apply only in capital cases; those convicted of lesser offenses who go mad after committing a crime may indeed be judged and punished. Since defendants who go mad but do not face execution are in no better position to aid in their defense, the rule seems to reflect not only the finality of capital punishment but also the competing desires of the culture which at once wants to suppress crime and adhere to a certain idea of the responsible individual. At the end of *Oliver Twist*, Fagin has moments in which he appears to have lost his senses, but he is sane enough to try to convince Oliver to help him escape and to threaten Morris Bolter.

18. Locke, *An Essay Concerning Human Understanding*, 335. This idea also can be seen at work in *Hopps v. People*, a 1863 Illinois case (31 Ill. 385), in which a defendant who admitted to killing his wife but pleaded insanity was kept from introducing evidence of good character during his trial on the ground that he did not deny that he murdered her. The Supreme Court of Illinois found the trial judge in error for excluding the testimony:

> In a case where the defense is insanity, we cannot have a doubt that evidence of good character as a man and a citizen, is proper for the jury to consider; whether a person whose character has been uniformly good, has, in a sane moment, committed the crime charged. It is undoubtedly true, a sane man, whose previous conduct has been unexceptionable, may commit an atrocious homicide, no doubt may exist of the fact, yet, under his plea of insanity, should he not be entitled to all the benefit as tending, slightly, it may be, to the conclusion that he could not have been sane at the time the deed was done? Generally, a

person of good character does not, of a sudden, fall from a high position to the commission of outrageous crimes; should he do so, would it be an unnatural or forced inference, that he may have been affected by insanity at the time?

19. Bradley, *Ethical Studies*, 5.

20. Ibid., 6.

21. Knapp, *Literary Interest*, 123.

22. The publication history of the preface needs explanation: the first preface (then called an "Introduction") Dickens composed for *Oliver Twist* was published in 1841 with the third edition of the novel. In 1850, a Cheap Edition of the novel was issued, and Dickens made major revisions to the 1841 preface for that edition. Most significantly, he added several paragraphs in response to an epidemic of cholera that broke out in London in 1849. Dickens revised the preface again in 1867 for the Charles Dickens Edition of the novel. In the 1867 edition, Dickens deleted his discussion of the 1849 epidemic and, with a couple of significant exceptions, reprinted the 1841 text.

23. Considering the conflict between character and conduct in *Othello*, William Empson in *The Structure of Complex Words* observes: "That there is usually a tension between a Shakespearean character (as judged by his speech-rhythms and so on) and his actions no one need be anxious to deny; the dramatic effects are heightened to the verge of paradox; but that the audience is not meant even to *try* to resolve the contradiction, however inadequate, seems to be more than Professor Stoll [a critic with whom Empson here takes issue] always wants to maintain" (240). In *Oliver Twist*, we have more to go on than speech-rhythms, or even "speech-rhythms and so on," and the need to resolve the paradox is as intense and intensely realized in the context of this crime novel.

24. For articles which take up the contradictions in *Oliver Twist*, see note 4 to this chapter. Rosenberg, in "The Language of Doubt in *Oliver Twist*, 91, assembles a list of critics who have themselves identified paradox as central to the way the novel operates. Like these critics, I find this term a necessary one in describing *Oliver Twist*, all the more so since in his preface, Dickens in essence identifies Nancy as the paradox at the heart of the novel.

25. "Conduct and character" as a pair appears twice in *Old Curiosity Shop*, 44 and 275, and once in *Pickwick Papers*, 575. In *Pickwick*, the phrase pops up during Pickwick's trial. The pairing of "Character and conduct" shows up in *Bleak House*, 267, as well as in *Dombey and Son*, 155, *Nicholas Nickleby*, 447, in a May 1837 piece for *Bentley's Miscellany*, "Some Particulars Concerning a Lion," 511, and in the concluding chapter of *American Notes for General Circulation*, 267.

26. T. S. Eliot, *Notes Toward the Definition of Culture*, 32.

27. Foucault, *Discipline and Punish*, 17–8.

28. (1865) *R. v. Rowton*, All E.R. Rep. 549.

29. Ibid., 550.

30. Ibid.

31. Ibid., 551.

32. Ibid.

33. Ibid., 554.

34. Ibid., 552.

35. Ibid., 554. In his *Digest of the Law of Evidence*, 152–3, Stephen makes the absurdity of the ruling more explicit: "One consequence [of *Rowton*] is that a witness may, with perfect truth, swear that a man, who to his knowledge has been a receiver of stolen goods for years, has an excellent character for honesty, if he has the good luck to con-

ceal his crimes from his neighbors. It is the essence of successful hypocrisy to combine a good reputation with bad disposition." But, Stephen adds, the *Rowton* rule is regularly ignored in practice. "The question always put to a witness as to character," Stephen reports, "is, What is the prisoner's character for honesty, morality, or humanity? as the case may be, nor is the witness ever warned that he is to confine evidence to the prisoner's reputation."

36. Stephen, *A General View of the Criminal Law* (1863), 309.

37. Ibid.

38. J. M. Beattie, *Crime and the Courts in England: 1600–1800*, 436. See also John H. Langbein, "The Criminal Trial before the Lawyers," 303, where Langbein offers Old Bailey Sessions Papers from the mid-1670s to the mid-1730s which show that the courts of this period had "no concern with the potentially prejudicial effect of past conviction evidence; there is no hint of instructions to the juries about the limited bearing of such evidence. Rather the impression conveyed by the reports is that past conviction evidence was often influential or decisive in the juries' adjudication."

39. Weiner, *Reconstructing the Criminal: Culture, Law and Policy in England 1830–1914*, 60–1.

40. Ibid., II. See also J. M. Beattie's *Crime and the Courts in England, 1660–1800*, 189, where Beattie notes that "It was a common view throughout the [eighteenth] century that receivers contributed massively to the prevalence of crime in the capital and that they operated virtually with impunity, both the major receivers who provided capital and support and a fencing network for the large-scale criminal confederacies, and the shopkeepers and merchants who simply failed to enquire closely into the ownership of goods offered to them for sale." This "common view" seems to inform the representation of Fagin's activities in *Oliver Twist*.

41. "Browning's Dramatic Idylls," 774–5.

42. Bouchier, "Dickens on English Criminal Law," 6.

43. Sutherland, "Why Is Fagin Hanged and Why Isn't Pip Prosecuted?" in *Can Jane Eyre Be Happy*, 52–63.

44. Renton, ed., *Encyclopedia of the Laws of England*, 68. I will take up the problem of "association" that this definition raises later in my argument.

45. Of liability that reaches beyond the actual perpetrator, K. J. M. Smith writes: "The need to supplement penal laws formulated for, and most immediately aimed at, the culpable perpetrator and to bring in and incriminate other less directly involved participants has been obvious to law makers for as long as the criminal law has existed" (*A Modern Treatise on the Law of Criminal Complicity*, 2). Obvious, yes, but also obviously difficult: when does involvement become criminal?

46. In *A History of the Criminal Law of England*, 2:211, James Fitzjames Stephen names Sir Matthew Hale's *History of the Pleas of the Crown* as "the most remarkable circumstance" associated with criminal law in the seventeenth century. Of this work, which was not published until the eighteenth century (after Hale's death), Stephen notes that it "shows a depth of thought and a comprehensiveness of design which puts it in quite a different category from Coke's *Institutes*. It is written on an excellent plan, and is far more of a treatise and far less of an index or mere work of practice than any book on the subject known to me."

47. Foster, *A Report of Some Proceedings on the Commission of Oyer and Terminer and Gaol Delivery for the Trial of the Rebels in the Year 1746 in the County of Surry and of Other Crown Cases to which are Added Discourses Upon a Few Branches of the Crown Law* [hereafter *Crown Cases*], 346.

48. So by 1763 Foster could remark: "Nothing needeth be said by way of Explanation touching Principals in the First Degree" (*Crown Cases*, 48).

49. I do not address the category of accessory after the fact because this category is different in kind from principals in the second degree and accessories before the fact. An accessory after the fact "is one who assists a felon after his crime, with a view to shielding him from justice" (Williams, *Criminal Law*, 409). While offenses involving principals in the second degree and accessories before the fact are part of the law of complicity, offenses involving accessories after the fact are obstructions of justice.

50. This procedural distinction was unequivocally dissolved in the Aiders and Abettors Act of 1861. But the distinction was still operative when *Oliver Twist* was published.

51. In the law of principal/accessory liability, "presence" can itself be considered evidence of participation, and I will say more about this concept when I take up *R. v. Coney, Gilliam, and Tully* (1882) 8 Q.B.D. 534.

52. Coke, *The Second Part of the Institutes*, 182–3.

53. The same difficulty arises in the definition of incitement, which is a common law misdemeanor and closely related to accessory liability historically and practically.

54. The *OED* gives as an obsolete meaning of assent "To come to an agreement as to a proposal; to agree together, determine, decide" (2a). Consent is "To agree with" (1) and "To come to agreement upon a matter as to a course of action."

55. In the *Corpus Juris* of 1918 (a British publication), the editors report the ambiguities of "consent" itself. Since (as I later discuss) presence at the scene of a crime is not a sufficient basis for liability as a principal in the second degree, the courts have been nervous about instructions that suggest presence as consent. The editors of the *Corpus Juris* of 1918 quote the following passage from an Illinois case, *White v. People* (1876) 81 Ill. 333, 337, to illustrate the court's caution: "'There is a plain distinction between 'consenting' to a crime and 'aiding, abetting, or assisting' in its participation. Aiding, abetting, or assisting are affirmative in their character. Consenting may be a mere negative acquiescence, not in any way made known at the time to the principal malefactor. Such consenting, though involving moral turpitude, does not come up to the meaning of the words of the statute" (*Corpus Juris*, 16:132, n. 4(a)). The editors also adduce *Plummer v. Commonwealth* (1866) 1 Bush [Ky.] 76–8, in which the court asked: "Is it a participation in an act to merely be present and consent to it?" What the court registers is the closeness of consent and acquiescence. Reviewing an instruction that put forth consent to a crime as the basis of liability, the court worried that "the jury may have been misled by [the use of the word 'consent'] as to attach to the instruction a different signification from that which the court intended; and to have felt authorized by it to convict the prisoners, merely on being satisfied that they were present and acquiesced in the homicide, without aiding and abetting the perpetrator, or having any participation in the deed" (ibid.).

56. Hale, *History of the Pleas of the Crown*, 435.

57. Notably, Stephen puts Foster in the same category as Blackstone. These are the major writers on the criminal law in the eighteenth century. While conceding that "The scope of Foster's work is narrow," Stephen recognized Foster as "the last, or nearly the last, author who has done much toward making the law by freely discussing its principles on their merits. . . . I do not think it would be possible to cite a better illustration of the good side of what has been called judicial legislation" (*History of the Criminal Law of England*, 2:213).

58. Foster, *Crown Cases*, 130.

59. Ibid., 131.

60. J. C. Smith, "Aid, Abet, Counsel, or Procure," 125.

61. J. C. Smith's comment also raises an eyebrow because, as other commentators have noted of the common law of secondary participation, "clear rules, and agreed upon statements of principle, are conspicuously lacking from it" (*Assisting and Encouraging Crime: A Consultation Paper*, section 1.1). So what *are* the common law concepts to which Smith refers?

62. Foster, *Crown Cases* 125.

63. Ibid.

64. As Glanville Williams explains, "Judges in the eighteenth and nineteenth century did not construe penal statutes literally; they construed them strictly, which was a different thing. Strict construction was a most excessively literal construction, but it worked only in favour of the accused" (*Criminal Law*, 217). This is understandable enough, since, as Williams notes, "the power of punishment is vested in the legislature in which lies the authority to define crimes and ordain punishment." Williams goes on to quote from an 1872 case in which James, L.J., declared: "No doubt all penal statutes are to be construed strictly—that is to say, the court must see that the thing charged as an offence is within the plain meaning of the words used; must not strain the words on any notion that there has been a slip, that there has been a *casus omissus*; that the thing is so clearly within the mischief that it must have been intended to be included, and would have been included if thought of" (217).

65. Foster, *Crown Cases*, 130.

66. Ibid.

67. Very recent commentators continue to follow Foster's lead: "Overall, the range of general complicity liability should not be, and is not, determined by the strict literal construction of the terms employed for, as Bentham reminds us, a verb 'slips through your fingers like an eel.'... Rather than terminological, complicity's limits . . . are conceptual . . ." (K. J. M. Smith, *Modern Treatise on the Law of Criminal Complicity*, 33–4).

68. Stephen, *History of the Criminal Law of England*, 2:235.

69. Ibid., 2:236.

70. Stephen remarks with some irritation that "It might have been thought that this enactment put an end to the distinction between principals and accessories before the fact, but this was held not to be its effect. It was considered that it did not make those accessories triable who were not triable before" (*History of the Criminal Law of England*, 2:236).

71. Foster, *Crown Cases*, 363.

72. Ibid., 343.

73. This range of response to accessory liability is detectable in the most recent edition of Andrew Ashworth's *Principles of Criminal Law*, an oft-required text for would-be English lawyers: "It is true that accomplices are normally less blameworthy than principals and therefore deserve less severe sentences. It is also true that a law which produces a conviction of murder and a sentence of life [or, as was the case in the nineteenth century, a sentence of death] for giving relatively minor assistance to a murderer is unjust (though injustice stems as much from the mandatory penalty for murder as from the law of complicity). But systems like the German seem not to provide for those, admittedly rare, cases in which the accomplice is no less culpable, and even more culpable, than the principal—as where a powerful figure orders a weak-willed person to commit a certain crime" (412).

74. K. J. M. Smith, *Modern Treatise on the Law of Criminal Complicity*, 2.

75. *Assisting and Encouraging Crime*, 32.

76. Ibid., 20.

77. Stephen, "Mr. Dickens as a Politician," 8.

78. However, as I discuss later, Oliver's timely swoon does much to divert the reader from considering in any full way what Oliver's culpability might be.

79. This said, it is true that the verb *accede* is taken up in *accessory*. *Accede* gives us the sense of consent within *accessory*, which is a salient part of the relation between the accessory and the principal. "Accessorize" as part of fashion lingo emerges, according to the *OED*, in 1939.

80. (1882) 8 Q.B.D. 534.

81. Coney and Tully were charged as principals in the second degree and not accessories because they were *present* during the commission of the crime. Presence determines whether or not a suspect will be charged as a principal or an accessory.

82. Ibid.

83. Ibid., 536.

84. Ibid., 537.

85. The contrast can also be teased out of the words "onlookers" and "spectators." We have the casualness, the accidentalness, of onlookers against the premeditativeness and intentionality of spectators.

86. Charles Dickens to John Forster, October 6 or 13, 1838, *The Letters of Charles Dickens*, 1:441.

87. Sutherland, "Why Is Fagin Hanged and Why Isn't Pip Prosecuted?" in *Can Jane Eyre Be Happy*, 56.

88. Shakespeare, *Othello*, 3.1.203. Note also K. J. M. Smith's claim that Henry II was arguably an accessory to Becket's murder: "If 'Will no one rid me of this meddlesome priest!' was uttered with Henry's awareness of its possible effect on his henchmen, then his complicity in Becket's killing appears arguable under modern English law." But, as Smith notes, Hume would disagree: "According to Hume, there is neither instigation or complicity simply by 'proclaiming of it as a meritorious thing to destroy a hateful object; no words of mere permission or allowance to do the deed; no intimation of thanks or approbation it shall be done; not the strongest expressions of enmity to the person, or the most earnest wishes for his death'" (*Modern Treatise on the Law of Criminal Complicity*, 34, n. 71).

89. Stephen, *A Digest of the Criminal Law*, 155.

90. In *Causation in the Law*, Hart and Honoré take issue with Stephen's reasoning, noting that Stephen "thought it would not be murder for A to tell B of facts, e.g. that C had seduced B's wife, which operated as a motive for B to murder C since [quoting Stephen] 'It would be an abuse of language to say that A had killed C, though no doubt he has been the remote cause of C's death.' But [conclude Hart and Honoré] if the causal relation required between accessory and principal offense were that implied by the word 'kills' there would be no need to distinguish principals in the first degree in murder from accessories" (380).

91. Stephen, *A Digest of the Criminal Law*, 155, n. 6.

92. Stephen, *History of the Criminal Law of England*, 3:8.

93. "It is sometimes difficult to know what degree of assistance is to be regarded as aiding. In a Canadian case, a taxi-driver was asked by passengers where they might obtain some beer; and he drove them to a bootlegger. He was convicted of aiding the unlawful sale of liquor. The decision seems to go to the limit of the law" (Williams, *Criminal Law*, 356).

94. Fagin and Nancy also share a like moment (though not a violent one) when she realizes Fagin is suspicious of her attempts to leave the house alone. They too exchange meaning through a parting glance: "[H]e had taken the opportunity afterwards afforded him, of sounding the girl in the broken hints he threw out at parting. There was no expression of surprise, no assumption of an inability to understand his meaning. The girl clearly comprehended it. Her glance at parting showed him *that*" (306). Notably the exchange remains ambiguous. Fagin may think that Nancy understands the meaning he wishes to convey, but he is operating under the mistaken assumption that she has taken another lover, so in fact, he may be misreading the look she gives him, as she may be misreading the look he gives her. His intentions are not transferred to her in the way that his later intentions are transferred to Sikes. Strangely, there is much in this scene that is echoed in the later one between Sikes and Fagin. When Fagin, on his way out of Sikes's rooms, hints to Nancy that she should take revenge on Sikes ("If you want revenge on those that treat you like a dog . . . come to me, I say, come to me," 305), she "shrunk back, as Fagin offered to lay his hand on hers, but said good night again, in a steady voice, and, answering his parting look with a nod of intelligence, closed the door between them" (305). Then we have later, just before Sikes sets off to murder Nancy, Fagin "laying his hand upon the lock" (321) to keep Sikes from leaving the room. Nancy rejects Fagin's offer "to lay his hand on hers" and shrinks from him, whereas in the later scene, Fagin's "laying his hand upon the lock" may allow the completion of the exchange between him and Sikes.

95. Ashworth, *Principles of Criminal Law*, 410.

96. Threatening Fagin, Sikes claims, "I've got the upper hand over you, Fagin," but Fagin shrewdly replies, "Well, well, my dear, . . . I know all that; we — we — have a mutual interest, Bill, a mutual interest'" (93). Fagin's "we — we — " is telling here.

97. Surprisingly, the first entry for "guilt by association" in the *OED* is as late as 1941: "The doctrine of guilt by association is abhorrent enough in the criminal deportation fields without being associated with lawyer and client." The next *OED* entry, from 1960, links association and intention: "He introduced those concepts of guilt by association and guilt by intention which have always been a feature of political trials and disputes in Russia." The phrase never turns up in Dickens, though the idea of it is certainly in *Oliver Twist*. "Associate" and its cognates appear several times in *Oliver Twist*.

98. Stephen, *History of the Criminal Law of England*, 2:98.

99. Hale, *History of the Pleas of the Crown*, 1:26. See also Blackstone, who argues that "the capacity of doing ill, or contracting guilt, is not so much measured by years and days, as by the strength of the delinquent's understanding and judgment" (*Commentaries on the Laws of England*, 4:23, quoted in Turner, *Russell on Crime*, 99). See also Weiner, *Reconstructing the Criminal: Culture, Law, and Policy in England, 1830–1914*, 51, where Weiner claims that during the period spanning approximately 1800–1850, "the traditional common law doctrine that a child under 14 could not be presumed legally responsible was usually ignored." Weiner adduces persuasive evidence which demonstrates that far from being exempt, children in Oliver's position would be "treated as being even *more* liable to criminal sanctions than earlier."

100. K. J. M. Smith, *Modern Treatise on the Law of Criminal Complicity*, 239–40.

101. (1894) 1 Q.B. 710 (C.C.R.).

102. Ibid.

103. Bayley, "Things as They Really Are," 49–64.

104. In *History of the Criminal Law of England*, Stephen makes the case that a person who is insane can be held no more responsible for his actions than a person who

dreams he has committed a crime, and what connects the insane person to the dreamer is the concept of the waking dream:

> There is a sense in which a person in a dream knows the nature and quality of his imaginary acts, and that they are wrong; but all the mental processes in dreaming are so feeble and imperfect, that I should suppose that no one who dreamed that he had committed a crime, even if the dream had included some feeling of conscientious reluctance, and of giving way to temptation, would on waking suffer any remorse, as he would if being awake he had formed an intention to do wrong and had afterwards abandoned it. If it be the case that certain forms of insanity cause men to live as it were in waking dreams, and to act with as faint a perception of reality as dreaming men have when they suppose themselves to act, surely they could not be said to 'know' that any particular act was wrong. (2:165-6)

On degrees of voluntariness and responsibility, see Silber, "Being and Doing: A Study of Status Responsibility and Voluntary Responsibility," 47-91.

105. For a very persuasive discussion of Oliver's fainting, see Rosemarie Bodenheimer, *The Politics of Story in Victorian Social Fiction*, 119-34. In her chapter on *Oliver Twist* and pastoral, Bodenheimer demonstrates that Oliver's fainting keeps him from obtaining any kind of social (including criminal) record. In her words, "Each time Oliver is nearly apprehended as an accomplice in a criminal act, he falls into a faint followed by an illness that erases his immediate past like a little death. After a rebirth, he wakes up among the social remnants of his natural history—Brownlow and the Maylies" (124). Dickens thus allows Oliver to resist social experience that, in turn, is evidence of Dickens's own resistance to the environmentalist view of character itself, according to Bodenheimer. Since Bodenheimer's argument is not about the relations between the novel and the criminal law, her discussion does not take up the complexities of calling Oliver an "accomplice," nor does it address Dickens's struggles with the long reach of criminal law, a reach necessarily long enough to capture Fagin but so long it also (almost) captures Oliver.

106. Dickens on occasion tries to protect Nancy by using the same device. The more implicated she appears in the attempted corruption of Oliver, the more delirious, even mad, she becomes.

107. J. Hillis Miller, *Victorian Subjects*, 43.

108. Williams, *Criminal Law*, 350.

109. Although Oliver fully intends to warn the Maylies during the great break-in and attempted robbery ("In the short time he had had to collect his senses, the boy had firmly resolved that, whether he died in the attempt or not, he would make one effort to dart up stairs from the hall, and alarm the family") and even takes a few steps in the direction of the sleeping family, at the moment when he must make his move Oliver "let his lantern fall, and knew not whether to advance or fly" (143).

110. See Weiner, *Reconstructing the Criminal*, 17, where he adduces persuasive evidence that in the Victorian period anxieties about female criminality were connected to concerns about more overt expression of female sexuality.

111. Charles Dickens to John Forster, November 3, 1837, in House and Storey, *Letters of Charles Dickens*, 1:328.

112. Nor was Dickens. In his autobiographical fragment, he conjures up his days at Warren's Blacking factory, and in so doing reveals the power that old companions and associates have over the self as the mind turns back to them: "No words can express the secret agony of my soul as I sunk into this companionship; compared these everyday associates with those of my happier childhood.... My whole nature was so penetrated

with the grief and humiliation of such considerations, that even now, famous and caressed and happy, I often forget in my dreams that I have a dear wife and children; and even that I am a man; and wander desolately back to that time of my life." John Forster, *The Life of Charles Dickens*, 1:53.

113. *Great Expectations*, 340.

114. Dickens would return to a Sikes-like character in *Barnaby Rudge*'s Hugh. In Hugh, Dickens would make his points about the social construction of character much more loudly and insistently.

115. In his essay on Dickens, George Orwell asserts the same half-truth: "If you ask any ordinary reader which of Dickens's proletarian characters he can remember, the three he is almost certain to mention are Bill Sykes, Sam Weller and Mrs. Gamp. A burglar, a valet, and a drunken midwife—not exactly a representative cross-section of the English working class." Sikes remains a burglar even though, it is safe to assume, Orwell knows him to be a murderer. Perhaps one answer to this is that Orwell is strictly identifying characters by profession, but if so, why identify Mrs. Gamp as a "drunken midwife"? See "Charles Dickens," in Orwell's *Critical Essays*, 4.

116. House, "Introduction to *Oliver Twist*," 197.

117. William T. Lankford in "'The Parish Boy's Progress': The Evolving Form of *Oliver Twist*" produces a lively and detailed analysis of Sikes that takes care to show that Dickens represents Sikes before the murder "entirely through his external appearance . . . And even while Sikes commits murder, his consciousness never enters the narrative" (29). Once Sikes commits the murder, however, Lankford registers what he calls a change in the "mode of narration. . . . Here the focus moves from external to internal, from Sikes's actions to the action of his mind" (29). While Lankford's observations serve a different argument, we share an interest in the sudden shift from the external to the internal.

118. In *Dickens and Thackeray*, 81, John R. Reed notes this change as well: "If Fagin is sly and insinuating, Bill Sikes is merely a cunning brute. Neither seems to have anything resembling a conscience, though Bill discovers something like one after he has killed Nancy." Later Reed adds, "Bill lacks a true conscience, but knows that he has committed an abominable crime, and thus superstitious fear serves the same function that conscience would."

119. Collins, *Dickens and Crime*, 286–7.

120. *Our Mutual Friend*, 546.

121. Ibid., 546.

122. Ibid.

123. Collins, *Dickens and Crime*, 284–5.

124. *Our Mutual Friend*, 708.

125. Ibid.

126. Collins, ed., *Charles Dickens: The Public Readings*, 467.

127. Ibid., 478.

PROLOGUE TO GEORGE ELIOT'S CRIMES

1. Hart, *The Concept of Law*, 172–3.

2. Ibid., 301.

3. Stephen, *A General View of the Criminal Law* (1863), 103.

4. Cohn, *Transparent Minds: Narrative Modes for Presenting Consciousness in Fiction*, 4.

5. Bentham, *The Principles of Morals and Legislation*, 73.

6. John Austin, *Lectures on Jurisprudence; Or, The Philosophy of Positive Law*, 1:433.

7. See *Some George Eliot Notebooks: An Edition of the Carl H. Pforzheimer Library's George Eliot Holograph Notebooks, MSS 707, 708, 709, 710, 711*, 1:194, 198, 200.

8. Ibid., 109.

9. *George Eliot's Middlemarch Notebooks: A Transcription*, 205.

10. Stephen, "English Jurisprudence," 456–86.

11. Noted in *The Journals of George Eliot*, 242.

12. Eliot, *The Mill on the Floss*, 164.

13. Ibid., 164.

14. Ibid., 165.

15. Ibid.

16. Ibid., 674, n. 29.

17. Sally Shuttleworth focuses on the intersections between Lewes's scientific work and George Eliot's novels in *George Eliot and Nineteenth Century Science*.

18. On the term "realism," see Levine, *The Realistic Imagination from Frankenstein to Lady Chatterley*, where Levine writes:

> Realism, as a literary method, can in these terms be defined as a self-conscious effort, usually in the name of some moral enterprise of truth telling and extending the limits of human sympathy, to make literature appear to be describing directly not some other language but reality itself (whatever that may be taken to be); in this effort, the writer must self-contradictorily dismiss previous conventions of representation while, in effect, establishing new ones. No major Victorian novelists were deluded into believing that they were in fact offering unmediated reality; but all of them struggled to make contact with the world out there, and, even with their knowledge of their own subjectivity, to break from the threatening limits of solipsism, of convention, and of language. (8)

I quote at length from Levine's introduction here because his subtle and detailed discussion of Victorian realism remains for me the most helpful and the most persuasive. The term "realism," Levine himself notes, seems to resist definition at every turn, so much so that Levine identifies his treatment of realism as a "study of its elusiveness" (7). Nonetheless, Levine moves toward a definition by describing realism as "the struggle to avoid the inevitable conventionality in pursuit of the unattainable unmediated reality" (8).

2. "TO FIX OUR MINDS ON THAT CERTAINTY"

1. The *OED* gives as one of its two examples a passage from Jane Austen's *Sense and Sensibility* (1796). The second citation is from *Boy's Own Book* (1869).

2. For a useful sketch of Austin's life to which this discussion is much indebted, see Wilfred E. Rumble's introduction to Austin, *The Province of Jurisprudence Determined*, vii–xii.

3. Rumble, introduction, xi.

4. Ibid., viii.

5. Stephen, "English Jurisprudence," 456.

6. Austin, *Lectures on Jurisprudence; Or, The Philosophy of the Positive Law*, 427–8.

7. See my discussion of objections to consequentialism hereafter.

8. Austin, *Lectures on Jurisprudence*, 434.

9. After Lewes's death, Sidgwick became a trustee of the George Henry Lewes Studentship on Physiology, and after Eliot's death, he collected signatures for the petition to have her buried in Westminster Abbey. See Haight, *George Eliot: A Biography*, 522 and 548.

10. Sidgwick, *The Methods of Ethics*, 202.

11. The letter as written does not actually mention "trouble." The letter reads, more cautiously, "I have told you where you are to direct a letter to, if you want to write, but I put it down below lest you should have forgotten. Do not write unless there is something I can really do for you" (333).

12. Stephen, *A History of the Criminal Law of England*, 2:111.

13. The rule remained in force until 1967. See *R. v. Maloney*, [1985] 1 A.C. 905, 910, where counsel for the Crown remarked that "Prior to the Criminal Justice Act of 1967 the approved direction to a jury was that a man must be presumed to intend the natural and probable consequences of his act: *DPP v. Smith* [1961] A.C. 290. The Criminal Justice Act of 1967 abolished any such irrebuttable presumption."

14. Turner, *Kenny's Outlines of Criminal Law*, 30, n. 3.

15. Griew, "States of Mind, Presumptions and Inferences," 67. Griew cites *R. v. Gathercole* (1838) 2 Lew CC 237 for the proposition that "natural" was interpreted as that which "must necessarily follow."

16. Section 8 of the Criminal Justice Act of 1967 provides that

A court or jury, in determining whether a person has committed an offence, —

(a) shall not be bound in law to infer that he intended or foresaw a result of his actions by reason only of its being a natural and probable result of those actions; but

(b) shall decide whether he did intend or foresee that result by reference to all the evidence, drawing such inferences from the evidence as appear proper in the circumstances.

Quoted in Griew, "States of Mind, Presumptions and Inferences," 71.

17. Griffin, "Consequences," *Proceedings of the Aristotelian Society*, 167–82.

18. Weiner, *Reconstructing the Criminal: Culture, Law, and Policy in England, 1830–1914*, 55.

19. Moore, *Ethics*, 72.

20. Griffin, "Consequences," 167. Griffin also cites Sidgwick's *Methods of Ethics* as the source for these ideas.

21. Moore, *Principia Ethica*.

22. Griffin, "Consequences," 181. See also Samuel Scheffler, ed., *Consequentialism and Its Critics*.

23. W. B. Yeats, "At Stratford-on-Avon," in *Ideas of Good and Evil*, 107. In "The Politics of Culture and the Debate over Representation," Catherine Gallagher observes that "before the 1860s, George Eliot's notions reveal a close but paradoxical relationship to liberal, even Utilitarian theories of value and representation" (115).

24. See Scheffler's introduction to *Consequentialism and Its Critics*, 3–4.

25. Irwine's reference to Nemesis, as well as his reading of Aeschylus (to which I will return later) reiterate the privileging of consequences over motives or intentions or any other kind of internal element. Irwine's pronouncement recalls Lord Acton's comments on the Greeks and human sacrifice in an 1863 essay. "It was not," wrote Acton, "the conscience of guilt, but the terror of its consequences, which overcame the humanity of the Greeks" ("Human Sacrifice," 413). Human sacrifice, for the Greeks, "did not wash away the guilt of the individual, but only warded off the consequences of sin

from the community. And these consequences remained after the guilt was washed away. Orestes though purified of his mother's blood, was still pursued by the furies." (Ibid.). In this I find provocative connections to *Adam Bede*, since one might read Hetty as the sacrifice offered up to "ward off the consequences of sin from the community" Eliot presents, while the consequences remain.

26. See Davis, "Child-Killing in English Law," 301–43; Smith, *Trial by Medicine*, 143–50.

27. Davis, "Child-Killing in English Law," 317.

28. See Green, *Verdict According to Conscience: Perspectives on the English Criminal Trial Jury, 1200–1800*, 269, where Green notes although he does not treat "such obvious instances of nullification (even where the facts were clear) as that practiced in prosecutions for rape and infanticide," such cases were "important," though rare and not as visible as the nullification in cases of theft, cases that were more common and had a greater impact on jury attitudes more generally.

29. Though beyond the scope of this study, one might pursue the questions that attend more closely to the intersections of gender and criminal states of mind that I merely touch on here. How did literary and legal narratives differentiate between the criminal states of mind of men and women? In her provocative article "Literary Defenses and Medical Prosecutions: Representing Infanticide in Nineteenth-Century Britain," 271–94, Christine Krueger argues that nineteenth-century literary representations of infanticide, including Eliot's in *Adam Bede*, helped to "protect women from the state by elaborating a representation of infanticide which insisted on its private character" (271). Of particular interest to me is Krueger's claim that in their representation of infanticidal mothers, literary narratives "mystify their motives as to render them inscrutable to legal reasoning" (272). Krueger's reading distinguishes itself from others in that it interprets this mystification—or perhaps annulment—of motive not as repressive but as protective. But if juries more frequently excused female defendants by rejecting prosecutorial allegations as to motive or intent, how was intention itself represented? Though fewer women were tried for crimes than men in the eighteenth and nineteenth centuries, more women were tried for homicide, and primarily for the murder of their own children. See Emmerichs, "Trials of Women for Homicide in Nineteenth-Century England," 99–109, cited in Krueger.

30. Bray, *The Philosophy of Necessity or, The Law of Consequences; as Applicable to Mental, Moral, and Social Science*, 1:178–9.

31. Eliot, "R. W. Mackay's *The Progress of the Intellect*," in *Selected Essays, Poems, and Other Writings*, 27.

32. Ibid., 271.

33. Other readers have noted the significance of Eliot's review of Mackay to *Adam Bede*. In Sally Shuttleworth's chapter on the novel, Shuttleworth quotes this passage from the Mackay review to suggest that Hetty Sorrel, like other Eliot characters, looks to chance rather than "what George Eliot termed in 'The Progress of the Intellect' that 'inexorable law of consequences,' which establishes the foundations for moral conduct and human duty. Unlike Adam, Hetty is not furnished with a rigid mathesis, a measuring line from which to assess all actions." *George Eliot and Nineteenth Century Science*, 46.

34. Ibid., 27. Carol Christ in "Aggression and Providential Death in George Eliot's Fiction" makes a similar point, noting that in all of Eliot's novels and in *Adam Bede* in particular, "Eliot sees herself as an historian, a modern-day Herodotus, who records changes in character and community that she sees before her, who observes and notes

down the 'varying experiments in Time'" (137). This claim serves Carol Christ's larger argument—that Eliot uses providential death to avoid the complications of aggression that she attributes to her characters—by showing how the providential deaths depart from the realistic writing Eliot often practiced and most admired. More telling is the observation that follows: "As an historian, Eliot characteristically emphasizes the inevitable consequences of her characters' actions. Arthur and Hetty, Lydgate and Rosamond, Bulstrode, Mrs. Transome are all studies in the tragic consequences of inconsequential deeds" (137). The move from inevitable consequences to inconsequential deeds in this sentence is puzzling but also provocative. While I do not agree that, for example, Bulstrode's deeds are inconsequential, I am interested in the implicit hierarchy Carol Christ registers here. Weight is assigned to consequences and denied to deeds.

35. (1859) 1 F & F 662.

36. Ibid.

37. (1811) *R. v. Farrington*, 168 ER 763.

38. White, *Misleading Cases*, 48.

39. Stephen, *A General View of the Criminal Law* (1863), 304.

40. Stephen, *History of the Criminal Law of England*, 2:111.

41. See *R. v. Whitmarsh* (1898) 62 J.P. 711, cited in Turner, *Russell on Crime*, 1:476.

42. Turner, *Russell on Crime*, 1:471.

43. Ibid., 1:471, n. 34.

44. Ibid., 1:468–9.

45. John Blackwood to G. H. Lewes, October 4, 1858, in Haight, ed., *The George Eliot Letters*, 2:483.

46. Boswell, *Life of Johnson*, 3:39–40.

47. As I will take up in my discussion of *Middlemarch*, Eliot would return to these complications in Bulstrode, thinking specifically in terms of the mind that casts out and then returns to a thought.

48. Stephen, *A General View of the Criminal Law* (1863), 304.

49. Ibid., 304–5.

50. Turner, *Russell on Crime*, I:468.

51. Eliot, *Daniel Deronda*, 645. Subsequent citations appear in the text.

52. Goode, "Adam Bede," 24–5.

53. Turner, *Russell on Crime*, 28.

54. Consider the use of "altered" here as compared to its use near the end of *Daniel Deronda*, when, in her confession to Deronda about Grandcourt's death, Gwendolen shrieks, "'It can never be altered . . . It can never be altered'" (648), and Deronda in his mind "could only have echoed 'It can never be altered—it remains unaltered, to alter other things'" (649).

55. Crane, "The Plot of *Tom Jones*," 72.

56. Ibid.

57. In his chapter "George Eliot and the Greeks," in *The Victorians and Ancient Greece* to which I am much indebted in my discussion of allusion in Eliot, Richard Jenkyns notes that Irwine's reading this *Aeschylus* is both anachronistic and unlikely:

> The action of *Adam Bede* opens in 1798. Irwine is presumably about forty-five; he would have been up at university early in the 1770s. His enthusiasm specifically for Greek authors, which would not have been strange in an intelligent country parson of George Eliot's day, would have been very abnormal in someone of his date. . . . And there is another implausibility. The Foulis *Aeschylus*

was a deluxe edition, illustrated by Flaxman, something more to look at than to read. (116)

Though a stickler for accuracy, it may well be that Eliot let these improbabilities slide for the sake of the tensions she wanted to bring to bear in this scene, so important are they to the development of her story. If, as Jenkyns suggests too, this scene with Irwine is "the turning point of the whole book" (116), it turns in part on our understanding these allusions.

58. Aeschylus, *Prometheus Bound*, 1361–5.

59. *Zeluco* was published in 1786 and reprinted in 1810 and 1820.

60. Buchen, "Arthur Donnithorne and *Zeluco*: Characterization Via Literary Allusion in *Adam Bede*," 16–7.

61. Coleridge, *The Collected Works of Samuel Taylor Coleridge*, 14(2):110.

62. John Blackwood to George Eliot, March 31, 1858, in *George Eliot Letters*, 2:446.

63. George Eliot to John Blackwood, December 28, 1858, in *George Eliot Letters*, 2:512.

64. Eliot, *Middlemarch*, 406–7. Subsequent citations appear in the text.

65. Monk, *Standard Deviations: Chance and the Modern British Novel*, 72.

66. Ibid., 73.

67. Eliot, *Felix Holt, the Radical*, 262. Subsequent citations appear in the text.

68. Gordon Haight reports Harrison's help on *Felix Holt* in *George Eliot: A Biography*, 384.

3. *MIDDLEMARCH, DANIEL DERONDA*, AND THE CRIME IN MIND

1. Alley, "George Eliot and the Ambiguity of Murder," *Studies in the Novel*, 61.

2. Ibid., 66.

3. Welsh, *George Eliot and Blackmail*, 216.

4. Carol Christ, "Aggression and Providential Death in George Eliot's Fiction," 131.

5. Austin, *Lectures on Jurisprudence*, 450.

6. Hobbes, *Leviathan*, 223–4.

7. John Blackwood to George Eliot, September 7, 1872, in *George Eliot Letters*, 5:306.

8. Blackwood shows some care with his words in this (and other) letters. Commenting in the same September 7, 1872 letter on Lydgate's situation in book 7, Blackwood remarks, "This 7th Book leaves Dr. Lydgate in a terrible mesh," turning the expected *mess* into an Eliotic *mesh*. Ibid.

9. Ibid.

10. In one of the few treatments of these issues, Henry Alley contends in "George Eliot and the Ambiguity of Murder" that Hetty Sorrel, Baldasarre Calvo, Nicholas Bulstrode, and Gwendolen Harleth demonstrate through their murderous acts (or omissions, as in the case of Gwendolen) "the frightening inextricability of guilt and innocence" (60). With Bulstrode, Alley argues that the representational difficulties at work when Bulstrode attempts to suppress his murderous thoughts manifest this inextricability of guilt and innocence. "We are led," remarks Alley, "to question the whole issue of crime and punishment, guilt and retribution, when the connections between sign and signifier fade" (64). Alley's language here—"the whole issue of crime and punishment, guilt and retribution"—is itself vague, but it registers the complications of representing states of mind and is true to the Bulstrode sections of *Middlemarch*. Eliot is

acutely aware of the complications of turning thought into speech. Of Bulstrode in prayer, the narrator avers, "Private prayer is inaudible speech, and speech is representative: who can represent himself just as he is, even in his own reflections?" (698). Putting reflection into words loses something in the translation. However, this recognition does not push the narrator into some postmodern spiral. The difficulties of turning thought into speech do not make guilt and innocence inextricable. The narrator's considerations of the similarities and differences between thought and speech anticipate the allusion to *Macbeth* that Eliot puts to good use in *Daniel Deronda*: "Who can be wise, amazed, temp'rate and furious, / Loyal and neutral in a moment?" (2.3.124–5). In *Daniel Deronda*, of which more later, Eliot imagines that while thought has the freedom to be at once wise and amazed, temperate and furious, speech has to conform itself to "clumsy necessities" (72). Bulstrode's "private prayer" occupies a position between thought and speech and is limited like speech itself by the limits of representation.

11. W. B. Yeats, *Ideas of Good and Evil*, 105.

12. Ibid., 106–7.

13. To illustrate the meaning of "to unfold" as "To disclose or reveal by state of exposition; to explain or make clear," the *OED* editors give a passage from *Locrine* 1.1.83 (1595), "I will unto you all unfold Our royall mind and resolute intent," and from Richard Flecknoe, *Epigrams & Epigrammatic Characters I* (1658), "Clearly unfolding and explicating the notions of her minde." From *Hamlet* 1.1.2, the editors give the reflexive use "Nay answer me: Stand and unfold your selfe."

14. Levine, *The Realistic Imagination from Frankenstein to Lady Chatterley*, 269.

15. During, "The Strange Case of Monomania: Patriarchy in Literature, Murder in *Middlemarch*, Drowning in *Daniel Deronda*," 88.

16. Ibid., 92.

17. Ibid., 93.

18. Ibid., 94.

19. Ibid.

20. Austin, *Lectures on Jurisprudence*, 423.

21. Ibid.

22. Ibid.

23. Ibid.

24. Ibid., 443.

25. Ibid., 441–42.

26. Wittgenstein, *Lectures and Conversations on Aesthetics, Psychology, and Religious Belief*, 21.

27. Fletcher, *Rethinking Criminal Law*, 440.

28. Austin, *Lectures on Jurisprudence*, 434.

29. Ibid., 436–7.

30. In *A History of the Criminal Law of England*, 2:111, Stephen provides this example:

> A puts a loaded pistol to B's temple and shoots B through the head deliberately, and knowing that the pistol is loaded and that the wound must certainly be mortal. It is obvious that in every such case the intention of A must be to kill B. On the other hand, the act itself throws no light whatever on A's motives for killing B. They may have been infinitely various. They may have varied from day to day. They may have been mixed in all imaginable degrees. The motive may have been a desire for revenge, or a desire for plunder, or a wish on A's part to defend himself against an attack by B, or a desire to kill and enemy in battle, or

to put a man already mortally wounded out of his agony. In all these cases the intention is the same, but the motives are different, and in all the intention may remain unchanged from first to last whilst the motives may vary from moment to moment.

31. Cox, *Yale Law Journal*, 659.

32. G. H. Lewes to Alexander Main, December 5, 1872, in *George Eliot Letters*, 5:337.

33. In During's essay "The Strange Case of Monomania," he claims of Laure that "At her trial she claims to have slipped and is discharged because 'no motive was discoverable'" (92). Not so. All that Eliot gives us are Lydgate's contentions for her innocence and his conclusion (in free indirect speech) that "no motive was discoverable." The most the narrator says is that "The legal investigation ended in Madame Laure's release." As any suspect might tell, there is a world of difference between an investigation and a trial.

34. Eliot, *Quarry for Middlemarch*, 54.

35. But what of the fact of Bulstrode's having disobeyed Lydgate's orders about the opium and the brandy? Since Hawley never interviews Lydgate, this piece of evidence never gets flushed out. Even so, it is difficult to know what difference, if any, it might have made. Since Bulstrode would have been following the course of treatment to which most other medical men subscribed, Toller and Wrench might still be left to conclude that his acts did not cause Raffles's death. They would interpret such acts as last attempts to prolong Raffles's life.

36. Stephen, *History of the Criminal Law of England*, 2:78. In the definitions of crime and sin set forth in *Leviathan*, Hobbes makes the same distinction:

> A Crime, is a sinne, consisting in the Committing (by Deed, or Word) of that which the Law forbiddeth, or the Omission of what it hath commended. So that every Crime is a sinne; but not every sinne a Crime. To intend to steale, or kill, is a sinne, though it never appeare in Word, or Fact: for God that seeth the thoughts of man, can lay it to his charge: but till it appear by some thing done, or said, by which the intention may be argued by a humane Judge, it hath not the name of Crime: which distinction the Greeks observed in the word ἁμάρτημα, and ἔγχλημα, or αἰτία; whereof the former, (which is translated Sinne,) signifieth any swerving from the Law whatsoever; but the two later, (which are translated Crime,) signifie that sinne onely, whereof one man may accuse another. But of intentions, which never appear by any outward act, there is no place for humane accusation. (224)

37. Stephen, *History of the Criminal Law of England*, 2:78–9.

38. Shakespeare, *Measure for Measure*, 2.1.17–8.

39. John Milton, *Paradise Lost*, 9.294–7 in *The Complete Poems*.

40. Turner, *Kenny's Outlines of Criminal Law*, 79.

41. Ibid.

42. Turner, *Russell on Crime*, 1:179.

43. Stephen, *History of the Criminal Law of England*, 2:224.

44. (1855) Dears. 515.

45. (1849) 1 Den. 432.

46. (1853) 1 E & B. 435.

47. For a discussion of the Victorian law of attempt, see Turner, *Russell on Crime*, 1:178–9. Victorian cases made fine distinctions that often depended on when intent was deemed to have been formed. The possession of indecent prints with intent to publish constituted an attempt to publish, while (by contrast) if an accused had possession of

indecent prints and thereafter formed an attempt to publish, he would not be not guilty of an attempt. See Stephen, *A Digest of Criminal Law*, 34.

48. Eliot, "Mr. Gilfil's Love-Story," in *Scenes of Clerical Life*, 155. All subsequent citations appear in the text.

49. Such expectations are encouraged by the obvious allusions to *Macbeth*. In addition to the daggers in the mind and hand of Caterina, one notes that the appointed meeting of Caterina and Wybrow is set to take place in a rookery.

50. (1864) L. & C. 471, 168 E.R. 1477.

51. Stephen, *History of the Criminal Law of England*, 2:225.

52. (1846) 2 C & K 293, 175 E.R. 121 (C.C.R), cited in Glanville Williams, *Criminal Law*, 635.

53. (1892) 17 Cox 491 (C.C.R.), cited in Williams, *Criminal Law*, 636.

54. Shelley, *The Cenci*, in *The Complete Poetical Works of Percy Bysshe Shelley*, 2.2.82–7.

55. Ibid., 2.2.93–6. In another moment that resonates with *Daniel Deronda*, mother, daughter, and brother are later executed for the murder of the count, committed by paid assassins. Faced with the charge of murder, the daughter Beatrice admits to having desired the death of the count, feeling that "some strange sudden death hung over him" (4.4.135), to which the pope's legate responds, before dragging them off to their trials, "Strange thoughts beget strange deeds; and here are both" (4.4.139).

56. Christ, "Aggression and Providential Death," 133.

57. Ibid.

58. Ibid.

59. Eliot, *Romola*, 300.

60. Ibid., 371.

61. Lewes, *Problems of Life and Mind* 2:459, quoted in Shuttleworth, *George Eliot and Nineteenth-Century Science*, 217–8, n.34.

62. Mill, "Bain's Psychology," in *Essays on Philosophy and the Classics*, 11:348.

63. Stephen, *A General View of the Criminal Law* (1890), 127.

64. Ibid.

65. G. H. Lewes to James Fitzjames Stephen, November 1872, unpublished letter, James Fitzjames Stephen Papers, Cambridge University Library.

66. Macaulay, *Notes to the Indian Penal Code*, in *Miscellaneous Works of Lord Macaulay*, 4:251–2. A bit later in the note, Macaulay again reiterates the less-than-satisfactoriness of this middle way: "It is with great diffidence that we bring forward our own proposition. It is open to objections; cases may be put in which it will operate too severely, and cases in which it will operate too leniently; but we are ignobly unable to devise a better" (4:253).

67. Bodenheimer, *The Real Life of Mary Ann Evans*, 101.

4. JAMES FITZJAMES STEPHEN
AND THE RESPONSIBILITIES OF NARRATIVE

1. A note on spelling: throughout this chapter, I will use "Nuncomar" and not the now more common "Nandacumar" to be consistent with Stephen's own spelling and to avoid confusion. For an instance of this alternate spelling, see Owen Dudley Edwards's pro-Macaulay/anti-Stephen essay, "Macaulay's Warren Hastings," 109–44. I follow Stephen with respect to the spelling of other Indian names for the same reason. Stephen himself was aware of orthographic concerns, and in his introduction to *The*

Story of Nuncomar and the Impeachment of Sir Elijah Impey he concedes: "With regard to the spelling of Indian names and words I have to admit ignorance. I have followed no system at all, but have spelt them as I found them spelt by others. In a few cases, however, I have adopted the more modern transliterations, instead of the old-fashioned ones, which have become obsolete. For instance, I write 'Khan,' not 'Cawn,' 'Shah Alam,' not 'Shaw Aulum,' 'Hindustani,' not 'Hindoostanee,' 'Diwani Adalat,' not 'Dewanny Adawlat.' 1:9. Hereafter citations for *The Story of Nuncomar and the Impeachment of Sir Elijah Impey* will appear in the text.

2. September 1884 unpublished letter, Stephen Papers, Cambridge University Library.

3. Leslie Stephen, *Life of Sir James Fitzjames Stephen*, 429.

4. Stephen to Lytton, February 23, 1885, unpublished letter, Stephen Papers, Cambridge University Library.

5. Stephen to Lady Egerton, April 29, 1885, unpublished letter, Stephen Papers, Cambridge University Library.

6. Leslie Stephen, *Life of Sir James Fitzjames Stephen*, 431.

7. Genette, "Fictional Narrative, Factual Narrative," 772.

8. Ibid., 762.

9. Davis, *Factual Fictions: The Origins of the English Novel*.

10. Macaulay, "Warrent Hastings," in *Macaulay: Prose and Poetry*, 405.

11. Leslie Stephen, *Life of Sir James Fitzjames Stephen*, 223.

12. On Governor Eyre, the Jamaica uprising, and the ensuing criminal investigations and trials, see Semmel, *The Governor Eyre Controversy*, and Dutton, *The Hero as Murderer: The Life of Edward John Eyre*.

13. Unpublished letter to his mother, March 26, 1867, quoted in James Smith, *James Fitzjames Stephen: Portrait of a Victorian Rationalist*, 137.

14. Quoted in Leslie Stephen, *Life of Sir James Fitzjames Stephen*, 228.

15. Stephen, "A Tale of Two Cities," 743.

16. Ibid.

17. Lyall, *Warren Hastings*, 70.

18. Ibid.

19. Stephen, "The Relation of Novels to Life," 162–3.

20. Chandler, Davidson, and Harootunian, Introduction to *Questions of Evidence: Proof, Practice and Persuasion across the Disciplines*, 3.

21. According to Greenblatt, empathy emerges in the Renaissance as part of a larger strategy of assimilation such that the object of the empathetic feeling becomes an object of conquest, as Iago conquers Othello and as, by extension, the explorers of the New World conquered that world's inhabitants. What surprises Chandler, Davidson, and Harootunian is that Greenblatt says little or nothing about "the thematics of evidence" that his assertions about empathy and about Othello seem to generate. The editors of *Questions of Evidence* invite Greenblatt to consider "the connection between evidence in interpretation and evidence in one's own interpretation." In short, if Iago's empathetic interpretive work constitutes an act of appropriation, what is Greenblatt's?

22. Ibid., 5.

23. Ginzburg, "Checking the Evidence: The Judge and the Historian," 298.

24. Ibid., 301.

25. Brooks has since published a full-length study of confessions in law and literature. See his *Troubling Confessions: Speaking Guilt in Law and Literature*.

26. Sarat, "Commentary: Ways of Telling Legal Events," unpublished paper read at the meeting of the Working Group on Law, Culture and the Humanities, March 29, 1998. My thanks to Professor Sarat for sending me his paper. In *Troubling Confessions*, Peter Brooks addresses Sarat's criticism by making his claims about motive less stridently. To take one example, Brooks asks "if confession implies a penitential state that may involve disgrace, even abjection, doesn't it often appear a violation of human dignity?" (9). The "may involve" begins to address but does not meet Sarat's objection. For further discussion and exploration of the "rich categories of resistance" Sarat refers to in his paper, see Ewick and Silbey, *The Common Place of the Law: Stories from Everyday Life*.

27. (1859) 4 Cox 55.

28. Ibid.

29. "Chelmsford–Friday, March 10. Charge of murder—Acquittal on the ground of Puerperal insanity," *Journal of Psychological Medicine and Mental Pathology* 1 (1848): 478–83, at 479, quoted in Roger Smith, *Trial by Medicine*, 109.

30. Stephen, "The License of Modern Novelists," 156.

31. Ibid.

32. Ibid., 125.

33. Stephen, "The *Edinburgh Review* and Modern Novelists," *Saturday Review*, 18 July 1857, 57.

34. Stephen, "The License of Modern Novelists," 141.

35. Ibid.

36. Stephen, "The *Edinburgh Review* and Modern Novelists," 57.

37. Stephen, "The License of Modern Novelists," 142.

38. Ibid., 143.

39. Stephen, "Novels and Novelists," 285.

40. Ibid.

41. Ibid., 286.

42. Stephen, "The *Edinburgh Review* and Modern Novelists," 57.

43. Stephen, "The Relation of Novels to Life," 159.

44. Stephen, "The *Edinburgh Review* and Modern Novelists," 57.

45. Stephen, "Mr. Dickens as a Politician," 8.

46. Stephen, "A Tale of Two Cities," 741.

47. Ibid.

48. Ruskin, "A Note on *Hard Times*," 159.

49. Stephen, "Little Dorrit," 15.

50. Levine, *The Boundaries of Fiction*, 111.

51. Ibid., 110.

52. Macaulay, "History," in *Miscellaneous Works of Lord Macaulay*, 1:153–4.

53. Ibid., 1:194.

54. Ibid., 1:192.

55. Ibid., 1:194.

56. Ibid., 1:155.

57. Ibid., 1:188.

58. Ibid.

59. Ibid., 1:190.

60. Ibid., 1:194.

61. Ibid., 1:177.

62. Ibid., 1:178.

63. Levine, *Boundaries of Fiction*, 116.
64. Ibid., 120.
65. Ibid., 121.
66. Stephen, "Lord Macaulay," in *Essays by a Barrister*, 102.
67. Stephen, "Lord Macaulay's Works," 207.
68. Stephen, "The Characteristics of English Criminal Law," 15–6.
69. Macaulay, "History," in *Miscellaneous Works of Lord Macaulay*, 1:197.
70. Feiling, *Warren Hastings*, 9. I am indebted to Feiling for his sketch of Hastings's early life.
71. Moon, *Warren Hastings in British India*, 30.
72. Lyall, *Warren Hastings*, 12.
73. Feiling, *Warren Hastings*, 47.
74. Ibid., 61.
75. Lyall, *Warren Hastings*, 57.
76. One central question both in the trial of Nuncomar and in the later impeachment trials of Impey and Hastings involved the application of 2 George II, c. 25 – the statute that made forgery a capital crime – to Nuncomar's case. In *The Story of Nuncomar*, Stephen takes up this claim in some detail:

> The really serious part of the charge of illegality may be shortly summed up by saying that Nuncomar was not subject to the law of England at all in 1770, when his offence was said to have been committed, and that if he was subject to it, the particular Statute (25 Geo. II, c.2) was not in force at Calcutta at the time when the offence was committed, or at the time when the trial took place. (2:19)

What follows is Stephen's careful rendering of the legislative history of the application of the criminal law of England in India, which goes on for several pages. Stephen concludes by remarking that the Supreme Court's application of the statute to Nuncomar's case may have indeed been mistaken, but that such a mistake "was innocent and in good faith. Every one who has much practical acquaintance with law is well aware that in many cases it varies from time to time" (2:34).
77. Feiling, *Warren Hastings*, 357.
78. According to Macaulay, Nuncomar exemplified to the nth degree the worst traits of the Bengalis. So, says Stephen in *The Story of Nuncomar*, "As an instance of the injustice of these super-superlatives, I may observe that Lord Macaulay's first remark on Bengalees is: 'The physical organization of the Bengalees is feeble to effeminacy.' Nuncomar, therefore, ought to have been hardly able to stand or even sit up" (2:41, n. 1).
79. Macaulay, "Warren Hastings," in *Macaulay: Prose and Poetry*, 400.
80. Ibid., 402.
81. Ibid., 387.
82. Ibid., 389.
83. Ibid., 389–90.
84. Rogers, *Recollections*, 93.
85. Macaulay, "Warren Hastings," in *Macaulay: Prose and Poetry*, 377.
86. Leslie Stephen, *Life of Sir James Fitzjames Stephen*, 162.
87. Ibid., 163 (ellipses in original).
88. Thomas Macaulay, "Milton," in *The Miscellaneous Works of Lord Macaulay*, 1:18.
89. Macaulay, "Warren Hastings," in *Macaulay: Prose and Poetry*, 439.
90. Ibid.
91. Ibid., 432.
92. Ibid., 433.

93. Ibid., 405.
94. Leslie Stephen, *Life of Sir James Fitzjames Stephen*, 431.
95. Ibid., 430.
96. Ibid.
97. Ibid.
98. Ibid., 430–1.
99. *The Waste Land: A Facsimile and Transcript of the Original Drafts*, 47.
100. Leslie Stephen, *Life of Sir James Fitzjames Stephen*, 431.
101. Ibid., 431.
102. Ibid., 433.
103. Ibid.
104. Ibid.
105. Stephen presents a similar hypothetical a bit later, while interpreting some remarks of Hastings. When asked during his impeachment trial whether or not he had ever countenanced the prosecution of Nuncomar, Hastings replied, "'I never did. I have been on my guard. I have carefully avoided every circumstance which might appear to be an interference in that prosecution'" (*The Story of Nuncomar* 2:61). Hastings's later prosecutors argued that this was an admission on Hastings's part, since only the guilty might be on their guard. In reply, Stephen asserted:

> The fact that he was on his guard against the appearance of taking part in the matter is only what might be expected if he really did take no part. A dies. The question is whether he died of arsenical poisoning or of disease of the bowels. The suggestion is that his doctor administered arsenic in the interest of B the heir. B is asked if he ever procured the doctor to poison A. He says, "I never did. I was on my guard. I avoided everything which could suggest such a thing." Would it be fair to remark, "Your answer admits your guilt. An innocent man would have taken no precautions." The utmost that the answer would really admit, would be that the witness knew he might be suspected.'" (*The Story of Nuncomar* 2:62)

That Stephen has recourse more than once to this family of hypothetical situations suggests how familiar a plot this was.
106. Leslie Stephen, *Life of Sir James Fitzjames Stephen*, 431.
107. De Quincey, "On Murder Considered as One of the Fine Arts (Second Paper)," in *The Collected Words of Thomas De Quincey*, 8:56.
108. For a full treatment of this subject, see Joel Black, *The Aesthetics of Murder*, where Black explores De Quincey's artist as criminal and the representations of murder as art.
109. The great legal critic Robert Cover reminds us, when we need reminding, that the violence of a legal opinion or interpretation is very real and makes certain legal narratives—like legal decisions, for example—different in kind from other narratives. In "Violence and the Word" (an essay I also refer to in my introduction), Cover effectively answers critics—and particularly Ronald Dworkin and James Boyd White—who do not recognize that the violence of legal interpretation puts this activity in a class by itself. "Legal interpretation," announces Cover at the very beginning of his essay, "takes place in a field of pain and death" (203). To put it plainly, "A judge articulates her understanding of a text, and as a result, somebody loses freedom, his property, his children, even his life" (203). And then later, "I do not wish us to pretend that we talk our prisoners into jail. The 'interpretations' or 'conversations' that are the preconditions for violent incarceration are themselves implements of violence" (211). At the end of a

trial report or a legal opinion, there issues a verdict and a sentence. It is useful to recall here that after Macaulay published "Warren Hastings," no one went to jail.

110. The first footnote of any substance (all the preceding footnotes merely provide references) offers information about Impey's intentions with regard to his written defense, a defense which he, apparently, intended to give to the British Museum. Shortly thereafter, a footnote must handle the intentions of the draughtsmen of the Charter of the Supreme Court of Calcutta, and then two pages later, Stephen must ask whether the Charter intended to exclude Irishmen from the jury pool.

111. Macaulay, "Warrent Hastings," in *Macaulay: Prose and Poetry*, 405 and 432.

112. For a more detailed analysis of "conduct and character," see my discussion of them in chapter 1.

113. Wimsatt and Beardsley, "The Intentional Fallacy," 2.

114. Stephen to Lady Grant Duff, October 7, 1883, unpublished letter, Stephen Papers, Cambridge University Library.

115. Acharya, *The Defence of Nundakumar: A Reply to Sir James Stephen's Book*, ii.

116. Ibid., 10.

117. Ibid., 25.

118. Ibid., 45.

119. Ibid.

120. Ibid., 44.

121. Ibid., 47.

122. Lyall, W*arren Hastings*, 70.

123. Ibid., 70.

124. Ibid., 70–1.

125. Ibid., 71.

126. Ibid., 73.

127. Mark Kelman, "Reasonable Evidence of Reasonableness," 179.

128. Ibid., 180.

129. Ibid., 177.

130. Ibid.

131. Ibid.

132. *The Private Life of Warren Hastings by Sir Charles Lawson: Opinions of the Press, 1895–6*, 10.

CONCLUSION

1. Hardy, *Tess of the D'Urbervilles*, 366. Subsequent citations appear in the text.

2. Ellen Rooney considers the "problematics of seduction" (93) in *Tess* and argues that Hardy at once presents Tess as a subject capable of intentions and choices and an object whose body acts of its own accord so that she is the victim of her own seductiveness. See "Tess and the Subject of Sexual Violence: Reading, Rape, Seduction," 87–114.

3. Shires, "The Aesthetics of the Victorian Novel: Form, Subjectivity, Ideology," 73.

4. Ibid.

5. Ibid., 72.

6. Conrad, *The Secret Agent: A Simple Tale*, 196.

7. Ibid., 197.

8. Ibid., 31.

9. Ibid., 59.

10. Though beyond the scope of my study, one might also take up as germane to this discussion Theodore Dreiser's naturalist novel *An American Tragedy*, a novel that offers a main character, Clyde Griffiths, imagining, plotting, and arguably carrying out the murder of his girlfriend Roberta. Dreiser creates the ambiguity of intentionality by making Roberta's death by drowning occur as at once the consequence of an accident and a premeditated act, but, as Philip Fisher has argued in "Looking Around to See Who I Am: Dreiser's Territory of Self," 728–48, where in most novels of "the age of individualism" (Fisher's term) the interior and its conflicts carried much weight and meaning, "it is one of the most interesting facts about the representation of modern characters in Zola or Dreiser that this territory of the self within the body has vanished or declined interest or investment" (733). Fisher further explains: "Clyde has no self to which he might be 'true.' Literally, he is not yet anyone at all. . . . He gets his 'self' moment by moment as a gift from the outside. He murders by imitation (after reading of a drowning in a newspaper) as he loves by imitation (his being mistaken for Gilbert)" (735). Fisher's essay itself expresses some ambivalence about calling Clyde's act a murder, noting first that "Roberta dies by accident really" (741) yet later referring to the act quite straightforwardly as "the murder of Roberta" (743). Fisher's ambivalence reflects the novel's ambiguity, for as Fisher claims, Clyde "seems particularly absent at the most decisive moments" (741). His acts are oddly not his own. It is no great leap to see the similarities between the imitations Clyde performs and the roles the Verlocs play.

11. Thompson, *Fiction, Crime, and Empire: Clues to Modernity and Postmodernism*, 171.

12. Waugh, *Feminine Fictions: Revisiting the Postmodern*, 9.

13. *R. v. Dias* (2001, December 13) EWCA Crim 2986.

14. *R.v. Cerovic* (2001, December 3). EWCA Crim 2868.

15. Capote, *In Cold Blood*, 245. All subsequent citations appear in the text.

16. In his comparison of *In Cold Blood* and *Handcarved Coffins*, Jack Hicks also notes that the former text "is decidedly realistic in philosophy and form." See Hicks, "'Fire, Fire, Fire Flowing Like a River, River, River: History and Postmodernism in Truman Capote's *Handcarved Coffins*," 170.

17. Capote, *Handcarved Coffins*, xviii. All subsequent citations appear in the text.

18. In his essay on *Handcarved Coffins*, Robert Siegle argues that Jake's reading tastes show that "he has no choice but to perceive events in terms of Dickens's search for hidden connections, people in terms of characters in nineteenth-century novels, referential 'facts' in terms of metaphorical figures—nonfiction in terms of fiction." "Capote's *Handcarved Coffins* and the Nonfiction Novel," 442.

19. Siegle claims that the text demonstrates the collapse of the divide between nonfiction and fiction. Ibid., 438.

⚔ BIBLIOGRAPHY ⚖

Acharya, Keshub Chandra. *The Defence of Nundakumar: A Reply to Sir James Stephen's Book*. Calcutta: Sadharani Press, 1886.

Acton, John Emerich Edward Dalberg. "Human Sacrifice." In *Selected Writings of Lord Acton: Essays in Religion, Politics, and Morality*, edited by J. Rufus Fears. Indianapolis, Ind.: Liberty Classic, 1988.

Aeschylus. *Prometheus Bound*. Translated by William Matthews. In *Aeschylus 2*, edited by David R. Slavitt and Palmer Bovie. Philadelphia: University of Pennsylvania Press, 1998.

Alley, Henry. "George Eliot and the Ambiguity of Murder." *Studies in the Novel* 25 (1993): 59–75.

Ashworth, Andrew. *Principles of Criminal Law*. Oxford: Clarendon Press, 1995.

Assisting and Encouraging Crime: A Consultation Paper. Law Commission consultation paper no. 131. London: HMSO, 1993.

Austin, John. *Lectures on Jurisprudence; Or The Philosophy of the Positive Law*. Edited by Robert Campbell. New York: Cockcroft, 1875–78.

——. *The Province of Jurisprudence Determined*. Edited by Wilfrid E. Rumble. Cambridge: Cambridge University Press, 1995.

Austin, J. L. *Philosophical Papers*. Edited by J. O. Urmson and G. J. Warnock. 2nd ed. Oxford: Oxford University Press, 1970.

Bayley, John. "Things as They Really Are." In *Dickens and the Twentieth Century*, edited by John Gross and Gabriel Pearson. Toronto: University of Toronto Press, 1962.

Beattie, J. M. *Crime and the Courts in England: 1600–1800*. Princeton, N.J.: Princeton University Press, 1986.

Bender, John. *Imagining the Penitentiary: Fiction and the Architecture of the Mind in Eighteenth Century England*. Chicago, Ill.: University of Chicago Press, 1987.

Bentham, Jeremy. *The Principles of Morals and Legislation*. New York: Hafner, 1948.

Black, Joel. *The Aesthetics of Murder*. Baltimore, Md.: Johns Hopkins University Press, 1991.

Blackstone, William. *Commentaries on the Laws of England*. London: Professional Books, 1982.

Bodenheimer, Rosemarie. *The Politics of Story in Victorian Social Fiction*. Ithaca, N.Y.: Cornell University Press, 1988.

——. *The Real Life of Mary Ann Evans*. Ithaca, N.Y.: Cornell University Press, 1994.

Boswell, James. *Life of Johnson*. 6 vols. Edited by G. B. Hill. Revised by L. F. Powell. Oxford: Clarendon Press, 1934.

Bouchier, Jeremy. "Dickens on English Criminal Law." *Notes and Queries*, July 5, 1879, 6.

Bradley, F. H. *Ethical Studies*. 2nd ed. Oxford: Clarendon Press, 1927.

Bray, Charles. *The Philosophy of Necessity; or the Law of Consequences as Applicable to Mental, Moral, and Social Science*. 2 vols. London: Longman, 1841.

Brooks, Peter. *Troubling Confessions: Speaking Guilt in Law and Literature*. Chicago, Ill.: University of Chicago Press, 2000.

"Browning's Dramatic Idylls." *Saturday Review*, June 21, 1870, 774–5.

Buchen, Irving. "Arthur Donnithorne and *Zeluco*: Characterization Via Literary Allusion in *Adam Bede*." *Victorian Newsletter* 23 (1963): 16–7.

Bulwer-Lytton, Edward. *Eugene Aram: A Tale*. Philadelphia, Penn.: Lippincott, 1891.

Burke, Edmund. *India: the Hastings Trial*. Edited by P. J. Marshall. Vol. 7, *The Writings and Speeches of Edmund Burke*, edited by Paul Langford. Oxford: Clarendon Press, 2000.

Capote, Truman. *Handcarved Coffins*. In *Music for Chameleons*. New York: Random House, 1980.

——. *In Cold Blood*. New York: Vintage, 1993.

Chandler, James, Arnold I. Davidson, and Harry Harootunian, eds. *Questions of Evidence: Proof, Practice and Persuasion across the Disciplines*. Chicago, Ill.: University of Chicago Press, 1994.

Chatham, Seymour. *Story and Discourse: Narrative Structure in Fiction and Film*. Ithaca, N.Y.: Cornell University Press, 1978.

Christ, Carol. "Aggression and Providential Death in George Eliot's Fiction." *Novel* 9 (1976): 130–40.

Cohn, Dorrit. *Transparent Minds: Narrative Modes for Presenting Consciousness in Fiction*. Princeton, N.J.: Princeton University Press, 1978.

Coke, Sir Edmund. *The Second Part of the Institutes of the Laws of England*. New York: Garland, 1979.

——. *The Third Part of the Institutes of the Laws of England*. New York: Garland, 1979.

Coleridge, Samuel Taylor. *The Collected Works of Samuel Taylor Coleridge*. 14 vols. Edited by Carl Woodring. Princeton, N.J.: Princeton University Press, 1971–90.

Collins, Philip, ed. *Charles Dickens: The Public Readings*. Oxford: Clarendon Press, 1975.

——. *Dickens and Crime*. 3rd ed. New York: St. Martin's Press, 1994.

Conrad, Joseph. *The Secret Agent: A Simple Tale*. Edited by Bruce Harkness and S. W. Reid. Cambridge: Cambridge University Press, 1990.

Corpus Juris. Edited by William Mack and William Benjamin Hale. London: Butterworth, 1918.

Cover, Robert. "Violence and the Word." In *Narrative, Violence, and the Law: The Essays of Robert Cover*, edited by Martha Minow, Michael Ryan, and Austin Sarat. Ann Arbor: University of Michigan Press, 1993.

Cox, Walter Wheeler. "Act, Intention, and Motive in the Criminal Law." *Yale Law Journal* 24 (1916): 645–53.

Crane, R. S. "The Plot of *Tom Jones*." In *Twentieth Century Interpretations of Tom Jones*, edited by Martin C. Battestin. Englewood Cliffs, N.J.: Prentice Hall, 1968.

Cross, J. W., ed. *George Eliot's Life as Related in Her Letters and Journals*. 3 vols. London: Blackwood, 1885.

Dancy, Jonathan, ed. *Reading Parfit*. Oxford: Blackwell, 1997.

Davis, D. Seaborne. "Child-Killing in English Law." In *The Modern Approach to Criminal Law*, edited by Leon Radzinowicz and J. W. C. Turner. London: Macmillan, 1945.

Davis, Lennard. *Factual Fictions: The Origins of the English Novel*. New York: Columbia University Press, 1983.

De Quincey, Thomas. *On Murder Considered as One of the Fine Arts*. In *The Collected Works of Thomas De Quincey*, edited by David Masson. Edinburgh: Adam and Charles Black, 1890.

Dicey, Albert Venn. *Law and Public Opinion in England during the Nineteenth Century*. 1905. 2nd ed. Macmillan: London, 1930.

Dickens, Charles. *American Notes for General Circulation*. Edited by John S. Whitley and Arnold Goldman. London: Penguin, 1985.

——. *Barnaby Rudge*. Edited by Gordon Spence. London: Penguin, 1973.

——. *Bleak House*. Edited by Nicola Bradbury. London: Penguin, 1996.

——. "The Demeanor of Murderers." *Household Words* 13 (1857): 505–06.

——. *Dombey and Son*. Edited by Alan Horsman. Oxford: Oxford University Press, 2001.

——. *Great Expectations*. Edited by Edgar Rosenberg. New York: Norton, 1999.

——. *Martin Chuzzlewit*. Edited by P. N. Furbank. London: Penguin, 1996.

——. *The Mystery of Edwin Drood*. Edited by Margaret Cardwell. New York: Oxford University Press, 1982.

——. *Nicholas Nickleby*. Edited by Michael Slater. Harmondsworth: Penguin, 1978.

——. *The Old Curiosity Shop*. Edited by Elizabeth M. Brennan. Oxford: Clarendon Press, 1997.

——. *Oliver Twist*. Edited by Kathleen Tillotson. Oxford: Clarendon Press, 1966.

——. *Our Mutual Friend*. Edited by Stephen Gill. London: Penguin, 1971.

——. *The Posthumous Papers of the Pickwick Club*. Edited by Robert L. Patten. Harmondsworth: Penguin, 1972.

——. "Some Particulars Concerning a Lion." In *Sketches by Boz and Other Early Papers 1833–39*, edited by Michael Slater. Columbus: Ohio State Press, 1994.

Dolin, Kieran. *Fiction and the Law: Legal Discourse in Victorian and Modernist Literature*. Cambridge: Cambridge University Press, 1999.

Douglas, Lawrence. "Discursive Limits: Narrative and Judgment in *Billy Budd*." *Mosaic* 27 (1994): 141–60.

Dreiser, Theodore. *An American Tragedy*. New York: Signet, 2000.

Duff, Anthony. *Intention, Agency and Criminal Liability*. Oxford: Clarendon Press, 1990.

During, Simon. "The Strange Case of Monomania: Patriarchy in Literature, Murder in *Middlemarch*, Drowning in *Daniel Deronda*." *Representations* 23 (1988): 86–104.

Dutton, Geoffrey. *The Hero as Murderer: The Life of Edward John Eyre*. Sydney: Collins, 1967.

Edwards, Owen Dudley. "Macaulay's Warren Hastings." In *The Impeachment of Warren Hastings: Papers from a Bicentury Commemoration*, edited by Geoffrey Carnall and Colin Nicholson. Edinburgh: Edinburgh University Press, 1989.

Eliot, George. *Adam Bede*. Edited by Stephen Gill. London: Penguin, 1980.

———. *Daniel Deronda*. Edited by Graham Handley. Oxford: Clarendon Press, 1984.

———. *Felix Holt, the Radical*. Edited by Fred C. Thomson. Oxford: Clarendon Press, 1980.

———. *The Journals of George Eliot*. Edited by Margaret Harris and Judith Johnson. Cambridge: Cambridge University Press, 1998.

———. *The Lifted Veil*. New York: Virago, 1985.

———. *Middlemarch*. Edited by David Carroll. Oxford: Clarendon Press, 1986.

———. *Middlemarch Notebooks*. Edited by John Clark Pratt and Victor A. Neufeldt. Berkeley: University of California Press, 1979.

———. *The Mill on the Floss*. Edited by A. S. Byatt. London: Penguin, 1985.

———. "Mr. Gilfil's Love-Story." In *Scenes of Clerical Life*, edited by Thomas A. Noble. Oxford: Clarendon Press, 1985.

———. *Quarry for Middlemarch*. Edited by Anna Theresa Kitchel. Berkeley: University of California Press, 1950.

———. *Romola*. Edited by Andrew Sanders. London: Penguin, 1980.

———. *Selected Essays, Poems, and Other Writings*. Edited by A. S. Byatt and Nicholas Warren. London: Penguin, 1990.

———. *Some George Eliot Notebooks: An Edition of the Carl H. Pforzheimer Library's George Eliot Holograph Notebooks, MSS 707, 708, 709, 710, 711*. Edited by William Baker. 4 vols. Salzburg: Universität of Salzburg, 1976.

Eliot, T. S. *Notes Toward the Definition of Culture*. London: Faber and Faber, 1948.

———. *The Waste Land: A Facsimile and Transcript of the Original Drafts*. Edited by Valerie Eliot. London: Faber and Faber, 1971.

Emmerichs, Mary Beth Wasserlein. "Trials of Women for Homicide in Nineteenth-Century England," *Women and Criminal Justice* 5 (1993): 99–109.

Empson, William. *The Structure of Complex Words*. London: Penguin, 1995.

Ewick, Patricia, and Susan S. Silbey. *The Common Place of Law: Stories from Everyday Life*. Chicago, Ill.: University of Chicago Press, 1998.

Feiling, Keith. *Warren Hastings*. London: Macmillan, 1954.

Ferris, Ina. *William Makepeace Thackeray*. Boston, Mass.: Twayne, 1983.

Ferry, Anne. *The "Inward" Language: Sonnets of Wyatt, Sydney, Shakespeare, and Donne*. Chicago, Il.: University of Chicago Press, 1983.

Fisher, Philip. "Looking Around to See Who I Am: Dreiser's Territory of Self," *ELH* 44 (1977): 728–48.

Fletcher, George. *Rethinking Criminal Law*. Boston, Mass.: Little, Brown, 1978.

Forster, E. M. *Aspects of the Novel*. New York: Harcourt, Brace, 1956.

———. "The Challenge of Our Time." In *Two Cheers for Democracy*. New York: Harcourt Brace, 1951.

Forster, John. *The Life of Charles Dickens*. 2 vols. Philadelphia, Penn.: Lippincott, 1873.

Foster, Michael. *A Report of Some Proceedings on the Commission of Oyer and Terminer and Gaol Delivery for the Trial of the Rebels in the Year 1746 in the County of Surry and of Other Crown Cases to which are Added Discourses Upon a Few Branches of Crown Law*. London: Professional Books, 1982.

Foucault, Michel. *Discipline and Punish: The Birth of the Prison*. Translated by Alan Sheridan. New York: Vintage, 1979.

Gallagher, Catherine. "The Politics of Culture and the Debate over Representation." *Representations* 5 (1984): 115–47.

Garner, Stanton. "Fraud as Fact in Melville's *Billy Budd*." *San Jose Studies* 4 (1978): 83–105.

Genette, Gerard. "Fictional Narrative, Factual Narrative." *Poetics Today* 11 (1990): 758–73.

Ginzburg, Carlo. "Checking the Evidence: The Judge and the Historian." In *Questions of Evidence: Proof, Practice, and Persuasion across the Disciplines*, edited by James Chandler, Arnold I. Davidson, and Harry Harootunian. Chicago, Ill.: University of Chicago Press, 1994.

Goode, John. "Adam Bede." In *Critical Essays on George Eliot*, edited by Barbara Hardy. London: Routledge and Kegan Paul, 1970.

Goodman, Nan. *Shifting the Blame: Literature, Law, and the Theory of Accidents in Nineteenth Century America*. Princeton, N.J.: Princeton University Press, 1998.

Green, Thomas Andrew. *Verdict According to Conscience: Perspectives on the English Criminal Trial Jury, 1200–1800*. Chicago, Ill.: University of Chicago Press, 1985.

Griew, Edward. "States of Mind, Presumptions, and Inferences." In *Criminal Law: Essays in Honour of J. C. Smith*, edited by Peter Smith. London: Butterworth, 1987.

Griffin, James. "Consequences." *Proceedings of the Aristotelian Society* 65 (1965): 167–82.

Grossman, Jonathan. *The Art of Alibi*. Baltimore: Johns Hopkins University Press, 2002.

Haight, Gordon S. *George Eliot: A Biography*. London: Penguin, 1992.

———, ed. *The George Eliot Letters*. 7 vols. New Haven, Conn.: Yale University Press, 1954–78.

Hale, Sir Matthew. *History of the Pleas of the Crown*. London: Professional Books, 1971.

Hardy, Thomas. *Tess of the D'Urbervilles*. Oxford: Oxford University Press, 1998.

Hart, H. L. A. *The Concept of Law*. 2nd ed. Oxford: Clarendon Press, 1994.

———. *Punishment and Responsibility: Essays in the Philosophy of Law*. 2nd ed. Oxford: Clarendon Press, 1970.

Hart, H. L. A., and Tony Honoré. *Causation in the Law*. 2nd ed. Oxford: Clarendon Press, 1985.

Hawthorn, Jeremy. *A Concise Glossary of Contemporary Literary Theory*. 2nd ed. London: Arnold, 1996.

Hicks, Jack. "'Fire, Fire, Fire Flowing Like a River, River, River': History and Postmodernism in Truman Capote's *Handcarved Coffins*." In *The Critical Response to Truman Capote*, edited by Joseph J. Waldmeir and John C. Waldmeir. Westport, Conn.: Greenwood Press, 1999.

Hobbes, Thomas. *Leviathan*. Oxford: Clarendon Press, 1909.

Holdsworth, William S. *Charles Dickens as a Legal Historian*. New Haven, Conn.: Yale University Press, 1928.

———. *A History of English Law*. 16 vols. London: Methuen, 1922–66.

House, Humphry. *All in Due Time*. London: Hart-Davis, 1955.

———. "Introduction to *Oliver Twist*." In *The Dickens World*. London: Oxford University Press, 1942.

House, Madeline, Graham Storey, and Kathleen Tillotson, eds. *The Letters of Charles Dickens*. 7 vols. Oxford: Clarendon Press, 1965–2002.

Jaffe, Audrey. *Vanishing Points: Dickens, Narrative, and the Subject of Omniscience*. Berkeley: University of California Press, 1991.

Jenkyns, Richard. *The Victorians and Ancient Greece*. Cambridge, Mass.: Harvard University Press, 1980.

Johnson, Edgar. *Charles Dickens: His Tragedy and Triumph*. 2 vols. New York: Simon and Schuster, 1952.

"Judicial Dignity." *Saturday Review*, May 16, 1857, 450–1.

Keats, John. *The Complete Poems*. Edited by John Barnard. London: Penguin, 1977.

Kelman, Mark. "Reasonable Evidence of Reasonableness." In *Questions of Evidence: Proof, Practice and Persuasion across the Disciplines*, edited by James Chandler, Arnold I. Davidson, and Harry Harootunian. Chicago, Ill.: University of Chicago Press, 1994.

Kenny, Anthony. *Free Will and Responsibility*. London: Routledge and Kegan Paul, 1978.

Knapp, Steven. *Literary Interest: The Limits of Anti-Formalism*. Berkeley: University of California Press, 1993.

Krueger, Christine. "Literary Defenses and Medical Prosecutions: Representing Infanticide in Nineteenth Century Britain," *Victorian Studies* 40 (1997): 271–94.

Kucich, John. *Excess and Restraint in the Novels of Charles Dickens*. Athens: University of Georgia Press, 1981.

———. *Repression in Victorian Fiction: Charlotte Bronte, George Eliot, and Charles Dickens*. Berkeley: University of California Press, 1987.

Langbein, John H. "The Criminal Trial Before the Lawyers." *University of Chicago Law Review* 45 (1978): 263–316.

Lankford, William T. "'The Parish Boy's Progress': The Evolving Form of *Oliver Twist*." *PMLA* 93 (1978): 20–32.

Leonard, David P. "In Defense of the Character Evidence Prohibition: Foundations of the Rule Against Trial by Character." *Indiana Law Journal* 73 (1998). Online. Available http://www.law.indiana.edu. Accessed February 7, 2003.

Levine, George. *The Boundaries of Fiction*. Princeton, N.J.: Princeton University Press, 1968.

———. Introduction. *The Cambridge Companion to George Eliot*. Cambridge: Cambridge University Press, 2001.

———. *The Realistic Imagination: English Fiction from Frankenstein to Lady Chatterley*. Chicago, Ill.: University of Chicago Press, 1981.

Lewes, G. H. *Problems of Life and Mind*. Vol 2. Boston, Mass.: Houghton Osgood, 1879–80.

Locke, John. *An Essay Concerning Human Understanding*. Edited by Peter H. Nidditch. Oxford: Clarendon Press, 1975.

Lyall, Alfred. *Warren Hastings*. London: Macmillan, 1915.

Macaulay, Thomas. *Macaulay: Prose and Poetry*. Cambridge, Mass.: Harvard University Press, 1970.

———. *Miscellaneous Works of Lord Macaulay*. Edited by Lady Trevelyan. 4 vols. New York: Harper, 1880.

Maus, Katharine Eisaman. *Inwardness and Theatre in the English Renaissance*. Chicago, Ill.: University of Chicago Press, 1995.

M'Carthy, Justin. "Novels with a Purpose." *Westminster Review* 82 (1864): 24–36.

Mill, John Stuart. *Essays on Philosophy and the Classics*. Vol. 11, *The Collected Works of John Stuart Mill*, edited by J. M. Robson. Toronto: University of Toronto Press, 1980.

Miller, D. A. *The Novel and the Police*. Berkeley: University of California Press, 1988.

Miller, J. Hillis. *The Form of Victorian Fiction*. Notre Dame, Ind.: University of Notre Dame Press, 1968.

———. *Victorian Subjects*. Durham, N.C.: Duke University Press, 1989.

Milton, John. *The Complete Poems*. Edited by John Leonard. London: Penguin, 1998.

———. *The Doctrine and Discipline of Divorce*. Vol 3. *The Works of John Milton*. New York: Columbia University Press, 1931.

Monk, Leland. *Standard Deviations: Chance and the Modern Novel*. Stanford, Calif.: Stanford University Press, 1993.

Moon, Penderel. *Warren Hastings and British India*. London: Hodder and Stoughton, 1947.

Moore, G. E. *Ethics*. Oxford: Oxford University Press, 1965.

——. *Principia Ethica*. Cambridge: Cambridge University Press, 1903.

Moore, John D. *Zeluco*. London: J. Limbard, 1834.

Moore, Michael. *Act and Crime*. Oxford: Clarendon Press, 1993.

Nussbaum, Martha. "The Window: Knowledge of Other Minds in Virginia Woolf's *To the Lighthouse*." *New Literary History* 26 (1995): 731–53.

Orwell, George. "Charles Dickens." In *Critical Essays*. London: Secker and Warburg, 1946.

Parfit, Derek. *Reason and Persons*. Oxford: Clarendon Press, 1984.

Petch, Simon. "The Sovereign Self: Identity and Responsibility in Victorian England." In *Law and Literature: Current Legal Issues 1999*, Vol. 2, edited by Michael Freeman and Andrew D. E. Lewis. Oxford: Oxford University Press, 1999.

Pollock, Frederick, and Frederic Maitland. *The History of the English Law Before the Time of Edward I*. 2nd ed. Cambridge: Cambridge University Press, 1968.

The Private Life of Warren Hastings by Sir Charles Lawson: Opinions of the Press, 1895–6. Madras: Madras Mail Press, 1897.

Pynchon, Thomas. *The Crying of Lot 49*. New York: HarperPerenial, 1999.

Radzinowicz, Leon. *A History of the Criminal Law and Its Administration from 1750*. 5 vols. New York: Macmillan, 1948–56.

——. *Sir James Fitzjames Stephen, 1829–1894, and His Contribution to the Development of the Criminal Law*. London: Quaritch, 1957.

Reade, Charles. *It is Never Too Late to Mend: A Matter-of-Fact Romance*. London: Chatto & Windus, 1913.

Reed, John R. *Dickens and Thackeray: Punishment and Forgiveness*. Athens: Ohio State University Press, 1995.

Renton, A. Wood, ed. *Encyclopedia of the Laws of England*. London: Sweet and Maxwell, 1897.

Rogers, Samuel. *Recollections*. 2nd ed. London: Longman, Green, 1859.

Rooney, Ellen. "Tess and the Subject of Sexual Violence: Reading, Rape, Seduction." In *Rape and Representation*, edited by Lynn A. Higgins and Brenda R. Silver. New York: Columbia University Press, 1991.

Rosenberg, Brian. "Character and Contradiction in Dickens," *Nineteenth Century Literature* 47 (1992): 145–63.

——. "The Language of Doubt in *Oliver Twist*." *Dickens Quarterly* 4 (1987): 91–8.

Rovane, Carol. *The Bounds of Agency*. Princeton, N.J.: Princeton University Press, 1998.

Ruskin, John. "A Note on *Hard Times*." *Cornhill* 2 (1860): 159.

Russell, Sir William Oldnall. *A Treatise on Crimes and Misdemeanors*. Edited by C. S. Greaves. 4th ed. 3 vols. London: Stevens & Sons, 1865.

Sarat, Austin. "Ways of Telling Legal Events." Unpublished paper read at the Meeting of the Working Group on Law, Culture and the Humanities, March 29, 1998.

Scheffler, Samuel, ed. *Consequentialism and Its Critics*. Oxford: Oxford University Press, 1988.

Schramm, Jan-Melissa. *Testimony and Advocacy in Victorian Law, Literature, and Theology*. Cambridge: Cambridge University Press, 2000.

Semmel, Bernard. *The Governor Eyre Controversy*. London: MacGibbon and Kee, 1962.

Shakespeare, William. *Macbeth*. Edited by Kenneth Muir. London: Routledge, 1989.
——. *Measure for Measure*. Edited by G. Blakemore Evans. Boston, Mass.: Houghton Mifflin, 1974.
——. *Othello*. Edited by G. Blakemore Evans. Boston, Mass.: Houghton Mifflin, 1974.
Shelley, Percy Bysshe. *The Cenci*. In *The Complete Poetical Works of Percy Bysshe Shelley*, edited by Thomas Hutchinson. London: Oxford University Press, 1952.
Shires, Linda. "The Aesthetics of the Victorian Novel: Form, Subjectivity, Ideology." In *The Cambridge Companion to the Victorian Novel*, edited by Deirdre David. Cambridge: Cambridge University Press, 2001.
Shuttleworth, Sally. *Charlotte Brontë and Victorian Psychology*. Cambridge: Cambridge University Press, 1996.
——. *George Eliot and Nineteenth Century Science*. Cambridge: Cambridge University Press, 1984.
Sidgwick, Henry. *The Methods of Ethics*. 7th ed. Chicago, Ill.: University of Chicago Press, 1962.
Siegle, Robert. "Capote's *Handcarved Coffins* and the Nonfiction Novel." *Contemporary Literature* 25 (1984): 437–51.
Silber, John. "Being and Doing: A Study of Status Responsibility and Voluntary Responsibility." *University of Chicago Law Review* 35 (1967): 47–91.
Sinfield, Alan. *Faultlines: Cultural Materialism and the Politics of Dissident Reading*. Oxford: Clarendon Press, 1992.
Smith, J. C. "Aid, Abet, Counsel, or Procure." In *Reshaping the Criminal Law: Essays in Honour of Glanville Williams*, edited by P. R. Glazebrook. London: Stevens, 1978.
Smith, J. C., and Brian Hogan. *Criminal Law*. 7th ed. London: Butterworth, 1992.
Smith, K. J. M. *James Fitzjames Stephen: Portrait of a Victorian Rationalist*. Cambridge: Cambridge University Press, 1988.
——. *A Modern Treatise on the Law of Criminal Complicity*. Oxford: Clarendon Press, 1991.
Smith, Roger. *Trial by Medicine*. Edinburgh: Edinburgh University Press, 1981.
Stein, William Bysshe. "*Billy Budd*: The Nightmare of History." *Criticism* 3 (1961): 240–8.
Stephen, James Fitzjames. "The Characteristics of the English Criminal Law." *Cambridge Essays* (1857): 1–63.
——. *A Digest of the Criminal Law*. London: Macmillan, 1877.
——. *A Digest of the Law of Evidence*. London: Macmillan, 1876.
——. "The *Edinburgh Review* and Modern Novelists." *Saturday Review*, July 18, 1857, 57–8.
——. "English Jurisprudence." *Edinburgh Review* 114 (1861): 456–86.
——. *Essays by a Barrister*. London: Smith, Elder, 1862.
——. *A General View of the Criminal Law*. London: Macmillan, 1863.
——. *A General View of the Criminal Law*. 2nd ed. London: Macmillan, 1890.
——. *A History of the Criminal Law of England*. 3 vols. London: Macmillan, 1883.
——. *Horae Sabbaticae*. 3 vols. London: Macmillan, 1892.
——. *The Indian Evidence Act of 1872 with an Introduction on the Principles of Judicial Evidence*. London: Macmillan, 1872.
——. *Liberty, Equality, Fraternity*. Edited by R. J. White. Cambridge: Cambridge University Press, 1967.
——. "The License of Modern Novelists." *Edinburgh Review* 106 (1857): 124–56.
——. "Little Dorrit." *Saturday Review*, July 4, 1857, 15–6.
——. "Lord Macaulay's Works." *Saturday Review*, August 18, 1866, 207–8.

——. "Mr. Dickens as a Politician." *Saturday Review*, January 3, 1857, 8–9.

——. "Novels and Novelists." *Saturday Review*, September 18, 1858, 285–6.

——. "The Relation of Novels to Life." In *Cambridge Essays*. London: Parker, 1855.

——. *The Story of Nuncomar and the Impeachment of Sir Elijah Impey*. 2 vols. London: Macmillan, 1885.

——. "*A Tale of Two Cities*." *Saturday Review*, December 17, 1859, 741–2.

——. Unpublished letters. Stephen Papers. Cambridge University Library.

Stephen, Leslie. *The Life of Sir James Fitzjames Stephen, bart., K.C.S.I., a Judge of the High Court of Justice*. 2nd ed. London: Smith, Elder, 1895.

Sutherland, John. *Can Jane Eyre Be Happy?* Oxford: Oxford University Press, 1997.

——. *Who Betrays Elizabeth Bennet?* Oxford: Oxford University Press, 1999.

Taylor, Charles. *Sources of Self*. Cambridge, Mass.: Harvard University Press, 1989.

Thackeray, William Makepeace. *Vanity Fair*. Edited by Geoffrey and Kathleen Tillotson. Boston, Mass.: Houghton Mifflin, 1963.

Thomas, Brook. *Cross-Examinations of Law and Literature: Cooper, Hawthorne, Stowe, and Melville*. Cambridge: Cambridge University Press, 1987.

——. "Narratives of Responsibility and Blame in Nineteenth-Century United States Law and Literature." *Narrative* 5 (1997): 3–19.

Thompson, Jon. *Fiction, Crime, and Empire: Clues to Modernity and Postmodernism*. Chicago, Ill.: University of Chicago Press, 1993.

Turner, J. W. C. *Kenny's Outlines of Criminal Law*. 16th ed. Cambridge: Cambridge University Press, 1952.

——. *Russell on Crime*. 2 vols. 12th ed. London: Stevens, 1964.

Waugh, Patricia. *Feminine Fictions: Revisiting the Postmodern*. London: Routledge, 1989.

Weiner, Martin J. "Judges v. Jurors: Courtroom Tensions in Murder Trials and the Law of Criminal Responsibility in England," *Law and History Review* 17 (1999). Online. Available: http://www.historycooperative.org/journals/1hr/17.3/weiner.html. Accessed February 5, 2003.

——. *Reconstructing the Criminal: Culture, Law and Policy in England 1830–1914*. Cambridge: Cambridge University Press, 1990.

Weisberg, Richard H. "Literature's Twenty-Year Crossing." In *Law and Literature: Current Legal Issues 1999*, Vol. 2, edited by Michael Freeman and Andrew D. E. Lewis. Oxford: Oxford University Press, 1999.

Welsh, Alexander. *George Eliot and Blackmail*. Cambridge, Mass.: Harvard University Press, 1985.

——. *Strong Representations: Narrative and Circumstantial Evidence in England*. Baltimore, Md.: Johns Hopkins University Press, 1992.

White, Alan. *Misleading Cases*. Oxford: Oxford University Press, 1991.

Wiggins, David. *Identity and Spatio-Temporal Continuity*. Oxford: Blackwell, 1967.

Williams, Glanville. *Criminal Law: The General Part*. London: Stevens, 1961.

Wilson, Luke. *Theatres of Intention: Drama and the Law in Early Modern England*. Stanford: Stanford University Press, 1999.

Wimsatt, W. K., and M. C. Beardsley. "The Intentional Fallacy." In *On Literary Intention*, edited by David Newton-De Molina. Edinburgh: Edinburgh University Press, 1976.

Wittgenstein, Ludwig. *Lectures and Conversations on Aesthetics, Psychology, and Religious Belief*. Edited by Cyril Barrett. London: Blackwell, 1966.

Yeats, W. B. *Ideas of Good and Evil*. London: Bullen, 1903.

LIST OF CASES

DPP v. Smith (1985) 1 AC 905

Hopps v. People (1863) 31 Ill 385

Lee v. Danger (1892) 2 QB 337

Macdaniel and Others (1755) Foster 121

Plummer v. Commonwealth (1866) 1 Bush (Ky) 76

R. v. Cerovic. (2001, December 3). EWCA Crim 2868. *Lexis-Nexis.* Wellesley College Library, Wellesley, Mass. 10 July 2002. <http://o-web.lexis-nexis.com>

R. v. Chapman (1849) 1 Den 432

R. v. Cole (1810) 1 Phill. Evid. 499

R. v. Collins (1864) L & C 471, 168 ER 1477

R. v. Coney, Gilliam, and Tully (1882) 8 QBD 534

R. v. Cox (1859) 1 F & F 662

R. v. Dias, (2001, December 13) EWCA Crim 2986. *Lexis-Nexis.* Wellesley College Library, Wellesley, Mass. 10 July 2002. <http://o-web.lexis-nexis.com>

R. v. Dugdale (1853) 1 E & B 435

R. v. Eagleton (1855) Dears 515

R. v. Farrington (1811) 168 ER 763

R. v. Gathercole (1838) 2 Lew CC 237

R. v. Goodchild (1846) 2 C & K 293, 175 ER 121

R. v. Maloney (1985) 1 AC 905

R. v. Monkhouse (1849) 4 Cox 55

R. v. Murphy (1833) 6 C & P 103

R v. Ring (1892) 17 Cox 491 (CCR)

R. v. Rowton (1865) All ER 549

R. v. Tyrell (1894) 1 QB 710

R. v. Whitmarsh (1898) 62 JP 711

R. v. Woodward (1846) 15 M & W 404, 153 ER 907

State v. Douglass 44 Kan 618

White v. People (1876) 81 Ill 333

⊰ INDEX ⊱

Griffin, James, 100
Grossman, Jonathan, 226n.13, 230n.67

Haight, Gordon S., 248nn.9, 69
Hale, Sir Matthew, 50, 51, 69
Hardy, Thomas, 34, 213–17
Harrison, Frederic, 130
Hart, H. L. A., 26, 27, 29, 30, 83–84, 91,
    231n.88, 240n.90
Hastings, Warren, 25, 171–72, 174, 189–93
Hawthorn, Jeremy, 229n.62
Hicks, Jack, 257n.16
Hobbes, Thomas, 134, 147–49, 250n.36
Holdsworth, William, 5
Holmes Jr., Oliver Wendell, 28
Honoré, Tony, 30, 240n.90
Hopps v. People, 235n.18
House, Humphry, 78

Impey, Elijah, 25, 172, 174, 191–93
Inchoate offenses, 30, 65
Infanticide, 103–4, 181
Inner life, 9–10. *See also* Interiority
Inner self, 9–10, 12, 22. *See also* Interiority
Insanity, 97, 181, 235nn.17, 18, 241n.104
Intent. *See also* Austin, John; *Daniel
    Deronda*; *Mens Rea*; *Middlemarch*;
    Stephen, James Fitzjames
  and acts, 90
  defined, 29, 141–42, 145
  in homicide laws, 83, 98
  imputed from consequences, 97
  as separate from desire in nineteenth
    century, 144–45
"Intentional Fallacy," 205
Interiority, 8–10, 21, 178–80, 210–11,
    227n.20. *See also* Narrator, third-
    person; State of mind

Jaffe, Audrey, 12–13, 23, 227n.32
Jenkyns, Richard, 247n.57
Johnson, Edgar, 234n.6
Johnson, Samuel, 28, 114
Joyce, James, 217
"Judicial Dignity," 5

Keats, John, 232n.112
Kelman, Mark, 209–11
Kenny, Anthony, 26, 231n.81

Knapp, Steven, 40–41, 75
Krueger, Christine, 246n.29
Kucich, John, 233n.4

Langbein, John H., 237n.38
Lankford, William T., 233nn.3,4, 243n.117
Law and literature, 8, 21, 179–80, 226n.16,
    232n.107
Law and morality, 83–84. *See also Adam
    Bede*; Consequences; *Middlemarch*;
    State of mind
Leonard, David P., 229n.60
Levine, George, 186–88
Lewes, G. H., 86, 90, 95, 140, 149–50,
    166–68
Locke, John, 8, 40–41, 79, 235n.17
Lyall, Alfred, 177, 190, 208–9

Macaulay, Thomas
  Essays, 188
  "History," 175, 186–88
  History of England, 188
  "Milton," 196–97
  "Notes on the Indian Penal Code," 168,
    202, 251n. 66
  "Warren Hastings," 32, 34, 172, 174, 188,
    193–98, 202, 255n.109
Macdaniel and Others, 52–53
Mackay, R. W., 101, 107–8, 121
Mailer, Norman, 220
Maine, Henry, 86, 93
Maus, Katherine Eisaman, 8
Maxims, 30–31
M'Carthy, Justin, 4, 225nn.3–4
Melville, Herman, 13
Mens Rea, 26–30, 39, 86, 105, 119, 156, 218,
    231n.89, 232n.103
Middlemarch, 31–32, 40, 85, 86, 90, 99,
    132–54, 184–85, 202, 250nn.33,35
  and acts, in relation to state of mind,
    90–91, 132–33, 137–39, 148–50, 154
  attempted murder in, 132
  Bulstode in, 90, 145–51, 247n.47
  intent and desire in, 141, 143, 144–46, 149,
    153
  monomania in, 140–41
  moral responsibility as against legal in,
    91, 132, 141, 145–46, 148–49, 153–54,
    169

and judicial murder, 176
Liberty, Equality, Fraternity, 32
"The License of Modern Novelists,"
181–82
"Little Dorrit," 186
"Lord Macaulay," 189
"Lord Macaulay's Works," 188
as member of Jamaica Committee, 176
on morality, as against positive law, 84,
153
on motive and intent, distinctions be-
tween, 147–48, 249n.30
"Mr. Dickens as a Politician," 5–6, 185
"Novels and Novelists," 183–84
on novels, 4–6, 173, 177, 181–84
"The Relation of Novels to Life," 4,
177–78, 184, 206
*Story of Nuncomar and the Impeachment of
Sir Elijah Impey. See separate entry*
"A Tale of Two Cites," 176, 185
on voluntariness, 29
Stephen, Leslie, 32–33, 172, 175, 196,
199–201
*Story of Nuncomar and the Impeachment of
Sir Elijah Impey* (Stephen, James
Fitzjames), 25, 32–33, 34, 171–81,
189, 193–212
assessment of evidence in, 201
on the book as a novel, 172–73
critique of Macaulay in, 34, 174, 193,
197–98, 202–4
on forgery as a capital crime, 254n.76
and intent, representation of, 204
in *The Private Life of Warren Hastings by
Sir Charles Lawson: Opinions of the
Press, 1895–6,* 212
questions of motive in, 205–6, 208–9

spelling in, 25n.1
and *State Trials* report, 204
summary of facts of the case in, 171–72,
189–93
Strict liability, 26
Sutherland, John, 49, 56–57, 61, 233n.2

Taylor, Charles, 8
Thackeray, William, 7, 14–15
Thomas, Brooke, 8
Thompson, Jon, 217–18
Trollope, Anthony, 7
Turner, J. W. C.
Kenny's Outlines of the Criminal Law,
26–29, 87, 230n.81, 231n.97
Russell on Crime, 19, 111–12, 119, 156,
241n.99, 250n.47

Utilitarianism, 100, 245n.23

Waugh, Patricia, 218
Weiner, Martin, 47, 231n.103, 237n.40,
241n.99, 242n.110
Weisberg, Richard, 226n.16
Welsh, Alexander, 8, 21–23, 132
White, Alan, 109–10
White v. People, 238n. 55
Wiggins, David, 235n.11
Williams, Glanville, 26–27, 38, 71,
238n.49, 239n.64, 240n.93
Wilson, Luke, 225n.12
Wimsatt, W. K. and M. C. Beardsley, 205
Wittgenstein, Ludwig, 148
Woolf, Virginia, 15–16, 217
Wuthering Heights, 12

Yeats, W. B., 101, 136, 245n.23